**SACRAMENTO PUBLIC LIBRARY**
**828 "I" STREET**
**SACRAMENTO, CA 95814**

11/2010

D0978884

# Endless Money

# Endless Money

## *The Moral Hazards of Socialism*

## William W. Baker

**WILEY**

John Wiley & Sons, Inc.

Copyright © 2010 by William W. Baker. All rights reserved.

Published by John Wiley & Sons, Inc., Hoboken, New Jersey.
Published simultaneously in Canada.

No part of this publication may be reproduced, stored in a retrieval system, or transmitted
in any form or by any means, electronic, mechanical, photocopying, recording, scanning,
or otherwise, except as permitted under Section 107 or 108 of the 1976 United
States Copyright Act, without either the prior written permission of the Publisher,
or authorization through payment of the appropriate per-copy fee to the Copyright
Clearance Center, Inc., 222 Rosewood Drive, Danvers, MA 01923, (978) 750-8400, fax
(978) 750-4470, or on the web at www.copyright.com. Requests to the Publisher for
permission should be addressed to the Permissions Department, John Wiley & Sons, Inc.,
111 River Street, Hoboken, NJ 07030, (201) 748-6011, fax (201) 748-6008, or online at
http://www.wiley.com/go/permissions.

Limit of Liability/Disclaimer of Warranty: While the publisher and author have used their
best efforts in preparing this book, they make no representations or warranties with respect
to the accuracy or completeness of the contents of this book and specifically disclaim any
implied warranties of merchantability or fitness for a particular purpose. No warranty
may be created or extended by sales representatives or written sales materials. The advice
and strategies contained herein may not be suitable for your situation. You should consult
with a professional where appropriate. Neither the publisher nor author shall be liable for
any loss of profit or any other commercial damages, including but not limited to special,
incidental, consequential, or other damages.

For general information on our other products and services or for technical support, please
contact our Customer Care Department within the United States at (800) 762-2974,
outside the United States at (317) 572-3993 or fax (317) 572-4002.

Wiley also publishes its books in a variety of electronic formats. Some content that appears
in print may not be available in electronic books. For more information about Wiley
products, visit our web site at www.wiley.com.

*Library of Congress Cataloging-in-Publication Data:*

Baker, William W.
  Endless money : the moral hazards of socialism / William W. Baker.
      p. cm.
  Includes bibliographical references and index.
  ISBN 978-0-470-47615-4 (cloth)
  1. Monetary policy. 2. Banks and banking. I. Title.
  HG230.3.B354 2009
  330.15'7—dc22

                                                    2009021625

Printed in the United States of America

10  9  8  7  6  5  4  3  2  1

*For my wife, Maris; our children, Chase and Ian; and all our family and descendants to come…*

# Contents

# Foreword

I t's an interesting—even entertaining—time to be a student of financial markets and government policy.

Never before has the world witnessed what the economist Ludwig von Mises called a "world-wide crack up boom." History reveals isolated events: the crack up of the Continental currency in America in 1781 or the bust of the German mark in 1923, which famously resulted in wheelbarrows full of paper currency just to buy bread. But never before has the world seen an event which engulfed the entire planet.

We may go down in history as the first generation to live through one, what do you think of that?

With the seizure of the credit markets in the fall of 2008, the jig was up for just about every major market in the global economy. The emerging BRIC economies—Brazil, Russia, India, and China—fell in unison with stock markets in the United States, Canada, Great Britain, France, and Germany. The commodities markets, which had been beneficiaries of immense speculation for the better part of the trading year, suddenly dropped, squeezing even the true believers from the market.

Price for oil, gold, copper—thought to provide refuge from the mayhem in the stock market—crashed along with everything else. The Reuters/Jeffries CRB Index, a broad measure of commodities in general, suffered its worst three-month spell since the Great Depression. Fine art, real estate, exotic financial derivatives—all boomed, then busted. What a sight it was.

In 2008, "there is simply nowhere to hide" was a common refrain among analysts, traders, and individual investors alike. It was a brutal time for anyone who had laid even a portion of their assets on the roulette table that had become the economy. Of course, there were plenty of voices cautioning against irrational exuberance as far back as the mid-1990s—before successive asset bubbles puffed their way through emerging economies in 1994–1997, the tech markets during 1996–2000 and the U.S. housing market during 2003–2007. Still barely anyone noticed that paper shuffling for profits is hardly a sustainable economic strategy until they opened their 401(k)s and noticed paper assets don't always go up like Larry Kudlow or Jim Cramer said they would.

No harm no foul, we say. You win some, you lose some. That is, until politicians get in touch with the electorate's emotions.

The crack up of the global financial markets in 2008 was a triumph for central planners. "The free market failed," they're only too happy to remind you. Lack of regulation and greed on Wall Street were to blame for the crisis. (Never mind, of course, that Fannie Mae and Freddie Mac, government sponsored firms with their own congressional oversight committee, fostered, encouraged—enabled—the market for mortgage-backed securities. On the eve of the bankruptcy of Lehman Bros., Fannie Mae and Freddie Mac together were directly or indirectly involved in about 8 out of 10 mortgages in the United States.)

On the wave of populist outrage over the crisis, Congress panicked and then went on the offensive.

The conventional wisdom of the day suggested if consumers can no longer spend because they have no money and corporations can't get the credit they need to finance new ventures or cover up sagging sales figures, then the federal government is the only actor in the economy that can spend, spend, and spend some more to get the economy "back on track." Unfortunately for all involved, an economy that requires people to spend more than they earn ad infinitum was on the wrong track in the first place and no amount of spending is going to get the national economy back on the road to building prosperity. Say nothing of the natural headwinds already presented by globalized labor markets and cheap production costs found in world's more industrious economies. Or the fact that the crisis itself has cut tax receipts to the federal government by nearly 20 percent—the largest single-year depletion of federal funds since 1932. Before the crisis peaked, federal spending was already creating historic deficits approaching half a trillion dollars. Now with the bailouts of the banking and auto industries—and the political desire to overhaul the health care industry—the nation is facing deficits in excess of a trillion dollars for years to come.

The trouble with running ever-persistent deficits is that when a real crisis approaches the government—your government—is left without the resources to deal with it. At some point, policy makers will come to realize the only way out of unsustainable debts is to rapidly debase the currency. Because they're in control of the printing press, they will attempt to do what governments since the beginning of written communication have always done, they will attempt pay off their mounting debts with cheaper and cheaper dollars.

This next phase in our history will be messy, at best. But the greatest danger is that even more ambitious demagogues will come along and do "some very foolish things," as warned by Warren Buffett in the recent documentary, I.O.U.S.A. Those setting policy in the capitol are under the mistaken belief that a free market economy can produce as much as they can legislate into the hands of others and then produce more. Those who respect the virtues of the market know that it's a fragile, rare occurrence in history that has produced the level of prosperity we enjoy. Sure there were hiccups in the credit markets. Yes, we witnessed what may be considered the largest global crash in markets in history. But as the economist Joseph Schumpeter observed during the Great Depression—the only challenge to capitalist values within immediate reach—"the capitalist reality is first and last a process of change." Not the type of change promised by politicians, but the reality that one economic system has been destroyed under its own weight. Let's not forget to respect private property, thrift, and the spirit of enterprise as we rebuild.

When Bill Baker contacted me about his book on the moral hazards of socialism, I thought, "Yes, another voice of reason!" With so many people confused and swayed by the sound byte news cycle, it's truly refreshing to find someone nutty enough to research real estate bubbles, the late degenerate period of the Roman Empire, and try to derive principles therein to apply to his own trading practice today. At the very least, Endless Money is a good read. But if you take the time, you'll find there are many more lessons to be learned from its pages—even if you're a dog-eared student of markets and governments yourself.

Addison Wiggin
Best-selling author
Executive Publisher of Agora Financial

# Introduction

I n 2008 the meltdown of the financial sector took the world by surprise. Yet credit crises have been a part of the human experience since before the birth of Christ. Even in the best times of the Roman Republic, a span of about two centuries, there were about a half-dozen credit crises. Man has a penchant for borrowing excessively, which is also to say that we lend our wealth unwisely. Until recently, that is the last century or two, there has been a sharp line of demarcation between money and credit. Now currency is amorphous. It is created at the click of a mouse at a ratio of ten-to-one or more whenever a deposit is made at a bank, or it can be produced in quantity when a central bank credits its balance sheet in exchange for government debt, mortgages, or the equally formless currency of other nations. It is essentially credit. Its value is tied to the promises of others, a function of their character or lack of it. Should that value vanish, it becomes a renewable resource. Like new trees that may become lumber to replace rotten planks, the Federal Reserve System (Fed) can produce some more. It is becoming a disposable element, and it has lost its permanence—an unsustainable trend because wealth has been placed at risk for systemic reasons.

Money facilitates many things. It enables the specialization of production and trade. It permits us to store wealth, that is, to defer consumption.

And it entitles our union, government, to extract taxation. The major debt crises of millennia ago generally arose from the enormous, recurring costs of war, but they also were inexorably linked to a human inability to gauge the ideal tradeoff between expenditure today and tomorrow. In recent times, financial crises have been extremely rare, because we have chosen a scientific, technocratic path of managing our monetary affairs. The Federal Reserve System has created credit growth of about 7 percent annually since its inception a century ago, sometimes (as recently) allowing it to accelerate into the double digits. In so doing, it bulldozed over any chance of asset prices declining deeply or for long ever since the Great Depression. Until recently this has boosted the confidence of speculators of all types, and repeatedly weakened those who might exercise caution. Our accomplishment bewitched us into a conceit that we had banished our ancient penchant for excess.

Central bankers in the United States and Europe have had a primary mission to keep inflation under control. They may have well proclaimed "mission accomplished" with inflation having consistently averaged less than 3 percent in the last 10 years, only to be rudely awakened. Like a doctor judging an athlete by muscle tone and not internal organs or functions, our underlying condition went undetected. The steroids of credit made consumer prices grow when otherwise buyers would have enjoyed a reduced cost of living, thanks to the productivity gains of capitalism and globalization. In a league filled with contestants on steroids, who could compete without them?

Academia has been supportive of the methodology behind the operation of our central banks and treasuries, but now its halls are aghast and repopulated with experts who would convincingly offer new, ever bolder solutions. Once challenged by a crisis of finance, it convincingly supported our effort to break free from the chains of gold that bound the world together, and our majority voted in landslides to adopt social contracts to protect the weakest. Twice confronted, our paper fetters are aflame and the institutions formed to protect us from the unkind strangers of the free market are dilapidated and looted, themselves in need of our wallet.

Have we the economic literacy to understand what has brought us here? Ignorance is widespread, and where it isn't, sharp disagreement between schools of thought has become germane to deploying a solution.

Our problem is simple: We have repeated a mistake of the ages. We have protected ourselves from harm for so long that we have extended our vulnerability beyond any previous scale. Until recently, the private sector was so encouraged by the prospects offered by the rising tide of paper money that it indebted itself to the tune of over $40 trillion; our government promised entitlements with a present value of over $50 trillion. Combined with public debt of over $10 trillion, these obligations are more than seven times as large as gross national product. But in defiance to this state of affairs, our experts are about to solve a debt problem by adding more debt, by adding banking credit, and by spending money raised from selling Treasury notes and bonds.

This book sympathizes with a long unnoticed sect of economic thought known as the Austrian School, whose "dean" was Ludwig von Mises and "founder" was Carl Menger. Murray N. Rothbard is a disciple of extraordinary ability whose thoughtful analysis of American history in the Austrian theoretical context was heavily relied upon in this text. I wish to acknowledge the generosity of the Mises Institute in making voluminous quantities of his work available to the public at large and for promoting the dissemination of his ideas to scholars and ordinary financial commentators alike without oppressive copyright limitations. But my view departs slightly from these greats by incorporating some pragmatism and recognizing some moral obligation to undo the massive distortion that operating a fiat currency system and a central bank has caused. I respectfully apologize to all who possess greater knowledge of economics. My grounding comes only from the battlefield of performing equity research and managing money for more than 25 years, where I founded two firms: GARP Research & Securities Co. (an institutional equity research broker-dealer, member: FINRA and SIPC) and Gaineswood Investment Management Inc. (an SEC-registered investment advisor). In this text I delight in taking apart the observations of some of the most respected economists of our time. They have earned advanced degrees and pursued careers in the field, earning them Nobel Prizes as long as they did not veer in the Austrian direction (with the exception being Friedrich A. Hayek), whereas I merely majored in economics at one Ivy League college, received a Masters in Business Administration at another, and then sought to continue my learning in the crucible of the financial markets.

Providing research on stocks and managing equity portfolios can be a very humbling experience, for in this endeavor theories are subservient to reality in the harshest way possible, through financial reward or loss. This book opens by relating some experiences of working under this pressure, and the respect for the unknown this brings to one's mental discipline. Most of all this experience reminds one that the machinations of men seeking to tame the vast unexpected interaction of economic forces that surround us are prone to hubris and error. It is not a giant leap then to question the wisdom of current academic orthodoxy surrounding central banking and fiat currency, for these interrelated institutions are most certainly constructs of man. The experience of analyzing companies and industries teaches one to be open minded, and macroeconomics should be subject to no less healthy respect for the unknown.

Part 2 of the book begins with a compressed monetary history of the United States and the global financial events of the interwar period, which may slow the progress of casual readers, but this frames the policy debate and investment outlook for the remainder of the book. The perspective this provides is that over the long term our nation has swung back and forth several times between operating a fiat currency and using hard money. Simple observation of this history could make a reversal in direction of the pendulum appear inevitable. The unanimous consensus during our lifetime that gold backing of liquid wealth is a barbarous relic could give way, but it would take painful financial circumstances, perhaps a funding crisis for the United States, to force the issue. The balance of Part 2 contains the critique of the mainstream academic interpretation that the Depression was made Great because of misguided adherence to the gold standard, which transmitted economic instability worldwide. Although it is a bit pedantic, readers will be richly rewarded with an alternative perspective that casts the professors of finance as flat Earth believers. While the concept of a flat Earth is probably an exaggeration of medieval scientific inadequacy, the analogy may have enough truth to it to pop the blister of condescension that has been expanding in academic literature, deflating the hauteur fed by the awarding of numerous Nobel prizes. This review also makes the case that World War I, coming on the heels of the founding of the Fed, ushered in an era of dollar diplomacy that promulgated the dilution of gold reserves held by banks and nations. When the burden of debt became too large relative to income by 1929, the United States responded by devaluing and confiscating gold, and then outlandishly embarking on a strategy of cornering the global gold market. Today's Fed might be similarly incongruous with the times, for it views the meltdown as an illiquidity crisis. With some assistance from the U.S. Treasury, its policy is to float more debt to alleviate the excessive issuance of debt that made the system unstable in the first place. Part 2 closes with a review of the numerous moral hazards inherent in operating a centralized banking system that has been friendly to expansive and redistributive fiscal policies. The structural change to finance over the last century has been enormous: The worst banks of 100 years ago would be pristine in comparison to the best banks and brokers doing business with the public today, because the responsibility of safekeeping has been palmed off onto the taxpayer.

With a cornerstone in history and theory thus laid in place, Parts 3 and 4 move to examine the realms of taxation and politics, respectively. The financial meltdown begun in 2008 provided ammunition to politicians who have been pressing to redistribute yet more income from the rich to the less than rich. Part 3 reviews the historical record, which shows that redistribution was immoderate from World War II until Reagan's presidency. Reagan succeeded in reducing the burden of taxation on the upper-middle class dramatically through the Tax Reform Act of 1986, whose impact was phased in by 1988. Still, from that time forward, income of the upper-middle class has been redistributed proportionately more than it was during the administration of Franklin Roosevelt, who ostensibly "soaked the rich." The top income tax bracket in 2008 applies to earnings above $357,700. The inflation-adjusted equivalent of this cutoff, $22,500, would merely fall in the 17 percent bracket of 1932. Roosevelt went after the super-rich; those earning $1 million annually paid a rate of 63% in the early 1930s, which rose to 77 percent by 1936. But adjusted for inflation, $1 million then equals over $15 million today.

The dunning of the upper-middle class to pay for swelling government expenditures, mostly for entitlements, is one untold story of our era. Another is the role of the super-rich, who can skirt taxation through withdrawal of debt capital and hedge this through the use of derivatives, and by minimizing ordinary income. They are the ultimate beneficiaries of the fiat currency system, because otherwise asset inflation through currency dilution would not route profits through this backdoor. Chapter 7 documents the political influence wielded by these elites, many of whom disingenuously call for higher taxation of income. Besides having broken the back of the banking system, where has this trend led us? The swerve to the left politically that occurred in 2008 will result in heightened redistribution and spending. But even without this added burden, the upper-middle class is incapable of paying down even a small fraction of our national debt, yet countries that support the Treasury note and bond markets seem incognizant of this national insolvency. Part 4 expands upon the politics of recent times. Recounting the saga of Fannie Mae and Freddie Mac, it takes a detailed look at the mortgage industry as a government-subsidized redistributive protectorate. It then notes the income shifting and expansion of a government set to begin as contemplated within the American Recovery and Reinvestment Act of 2009, comparing Obama policies to those that brought on the malaise of the Carter years. With a goal of establishing a majority of the electorate that pays no income taxes at all, the new economic overlords may have inadvertently harnessed democracy to strike a fatal blow to capitalism, a theme developed in Part 4's short concluding chapter.

Historians will write one day that 2008 marked the close of a great financial epoch, one whose heroes were financiers of the ilk of Soros or Buffett, neither of whom built essential institutions but instead were intermediaries that profited by being shrewd conduits of other people's money. True, a few modern-day industrialists, like Gates, Jobs, or Google founders Sergey and Brin, emerged. While our nation stretched its trade imbalance to the limit, and services as well as tangibles were increasingly produced offshore, even the software code that was the fabric of these great, new American corporations could not affordably be constructed here. Ending this epoch may mark the exile of the upper-middle class from our social and economic structure. This most productive group felt a rush of wealth from the inflation of the money supply, but it was simultaneously looted with confiscatory state and federal income and death taxes. Seeking to escape the progressive capturing of the fruits of its labor, it withdrew massive amounts of cash tax-free through mortgages and home equity lines, only to fall victim to asset price deflation. The beginning of the new era, one born of hope and change from those underneath, will be one of a flatter, more uniform society, unless the trickling down of impoverishment awakens us all to our heritage and unites us, a response we have experienced in other times of challenge. The über-wealthy have positioned themselves to collect the trinkets off the fallen bodies now that the battle has been convincingly won, and for this they owe allegiance to demagogues. In what may be one of the best public relations foils of all time, the pinnacle of society may have used class warfare to its own advantage, so for this Part 3 is named "Faux Class Warfare."

The exploitation of the lower classes to permit the aristocracy to consolidate the estates of the lesser nobles into their own is what happened to Rome. It can happen again here, but the trend might be so slow that future historians might argue whether the United States fell or evolved into a new and better system of global unity, or ponder precisely when or how it happened. Like some other authors have recently done, I draw an analogy to the fall of the Roman Empire, partly to weigh in with some common sense on a topic that is increasingly evoked by some on the left to justify their Marxist leanings. The Roman Empire did not "fall" as the title of the great historian Edward Gibbon's opus on that score implies. Its poor delighted in handing over the franchise to the barbarians, for their government had turned its citizens into serfs. In ancient times, the highest level of commerce occurred during the Roman Republic, before the birth of Christ. Activity began to tail off shortly after that, when the Roman Empire began to devalue its currency, essentially a tax on cash balances. It raised taxes a century or more later, and taken together these actions combined with legal changes systematically obliterated its middle class. This book takes aim at liberal analyses that draw parallels to the United States, claiming that privatization of government functions or military overextension are common elements that predestine us to lose our station in the world. These arguments could not be more patently wrong, and are exposed for what they are in Part 5.

Paralleling the enormous change in the world's financial system has been the degradation of our culture, the topic of the sixth part of this book. It runs beyond lewd music, violent movies, or the open acceptance of lifestyles that have been considered perverse for thousands of years. Libertarians, who are the minority that has proselytized for hard currency and fiscal restraint, celebrate the self-expression and self-actualization that has occurred thanks to the prosperity of capitalism, which unshackled us from hard labor on farms or in factories. But economic success has absolved the majority of the populace from the need to pay taxes. Success at the voting booth at securing additional takings threatens to realign incentives so much that producers may no longer see their rewards justified by risks. Such a majority would continue to egg on its representatives to dig surrounding our constitutional foundation, threatening private property rights and the freedom to conduct business without government intrusion. There is a paradox of freedom, that it can mean absolution from responsibility: from repaying debt to honoring familial commitments to enjoying sheer self-indulgence and neglecting to save or plan for the future, be it one's own or that of the nation. Although the clock could never be turned back, the societal impact that modern birth control (and abortion) had upon family formation and savings has been subversive. Affluent baby boomers uniquely would worship at the alter of consumption early in life, deferring marriage. Then, thanks to government policies that subsidized housing in multiple ways, they would stretch already thin balance sheets to invest in McMansions and second homes that carried mortgages payable well into old age. The more plebeian of that generation would not miss out either, leasing cars, maxing out credit cards, and eventually grabbing for the brass ring through variable rate interest-only primary mortgages augmented with home equity loans that could extract any accumulation of net worth to be devoted to more pleasurable ends. Character in the Victorian sense is obsolete; so to pick up the pieces from the financial meltdown we are choosing to embark on an orgy of fiscal stimulus, national debt accumulation, and taxation of the entrepreneurial class, which has been the locomotive of our good fortune.

The book closes by venturing a look into the future, which as the great wordsmith of our time, Yogi Berra, opined, "ain't what it used to be." This last part begins by reminding us how reluctant concern over creeping socialism is, and how incognizant everyone from the least to the most educated are concerning the moral hazards of operating a fiat currency in conjunction with a state that is hell-bent on fiscal expansion and providing entitlements. Although we have veered far off the course that our founding fathers set for us, the financial crisis begun in 2008 may contain pressures that should be sufficient to trigger a reexamination of our banking sector and the powers granted to government over the last hundred years or so in a way that is much more deeply fundamental than anything currently under consideration. As of this writing in May 2009 the stock market is booming, but the real economy has yet to respond to the printing of money ordered by the Fed or the stimulus spending voted upon by Congress. Debt levels remain higher than ever, and income and employment is thought to have merely stabilized. How reduced income can support higher debt is a mystery, but then again the scale of government intervention has never been this great in peacetime. In the epilogue, a policy solution that is an alternative to this forceful intrusion is offered. It is not a purely free market approach as advocated by the Austrian School, the major difference being the necessity to protect depositors and account holders who were forced through Fed policy to trust deposits to a weak banking sector, and furthermore were taught to borrow heavily in order to keep up with inflation of asset prices, particularly real estate. But once these wrongs are undone, then the virtue of operating with a hard currency and drastically smaller government sector could be realized.

So the radical solution I would choose would require a shift in thinking to focus upon *greatly* reduced spending, lopping off most of the functionality of the government's regulatory apparatus. It would require at least a 50 percent devaluation of the dollar in terms of gold, to be accompanied through printing dollars to compensate busted deposits, insurance contracts, or securities held by those who foreswore conspicuous consumption and saved in supposedly safe bank accounts, annuities, or U.S. Treasuries. In fact, near the end of the book I explore what might be the equilibrium price of gold were it to be used to back the dollar; a price between $5,000 and $10,000 might be expected. When this process is complete, we could then scale back the role of the Fed to limit its policy actions only to times of truly desperate liquidity contraction, if at all. The repeal of the Sixteenth Amendment would be imperative; it should be replaced with a moderate and flat wealth tax. Interestingly, when Augustus restored the flat wealth tax in about 25 BC, it lit a fire under economic growth in the Roman Empire, for it reduced the marginal tax rate on income to 0 percent! Without constitutional tax reform, the gold purchased by the Fed to back the currency would hastily be shipped back to where it came.

Democracy is a privilege, for which generations of brave Americans have fought. To allow it to implode from the poisonous effects of socialism is to repeat the mistake of the Romans, and to condemn our children to lifetimes of servitude and close supervision by the cold, unfeeling tentacles of the state. There are two types of people who will read this book. One will feel empowered and may rediscover his civic duty. He is also likely to act by reallocating his investment choices, thinking he now has insight as to where we are headed. The second type of reader will feel somewhat impotent and overwhelmed by the changes at hand. But both camps of individuals have more in common with each other than they would like to admit.

# Endless Money

# Part One

# THE CALM BEFORE THE STORM

Wall Street is populated by many types of professionals: those who gather assets, those who package and sell securities, and those who trade them, to name a few. The portfolio manager is unique in that he is solely charged with investing to make money and avoid risk, although in the hypercharged atmosphere near the close of the 20th century such objectivity was subverted by new incentives.

This opening chapter is expressed in a familiar tone, through the eyes of one who participated with this awesome responsibility from the inception of the great 1982-2008 bull market through its collapse. Initially it captures the mood of downtown Manhattan, and then meanders through time to relay the money management mindset as it evolved. To know the collective mental state of the financial markets and of those who manage the money invested in them is to know the reduction of pecuniary thoughts of everyone—consumers, savers, government leaders—into one thing: price. Sometimes price anticipates the future, and other times it is backward looking and completely unable to see what is coming. Because of this unreliability, it confounds analysis by a rational mind. Those able to understand it can feel like the signal-man of Charles Dickens, who sees the future but is disbelieved.

The irrationality of inflection points is discussed in this context, with examples of the fate of heretic signal-men as well as those who enjoyed success when acting on completely sham information. These two odd bedfellows are explained by an outside and ignored dimension, typified by the onset of the banking crisis, when CEOs of banks thought their institutions were sound because of low defaults and delinquencies, but loan balances were perilously close to inflated home values.

In fact, those who apply scientific methods and construct sophisticated portfolios around them eventually see what they have assembled abandoned by the flows of capital, like the dispersion of the peoples who came together to build the Tower of Babel before the job was completed. This chapter begins its conclusion in homage to Nassim Taleb, critic of the modern day builders of risk models, who was one of the few who warned of just such a predicament awaiting us. But the chapter goes further by reminding us, as C.S. Lewis did, that feeling the "clean sea breeze of the centuries" can provide a glimmer of the future, even when it is seemingly irrational. It ends by carrying forward these humbling lessons of the world of finance to the political sphere, which over the decades has become divisive and summarily dismissive of solutions that might unite our moral sentiment, instead embracing socialism and statism. By providing this personal-tone poem of sorts before diving into the observations of this book, a hope is nourished that readers may welcome new opinions and recognize some transcendent ideas that shed light on the danger of our monetarist, political, and cultural impasses.

# Chapter 1

# Unknown Unknowns

*"After partaking of a slight refreshment in almost breathless silence the Gen. filled his glass with wine and turning to the officers said, 'With a heart full of love and gratitude I now take leave of you. I most devoutly wish that your latter days may be as prosperous and happy as your former ones have been glorious and honorable.' After the officers had taken a glass of wine the Gen. said, 'I cannot come to each of you, but shall feel obliged if each of you will come and take me by the hand.'*
*Gen. Knox being nearest to him turned to the Commander in Chief Who suffused in tears was incapable of utterance but grasped his hand when they embraced each other in silence. In the same affectionate manner every officer in the room marched up, kissed and parted with his general in chief. Such a scene of sorrow and weeping I had never before witnessed and fondly hope I may never be called to witness again."*

COL. BENJAMIN TALLMADGE, *THE MEMOIR OF COL. BENJAMIN TALLMADGE*, COLLECTION OF FRAUNCES TAVERN MUSEUM, P. 103

To be prosperous and happy, in the words of Washington, is the hope he bestowed upon his officers in 1783. Today the average salary in Downtown Manhattan is $115,000, and this mixes in everyone: from the brigade of 20-something women with vampish nails from Staten Island who commute by ferry to their first jobs as adults, to the tired older men who squeeze in and out of the Lex subway line in perspiration on a

3

hot July day or wearing rain-drenched pinstripes. One wonders if they might still be working from joy of doing battle with the market or because they lost nearly everything at Drexel Burnham, Bear Stearns, or if it were in the days of yore, that they "took a loss with Auchincloss." For years, the best and the brightest from Harvard, Stanford, Amos Tuck, and other elite graduate business schools came here alongside the pugnacious of Brooklyn or Jersey who might simply pass a Series 7 exam, all in the quest for profit and a better life. Most might now sit behind a Bloomberg terminal in midtown, in Boston's financial district, or even in a comfortable class "A" space in suburban Dallas, Minneapolis, or San Diego.

As an institutional portfolio manager, you might lunch with industry analysts, CEOs, CFOs, economists, or strategists. Dick Cheney was on tap for this highly paid entertainment circuit well before becoming Veep or taking the reins of Halliburton. Oddballs sure to stimulate, such as Iben Browning, climatologist and raconteur extraordinaire, might have regaled students of the markets with billions to manage with tales of tree rings and revolutions, long before anyone had even thought about global warming. Lunch might be served for these occasions at Fraunces Tavern, the scene of Washington's farewell to his officers. Or it might be at the India House or Delmonico's, which dates back to 1837, or atop a skyscraper with a sweeping view of the harbor, the bridges, and the Statue of Liberty. If you gaze on the horizon, you can see the Atlantic Ocean.

The walk there takes you through narrow, crooked streets between tall buildings that block the light more than would be the case further uptown, save for refuges like Trinity Church or its parish, St. Paul's Chapel. Buried in its graveyard is Alexander Hamilton, who issued bonds for the Revolutionary War, founded the Bank of New York, and created the national bank, later dismantled by Andrew Jackson; he was laid to rest there not even having turned 50 in 1804, dead from the gunshot wounds from the historic duel with Aaron Burr. William Bradford, Robert Fulton, and others whom school children would not know rest in peace there, too, and there are many graves whose headstones have been erased by the grit of time. A sycamore tree in the chapel graveyard was stripped and broken while deflecting debris when the World Trade Center came down; St. Paul's Chapel, Manhattan's oldest structure, was hardly touched thanks to the heroism of the tree, which succumbed alongside the 3,000 who fell that day.

But most of the dead of Manhattan are gone, literally disinterred and escorted off the island long ago to make room for buildings that capture $50 per square foot annually for each floor that rises up from the earth. A 70-story building might bring in $100,000 each year from the sliver above what was a final resting place, so the capitalized value of a cemetery plot might be $1 million to a developer if he could buy enough together to have several contiguous acres. The living of Wall Street are younger than you might think; a cartoon draws a chuckle by depicting a young man in pinstripes, cufflinks, suspenders, Hermes tie and spread collar responding to a bartender's request for ID by saying, "Of course I'm over 21. I'm a managing director of Morgan Stanley."[1] Few have time to think about the past.

Walking through these canyons in rapid pace or squeezed in "pedlock" waiting to cross the street to get back to work does not promote reflection. Occasionally you might be tempted to rest in the chapel, but you can't, for the pews of St. Paul's were removed to accommodate those who might browse rather than sit and cogitate, making the chapel more a secular museum than a spot for contemplation. In the bull market of the late 1960s, a vigorous young curate of the Trinity Church, Francis C. Huntington, sought to explore the work-related problems of the professionals on Wall Street, holding discussion groups wherein he would ask them about "what was bugging them about their jobs." Discouraged by tepid interaction and admonition from his superiors to not overstep the bounds of this conservative church's spiritual mission, he set up another congregation down the street. But instead of uncovering gutsy problems among his new fold, he found evasiveness. Problems were always someone else's. Eventually his new "church," the Wall Street Ministry, would be watered down through renaming to the Wall Street Center, a less provocative appellation. It probably exists no longer, but a search for it turns up help from social workers at the Wall Street Counseling Center. Instead of contemplation, it offers assistance with substance abuse, psychotherapy, and marriage counseling.[2]

After your first walks about the neighborhood as a young professional on Wall Street, the sense of the past might fade into the background, and as you step, your own thoughts of financial markets cling instead. You remember the digital screen, nowadays two or more, that keeps you focused on what is happening today, this very moment.

More than anything you want insight; the unique arrangement of ups and downs you see are a compelling truth, but they will be forgotten by tomorrow. Perhaps the long view might help. What would Hamilton say if he were here? Or Jefferson, Burr, or Madison?

## The Signal-Man

If I telegraph Danger, on either side of me or on both, I can give no reason for it," he went on, wiping the palms of his hands. "I should get into trouble, and that is no good. They would think I was mad. This is the way it would work,

Message: 'Danger! Take Care!'

Answer: 'What Danger? Where?'

Message: 'Don't know. But for God's sake, take care!'

They would displace me. What else could they do?"

His pain of mind was most pitiable to see. It was the mental torture of a conscientious man, oppressed beyond endurance by an unintelligible responsibility involving life.

Charles Dickens, *The Signal-Man*, 1866

Humans are adaptive. Our history is one of making alterations to our routines, mostly small, but sometimes there are breakthroughs. Most of the time, we see from experience what worked and what did not. We are focused on objectives, so much so that sometimes this might even color our perception of the past, like the conflicting accounts of witnesses in the classic 1950 film, "Rashomon." Austrian School economist Friedrich Hayek believed that capitalism evolved through this adaptive process, and as a broad, intricate system of incorporating market signals it contained intelligence greater than any that could be assembled by central planners.

The complexity of this adaptive, broad system of intelligence makes forecasting nearly impossible. But like the signal-man of the Dickens story, we are treated to flashes of the future. The signal-man is not sure if he is hallucinating, but he gets the ear of the protagonist, who listens sympathetically to his recounting of premonitions that certain recent rail disasters would occur. In the end, the signal-man's third vision is indeed accurate, for it foretells his own death. But without certainty and being able to color in the details, neither the signal-man nor his new friend could make use of his limited clairvoyance, much less give him peace that he was not losing his mind. Indeed, economic or investment forecasting is a perilous occupation, sure to madden most who try to master it.

Today the economy and the capital markets are faced with the long-term buildup of public and private credit. Moreover, promises to tax and spend future income may even be the greater influence. How we got here is more a story of what has happened to our culture than it is one of a particular central bank or government policy. Combined, our private and public liabilities are multiples of the income of the United States, and the situation is no different in Europe. The change to a system wherein liabilities could pile up without eliciting much concern happened so slowly that few noticed any change, yet a time traveler from a century ago would not recognize the financial or governmental institutions of today. Interestingly, a citizen of the Roman Empire would see certain parallels: His empire spared the aristocracy from taxation, and protected it in credit crises. The treasury of the Roman Republic flooded its economy with 50 tonnes of freshly minted silver denarii annually at its peak, driving up real estate prices. Yet the cost of living remained subdued with free bread and entertainment.

Often long-term trends such as this work in the background, like the Coriolis force giving birth to a tropical storm which then builds into a hurricane. Save for the 1970s, the system of fiat currency has been spectacularly successful: Recessions have been tame and short, while the cost has been tolerable inflation during expansions. Ironically, tapping into the people's credit and spending power through Keynesian fiscal policy and aggressive central banking builds up more Coriolis force, but dampens the perception of risk in the near-term. The credit crisis of 2008 may be remembered as a gentle rain, with downpours in certain small regions. Or what we feel may be bands of moisture preceding a category five deluge, or a reminder that the next season might be worse. There is a huge difference between forecasting the weather and being prepared for inevitable dangers. The former is almost impossible to do; the latter ought to be easy. But, as the victims of Katrina in 2005 would attest, not having known of such loss of life since the 1928 Okeechobee Hurricane bred complacency.

It is almost impossible for humans to be concerned with what in retrospect seems so logical a course of action when the benefit from doing so is actually the denial of some short-term pleasure. Shoring up levees is a costly and constant necessity. Even simply leaving town for a few days is inconvenient. Before advance warning and flood insurance was available, folks simply did not build in the flood plain.

The timing or eventuality of financial calamity is unable to be forecast. At best it might be like a hurricane warning: The tempest may strike here, it may hit there, it may be downgraded to a tropical storm, or it may go elsewhere entirely. But that doesn't mean one should whistle through the graveyard. Man has developed ways, though crude, to help those who dare to live in dangerous regions.

The capital markets are the nerve center for all things economic. They flash signals of future events, sometimes warning of danger, sometimes transmitting aggregate foolishness: a mirror to our psyche. But many times the commentary from the experts is dead wrong when longstanding trends give way. What follows here is a framework for thinking about how to recognize what might be happening beneath the surface and affecting the long term. A few anecdotes from times past are salted in to provide more color—one insider's view from the highest level of money management.

Humans are especially prone to faulty judgment at points of inflection, that is, when a trend is reversing. This is particularly so when what is to come is well outside the realm of expectations. At such points, there is a minority of market participants who are sensitive that the change is occurring. Members of this group, like Dickens' signalman, have glimmers of the change to come. It is not necessary that they completely understand what is occurring. In fact even completely bogus input could yield the proper result to those acting upon the new information.

On the other hand, the majority are so hardwired to the established direction they will insist that the reams of information put in place during the historical trend prove they are in the know. Another way to think about inflection points being invisible to the majority is to draw an analogy to how fish might view swimming in a pond that is surrounded by the first winter cold front capable of freezing it. They live in the dimension of water, and cannot know what the air is doing unless they are among the few who might be jumping. Similarly, humans have an inherent difficulty with factors existing in another dimension, for these can remain unapparent to observers even some time after an inflection occurs. In 2007, banking CEOs were saying their institutions were sound and some even had their boards of directors authorize massive share repurchases to defend against slight drops in valuation. Charge-off ratios and delinquencies were manageable. But depositor funds, leveraged near 20-to-1, had been invested in mortgages secured by real estate whose value had skyrocketed; a slight drop might wipe out the thin coverage inherent in loan-to-value ratios and the banks' capital ratios. To many banks it did. Even well into the crisis there was little acknowledgement of the debacle that has occurred in the real estate market. One of the real estate industry's principal news sources, *Inman News*, published an article in late August 2008 by economic commentator Lou Barnes that typifies the real estate agent mindset of denial. Barnes rants, "Case Shiller continues its hysterical mismeasurement, insisting that home prices fell 15.9 percent in the last year. The excellent www.ofheo.gov data has national prices down 4.8 percent."[3]

There are anecdotes galore that one might cite where trend followers were humbled. In a twist to logic, Bill Miller, who recorded one of the longest streaks of besting the S&P 500 of any mutual fund manager, suddenly saw a 34 percent drop in his $9.7 billion LMVTX fund in the 12-month period through July 2008 when the financial sector began its collapse, but still before the financial markets as a whole melted down. This plunge far exceeded a 12 percent correction in the S&P 500 over the same time span.[4] Legg Mason held 80 million shares of Freddie Mac as of July 31, 2008, in Miller's fund and in its institutional accounts, up from 50 million earlier in the year. On September 8 these sank below $1 per share after the U.S. Treasury moved in to rescue this firm and Fannie Mae. As Miller's comments reveal, he has followed a strategy of being a contrarian, not a trend follower. Yet somehow, under the penumbra of the reversal of a long-term trend that may be unfolding in the credit crisis, Miller might unwittingly have become one with a powerful tendency to overextend credit and flex governmental muscle to avoid recessions. The frustration of Miller, who deservedly achieved financial stardom for a lifetime of achievement, is evident in the comments he made to his mutual fund shareholders in a July 27, 2008, letter:

> I have used the mantra to our analysts that if it's in the papers, it's in the price—which used to be correct. Indeed, it borders on cliché in the business that by the time something makes the cover of the major news or business publications, you can make money by doing the opposite. There is solid academic research to back this up. But in the past two years, you didn't need to know anything except to sell what the headlines were negative about (anything related to real estate, the consumer, or finance) and buy anything that was going up and that everybody liked (energy, materials, industrials).
>
> … It has been explained to me that it was obvious we should not have owned homebuilders, or retailers, or banks, and that I should have known better than to invest in such things. It was also obvious that growth in China and India and other developing countries would drive oil and other commodities to record levels and that related equities were the thing to own. "Don't you even read the papers?" was a common comment.
>
> … Is it obvious financials should be bought right now, having reached the most oversold levels since the 1987 Crash, and the lowest valuations since the last great buying opportunity in 1990 and 1991? Or is it obvious that they should be avoided, since the credit problems are in the papers every day and write-offs and provisioning will likely continue into 2009?[5]

One might also gain insight from examining the psyche of investors at other major inflection points, chosen from long ago since even a year or two after a crisis it seems the human mind can't always comprehend how big a change might have been afoot. The Dow Jones Industrial Average was below a ceiling of 1,000 from 1969 to1982. The mutual fund industry was in net redemption for many of these years. One such fund complex, which shall remain unnamed, coped with this challenge by keeping an extremely tight lid on expenses. Its portfolio managers were woefully underpaid, and professionals hired to direct the sales force turned over nearly once each year. Very close to the end of this decade of moribund stock market behavior, the firm could only entice someone to head the sales operation by offering him a significant percentage of firmwide net sales. Once the market broke through 1,000 and money began to pour in like a monsoon after the dry season, his compensation ballooned well beyond that of the CEO of the conglomerate that owned the fund company. Portfolio managers, still earning the compensation of mid-level administrators, started to get picked off by Wall Street firms desperately needing to staff up for the bull market. The independent directors of the funds under advisement threatened to award the contract to manage them to another firm, which led to a hastily arranged sale. Within a year, profits had risen so much that this transaction had, in retrospect, taken place at just two times earnings, and the extraordinary rise in profits would continue for decades.

In the meantime, the portfolio managers of this fund complex had their own issue to resolve, which ran concurrently with this change in trend. Being heavily weighted in energy stocks during the 1970s had been rewarding, but suddenly this tailwind had reversed. What happened next demonstrates how at an inflection point, factually incorrect information, can counterintuitively lead to the correct decision being made. This is so because due to the complexity of the capitalist system, all information embedded within its millions of transactions sometimes is not arranged into a logical pattern (such as a trend) until well after the fact. Obfuscation of the truth at major turning points applies to foreign affairs and politics as well: Only Churchill could recognize the menace of Hitler; the CIA and FBI as a whole could not weigh the threat from Islamic fundamentalism despite repeated attacks from Al Qaeda (but John O'Neill, the former head of counterterrorism in the FBI's New York field office who perished as director of security at the World Trade Center could).

The scenario was this: In the waning days, months, and weeks of the peak in the oil market (1980), energy stocks carved an ever more vertical trajectory. At this apex, volatility became extreme. On a large down day during the top of this formation, news spread that in the remote regions of Siberia a massive new oilfield had been discovered that would dwarf the reserves of Saudi Arabia and cause the supply of oil to overwhelm demand globally. Pondering the significance of this, the portfolio managers asked their in-house energy expert what to do. His instinct was to chase down the rumor to see if it was real. Its fabricators knew it would be nigh impossible for anyone to obtain confirmation from the Soviet authorities, so doubt would linger, enhancing their ability to make the most of their lie through shorting energy. Eventually, various so-called experts on Wall Street would emerge to refute the report. Thus, the in-house expert chose to parlay his access to these revered gurus on the street rather than jump to a conclusion and possibly be proven wrong. Emboldened by possessing the right information certified by the most expert of the experts, he concluded that his firm should continue to weight energy stocks heavily in portfolios. To his chagrin, energy stocks plummeted month after month, eventually bottoming out six years later, which is what one would have expected had the rumor been true.

Institutional investors are revered because they know more than the little guy. Indeed they always do, but knowledge does not always guarantee them better performance than the market gets as a whole, because in essence they *are* the market. They are subject to the same blindness and emotion as the rest of us. Humans are predisposed to seek out facts in the present, but we are poor at crafting these into descriptions befitting inflection points, or even during the considerable period of time that follows. By nature most will fall back upon the comfort of possessing expert knowledge and be dismissive of almost any hypothesis well outside the range of current forecasts. The best kept secret is one that is told to everyone, but not believed (the verbal equivalent to Poe's *Purloined Letter*). Perhaps the reason is that collectively our ability to forecast, even among those who are emboldened to stake out turf outside the boundaries of evidence, is poor. Among us are too many boys crying wolf who are perennially wrong that the evidence-based majority of investors would reject any true prophet.

For those who have managed institutional money on Wall Street for decades, one of the most memorable outside-the-box forecasts came from First Boston strategist Suresh Bhirud, who in the spring of 1983, at a time when the Dow Jones Industrial Average was at 1,200, predicted correctly that it was headed much, much higher. Titled *On a Clear Day*

*You Can See 2,000*, the research report seemed unbelievable, since the market had been stalled beneath 1,000 for about a decade.[6]

On the other side of the coin is a graveyard filled with the intellects that have sought to challenge the wisdom of compounding credit growth at a rate significantly greater than real economic growth. There is a good reason for this: as Ibbotson and Sinquefield have shown, long-term returns of the stock market have been high, reflecting risk and a premium over inflation. From 1925 to 2007, large-cap stocks averaged a total return of 10.4 percent, while inflation was just 3 percent (using the official yardstick).[7] There are no straightforward decision rules for asset allocation that can be gleaned from fundamental data that are stable and reliable over time; so the conventional wisdom is that it is best to stick with stocks unless you have some need for money in the next few years.

In the late 1980s, Charlie Minter and his partner Stan Selvigson warned of a coming credit crisis. Although they were utterly wrong, their convincing graphics and articulate commentary was welcomed (but rarely acted upon) by institutional investors weary of continuously upbeat forecasts from other strategists. This duo was among the most requested in the infotainment office-visit circuit run by the big brokers, which provided them a foundation for leaving their employer, Merrill Lynch, and forming Comstock Partners. Public figures have mistakenly sounded the alarm of excessive speculation, too. In 1955, the Senate Banking Committee investigated the stock market, issuing a report concluding there was too much speculation, even though dividend yields on stocks were about 40 percent *above* those available in the bond market, indicating continued public wariness of equities caused by memory of the Great Depression. (Currently dividend yields are 60 percent lower than bond yields, and bond yields themselves are near record lows). Federal Reserve Chairman Alan Greenspan thought the stock market was giddy with "irrational exuberance" in December 1996, only to find it would ascend more rapidly than ever, by 27.6 percent annually from the beginning of 1997 through the end of 1999.[8]

There is a long list of others who have bucked the conventional wisdom by being bearish. In fact, a cottage industry exists that exploits investor fears with dire predictions usually recommending ownership of gold coins or Treasury bills. They may have gained some converts during downturns, but each time the central bank has acted swiftly to spray more cheap credit out of its hose to put out the fire. With the exception of the malaise of the Jimmy Carter era, prolonged credibility has eluded those who would sound a systemic alarm.

In the last 50 years or more there has been a shift in the way the public invests. Before the Great Depression, stockbrokers were unregulated and might be involved in functions such as corporate finance, mergers, trading, or private capital. In the 1950s and 1960s, they were known for picking stocks. The go-go years of the 1960s produced a mutual fund star system, with performance aided by ownership in conglomerates such as Ling-Temco-Vought or ITT. An example of alchemy, conglomerates could buy almost any company and manufacture earnings per share through pooling merger accounting, now not permissible under generally accepted accounting principles (GAAP). "Derived from the Latin word *glomus*, meaning wax, the word suggests a sort of apotheosis of the old Madison Avenue cliché 'a big ball of wax, and is no doubt apt enough; but right from the start, the heads of conglomerate companies objected to it'."[9]

The net redemption of mutual funds in the 1970s gave way to the bull market of the 1980s, and by this time there were more mutual funds than NYSE-listed stocks. Large brokerage firms and their retail representatives realized that a separation of skills held advantages. Brokers were best at asset gathering and holding hands to retain accounts; if they were charged with selecting specific equities, they might be second-guessed for specific mistakes in client portfolios. Professional managers, in particular those in charge of in-house mutual funds, could be used instead. If clients were performance hungry, they could be shown independent managers with good three- or five-year track records. If *they* made mistakes, they could be jettisoned and easily replaced by the next one who had risen to the top of the statistical heap. During comparatively short periods of time the emergence of investing themes (Internet, energy, small-cap value, hedged portfolios, etc.) creates winners, so prospective clients always think the current menu looks appetizing. In this way Wall Street has inventively adapted to the threat raised by passive management, the case for which seemed airtight once the efficient market theorists were given their due. What is it about human nature that we value the present so highly, but we lose sight of the big picture?

## Unknown Unknowns

There are known knowns. There are things we know that we know. There are known unknowns. That is to say, there are things that we know we now know we don't know. But there are also unknown unknowns. There are things we do not know we don't know.

Donald Rumsfeld, statement from Defense
Department briefing, 2002[10]

In his bestseller, *The Black Swan*, the financial commentator Nassim Taleb claims that investors and economists err in understanding the direction of markets because they underestimate what they do not know, a concept he names "tunneling." (Before the sighting of a black swan in Australia, all swans were believed to be white.) Taleb tells the story of visitors to the medievalist and philosopher Umberto Eco's library of 30,000 books: Most compliment his knowledge by asking in amazement how many has he read; others understand that his wisdom comes from his habit of turning to the large number of unread books at his disposal for reference. When results come in outside the bounds of their forecasted outcomes, experts claim they were correct "except for certain unforeseeable influences." He notes a general tendency for costs of public and private projects to be greater than expected, often by orders of magnitude, because factors "outside the control" of forecasters are systematically excluded.[11] Taleb hints that forecasting may be error prone because of a feedback mechanism. For example, if economists predict inflation, it may not occur because the Fed may subsequently act by tightening credit.[12] Another insight is that the economic system (like global weather) is too complex to model. Inklings of the future suggested by the causal relationships hypothesized by a forecaster or known from historical evidence may indeed be valid, but they may not occur on schedule due to unforeseen circumstances. As John Maynard Keynes proclaimed, the market can remain irrational longer than one can remain solvent.

The religious and cultural observer C.S. Lewis spent much of the later portion of his life taking on what he termed "chronological snobbery," arguing that we cannot understand the implications of current day cultural or religious beliefs without an appreciation of the point of view from days past. He urged us to read old books "in order to let the clean sea breeze of the centuries" reveal the assumptions of our present era. C.S. Lewis, an intellectual genius with photographic memory, liked to demonstrate his ability to recall the written words of his own library. He would sometimes direct a guest at his home to select from 40 shelves of 20 books each. The guest would read one line from a random page, and C.S. Lewis would then recite the rest of the page from memory.[13]

Taleb sees no value in the role of financial market experts, because they cannot know the unknown and thus are unable to forecast reliably. This is a bitter pill for self-proclaimed experts such as this author. However, taking a cue from C.S. Lewis, we might find insight from appreciating where the credit, equity, and currency markets are in the context of a century or more of observing investment behavior. With the heat of the moment cooled by the "clean sea breeze" of knowing how we got to where we are, we may get glimmers of where we will go. Dicken's signal-man was open to the future, whereas those to whom the prescient signal-man would telegraph danger were not. Donald Rumsfeld was mocked for his poetic reference to unknown unknowns, the very things that Nassim Taleb says we exclude from our forecasts because they are outside our tunnel of vision. Anyone who dares to venture outside the reality of the recent past invites ridicule, for he is easily proven wrong by facts.

This book's observations about the world's financial meltdown that began in 2008 is an adventure into the past, into our American culture, and a reexamination of the very principles of this country's founding, including foregone conclusions about the viability of democracy. We have forgotten our forefather's debates about central banking, hard currency, and taxation. So too have we adopted a very different understanding of morals that guide us and our decisions. Theirs was a world of uncertainty, of setting a course that might produce a result greater than the world has seen since the Roman Republic, an epoch when global commerce and monetary exchange spontaneously erupted on the scene and brought forth a middle class with more than a subsistence livelihood.

In vivid contrast, the leaders of the present world are so certain that their solutions will provide for us that there is no substantive debate.

Yes, there is acrimony between Democrats and Republicans. But nearly every program that might strengthen our nation is off limits, the well poisoned by political correctness. A bipartisan solution to the crisis of cancerous growth in both private and public credit is to tweak entitlement benefits and raise taxes. To suggest that government is the problem, not the solution, is pure heresy. To suggest restoring the safe-keeping role of the financial system to banks would bring the zombies that hold the nation's deposits back to life is so unthinkable that no one in the private or public sector would seriously broach the thought. To suggest the removal of rules, not more rule-making for financial institutions, would never be considered by the commissioners of the SEC. A bill demanding the downsizing of any regulatory agency would never be entertained by a Congressional committee. Tax reform does get discussed occasionally, but gets about as much serious consideration as the purchase of a Mercedes Benz by a poverty stricken family. It is the domain of kook candidates such as Ron Paul or Mike Huckabee. Introducing some aspect of hardness to management of the money supply—even if it does not involve backing with gold—is academically dismissed as barbaric and earns its advocates the label of "crackpot." To question the spread of immoral behavior, be it in whole neighborhoods that are rife with crime or on the public airwaves, earns one the label of being uncaring. To return the public schools to the people, even with the subsidy of vouchers, is uncaring as well. Worst of all, to acknowledge that our democracy has given way to a new form of government—socialism—is unspeakable and will be denied out of hand. Only through the fresh breeze of history can we see how our course has veered in a direction that might irretrievably weaken us, unless we lose our hubris and our certainty that central control is the better way. We must rebuild our character, person by person.

# Chapter 2

# Wings of Wax

*So saying he applied his thought to new invention and altered the natural order of things. He laid down lines of feathers, beginning with the smallest, following shorter with longer ones . . . His son, Icarus, stood next to him, and, not realizing that he was handling things that would endanger him, caught laughingly at the down that blew in the passing breeze . . .*

*. . . when the boy began to delight in his daring flight, and abandoning his guide, drawn by desire for the heavens, soared higher. His nearness to the devouring sun softened the fragrant wax that held the wings: and the wax melted: he flailed with bare arms, but losing his oar-like wings, could not ride the air. Even as his mouth was crying his father's name, it vanished into the dark blue sea . . .*

METAMORPHOSES BOOK VIII, DAEDALUS AND ICARUS, OVID[1]

In a Greek myth, Daedalus escapes Crete where with his son, Icarus, is being held prisoner by King Minos, the keeper of the labyrinth Daedalus had built to hold the Minotaur. A master craftsman and intellect, he fashions wings from feathers, thread, and wax, and the pair escape. But Icarus, not heeding his father's warnings about the wax, flies too close to the sun, which melts his wings, plunging him to his death. When Daedalus lands safely in Sicily, where he hangs up his wings forever, he dedicates them to Apollo, the god of the sun (who not so incidentally melted the wax on Icarus' wings).

It is ironic that in the last decade more attention has been placed upon risk management than ever before. Every failed bank in this cycle manned a risk department with a veritable army of experts, but like the Romans feeling secure that Hannibal would never cross the Alps with elephants to attack them, the unexpected did happen. The primary reason why there is stress in the financial system today is real estate. Its value appreciated quickly, and at that point loans were taken out against its value. Yet it was perceived to be a low-risk asset until just before the crisis hit. In 2004 Franklin Raines, CEO of Fannie Mae, was asked in a House committee meeting why his company's equity was 3 percent of assets, whereas when a bank's equity ratio dips below 4 percent it is deemed to be in deep trouble. Raines replies, "There aren't any banks that only have multifamily and single-family loans. Those assets are so riskless that their capital for holding them should be under 2 percent."[2]

To understand what ails the capital markets, one must appreciate the progression of thought that accrued over the three decades prior to the panic of 2008.

The 1970s began with P-E multiples on stocks withering from over 50x during the "nifty fifty" phenomenon (pay any price for "greatness"—think Xerox, IBM, Polaroid, Avon) to the mid-single digits by 1973-74. Valuation remained depressed, and short-term yields topped 20 percent before that decade was over. The investment management industry saw its talent migrate elsewhere; jobs were scarce, and those few available in the industry were paid a pittance, especially when compared to investment banking. The superstars of that era were attracted to value, or they succeeded by heavily weighting the energy and capital goods sectors almost to the exclusion of all else. Investment management was a financial backwater, undesired by MBAs from Harvard, Stanford, or Tuck. Although the culture of each firm was unique, generally managers were left alone and permitted to concentrate sectoral bets. They did not engage in complex hedges to ameliorate risk. Although theoretically known, alpha (outperformance of an index used to benchmark) and beta (returns achieved solely through being invested in the stock market in general) were inseparable, and the principal tactic to deal with risk was to know when to move away from the crowd. Because commissions were $1 per share, 100-page long reports from boutique firms such as Donaldson Lufkin, Jenrette were easily paid for with client funds to guide decision making, and trading was extremely infrequent. Portfolio managers knew what they owned intimately and made strategic investments to last over time. Today, thanks to "dark pools" and ECNs (electronic communication networks), institutional stock commissions are zero or near zero. The emphasis is on getting in and out, hedging, pursuing an activist agenda against management for a quick buck, deftly reacting to news, getting a jump on proximal indicators of next quarter's sales and earnings—almost anything but avoiding risk by exercising sound judgment and simply buying a good company at a reasonable price and holding it.

The 1980s ushered in portfolio insurance, which parlayed an academic breakthrough that rapid, mechanistically enforced selling at a key inflection point of momentum would theoretically save holders of stocks from a bear market. This it failed to do, instead being a key accelerant to the collapse of equities in October 1987. By the millennium, risk management came into its own, employing vast ranks and seemingly effectively dampening poor performance. With everyone employing it, we were like the children of Lake Wobegone, who are all above average. But in its essential form, its primary message was to force portfolio managers not to manage as they learned in the 1970s, that is exploiting and then avoiding movements from one investment concept to another, but instead to spread out their bets by minimizing something known as *value-at-risk* (the sum of the variance inherent in all positions in one's portfolio). In plain English, this meant that having many small positions would reduce variation, but if a manager possessed true stock picking skill, his methodology applied consistently across hundreds or even thousands of choices would maximize alpha. His beta could then be laid off in the burgeoning markets for derivatives: futures and options.

Counterintuitively, demand for beta increased, for the academic community recognized that in an efficient market, it was senseless to do anything other than hold an index of stocks. A sort of truce in the institutional marketplace developed, with one faction mining alpha with increasingly sophisticated strategies (which required massive leverage to work, since excess returns were arbitraged to skinny possibilities) and another accommodating that group by dutifully accepting its offloaded beta.

With the sharp downturn following the Internet boom, demand for hedged, active return strategies skyrocketed. Although most hedge funds would provide transparency to their investors, many would instead choose to keep information about their portfolio holdings close to the vest. Promising a serving of cake and being able to eat it, too, they would assure potential and actual partners that their desire for risk aversion *and* high return on investment was being met. They would grind out monthly returns that were very good but almost never great or poor, suggesting all systems were working like a well-oiled machine. They would walk them through dazzling software-based control mechanisms designed to constantly react to sophisticated statistical measurements not only of the old standby, value-at-risk, but also geeky quantitative output such as gamma, rho, or delta. Returns were sliced and diced by ratios such as Sortino, Sharpe, information, tracking error, or downside deviation. Meanwhile, by not really offering a look under the hood and instead just passing out copies of the owner's manual, the deck was cleared for delivering precisely what the client was asking for—the impossibility of high, risk-reduced returns.

## Fake Alpha and Derivatives

In December 2008, Professors Dean Foster and H. Peyton Young, of the Wharton School and Oxford University, respectively, documented a basic methodology that could be practiced by hedge fund managers that could reliably produce "fake alpha."[3] In its simplest form it entails making a bet that a small degree of outperformance, perhaps 7 percent to 8 percent will result about 90 percent of the time, with the downside being a loss of everything in the other 10 percent of cases. There are no known cases of hedge funds deploying this strategy, but its mechanics are identical to what happens when a fund manager uses derivatives to boost current income that is uncorrelated with the market at the expense of suffering a major loss due to default. Might not the managers of Bear Stearns, who banked large bonuses each year, been inspired to do this because they could reshape financial contracts to produce high yields through option-like structures, with the consequences of their excess seemingly never to be felt due to the salutary effects of inflation, or deferred to some indistinct future moment?

What is intriguing is that to attract prodigious amounts of investment capital, hedge funds no longer needed to post eye-popping returns, just a constant stream of respectable profits and maybe a few mildly down months, a model that shysters like Bernie Madoff mastered to the pleasure of their sheep.

How were derivatives used to enhance return in a way suggestive of fake alpha? An oft-quoted example is the case where a small hedge fund set up a subsidiary backed by a paltry $4.6 million guaranteed $1.3 billion of subprime mortgages for the Swiss banking giant UBS. When it was called upon to put up additional collateral, it failed. However, the hedge fund had posted attractive returns of some 44 percent annually through the leverage on the fees while things were going well, making them an exquisite example of a legitimized producer of fake alpha that fed off the option premium collectible from the credit default swap gravy train.[4] But this gross example trivializes the systemic practice. Goldman Sachs was willing to borrow 30 times its equity base because it could lay off its credit risk through default swaps with AIG, which took in fake alpha earnings from booking premiums from the sale of premiums to Goldman.

Derivatives appealed to hedge funds that could use them in combination with borrowing. Both are a form of leverage. Derivatives became ubiquitous, extending well beyond the small hedge fund community and distributed through a network controlled by the world's largest banks. The 10 largest players in credit derivatives control 90 percent of the trading volume; assuming the global value of contracts is $530 trillion, this is 17 times the size of world GDP.[5] The industry's gross credit exposure before netting is estimated at $12.7 trillion and after netting is only $2.7 trillion.[6] The forced marriage of J.P. Morgan and Bear Stearns in March 2008, the two top holders of derivatives, pooled together $77 trillion and $13.4 trillion of derivatives, respectively.

If derivatives are so large and so involved in disguising risk and return among market participants, then why is there so little transparency in their disclosure? They are merely a line item footnote. When Enron collapsed, the financial community got a shot over the bow that it should be paying closer attention to the footnotes of financial statements. Enron aggressively used special purpose entities (SPEs), some 3,000 in off-balance sheet partnerships in which it effectively sold parts of itself to itself. Their nature was so complex that Enron's directors failed to understand the "economic rationale, the consequences, and the risks" of its deals,[7] and author Kurt Eichenwald (*Conspiracy of Fools*) makes the case additionally that even the firm's CFO, Andrew Fastow, didn't either. Yale law professor Jonathan Macey posits, "Enron was vanishingly close, in my view, to having complied with the accounting rules. They were going over the edge, just a little bit." Malcom Gladwell adds in the *New Yorker*, "It's almost as if they were saying, 'We're doing some really sleazy stuff in footnote 42, and if you want to know more about it ask us.'" Indeed, people did, from a business school project team at Cornell in 1998, to Jonathan Weil at the Dallas bureau of the *Wall Street Journal* in September 2000, to *Fortune's* Bethany McLean in March 2001. By December 2001 the company filed for bankruptcy.[8]

Would not a requirement of extensive transparency in the financial reporting of large financial institutions for derivatives combined with banning the research function from these same behemoths have produced a vibrant independent research industry with the fodder to have rung an alarm bell before the credit crisis emerged in 2008? Or were our taxpayer funds better spent doubling the staffs of the SEC and FINRA, which are thoroughly unequipped to make such important subjective judgments and, furthermore, never will be?

As with Enron, through late 2007 and 2008 headlines of articles repeatedly warned about the dangers of derivatives:

*Beware Our Shadow Banking System* announces the headline quoting Bill Gross in November 2007 on CNNMoney.com[9]
*A Way (Bank) Charges Stay Off the Bottom Line* informs David Reilly in the *Wall Street Journal* in April 2008[10]
Bloomberg's Yalman Onaran notifies us, *Banks Hide $35 Billion in Writedowns From Income, Filings Show*[11]

Independent analysts have done a great job of looking into the affairs of Enron and other disasters on an ex-ante basis, but regulators propagate a system that disadvantages them relative to proprietary research where large broker-dealers responsible for raising capital, trading, and other conflicting functions generate reports about investments. Due to technicalities it defines in detail, the SEC has determined these functions are operating conflict-free. And since coveted government posts such as SEC commissioner are tickets to partnerships and managing directorships at the highest-paying financial institutions in the world, the rules determined by those who would safeguard the public are friendly to this deadly form of cross-subsidization that suffocates the public's one best chance for objective analysis of investments. At the same time it refuses to mandate transparency as to where dollars flow for research on the investment advisor side of the investment world. Is it any wonder that the research business remains dominated by the subsidized ranks of analysts at large broker-dealers?

## Operational Risk

Operational risk accounts for a significant category of investor losses; it is fraud or more often the case plain old mismanagement (think of the preposterous assumptions of Long-Term Capital Management). We are told it is hard to guard against it and that there are no software packages that can avert it. Of course, the disinfectant of transparency goes a long way, but common sense is the most effective tool at our disposal to avoid being sucked into such schemes.

The centerpiece of operational risk for our time has to be the Bernie Madoff scandal, which broke in December 2008. However, the continual financial market meltdown has revealed other giant Ponzi schemes, such as the failure of the $50 billion Stanford Group in February 2009. Oddly, most mainstream professional money managers had never heard of Madoff, yet he had raised over $50 billion. The public response will likely be a vociferous demand for yet more intensive regulation of the financial industry (a topic examined in detail later in this book), yet Madoff's operation was not in fact a hedge fund. Instead he ran an SEC-regulated broker-dealer, offering separately managed accounts whose owners—the ones being duped—were a type of hedge fund known as a "fund of funds." Even more mystifying, is that the type of hedge fund that fed Madoff his funding offers as its sole expertise its ability to select other hedge funds in which to invest. While selection of and access to funds with high returns is a key determinant of the success of funds of funds, an equally large selling point for them is usually their procedures for due diligence (how well they kick the tires).

The most amazing part of the Madoff affair is that experienced hands in the industry which practiced the investment strategy Mr. Madoff professed to employ, an options trading technique long known as "risk-less arbitrage," loudly proclaimed that it was impossible to produce a track record with it akin to what Madoff reported to his investors. When practiced in its purest form, it involves buying and selling calls, puts, and an underlying equity such that risk of price movement is hedged away. Under these circumstances the market has long offered essentially Treasury bill type returns, because arbitrage has narrowed spreads since at least the 1970s. In contrast to other risky investments, Madoff's returns were not off the charts. Just like any good Ponzi scheme they were plausibly in the low double digits, with never a down month and rarely if ever a sub-par result. However, they aroused suspicion in the options community. Madoff's competitors, assailed with feedback from the capital-raising specialists that they were incompetent because they could not replicate the effortlessly sellable Madoff track record, were appalled. One in particular, Harry Marcopolos, took it upon himself to pen a 19-page examination of Madoff complete with a recitation of no less than 29 "red flags," which he presented seemingly on a silver platter to SEC officials titled, *The World's Largest Hedge Fund is a Fraud.*[12]

Marcopolos is a derivatives expert, having traded portfolios in the billions of dollars in various options strategies for hedge funds and institutional clients. The general thesis Marcopolos advances is that for Madoff to have outdone the returns the market permits for riskless arbitrage, he would have had to deviate from it and consistently made bets that were winners for nearly 200 months, consecutively. (Madoff had seven months in which he claimed losses of less than 1 percent.) Zeroing in on periods of time when the market was pricing options such that riskless arbitrage was essentially inoperable, such as the Asian currency crisis, he concluded the likelihood of Madoff not having suffered more than a few skin lacerations is statistically almost impossible. (It could also be said it was strange he never hit the cover off the ball if he had needed to deviate from riskless posturing during such unusual market conditions.) He goes on to question the firm's overall structure, whereby it leaves on the table the opportunity of collecting the customary 20 percent incentive fee for its fund of fund clientele to enjoy, which given its readily marketable track record would be irrational not to capture.

Also, knowing the depth of the marketplace and the approximate size of the Madoff assets (which he underestimated), Marcopolos, based upon his experience, believed Madoff could only have hedged its large portfolio by using nonexchange traded derivatives, which could only have come from UBS or Merrill Lynch, the only two firms dealing in the OTC derivatives market that would trade with Madoff. He alleges that these firms would not write contracts of that magnitude without extracting a usurious premium for the use of their risk capacity. He taunts the SEC to demand to see the order tickets for such transactions, being fairly certain these trades could not have happened. Even more suspiciously, Marcopolos asks why Goldman Sachs and Citigroup, which are larger than UBS and Merrill, refused to enter into the counterparty risk of dealing with what would have had to have been the juiciest plum of options accounts on the street.

Stanford Capital, a financial fraud equally large as Madoff, ostensibly sought to improve upon the investment returns it promised its depositors by placing capital into private investment deals, as suggested by a preliminary investigation. Stanford may not have stolen outright as did Madoff, but the incentives to collect fees for years and walk away when poor returns inevitably might follow were irresistible. Stanford offered the public exactly what it wanted—seemingly low risk yet high returns—and the public felt emboldened to accept this prima facie because regulators and sophisticated risk models implied legitimacy and safety. Perhaps not as boldly or behind as many offshore curtains, much of the hedge fund community was delivering solid but not eye-popping returns and promising to have little risk. Pershing, one of the largest custodial brokers on Wall Street, stopped doing business with Stanford Group in early 2008 (about a year before its collapse), because it became wary of Stanford's unwillingness to allow an independent investigation into its financial health.

No doubt the public, encouraged by a righteous media, will demand more regulation to prevent frauds like Madoff from recurring. In response their auditing and enforcement staffs will probably double once again as they did in the last eight years. It is far from certain that they would uncover the next broker-dealer committing large-scale fraud such as Madoff, but it is a certainty they will track down more technical violations from the sea of documentation required of the industry. One has to wonder, in the eight examinations the SEC performed over 16 years at Madoff, might it have caught him if it had demanded to see fewer pieces of paper produced by those in on the fraud that were expertly crafted to throw off the agency, and instead had its staffers cross-check just a handful with counterparties? According to a few SEC auditors interviewed off the record by the author, the firm's counterfeit DTC trade confirms were so good they were "better than originals." Wouldn't following through with the DTC or Madoff's trading partners, justified by the implausibility of Madoff's business model, have revealed as the trustee suggested in February 2009 that no trades had ever occurred? Might a tightly focused operation with fewer, more effective, and fraud-focused investigators and less paperwork be more productive and in alignment with what investors seek?

How much does the public rely upon the security blanket of knowing the SEC and FINRA are present at the investment advisors and broker-dealers it chooses to trust? If "Member–FINRA, SIPC" had not been emblazoned next to the firm logo, or if Madoff himself had not been chairman of the NASDAQ stock market, might more potential clients have scratched before they sniffed? A town that has 100 traffic cops and no murder detectives probably won't find any dead bodies, but its police force will be very busy and profitable.

## Evidence-Based Investing

How else could one get the courage to lever up to five-to-one or even 30-to-1 as was the case in some investment banks and statistical arbitrage proprietary trading funds, without "proof" that certain assets and liabilities would behave in correlation or within bands of normal distribution? One year before the equity market imploded due to the credit crisis, a class of hedge funds known as "statistical arbitrage" funds collapsed, foretelling the effect leverage was having on stability of the market. The premise of this fund category was that excess returns could be harvested from bets on mean reversion, such as spreads between certain categories of debt, or among equity sectors such banks that lend against real estate and REITs, which own property. Knowledge of correlations, which can be used to calculate probabilities, would in theory limit risk, because such historical data would quantify the likelihood that disparate performance could further widen from the mean or inverse correlations might be relied upon to offset unexpected movement. The funds hedge extensively, maintaining both long and short positions that by design should move in concert, but over time differ slightly enough to produce a net gain on the two opposites. Since these opposing bets cancel each other out so much, very high amounts of leverage must be employed to earn an attractive absolute rate of return. All is well and good if the tendency for the individual holdings to move together continues in line with history, but if a secular shift occurs, risk is magnified. Why? Because the structure of this strategy exchanges one type of risk for another. Being hedged, the fund loses its correlation with the overall market. But due to the mathematics, its sensitivity to the *change* in covariance of its positions is magnified fourfold.

Probably half of all statistical arbitrage funds that deployed this strategy have moved on to greener pastures. But the use of value-at-risk statistical models to control exposure in hedge funds or even for large pension funds that allocate between different asset types continues, and it is virtually a mandatory exercise for institutional managers. There is hardly a large pension plan that has not developed a PowerPoint presentation that boasts it realigned its investments to increase excess return (alpha) and also reduced risk (variance). So in this sense, statistical arbitrage exists in some diluted form almost everywhere.

Nassim Taleb decries the practice of evidence-based investing and value at risk models as conducted in the mainstream of Wall Street in his tome *The Black Swan*. In this book, he suggests that distributions of not only investment returns but most phenomena might follow a Mandelbrotian pattern instead of the mainstay assumption of normal distribution. In other words, outcomes are not clustered near a mean. That being the case, risk modeling in the investment community might work fine for long periods of time, but then when change occurs, the models would be wildly wrong.[13]

Evidence-based investing is so compelling numerically that it attracts vast amounts of capital to managers who have established track records of deploying it successfully. But it has produced a market full of capital awarded to funds based upon historical trends, which are subject to dramatic realignment, particularly in light of what may be a generational economic episode that may result in the realignment of trade between nations, the bankruptcy of major global entities, or even entire countries and their currencies, Iceland being the first to fall. Market participants can only seek to hedge against perceived risk, or known unknowns. When many stand on the same side of the boat in the belief that they are protected by the latest technology, the iceberg below the surface has a tendency to create a Titanic moment.

## The Greatest Risk

To combust, a fire requires three conditions: fuel, oxygen, and heat. Derivatives and evidence-based investing are not enough to cause a financial meltdown. What causes a generational event is the presence of a fiat based monetary system that encourages the printing of bank money. The reason is that it beguiles the public to embrace leverage with gusto, at twice the magnitude seen just before the Great Depression (See Figure 2.1). This bet was made based upon the assumption that

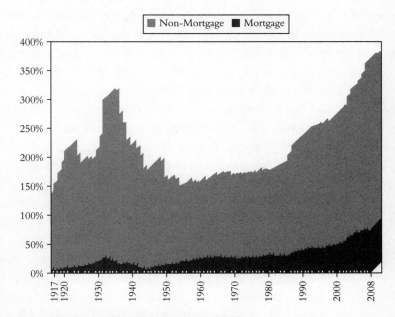

**Figure 2.1    U.S. Total Debt as a Percentage of GDP**
*Sources:* Historical Statistics of the United States, Federal Reserve System Data

real estate prices would continue to ascend, as they had historically, or at the very least not decline appreciably.

With the stock market downturn of late 2008, scales have fallen from the eyes of some observers such that leverage is now known to have built up excessively. The tremendous amount of debt that accumulated could only have occurred in a banking system that forced the creation of $1 trillion of new paper money annually from the peak of the Internet bubble in 2000 to the financial meltdown of 2008 through fractional reserve lending. And the creation of bank money was not much less prolific in the entire history of the Federal Reserve System.

The stability witnessed since World War II in the U.S. economy may ironically be a *cause* of economic instability, which could be deepened and extended in duration should cultural and political factors align in complete support of socialism. Whenever there has been a recession, rates have been lowered and liquidity injected such that the impact of credit default was diluted. Although this avoided long, deep recessions, it has encouraged greater and greater waves of risk taking.

What did the American public know of the credit crunch? Amazingly, a survey of 1,361 homeowners released in August 2008 and conducted by Harris Interactive for Zillow, an Internet-based provider of home valuations derived from the collection of last sale public records and proprietary algorithms, revealed that 62 percent of homeowners thought their home value had *increased* or remained the same in the last year! In fact, 77 percent of U.S. homes lost value in the 12 months preceding the survey. In the *next* six months, homeowners thought their own properties will increase in value or at least remain the same price, but they mused that 42 percent of other people's homes would drop.[14]

In addition to investing heavily in real estate, in aggregate the American public used borrowing power generated by that asset to save for retirement through the purchase of common stocks. According to Ibbotson Associates' database, which stretches from 1926 to 2007, the best 20-year period of return on investment for large company stocks was 1980-1999, where annual profit including reinvested dividends was 17.9 percent—better than any other of the 63 total sequences of 20-year stretches contained in the whole period. Highly correlated with stocks during this time period were long-term bonds, which turned in their best 20-year rolling return from 1982 to 2001. With this recent history still fresh in the mind of investors, confidence in the long-run returns of stocks remained quite high until the panic began in September 2008. Mutual fund complexes continued to exhort investors to "dollar cost average" their accounts through tithing their paychecks, thereby removing emotions from decision-making and vaccinating their company's income stream from sudden redemptions. With returns like these, why not invest with an indexed approach?

Since that is pretty safe and lucrative as the long-term data suggest, why not do it but also enhance returns by availing oneself to the fruits of modern scientific methods? At long last the bull market provided an escape from the dreary nihilistic world of efficient market dogma. In 1996, near the end of the best long-term equity return period of several lifetimes spanned by the Ibbotson data, appeared one Jeremy Siegel with his "definitive guide to high-return, low-risk equities," a book for the masses titled *Stocks for the Long Run*. Siegel has escaped from the world of academia into the lucrative world of Wall Street through establishing WisdomTree, a provider of ETFs and mutual funds. WisdomTree tweaks the major indicies to squeeze out a slightly better return with less volatility—all based upon statistical analysis thought-fully proven through roughly 40 years of backtesting. The strategy is to exploit a structural flaw that requires index funds to buy more of stocks that go up and sell as underperformers go down;—instead it does the opposite by slightly overweighting holdings of high dividend yielding or low P/E stocks. While the approach appears to be successful and probably improves upon the returns of individuals plunging their IRAs into hot tips heard at the country club tap room, demand for this product may be indicative of the public's unwavering faith in equities and bonds, and buying-on-dips right up until the end. In fact it enhances the buying on dips approach, which could put it in front of the same trend that eroded the performance of Bill Miller's Legg Mason Value Trust. What if we are at an inflection point at the end of a major long-term trend, such as the one that delivered the best 20-year stock and bond returns ever in the Ibbotson database?

Why were individual investors so quick to plunge back in to buy 10,000 share lots of Citigroup trading at $2 per share in March 2009 in an attempt to recoup their 50 percent drubbing in late 2008? It might or might not work, but either way it is a doubling down mentality. Treasury Secretary Geithner tapped in to this raw desire for the rocket fuel of optionality when he fashioned the Private Public Investment Program (PIPP) to lure capital to make a highly leveraged bet to buy toxic debt from ailing banks in that same month. What if our culture, which has rejected absolutes and embraced humanism, has substituted manmade, evidence-based thinking for moral thinking and humility regarding the unknown? Investors who lived through the Great Depression would not have bought into the WisdomTree approach or the idea of having confidence in the long-term and indexation at all. Why not? Because the evidence of their times told them not to do so.

Should the credit crisis have been expected? If one ascribes to the religion of fiat currency, credit can be comfortably grown with minimal inflation, and in so doing, deep recessions are arrested by intervention. Like the fish in the pond surrounded by sub-32°F air, most participants in the economy cannot yet feel an impact, nor do they anticipate the effects of having reached a tipping point from too much debt and the profligate spending of federal and state governments. Europe is no better. Its more hawkish central bank may have protected the foreign exchange value of its currency for a time, but credit expansion happened there, too. Moreover, Europe has even higher tax rates, entitlement commitments, and debt levels. As usual, we are hanging on to the implications of each minute piece of economic data and failing to grasp the overall picture: Our culture has rotted, and the resultant rise in socialism and the grotesque stretching of the credit market may be joining together to produce a very unanticipated change. Might the ever more elaborate risk models simply be wings of wax, giving young men like Icarus confidence that they can fly sublimely? For that matter, could the Fed governors be wearing wings of wax as well, now pumping them ever harder though some of the wax has begun to drip off?

# Part Two

# ENDLESS MONEY

The last century has been one of endless money creation, nearly all of it through the magic of commercial banking, which unbeknownst to most Americans prints money through the creation of new loans that get deposited back into banks as this money is spent on business ventures or consumption. Part 2 begins by discussing what our monetary system looked like prior to the last hundred years, when it was based upon silver and gold. Then moving into the modern era, accepted monetary theory is critically examined. Its applicability to understanding financial crises is weighed. The current meltdown has challenged its basic underlying assumptions, and it was predicted by not a single academic close to the Fed. Either debt deflation or inflation might occur, depending upon how monetary authorities interpret these theories and what this implies for their policy actions. While the political will to print could build in momentum, it may be difficult to ignore the downside pull of having established excess debt relative to our national income that is on the order of $20 trillion to $25 trillion. The idea that the Fed would lag behind pressure building that would be deflationary to asset prices is developed in Part 2, for providing credit has not restored equity and direct monetization has been small relative to funds advanced during multiple decades of credit inflation. The last chapter of this section closes with a review of the moral hazards that have been caused by operating a centrally controlled fiat currency and practicing Keynesian economic policies.

# Chapter 3

# The Rise and Fall
# of Hard Money

A fierce debate used to rage in America about what form of money and type of banking system we would use. The populace was well informed about the merits and demerits of using gold, silver, or paper and had strong opinions about whether or not there should be a central bank. About 100 years ago this debate was settled, and we embarked upon a century of abundance fed by technological innovation, so we as a people are now largely ignorant of these issues. The modern curriculum of American history contains almost no mention of monetary issues save abbreviated reference to controversy about establishing national banks. The solutions advanced by the losers of the debates over currency and banking seem impossible to adopt in a modern world; to do so would be like banning cars and using horses instead.

Those with great responsibility for managing money in the institutional setting know little of these basics, but with the violent downturn in the equity and credit markets that began in 2008, light has begun to shine on long discredited voices such as the Austrian School of Economics. Most who thus initiate their learning are surprised that

sound banking and currency are interwoven concerns, and that the issue
of gold backing is not solitary but fractured into many camps. The
bulk of this chapter explores the monetary history of the United States,
but without first beginning by highlighting the nuances between bullion, specie, gold-exchange systems, and free banking, the compressed
view of history that follows might be that much less understood. At
that point economic history pertinent to our present predicament is
reviewed sequentially from the colonial period to the interwar era,
when the focus switches from the development of the puerile domestic economy to the world stage. The analysis dwells upon this interesting latter moment, which is often neglected in discussions of the Great
Depression and in analyses of financial meltdowns. However, it was a
fulcrum between the old system and the new, one which began with
the birth of our modern financial world and its governmental institutions. These may some day come to be regarded as structurally flawed
and contributory to the present meltdown.

America's colonial history is imbued with the experience of fiat
currency, and this invention has remained a powerful force in the nation
and the world economy ever since. The term "fiat currency" applies to
any money declared by government to be legal tender, particularly for
the payment of taxes, but for this analysis one should exclude gold and
silver coins, known as specie.

Although technically the dollar only lost its backing with gold in
1971, other more subtle monetary constructs have made this linkage
increasingly irrelevant for a century or more. Gold or silver's capability to preserve wealth can be lost when banking is centralized, when
banks can issue notes against it as legal tender, and when specie is not
available or economic for public use. These three subtleties are examined briefly in the following review of the gold standard, and in this
context an examination of the historical record leading up to the Great
Depression will be explored after that.

The great economic historian and theorist Murray N. Rothbard
(1926-1995), whose mentor was Ludwig von Mises, wrote a definitive history of money and banking, *A History of Money and Banking in
the United States: The Colonial Era to World War II* (Ludwig von Mises
Institute, Auburn, 2002). This work begins by relating the horrendous
record of paper currencies issued by the colonies. He also lays particular blame of mismanagement of the nation's money supply on the

National Banking Acts of 1863, 1864, and 1865, which wiped out state banking and established a nationwide fiat currency. Although central banking would not gain permanence until 1913 (after two failed enterprises), these reforms paved the way for it by concentrating influence in the major banking centers through national banks.

Central banking allows one authority to regulate the expansion of credit for member banks. This discourages renegades from creating new bank money opportunistically in excess of established players. More cynically, it allows the group as a whole to expand credit rapidly and synchronously such that the banking industry can lay claim to new wealth at a maximal rate of increase. In contrast, decentralization limits systemic credit growth, because notes issued by a bank are discounted in circulation or may be redeemed for specie with their originating bank. Excessive issuance would threaten to exhaust reserves.

Centralization allowed the money supply to grow much more than it would have under a decentralized gold coin reserve system, even if banks had been permitted to issue their own notes. Long before the crisis of 2008, if expansive banks such as Countrywide had been allowed to issue notes in competition with other banks, their regular redemption by other clearing banks would have discovered weakness much more promptly than was the case today. Deposit insurance and regulation has structured the competitive landscape such that banks operate in uniformity, leveraging their deposit bases to the hilt and flooding the market with cheap loans. Notwithstanding the periodic practice of outright debt monetization (buying government debt with newly printed central bank notes) to finance wars, one must ask why our culture has changed such that the last 100 years can only permit a largely fiat-based system, yet in earlier times this structure would have been nearly as threatening as reversing the direction of the Earth's rotation.

Issuing loans or notes against a reserve of gold or silver (or in modern times, simply against deposits with the FED) creates new money, because funds disbursed to loan recipients find their way through the economy back into additional deposits, an expansive and circular process known as pyramiding. Seventeenth century goldsmiths of England learned that paper exchangeable for their inventory of gold might not be presented for redemption regularly, so they could earn interest income and in fact manufacture money up to the point that the redemption of notes would not exceed the supply of gold behind them.[1] Adherents of the Austrian theoretical monetary framework, such as the economist (and historian) Murray N. Rothbard, view this as counterfeiting. The issue of counterfeiting was swept aside legally through British court cases (*Carr v. Carr* in 1811 and *Devaynes v. Noble* in 1816).[2] By the 19th century it was generally accepted that banks could continuously pyramid loans against deposits, making fractional reserve banking the principle mechanism by which money could be created in the economy. Some point out that systems of circulating receipts for physical goods constituted paper money well before this time. In the medieval era families such as the Riccis and the Medicis extended credit to customers and accepted an additional fee for the time value of money, but the paper this created was not expanded beyond the value of goods sold. Such credit was non-inflationary, and it also benefitted commerce through the substitution of a less bulky medium of exchange.[3]

## The Gold Standard

What in fact is the classical notion of a gold standard, and how well did we adhere to that ideal? The classical gold standard holds considerable appeal because it produced an extraordinary interlude of per capita income growth and price stability in the 19th century. However, the gold standard has been honored more in the breach than the observance historically, even in that hallowed time. Under a classical gold standard countries hold stocks of gold in reserve, and they are ready to see these exported to settle up surpluses of paper foreign currency that gets accumulated through trade imbalances. There need not be a central bank, per se, but a government must stand prepared to buy or sell gold to maintain a steady value of its currency.[4]

In the United States, banks cartelized to temporarily issue clearinghouse paper in times of panic; central banks existed in Europe that were lenders of last resort. A government's commitment to its currency inspired market actors to assist in returning currencies to their fixed gold value. Central banks such as the Bank of England would aid the process of maintaining equilibrium through procyclical actions: For example if a trade deficit caused gold to flow out to other countries, the central bank would raise interest rates, shrinking demand for credit and the gold certificate notes. In turn, this would mean that private banks would delever and establish a higher ratio of reserves to assets. Deflation would result, improving the competitiveness of exports relative to trading partners, restoring trade equilibrium, and relieving the need to ship gold to other countries, since they would no longer be presenting currency for redemption.

For such a system to work, wages and prices must be able to adjust freely and no exchange controls or tariffs could impede trade. But in practice, not all goods or services are tradable. Other violations of the rules of the game might occur: Banks would sterilize gold movements, accumulating gold disproportionately by pursuing a contracyclical interest rate policy that would discourage expansion of gold-backed notes when gold inflows would normally trigger it. Reserves might be held in foreign currencies, usually sterling, rather than gold (an attractive option since interest could accrue).

In reality the mechanical adjustments envisioned in the classical gold standard rarely if ever took place. Instead, prices tended to rise and fall in concert internationally as if there were one world currency. In the 19th century, long-term capital investment supported a lower cost of capital for projects in the United States relative to the United Kingdom, allowing a U.S. trade deficit and gold inflows to persist. Probably most important to the classical gold standard's success was a culture and political acknowledgment that governments should limit spending, balance budgets, and above all not monetize debt. Ironically, the chief force working against this stability was that of industrialists seeking an elastic money supply that would help finance large-scale investments like railroads, aided by government subsidization such as the granting of real estate. Business magnates were generally Republicans, and they pressed for the formation of a central bank to promote elasticity.

A gold standard is weakened when the metal that forms its foundation is in a form that would not likely be sought for redemption by the populace. For this reason, the architects of the gold exchange standard restored after World War I (when exchangeability had been suspended) promoted the use of gold bullion over specie. A key feature of that variant of the gold standard was the recruitment of major trading partners to substitute English pounds or U.S. dollars for their central bank reserves, depending upon which currency or trading block in which they operated. From the perspective of the operator of the reserve currency, this simultaneously discouraged citizens from demanding gold in return for dollars, and it injected a cumbersome intermediate step before foreign currencies might be subject to the discipline of redemption. It also allowed British and U.S. banks to inflate and build up trade imbalances without fear of immediate settlement.

Eventually this would cause the British pound to accumulate considerable stress in the late 1920s when its value was erroneously pegged to prewar parity, leading Britain to be the first major nation to break from the gold standard in the depression. As cultural norms had changed, Britain would not adopt measures such as raising interest rates or allowing deflation as would have been necessary under a pure gold standard, thus causing unemployment to rise in the late 1920s and setting up a horrific speculative attack on its reserves.

Centralization, pyramiding, and removing readily used specie from circulation—the three twists to using precious metals as a currency reserve discussed above—offer nearly as much explanatory power over monetary trends through the beginning of the 20th century as do the use of gold or silver themselves as a reserve. The straining of our historic linkage to a hard reserve also mirrors a gradual shift in cultural norms from individual responsibility for failure and immediate financial correction to socialization of risk, redistribution of wealth, and statist economic intervention. The decentralized banking structure of the early 19th century kept moral hazard in check, as no institution was too big to fail, including national banks that would arise. By the 1920s restraining people and countries from converting cash to specie may have postponed the cleansing process of economic cycles, leading to a new height of speculation and the Great Depression.

Later in this work the role cultural norms play in the selection of monetary systems will be explored. The most strident supporters of gold would advocate a 100 percent gold-coin-backed banking system; in the years just before the crisis of 2008, at the opposite end of the spectrum in recent times Federal Reserve governors and academicians spoke of the possibility of not having any reserves at all. Even in the unlikely case the world returned to a 100 percent commodity-exchangeable currency, there would still be credit (though it would be securitized rather than provided through deposit lending). Even in ancient times there was lending activity. In the Sumerian era (3000-1900 BC) a loan of barley carried an interest rate of 33 percent (payable in barley), while borrowing silver cost only 20 percent.[5] But the phenomenon of very sudden systemic wealth destruction either through a deflationary spiral or inflation outside of war is modern and related to man's monetary inventions. There are many faces of gold, but the more distant they are to us, the greater the risk that mankind harms itself, and especially certain groups within society, through unforeseen consequences.

The courage of Rothbard to maintain intellectual purity and fealty to the concepts of gold and 100 percent backing of deposits is remarkable given his living in a time when people who identify with either the left or the right politically would roundly reject these notions as antique. Moreover, modern conservatives might part ways intellectually with either the use of gold as a reserve or to advocate the decentralization of banking and control over the currency. With our culture having deviated so far from the 19th century mindset, it is nigh impossible to see how either of these Austrian School concepts could gain traction, save for a grassroots preference to hold liquid wealth in gold or gold ETFs instead of legal tender. In the meantime the growing preference for socialism by voters in the developed nations parallels the growth of public and private debt. These two phenomena are ideally suited for each other, because they have in common the theme of men making use of the assets of other men. We need go no farther than the hijacking of Freddie Mac and Fannie Mae in the current era to see how slogans such as "affordable housing" became a lightning rod that give birth to the Frankenstein of a monster that has engulfed the credit markets in the name of socialism. While the difficult issues regarding the ideal structure of the world's monetary systems may not get resolved anytime soon, perhaps the simple mathematics of compounding debt will force a reexamination.

## America's Beginning: Paper, Silver, and Gold

Because finance has been predicated upon fiat currency for roughly the last half century or more (depending upon the technical definition), even veteran institutional money managers are at best vaguely aware that our nation vacillated between hard money and credit-backed currency repeatedly. At times just before the adoption of either extreme no doubt most would not have predicted complete systemic shifting from gold to paper or back again. Likewise in 2008 investors and policy makers were caught unaware of the meltdown. With greater awareness of a natural tendency for our financial system to alternate between hard and elastic currency, money managers might become cognizant that a return to gold could be unfolding. Likewise, voters might begin to evaluate their representatives with a renewed sense of imposing the ultimate regulator, gold, upon financial market activities and government excesses. The condensed history that follows chronicles our past to paint a detailed picture of the consequences of excessive bank lending and reckless fiscal expenditure. Those wishing to stick solely with the broad monetary, political, and cultural themes may feel free to advance to the end of this chapter, but its reading will reveal the laboratory of growth this nation once was when it mainly operated in an era of hard money, and why it continually chose to revert to such a system, usually after circulation of excess paper linked to speculative lending had dire consequences.

The account of that era from central bankers today sanitizes this experience and idealizes the evolution of money from the dark ages of specie. A March 2006 educational essay published by the Philadelphia Fed extols the view of Ben Franklin, who in 1731 at age 25 secures the contract to print Pennsylvania fiat currency and goes on to prosper as a printer, writer, scientist, and assemblyman. Franklin's view, as expressed in a pamphlet he circulated two years before securing his lucrative franchise, turn's Gresham's law on its head. He professed that without paper currency, local trade in his colony was impaired. His description of the state of affairs was that Pennsylvanians had exchanged their coins for manufactured goods from Europe, leaving behind so few that business was difficult to conduct. But in reality one of the greatest interludes of inflationary paper note printing had been underway in New England, and it would spread to nearly every colony by 1740. Pennsylvania had begun printing in 1723, the year Franklin first arrived in Philadelphia. The first great test of America's attitudes about credit began in 1690 in the Massachusetts colony, then still a puritanical refuge. Its government first issued paper money in payment of service to troops that had raided the French Quebec colony. Originally Massachusetts' government promised that the paper would be issued in restricted quantity and redeemable for specie raised from taxation. This early use of state credit thus linked fiscal policy to monetary policy. Massachusetts kept up its raids and broke its pledge to limit paper issuance. By 1711, the large quantity of paper used in payment of troops eventually displaced silver as the chosen medium of exchange in the economy at large, as predicted by Gresham's law that bad money chases out good. By that year the new currency traded at a 30 percent discount to specie, and by 1748 the depreciation was tenfold. The 1740s saw nearly every other colony also institute fiat currency. These notes, which were all denominated in English pounds, were usable across colonial borders. Thus Rhode Island caught on to the benefit of outdoing its neighbors, depreciating its currency by 23-to-1, while other colonies restrained printing to nine or 10 times dilution.[6] The printing of money became competitive, for any one colony could exploit its neighbor's wealth by exchanging newly issued certificates for trade or assets over the border.

But Franklin was well aware of the dangers of excessive issuance, and he was keen to resist unlimited expansion of the money supply that had overtaken other colonial land and specie banks. To Franklin's credit, Pennsylvania's fiat currency was the least inflated of all the colonies' at just 80 percent over par.[7] Under Franklin's persuasion, the Pennsylvania colony operated an innovative land-based bank that he professed would automatically stabilize the quantity of scrip issued. Landowners could borrow with their land as collateral for an amount up to twice the value of their property. The loan of paper from the government bank had to be retired over time (at which point title was restored and the money was permanently withdrawn from circulation), and new loans were not allowed until such a mortgage was entirely repaid. If the government issued too much scrip and caused inflation, then citizens might accumulate the depreciated currency and repurchase title to their land cheaply. A key advantage of basing the value upon land was that it could not be exported to Europe like gold could.[8]

Coincident with the conclusion of the war with France in 1748, King George ended the paper issuance of all the colonies, and plans were laid to retire colonial paper currency in circulation, culminating in the Currency Act of 1764. Notes in Massachusetts were redeemed at discounted market prices. The result was an inflow of silver coins and economic prosperity to that region, which was preferable to the intense inflation and damage to export industries that its fiat experiment had caused. Lucrative trade with the West Indies that had been pouring into Providence was diverted to Boston, appropriately because that trading partner was rich in specie needed for commerce in Massachusetts.

King George III may have lost the American colonies because he introduced the American Revenue Act of 1764, which differed from its predecessor, the Molasses Act of 1733. Instead of continuing the policy of 'salutary neglect,' the British navy enforced its punitive three cent per gallon levy, which equated to 100 percent. The result was a severe business depression, affecting merchants such as the bankruptcy of Nathaniel Wheelwright in Boston and planters in Virginia who suffered when prices and exports plummeted.[9] The crown forced colonists to pay taxes in hard money, having outlawed colonial currencies. Figures such as Ben Franklin appealed to the populace over the wealthy in society; his pamphlet in support of printing paper currency threatened the gentry, and his use of the media to influence public opinion was subversive. However, by the time the crown had reinstituted hard money he leaned somewhat towards the Tory cause, having been appointed deputy postmaster general, and his son William, governor of New Jersey. He raised no protest to the Revenue Act, and even helpfully suggested a tea tax. But he would reverse this sentiment by the time of the Stamp Act in 1765.[10]

By the 1770s enough tension had built between England and the American colonies to ignite rebellion. The ensuing war required massive financing, and once again the new world turned to the borrowing and printing of new dollars. Murray Rothbard estimates that the Continental Congress issued over $225 million of paper money in the five years through 1779, dwarfing the money supply of just $12 million prior to independence. States issued another $210 million of currency. Additionally, loan certificates of some $600 million were issued to pay for army supplies. By 1781, Continental dollars were nearly worthless; 168 were equivalent to one dollar of specie.[11] When faced with unexpected high budget outlays, usually caused by large-scale wars, governments face a choice of either raising taxes or issuing debt. With fiat currency, the latter option tends to avoid revolutions or plebiscites. After independence, in the state of Massachusetts, the collection of the poll tax in hard money inflamed the ire of farmers in the western part of the state, triggering Shay's rebellion, a seminal event that was the proximate cause of the Convention of 1787.

Colonial American history was characterized by money supply expansion through outright printing, interspersed by usage of specie. The American embrace of fiat currency benefitted colonial governments, since its first usage was to finance public obligations, after which it would be circulated. It added wealth to the colonies and undermined the monetary base of Britain, essentially making the colonists legal counterfeiters. It also underscores that government has two means of financing: one is to tithe the income of its citizenry; the other is to tax the value of circulating medium simply by printing money. The latter benefit to government is known as "seigniorage," and it accrues directly to the holder of the press.

Perhaps on account of living through such an extreme episode by necessity, or perhaps from its repeat in France during that country's revolution (1789-1797), blatant issuance of paper money came to an end. The Founding Fathers expressly wrote into the U.S. Constitution that the nation's currency would be gold and silver coins, fixed at a ratio of 15-to-1 such that a dollar would equal 371.25 grains of silver or 24.75 grains of gold. Foreign coins made up 80 percent of the money supply, with the bulk of this being Spanish silver dollars.

Although the founding fathers had succeeded in creating a Constitutional hurdle against the outright printing of money by the states, by the early 19th century a new form of paper money production would take root: Fractional reserve lending. It would be particularly pernicious when associated with the government sanction of a central bank that would be supportive of heavy public spending for projects such as canal building or the purchase of frontier land.

## Bank Money and Public Works: From Boom to Bust

Early in the nineteenth century the manufacture of money through leveraging multiple loans against a reserve of specie took hold in the new nation. "Bank money," as it is sometimes called, rapidly exceeded specie reserves handily. Its growth, periodic overexpansion, and contraction became the DNA encoding cyclicality to the economic corpus, but the use of silver and gold at the base provided restraint that would reign in moral hazard and provide a safe haven for savers. However, when specie conversion was suspended, it would set the stage for even larger catastrophes, a point that might well be taken when evaluating the Fed's actions in combating the credit crunch of 2008.

The practice of using credit as currency had actually begun in England. Charles I borrowed gold on deposit from merchants at the mint to help finance a civil war. After this gold was returned, merchants sought to avoid the state's involuntary usage of their wealth by keeping it at goldsmiths instead, who issued receipts for the inventory. The receipts were used as a form of currency and were issued in excess of the gold held, thus giving birth to "fractional reserve" banking at about the same time as the Massachusetts colony began its paper currency system.

This expansion of credit built upon a hard base such as the goldsmith's gold stock is the model of a gold standard such as that adopted by England in 1816 or by the United States in 1879. An important variant was the emergence of state chartered banks as well as the establishment of a central bank. The first national bank was founded by Robert Morris in 1782 (Bank of North America) using appropriated specie loaned to the United States by France. Lack of confidence in its notes quickly caused Morris to exit federal banking and focus only on private commercial business. This brief experiment was followed by a more permanent one within a decade. Alexander Hamilton, the protégé of Governeur Morris, founded the Bank of the United States in 1791. It lent heavily to the federal government, and it formed the core of a system of new commercial banks that expanded the money supply. In 1811, its 20-year charter was not renewed in a battle won by Jeffersonian Democrats, which opposed state monopoly power over finance. All along, state-chartered banks proliferated. These grew the money supply through extending loans on deposits that were redeemable in specie. In 1800 there were only 28 such banks, but their ranks swelled to 117 by 1811 when the first Bank of the United States closed its doors.[12]

Rothbard's assertion that relending bank deposits multiple times is counterfeiting is alien to today's financial orthodoxy. But when thinking of money as a store of value, it is diluted by the expansion of credit (sometimes referred to as bank money). If population and the quantity of goods and services grow slowly but bank money expands at a faster rate, then those who hold wealth in monetary form (instead of in hard assets) are cheated. Moreover, he asserts that the beneficiaries of watering down the money supply are the banks that do it and the individuals who receive the loans that initiate the expansion. When social programs soak up central bank accommodation of Treasury issuance through monetary expansion, savers see their wealth diminished in relative terms, as if a tax had been placed upon them. In such an arrangement socialism flourishes, because there is no perceived cost to those who hold wealth. In actuality, the difference between the low single digit inflation of modern fiat currencies and the natural deflation that would accrue from productivity gains, and from the integration of billions of low-wage laborers into the world economy represents seigniorage transferred to the political beneficiaries of socialized credit. It is a staggeringly large number annually. Taken to the extreme, bank reserve requirements could be set near zero to permit infinite expansion of the money stock. The panic of 2008 may have this very characteristic.

The experience of the early 19th century provides some evidence of Rothbard's observation of how strong the profit opportunity was when the United States first witnessed fractional reserve banking. Howard Bodenhorn, an academic authority on the topic, described the rush to set up banks in that era in two books published this decade. What is interesting is that the process was particularly political and intertwined the state with banks, since charters were granted by legislatures. "Charter mongering" by opportunists was so brazen that "bribery on this scale offends modern sensibilities."[13] Many varieties of enticements were offered to elected officials and whole states or lawmaking bodies, from cash bonuses to participation in guaranteed profits to stock grants, naming just a few. Shareholders and officers were the most favored borrowers, and their institutions essentially were a license to print money. The first recipients of the banking bonanza were the wealthiest, who were Federalists. Soon partisan alignments were so strongly embedded that Republicans became fearful of borrowing from these institutions. With bank nationalization recurring under the Obama administration, this situation could be repeated.

"Republicans claimed that the Federalist banks were tainted by bribery, corruption, and charter mongering. But because the charters were irrevocable, the best the Republicans could do was charter their own partisan banks, which elicited Federalist howls of protest ... The sheer size of the bribes and bonuses and the eagerness with which they were handed out demonstrated the profits to be had in banking, especially for the first to obtain a charter in a community."[14]

The War of 1812 required enormous sums of money for troops and ships, which were accommodated by note issuance of banks that stretched loan-to-specie reserve ratios to roughly 18-to-1 among mid-Atlantic state banks, as contrasted to conservative measures of about two-to-one in New England, where most of the war manufacturing occurred. New England did not support the war effort with either troops or financing, and it continued to trade with Britain in defiance of national decrees. After the war when the paper was presented for payment, the insolvency of the mid-Atlantic banks was clear. This lead to a crisis and federal suspension of specie repayment by banks in August 1814, just five months before the conflict with England ceased. The result was inflation, from this time to the resumption of specie requirements in February 1817, there was both an expansion of bank notes and a massive issuance of Treasury Notes, which could also be used for payment in commerce.[15]

The second central bank formation, the Bank of the United States, occurred in 1816. It attempted to foster a uniform currency, which meant that the regional disparities in loan-making evident during the war turned the tables on New England banks, placing them on the hook for converting notes from other states into specie at par. Land speculation was rampant, because the United States Treasury would accept notes from state banks in payment for western lands. Agricultural commodities rose in price partly due to a healthy export market to fulfill demand from Europe, whose output was curtailed from the Napoleonic Wars. British policies that restricted westward migration of colonists were done with, and other foreign powers and Indian nations receded. In the south, for example, probably between $5 million and $10 million of new paper was issued to pay for lands suitable for cotton in the Mississippi territory in about a five year time span, a considerable sum compared to the grand total of $58 million for all forms of currency in circulation in 1810, as related by Thomas Perkins Abernathy:

> The binge in land speculation was given tremendous impetus by bank notes issued by the United States Bank and by about seventy local banks founded in Tennessee and Kentucky in 1818. Also, five million dollars in scrip, issued by the federal government to the Yazoo claimants, was redeemable only in payments for lands Georgia had once claimed in what became Mississippi and Alabama. All these paper notes made it easy to make at least the down payment on public lands. Millions of dollars in Alabama public lands were sold on credit at Midgeville, Georgia, in 1817 and in Huntsville, Alabama, during 1818. Frequently those who bought could not complete payment, and credit sales had to be abandoned by the government in 1820. [16]

The new central bank had expanded loans above its specie reserves by a factor of more than nine-to-one. Its stretched balance sheet and the need to repay in specie a $4 million debt used to finance the purchase of Louisiana, triggered a 47 percent collapse in the money supply in the Panic of 1819.[17] The depth of this contraction, which persisted through 1821, combined with substantial corruption at the bank, provided two persuasive arguments for Andrew Jackson to shut it down in 1833.

However, not all banks were wanton lenders, and a system known as the "real bills" doctrine, which restricted loans to the financing of business transactions for up to 90 days, was prevalent through 1830. In fact a study of antebellum banks by Bodenhorn calculated an average of 80 days for a sample of institutions from 1815 through 1860, but these were in New York state and several areas not swept up in land speculation or public works. Many other state-chartered banks continued to lend against their specie redeemable deposits, particularly for land speculation as the nation moved westward. By 1836, Jackson issued the Specie Circular, which required sales of public lands to be paid for in specie, thus crimping the bull market in real estate.

However, Jackson still could not hold back efforts of the states to inflate the money supply. State governments took on enormous debt that was spent on public works such that aggregate state debt approached $170 million by 1839. At the time, this was nearly as high as the entire money supply of the United States ($240 million).[18] A prominent example was Pennsylvania's heavy spending on canals, begun in 1826. The backbone of this system was the Main Line Canal, which stretched 395 miles and was completed in 1834. Due to the topography of Pennsylvania requiring its reaching an elevation of 2,200 feet, it could not compete with the Erie Canal, needing 174 locks to the latter's 84. Its cost was $10 million, while that of the overall canal system was $65 million. The spending spree pumped up the state's debt to $36 million, the interest on which was unpayable by 1841. Canal building took up much of the capital of Pennsylvania banks. When the state defaulted, the Pennsylvania legislature encouraged banks to subscribe to a $3.1 million issue of "Relief Notes," which turned out to be the final straw for many country banks that subscribed to the offering. The spectacular failure of the Bank of the United States in 1842 pulled down two large Philadelphia banks, capping an era of public finance that eventually froze private credit. Yet the Pennsylvania legislature pinned the blame on the financial sector and refused to issue new bank charters.[19] An analogy might be drawn to Public-Private Partnership (PIPP) introduced in 2009, which encourages financially strapped financial institutions to provide capital to buy toxic debt securities. However, this modern innovation uses federal lending and guarantees, which ultimately rely upon taxation or the monetization of government debt with newly issued fiat currency. Consequently, the final straw will rest upon either taxpayers or savers.

The depression of 1839-1843 liquidated over a third of the money supply, causing ten states to either default or repudiate their debts. The Democratic Party continued to press for a hard money system including the elimination of fractional reserve banking, but ultimately it was foiled within many states, where Whigs persuaded some 18 of the 33 states in the Union by the start of the Civil War to adopt banking that permitted credit expansion built not upon specie but state bonds. Known as "free banking," the practice meant elasticity of money could be permitted through periodic suspensions of specie redemption for deposits, and new banks could be set up easily—only if they met high requirements for holding state debt in reserves. Whigs as a party advocated government intervention in funding infrastructure, a precursor of the Keynesian logic of the 1930s, which appealed to many burned in the depression of 1839-1843. While the Whigs would splinter apart from division on the slavery issue and from the reduced appeal of opposing Jacksonian hard money precepts in an expanding economy, this fundamental change in banking would lay the groundwork for marrying the heavy issuance of public debt and its monetization by printing money through a banking system free of linkage to specie.[20]

## From Greenbacks to Gold

The Civil War required heavy spending that could only be supplied by the accumulated wealth of the nation; taxes on goods or income would not be sufficient. Building upon the theme of basing currency on government debt rather than gold, the National Banking Acts of 1863, 1864, and 1865 ushered in the greenback era. Control over money creation was centralized into a select group of national banks in the spring of 1865 through the passage of a 10 percent tax on state bank notes, an imposition made when it became clear these banks did not want to join a new hierarchical federal bank system and be subservient to Wall Street.[21] The obligation of national banks to pay out specie on demand was suspended, echoing the precedent set during the preceding war. Federal debt, which was issued through a monopoly granted to Jay Cooke & Company, swelled and reached the unthinkable sum of $2.3 billion by 1866, almost all of it new.[22] It formed the basis of the new federal banking system, which by then used the debt for reserves to back state-chartered banks.

Cooke, whose father had been a Whig member of Congress, possessed unbridled enthusiasm for federal control over money. Other greenback enthusiasts desired printing of fiat notes to pay for massive public works; one Richard Schell lobbied for digging a canal from coast to coast. The buildup of federal and private debt in the banking system was promoted through the Cooke & Co monopoly. It had speculated in building the Northern Pacific Railway, which grandiosely sought to bring Duluth on par with Chicago, and received the greatest giveaway of federal land (47 million acres) of all the railroads, probably thanks to the relationship between Treasury Secretary Salmon P. Chase and Jay Cooke. The failure of Cooke & Co. is generally credited with triggering the panic of 1873, which saw many other railroads fail. Most were highly leveraged.[23]

In the mid-19th century before the era of the classical gold standard, England and France held most of the world's gold that was otherwise circulating. Silver was in fact prominent prior to then, and major gold discoveries at Sutter's Mill, CA, in 1848 and in Australia three years later dramatically increased quantities available. Historically when a gold- or silver-backed system was in effect, reserves were created through the public delivering gold or silver to the mint for the production of specie, or when foreign supplies of specie or bullion were imported into the banking system. So in periods of rising mining activity, the money supply would increase. "The discoveries of gold in Russia, Australia, and California, by which the gold product reached its highest amount soon after 1851, form an epoch in the monetary history of every modern state with a specie circulation" wrote Laurence Laughlin in 1885.[24] Later the innovation of cyanide leaching concurrent with the exploitation of tailings along the Rand in South Africa would increase supply in the 1890s.[25] In 1871 Germany was first to join the United Kingdom in a purely gold system, and it was quickly followed by other European nations in 1878, the year before the United States also retired the inflationary greenback.

Congress shifted into the hands of the Democratic Party, which passed the Resumption Act of 1875, providing for a return to the gold standard in 1879. Simultaneously a bill in Congress that demonetized silver coins was passed quickly and with little fanfare, and later became known as the "Crime of 1873," which was followed by a complimentary measure the next year.[26] By weight, silver had historically enjoyed a ratio of 15 to 1 compared to gold, which was acknowledged in the Coinage Act of 1792, but mainly due to prolific Mexican mines this relationship deteriorated to 16 to 1 in the 19th century through 1872.[27] Silver, particularly Spanish dollars, had been the predominant coinage in most of the world, even in America, for many years. European nations had begun to switch to a gold standard, which in combination with the United States legislation led to silver eventually crashing in value to a ratio of 323 to 1 by 1894. The experience of silver suggests the metal's value is quite different when consumed for everyday use compared to finding utility as money, which requires its deployment in quantity. There may be a parallel in the modern gold market. At $900 an ounce in mid-2009 the yellow metal could be argued to be slightly overvalued relative to historical prices inflated using the consumer price index, but it is only a fraction of its worth should above ground tonnage be required to equal the face value of a small reserve of M3, say 20 percent. In the closing section of this book alternatives for arriving at an equilibrium price are calculated, and these place gold's value in the thousands of dollars per ounce.

The resumption of 1879 ushered in prosperity, although economists tend to label the ensuing years as well as the six years leading up to resumption as a dark economic period, because deflation occurred. Yet output rose in both instances, and in fact prices fell less under the gold standard than they did during the downside following the inflationary bubble of the greenback era ending in 1873. Deflationary periods such as the six years following the panic of 1873 in the United States have long been assumed to have been difficult eras by historians because of falling prices, especially for agricultural products, an economic mainstay. But real GDP rose 6.8 percent per annum during that interlude, and 4.5 percent per capita, while the money supply expanded 2.5 percent annually.[28] Through Rothbard's steadfast view that pyramiding loans on top of reserves of any kind, gold or otherwise, is counterfeiting, the panics of 1884, 1893, and 1907 were caused by banks stretching their balance sheets speculatively and being vulnerable to deposit redemption. Thus, the credit and not the underlying reserve would be to blame for the vulnerability of the financial system.

The rejection of silver by European and American governments would not extend into most of the rest of the world, where Mexican dollar coins remained popular until the turn of the century. Silver's depreciation coincided with a rise in imperialist ambition in the United States and the obvious success of Victorian England, for it opened the door to establishing currency spheres of influence. The Jacksonian tradition of hard money insulating the common man from the credit manipulations of money center banks was a mainstay of the Democratic Party in the 19th century, and it sprang from Jeffersonian ideals of the century before. But by the end of that time industrialists comfortable under the Whig and later the Republican banners came around to the view that building an elastic credit system on top of a gold reserve base could promote hegemony internationally and still provide ample credit expansion. Many hard money Democrats defected to the Republican Party in the election of McKinley in 1896 after a deal was brokered wherein he supported a gold base to the monetary system. Rothbard's approach of "specific understanding" of the actors of this era goes far to explain how the gold standard and eventually the addition of hier-archical layers of American regional and foreign banks upon a Federal Reserve System came into being. He observes: "Once gold was secured by the McKinley victory of 1896, (the Morgans) wanted to press on to use the gold standard as a hard money camouflage behind which they could change the system into one less nakedly inflationist than pop-ulism but far more effectively controlled by the big banker elites. In the long run, a controlled Morgan-Rockefeller gold standard was far more pernicious to the cause of genuine hard money than a candid free-sil-ver or greenback Byronism."[29]

Evangelist and populist William Jennings Bryan was the most promi-nent silverist, best known for mesmerizing the masses with his Cross of Gold speech in 1896, which merely advocated bimetallism as an anti-dote. His brand of populism was criticized by hard money Republicans who saw the "free silver" movement that advocated permitting the mints to produce dollars at a ratio of 20:1 as inflationist, especially since ore was plentiful from Nevada discoveries. An overlooked facet is that by this time silver was practically worthless relative to gold in the open mar-ket, because silver had been demonetized in Europe in favor of gold, causing its value to sink to that suggested by its utility for flatware. The momentum of the silverite movement was effectively blunted by the Silver Purchase Act of 1878, which mandated Treasury stockpiling of sil-ver and may be seen as a massive subsidy program.[30] Eventually the shift in Treasury metal holdings from gold to silver would undermine the gold standard in the last decade of the 19th century. Rothbard attributes the panic of 1893, which damaged Grover Cleveland politically, to foreign outflows of gold caused by fears of abandonment of the gold standard.[31]

The "free silver" ideology should not be confused with "free metal-lism," which allows coins to circulate as weights unlinked to specific paper currency values. This laissez faire system would attract a sufficient amount of specie for commerce. Otherwise when ratios of value are etched in stone, Gresham's law dictates behavior, and improperly priced coins are driven out. Since free silver specified an artificially high, non-market price, it would have demoted gold and caused inflation.

## When Banks were Strong

In the midst of a deep depression in the early 1890s many national banks failed. However, the reserve balances set aside in gold and other non-interest bearing assets were 60 percent of the capital of National City Bank, the precursor of Citibank. Equity was 16 percent of its assets. In that era, many banks would not lend against real estate, and debt could not be counted as capital. Chemical Bank, now part of JP Morgan Chase, held shareholders equity of some 19 percent of assets and 38 percent of its individual deposits in 1904, a few years prior to the famous Panic of 1907. At the time of this panic, reserve city banks were required to hold 25 percent of their deposits in reserve and half those reserves in cash.[32] Prior to the National Currency Act of 1863, banks issued notes privately, which provided ample opportunity for fraud. Yet losses then are estimated at only 2 percent, far less than the inflation to which the government subjected the people once the Act was legislated and the need to finance the Civil War became pressing.[33]

By 1903 the weakened state of silver globally provided the perfect opportunity for Britain and the United States to approach friendly countries with an opportunity to base their national currencies upon the pound or the dollar, respectively, which were grounded upon gold and could serve as a reserve base underneath foreign money supplies instead of silver. Seigniorage as well as control over financial affairs would accrue to the issuer of the reserve currency, the United States or Britain, and their client states would be subservient.

> The idea was to replace a genuine gold standard, in which each country (or, domestically, each bank) maintains its reserves in gold, by a pseudo-gold standard in which the central bank of the client country maintains its reserves in some key or base currency, say pounds or dollars . . . during the 1920s, most countries

maintained their reserves in pounds, and only Britain purported to redeem pounds in gold. This meant that these other countries were really on a pound rather than a gold standard, although they were able, at least temporarily, to acquire the prestige of gold. It also meant that when Britain inflated pounds, there was no danger of losing gold to these other countries, who, quite the contrary, happily inflated their own currencies on top of their expanding balances in pounds sterling.[34]

Before the government guaranteed deposits and chartered the Fed, the free market induced some of the nation's largest, fastest growing, and most successful banks to conservatively manage their finances as a business strategy. Anyone seeking safe haven then could place his money on deposit at National City Bank and earn 0 percent, and it was actually safer than holding U.S. Treasuries. The strategy paid off for Chemical Bank, which saw its deposits skyrocket from $20 million to $29 million in less than a year during the 1907 panic. The year 1907 saw a dramatic collapse of the banking system, but depositors largely recovered completely without any governmental intervention and economic growth returned swiftly. This would mark the end of our nation's self-reliance, when government was contained and citizen actions controlled the financial system.

What is inconceivable to us today is that in the 1890s the nation's leading banks were so sound that they actually repeatedly stepped in to rescue the U.S. Treasury. And interestingly, notably large collapses showed the problems of even such a severe downturn were more matters of illiquidity than insolvency. For example, the most visible one in the 1907 panic, the Knickerbocker Trust, paid off all its depositors in full within three years.[35] Later, in the midst of the severely weakened asset prices of the Great Depression, the notoriously risky Bank of United States paid off 83 cents on the dollar to its depositors, and four-fifths of this was repaid within two years of its closure in December 1930. This bank had served 440,000 depositors in New York City and placed about one-quarter of its loans in speculative commercial real estate through related entities, something regulators would never permit today (See Figure 3.1).[36]

By comparison, well before the Panic of 2008 set in, America's financial institutions had weak balance sheets despite having been fantastically

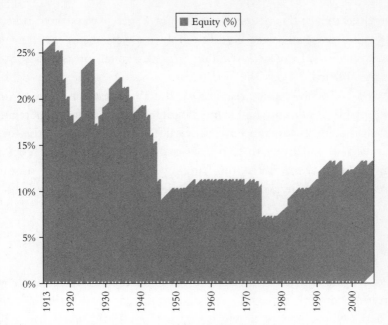

**Figure 3.1  Equity as a Percentage of Commercial Bank Credit**
*Source:* Federal Reserve Statistical Release H.8 Assets and Liabilities of Commercial Banks in the
United States from 1973 forward.  Statistical Abstract of the United States for earlier periods.  Precisely
which bank accounts are measured in these two series causes a difference of less than 3 percent to
produce three-fourths of the total one-time drop visible from 1972 to 1973 in the chart.

profitable in the prior decade. A survey of March 31, 2008, balance sheets
is revealing: Goldman Sachs is deemed the most conservative investment
bank, but its equity capital was just 3.6 percent of assets. JP Morgan Chase
(prior to bailing out Bear Stearns) had equity measuring 7.7 percent
of assets, but, this net of goodwill and intangibles was only 4.5 percent.
Moreover, in footnotes to its year-end 2007 balance sheet, it disclosed
some $77 trillion of gross notional value of derivatives. At mid-year
2008, Citigroup traded at less than 70 percent of its book value, which
after subtracting goodwill and intangibles was less than 3 percent of its
assets. By the end of the year Citigroup was counting some $44 billion
of deferred tax assets as over half of its Tier 1 capital, even though this
sum merely represents the present value of the tax benefit its losses would
have if they might be used at a later time to shield profits. Almost all
of the banks (such as Wachovia and Washington Mutual) that stum-
bled near the end of 2008 had healthy looking Tier 1 capital ratios, yet

at the time they merged into the safety of larger players they indicated they would have had severe liquidity problems were it not for their government lifelines. In May 2009, after massive capital injections from the Treasury and loans from the Fed, Treasury Secretary Geithner declared there was "zero" insolvency risk among the 19 largest banks, based upon an acceptable minimum of having tangible equity at just 4 percent of assets, a ridiculously low ratio by historical standards. Thanks to the socialization of risk and more than 100 years of growing cultural acceptance of this practice as the norm, the banking system is uniformly unsound, whereas it was only irregularly unsound before.

## The Triumph of Public Debt

The classical gold standard could not survive the first worldwide war, wherein governments found it easy to confiscate wealth through buying their own debt with newly issued money. World War I had a profound effect on the world economic order. For the United States, it began an up-cycle of issuing public and private debt. Taxes were increased sharply. To help service the cost of war and reconstruction, the top income tax bracket was pushed to 67 percent in 1917, something made possible by the ratification of the Sixteenth Amendment in 1913, which established the federal income tax. In essence this rescinded the citizenry's constitutional right to private property. Through the founding of the Fed, also in 1913, the United States government regained the ability to print money extensively, which led to inflation that undercut the value of the dollar by nearly 50 percent over the ensuing three years. This eroded the purchasing power of those who bought some $17 billion of Liberty Bonds or otherwise lived on fixed income streams. (For comparison, nominal GDP had been about $32 billion in the 1907-1911 period.) While gold could still be demanded in exchange for dollars, an inconvenient check on government, during the interwar years creditors and debtors would become more apt to expand their balance sheets by pyramiding paper atop gold reserves. The scale of this fiscal and monetary intervention would sow the seeds of the destruction of what was left of the diluted gold standard by the advent of the Great Depression, a period discussed later in this chapter.

Most commentators see the 1925–1931 period as the last gasp of the gold standard, an era marred by Britain's resumption at prewar parity that caused its economy to fester under the burden of 10 percent overvaluation that could not be expunged by deflation. Recalcitrant unions in old line coal and textile export industries, in some cases made up of soldiers who had returned from the brutal front lines of the war, eventually called a general strike in 1926. Cultural rejection of deflation clearly undermined resumption of the gold standard by Britain, and its custodianship of the world's reserve currency. Britain had allowed its share of world gold reserves to recede to 6 percent, a far cry from Russia (21%), France (17%), the United States (19%), or even Austria-Hungary (10%).[37] It is for this reason that some draw a parallel to present times and warn that the United States has abused its stewardship of the dollar by allowing pyramiding to reach an extreme and by backing itself into a fiscal corner where tax revenue may never adequately fund commitments.

By 1913 almost half of the forex reserves of the world were denominated in sterling and London was still the financial center of the universe. But by then the U.K. held just 3 percent of world gold reserves, setting the stage for the spectacular failure of the gold exchange standard in 1931.[38] Still, this conventional conclusion fails to account for what would follow, a tectonic shift to America, which through unsound policy likewise would gradually debase gold during the interwar years. Most observers date the global end of the gold standard at 1931. Actually the United States and Britain merely substituted devaluation (and at least initially sterilization with low interest rates) for the old rules of the game that had demanded a pro-cyclical interest rate policy. This was followed by gold hoarding. From 1925 to 1945 Britain's central bank gold holdings rose 64 percent, and those of the U.S. Treasury nearly tripled.[39] The United States and French sterilization of their abundant gold inflows in particular forced other countries to abandon gold altogether or feel a disproportionate transmission of deflation.

Cessation of hostilities in November 1918 did little to dispel intense mutual distrust among the nations of Europe—no wonder with 20 million dead and a like number of injured. Initially a boom occurred for the replenishment of foodstuffs and raw materials. But each country pursued autarkic policies that crippled trade. The Austro-Hungarian

Empire was divided into small states that protected individual components of manufacturing. No longer might Czechoslovakian coal supply
Austrian iron works, or Austrian yarn be exported back in return to that
country's weaving mills. Millions were unemployed in central Europe
during the downturn of 1921.[40]

The reparations burden laid at the feet of Germany after the Treaty
of Versailles in 1919 was suffocative. Within a year this unrealistic reparations tithe would be cut in half. A hypothetical comparison to the
present time is instructive: Imagine if the United Nations could impose
a $23 trillion interest-bearing debt burden upon the United States,
payable to a handful of countries. The interest on this, calculated at
5 percent, would amount to $1.15 trillion annually. By comparison, the
tax revenue raised in the United States in 2006 from the individual
income tax was slightly over $1 trillion, which was taken from salaries
and wages of some $5.5 trillion and other income of $2.6 trillion (pensions, capital gains, business and partnership income, Social Security).
The imposition of such a burden would thus double the tax burden
of Americans. Europe as a whole was crippled. At war's end, Germany
was stripped of its colonies and maritime assets. Fifteen million out of
its 67 million of population had been involved to some extent in foreign trade relating to these imperial holdings, broadly defining this to
include workers in industries reliant on certain commodity imports.[41]
High tariffs and debt perpetuated capital and trade account imbalances.
There was an element within Germany that astutely believed that having an unrealistically large amount of debt due would enlighten the
allies such that they would loosen restrictions on the export of German
machinery and capital goods, and attract financial inflows to rebuild the
power plant of Europe.

The German government was forced to print money, since it could
not raise taxes further, causing the famous Weimar hyperinflation of
1921-1923. The German default of 1923 was met by the occupation
of the Ruhr Valley, but this so inflamed tensions that workers there
were encouraged to strike. In 1924 reparations once again would
be modified under the Dawes Plan. Foreshadowing today's global trade
imbalances being propped up with massive capital account movements,
the United States chose a strategy of being the crutch for an unsustainable situation in Germany. Germany became the largest debtor nation

by 1924. Despite restructurings, by 1928 it would still owe $1 billion, mirrored by the great creditors: the United States ($1.1 billion) and the United Kingdom ($0.6 billion).[42] Similarly the currencies of Austria, Hungary, Poland, Germany, and Russia became valueless, and intense inflation ravaged Romania, Bulgaria, Portugal, Greece, Yugoslavia, Finland, Czechoslovakia, France, and Belgium. Of these more fortunate victims, the best-performing currency versus the dollar (Belgium) lost 87 percent of its value by the early 1920s.[43]

The commodity boom that began just after the war quickly subsided by the early 1920s. Writing in 1924, Chase National Bank's Economist Benjamin Anderson writes of the dangers of "cheap money" crowding into New York, but scarcity elsewhere:

> ... even if we have not blown up a price bubble, we have been blowing up a credit bubble, especially in the form of long-term debts. States, municipalities, agriculture, and other borrowers have borrowed excessively because money has been cheap. Banks have invested heavily in long-time bonds. A great volume of short-time money market funds has been diverted to capital uses ...

> For the world as a whole, capital is scarce after ten years of war and disorganization. Its apparent abundance is due to abnormal money market conditions, both in the United States and abroad, and to the fact that capital is unwilling to venture into many countries and great industries which badly need it, and which, with a restoration of confidence, would be effective bidders for it. Men who use money market funds at low rates for capital purposes may expect a rude awakening when the tide turns ...

> Capital in London and New York prefers the 2% or 3% it can get with safety to the 10%, 15%, or 30% which it might have in these countries under existing conditions of grave risk ...[44]

Although, for example, the investing public in New York did eventually snap up bonds marketed at high interest rates and face value discounts ($200 million of German bonds sold out in one day after the

Dawes plan was approved), generally the debt saddling the world was intergovernmental and related to the triangle of the United States, the allies, and the Germans. This arrangement would have largely transmitted reparations through to the United States, but Germany and Europe were starved for capital as well as on the hook for debt. So capital would have to flow in the opposite direction, which it did for most of that decade.

Ostensibly the United States remained uninvolved in European affairs, and held this stance as a negotiating gambit since it wished to keep from having to reduce its war debts to the allies. But in practice New York became the source of *new* financial deals, supplementing London's maintenance of old relationships in a handoff of wearing the crown of world financial affairs. It supplied Germany (and later Poland) with loans, through a diluted version of the "private loan with supervision" model then being effectively used in a score of developing nations in the new dollar diplomacy spreading across the world under the auspices of the "money doctor" Edwin Kemmerer and other professional currency experts. His predecessor, Charles Conant, had been paid handsomely in deals, such as when he obtained 50 percent of the total seigniorage of displacing the Philippine's silver specie system in favor of dollar-backed paper money for his banker, J.P. Morgan, in 1903-1905.

Kemmerer's controlled loans did not rely upon gunboat diplomacy as those of the Conant era had, but they involved the insertion of a U.S. advisor to control tariff receipts. It may be argued that his success mostly stemmed from tapping into the surplus of capital being printed by the banking system during the 1920s. He advised for the Dawes Plan, which installed the 32-year-old Seymour Parker Gilbert to watch over Germany as its "agent general for reparations payment." Gilbert and Reichsbank head Hjalmar Schact jointly feared the funneling of U.S. loans for social and other unproductive programs such as unemployment relief, parks beautification, and maintaining local deficit spending. In fact Germany cut taxes in 1925 in response to economic weakness, and saw its deficit grow in 1926 and 1927. But otherwise he ruffled feathers in this country, being little involved in social affairs and working long hours alone, offending nationalist sensibilities, and unwittingly becoming the whipping boy for deleterious foreign involvement.

In 1927 after permitting a loan to support Prussian deficit spending, he penned a memo to the German finance minister that rebuked its policies. The financial world interpreted this as a red flag and cut off funds from Germany by 1928. Some 40 percent of the country's financing had been short-term. May 1929 brought the Young Plan to rescue Germany from plummeting economic activity, and Gilbert was terminated.[45]

The gold exchange standard would emerge by the mid- to late-1920s, with France rejoining in 1926, followed by Belgium in 1927, and Italy in 1928, among others. However, the new order was not really a gold standard, for these countries could hold a large part of their reserves in sterling or dollars, and their central banks could not establish adequate reserves without reliance upon short-term borrowing. When credit began to tighten in 1928, pressure mounted and was unleashed after the stock market collapse in New York in late 1929, exposing the leverage and weakness underlying numerous central banks and their currencies—especially Britain and Germany.

In contrast to Europe, the United States enjoyed an industrial boom in the mid-1920s, seeing a solid rise in auto production and the doubling of electricity generation, as well as a housing boom that lifted construction to 12 percent of national income by 1927, its peak year. By 1925 its manufacturing had increased 48 percent from 1913, driven in part by supplying Germany, which paid for purchases with American supplied capital. Another star of that era was Japan. It benefitted from insatiable demand for the export of silk for women's stockings, among other things, and it had used World War I as an opportunity to jump-start its export base. By 1925 its manufacturing had increased 122 percent from 1913.[46]

From 1928 on, Western Europe was subdued with France only growing its manufacturing some 14 percent and Germany contracting 5 percent. Germany might have saved itself by providing credit internally. However, with the experience with hyperinflation fresh in the public's mind, which had destroyed middle class savings, made this impossible.

Thus, between the wars, economic performance varied greatly among nations. While the United States and Japan benefitted from the misfortunes of continental Europe after World War I, Britain could not. It can be seen as an empire that continued a decline from its pinnacle

achieved in the 1870s. It had gotten a major jump on the world's industrialization, capturing 38 percent of all world manufacturing exports
at the peak of its influence, with this being done largely on the back of
textiles, which disproportionately had been some 60 to 70 percent of its
exports. It had diversified into producer goods by the 1920s, but even
these chosen industries were slow growing compared to the up and coming businesses of the United States, and they were subject to competition
from the industrialization of other nations. During the 1920s, its unemployment was 10 to 11 percent, largely due to the structural lack of competitiveness of these sunset export industries. Its coal industry had lost its
cost advantage to new mines on the continent, causing exports to decline
by 12 percent from 1924 to 1929; likewise cotton and woolens fell 10
percent and 20 percent under pressure from Indian mills, respectively. The
United Kingdom sought to reestablish gold backing for sterling at par
with its prewar value, despite there having been wholesale price inflation
of over 200 percent from 1913 to 1920, which had subsided to just 48
percent by the time of resumption in 1926.[47]

Initially Britain's industrial decline was not worrisome, for it
retained a large services surplus from the shipping, insurance, and
financial services it could dominate due to its former world leadership. London was a financial hub (and is today) through which it
placed investments. Whereas it had financed these with a trade surplus
previously, by the 1920s it had become reliant upon short-term debt
financing for these deals. Like her continental neighbors, this would
prove to be an Achilles' heel. The Bank of England ambitiously re-
established the pound at £4.25 per troy ounce of gold (the dollar had
been $20.67 per ounce, for a cross-currency ratio of 4.86), and there
was little hope for corrective deflation due to the rise of trade union-
ism and the central bank's expansion of credit. Perhaps anticipating the
modern era of coordinated policy with ever expanding money supplies, Benjamin Strong dutifully inflated the U.S. money supply, but his
effort was undermined by Britain's sterilization, which was a growth in
credit that never before had been contemplated under the rules of the
game of the classical gold standard. It left the world system precariously
balanced when the signal of falling stock prices enticed deleveraging of
the excessive amount of debt that was building up thanks to copious
supplies of cheap money on both sides of the Atlantic.[48]

Had the pound been set at £6.00 or £6.50 per troy ounce (i.e. for a cross-currency ratio of 3.2 to 3.5), stability might have ensued. Most economists agree that the pound was overvalued when it was reset at prewar parity. Some of the trade patterns suggest this, with the coal, steel, and basic industries losing foreign markets and manufactured imports rising sharply (33%) from 1924-1929, and even through 1931. But wholesale price inflation in some other countries had been similar, with the United States, Sweden, and Holland seeing 43 to 49 percent rises— right in line with Britain's. The exception was where inflation was allowed to burn out of control in much of Europe. France, which pursued inflationary policies to rebuild after WWI, saw the franc plummet some 80 percent while its price level increased about four and a half times. Six governments failed in quick succession within 18 months, bringing in the conservative Poincaré regime in 1926, which balanced the budget and resumed gold backing by 1928. However this was done at a low level, stimulating French exports and causing accumulation of currency reserves, particularly of sterling.[49] Much emphasis is placed upon the role of exchange rates in setting up the severe economic weakness that began in 1928 and eventually spun out of control by 1931 when Creditanstalt would collapse and bring the international house of cards down. But in reality more is explained simply by recognizing that excessive leverage would invariably cause a multi-year hangover, especially when bad policy would prolong imbalances by layering on yet more debt.

Truly authorities wanted to return to a gold standard after World War I, but in reality cultural change had occurred that made success impossible. The general strike in Britain in 1926 pitted the deflationary reality of returning to gold against a powerful new labor movement. Its gold was depleted, and its trade deficit gradually wore away at its remaining wealth, mainly overseas investments and services. Germany being stripped of all its resources—ships, foreign investments, gold— was completely reliant upon short-term credit priced at 8 to 9 percent. France and Japan operated undervalued currencies, taking advantage of the wild resetting of wholesale prices that occurred in response to war shortages, undercutting stability because these would require permanent deflationary adjustment among their trading partners. France did this through accepting inflation and then locking in undervaluation versus gold. Japan devalued 20 percent after a major earthquake in 1923 and did not link to gold until 1930, and then this was maintained for only one year. The compromise for the rest of the world was a pseudo-gold standard. From a global perspective it was highly leveraged, because it pyramided multiple countries' currencies upon the thin reed of Britain or upon the United States, establishing international central bank reserves partly backed by paper. By centralizing banking, monetary management fell under the purview of government more than being beholden to risk-averse depositors, for specie was abandoned almost altogether, giving birth to numerous occurrences of hyperinflation.

Meanwhile, although global trade was not as important to the U.S. economy relative to these other nations, it too had drifted into a new era of central banking and emerging statism. The groundwork had been laid by the Banking Acts of 1863-64, which reduced the importance of state-chartered banks and proved to be the death knell for Jeffersonian and Jacksonian ideals, once the bedrock of the Democratic Party. It is telling that Republicans beginning with McKinley took over ownership of the gold issue at the turn of the century. But rather than doing so to protect the common man from dilution of his wealth through established mechanisms, they established new rules that concentrated risk and put control of credit expansion into the hands of a few, and eventually one, central bank. Central banking took hold abroad, generally with complete government control. The old way of self-regulation, through exchangeability for specie and fostering a distributed population of local banks that provided more particular public visibility and were subject to failure, could not survive amidst the new culture of progressivism and the Wilson technocracy.

## The Aftermath

Now that nearly a century has elapsed, most current analysis of the Great Depression is predicated upon Keynesian and Monetarist intellectual perspectives, largely focusing upon what happened in the 1930s. By editorial omission, the turbulence of the First World War and its aftermath might even be imagined to be serene by students unfamiliar with it, in comparison to the hardship of the Roosevelt years. But what happened in the interwar period was extraordinary. Certainly in the 19th century the United States had its share of volatility. It had suspended linkage to gold, monetized Treasury debt through printing, shifted between centralized and decentralized banking systems, and had witnessed private credit bubbles built despite the potential discipline of depositors' demanding conversion to specie. But in the interwar era, the world had detached itself significantly from sound money more or less permanently, rather than for brief interludes such as when necessary to finance the War of 1812 or the Civil War.

Once the Great Depression unraveled the artificial stimulus of growth through leverage that occurred under the gold-exchange standard, the United States did not exactly abandon gold. Instead it became the highest and in fact dominant bidder in the world market for gold, and exhibited a crazed preference for the metal. The price increase from $20.67 to $35 triggered a mining boom, and the United States bought more than the total production of the world's mines through the Great Depression. By the early 1950s, the United States would own three-fourths of all monetary gold and half of cumulative world production since the beginning of time.[50] The establishment of pegged exchange rates in the Bretton Woods Agreement of 1944 could be seen as a global gold-exchange standard pyramiding all the world's money upon gold held by the United States, placing America in a position not unlike that of Britain at the height of its empire. Ironically, from that moment forward, the United States mimicked the actions of its aging parent, repudiating this backing of its currency and providing a beacon for the world to follow it down the path of adopting a purely paper-based currency system. In a perverse way, the hoarding of so much gold by the United States might have destabilized a genuine return to a classical gold standard globally until decades later when the cumulative hefty expansion of credit would cause the country's stockpile to be drained to the point of severing the United States' link to gold entirely.

The farther the United States (and the world) departed from the use of gold, the more it built a currency that was primarily backed by credit. If the value of that indebtedness falls well below par, then the reserves that are negated are likely to need to be replaced by additional fiat money, although the popular hope has been that additional lending and

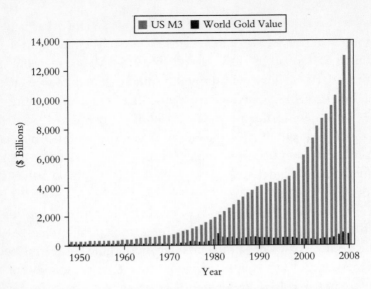

**Figure 3.2    Total Value of U.S. Money Supply (M3) & World Central Bank Gold Reserves ($ billions)**

liquidity provisioning might replenish equity as was the case in 1990. (See Figure 3.2.)

After steadily losing gold reserves through the 1960s, the Nixonian era ushered in the adoption of a purely paper-based pyramid of banking and foreign exchange established upon the dollar as the world's reserve currency. This would grease the skids for accelerated and completely unchecked leveraging of the banking system, securitization, and derivatives creation. Now that precious metals have been stripped of their role as a form of money, their value has shrunken to a low single digit percentage of the worth of the total stock of dollars (and other fiat currencies). Mainly relegated to jewelry (about 70% of annual demand), gold's value is mainly set by its utility as a commodity. Upon the occasional lapses when faith in government obligations has waned, especially in the context of inflation, its value was partially restored, because citizens saw it as an alternative to fiat currency. However, it held up well through much of the 2008 panic, but its strength then was correlated with fears of debasement when monetary authorities discussed quantitative easing or injected reserves. The thesis that gold should decline in price when deflation occurs is contradicted by the history of the metal having roughly doubled its purchasing power in the early 1930s. Silver was once the preeminent form of specie, but for a century its value relative to gold has remained depressed. The advent of gold-backed ETFs portends a permanent threat to silver, because divisibility is now possible, which might enable broad usage of a 100 percent backed gold currency. Obviously this is an extremely remote possibility, but the kernel of an idea is visible.

The Great Depression, briefly reviewed next, will provide academics and investors with fodder for many opinions about its origin and the causes for recovery from it for generations. The meltdown begun in 2008 is likely to also. Interpretations of both are likely to be politicized. The structure of government and monetary administration adopted in 1913 allowed for unprecedented capacity for a centralized response to such crises, which unbeknownst to many has enabled redistributionist policies. It should spawn a debate between capitalists and socialists. Instead, modern day capitalists are cheerleaders for monetary intervention by the central bank as a means of smoothing out economic cycles, bailing out risk takers, and injecting a near lethal overdose of moral hazard sure to foster a culture of dependency among the populace. When combined with a unique two-tiered tax system, it is stripping away the estates of the upper middle class, and it has propelled the riches of a select few elites to heights that would make barons of the gilded age envious.

# Chapter 4

# Flat-Earth Economics

*The curious task of economics is to demonstrate to men how little they really know about what they imagine they can design.*
FRIEDRICH A. HAYEK, *THE FATAL CONCEIT:*
*THE ERRORS OF SOCIALISM,* 1988

The Fed has the authority to create money out of nothing, a power greater than that possessed by most if not all sovereign rulers in the history of mankind. Having doubled the money supply in the seven years through 2007 and grown it at an 7 percent annual clip since its inception in 1913, the Fed has used its power with abandon, with only two uncomfortable outcomes: the Great Depression and the stagflation era of the 1970s. With the debate over gold-backed currency and bank reserves having been settled a century ago, its supreme sanction to print is now unquestioned. Voices of dissent have been marginalized, and proponents of the Fed's dominion have been honored by being hired as consultants by the hundreds by the central bank. These chosen gurus have fanned out into academia to spread the orthodoxy and stamp out alternative views such as the Austrian School.

In this chapter, the stultification of economic theory with an anti-gold bias is examined carefully. The modern precepts of central banking are discussed, revealing how and why inflation targeting has become the primary policy rule, and what this means for financial markets over a very long stretch of time. Several provocative figures are presented that challenge the conventional wisdom surrounding economic growth, inflation, deflation, and money supply growth. With this grounding, the latter half of the chapter ventures into the academic papers that Fed Chairman Bernanke has cited in his theories about the Great Depression and its relevance to today's meltdown. Chairman Bernanke has also written extensively on that era, perhaps even in greater quantity than some of the authors presented here. His style is far more thorough and granular, but essentially his mission has been to substantiate these early findings and build upon them with a wider focus. The Great Depression is highly relevant to the credit implosion that began in 2008, although a majority of observers today pointedly deny the applicability of the parallel. Of even greater importance is that the academic blueprint Bernanke might follow to escape the clutches of a liquidity trap may be fatally flawed, and in fact much of our present difficulties can be traced to Depression era institutions and practices.

By carefully probing the flaws of this body of economic research, a deeper understanding of our present dilemma is inescapable. Bernanke and his academic peers, who together have ossified around an academic consensus, lay the blame for the depth and duration of the Depression upon the gold standard. Yet via the convenient machination of assumption they neglect to discover the primary cause of that sharp downturn, which not only instigated the collapse, but doomed it to be deeper and longer than prior recessions. In so doing, these flat-Earth economists convict by association in such a way that the real culprit, fiat currency and the leverage it promotes, may be set free. The DNA of the killer may be long lost, but the reader as judge will have a chance to review data that exonerates gold and correlates 92 percent with the evidence, while the case built by the flat-Earth economists rests upon circumstantial clues that statistically explain just over half the crime. It does make for heavy reading at times, but given the unanimity of opinion expressed by mainstream economists and the economic illiteracy of the media, institutional and retail investors, and—worst of all—the voting public, this critique of the academic case against gold might, like the voice crying out in the wilderness, be enlightening.

## Misunderstanding Inflation

Fortunately, for consistency in any century, there is the classic definition of inflation that is an "inordinate expansion of credit." In the 1930s, Keynes in a number of letters to the Fed twisted this around to mean that inflation was simply rising prices that had very little to do with central bank manipulations.

Bob Hoye, Address to the Committee for Monetary
Research and Education, May 2009

Fed Chairman Bernanke's decision to use the tools of printing money through directly monetizing government debt and mortgages rests upon decades of academic theory, and in particular on work that blames the gold standard for the depth and length of the Great Depression. Although there is ample evidence that government intervention was injurious because it retarded the private sector's actions to save and reduce debt, Treasury Secretary Geithner has stated that economic recovery in the 1930s did not occur chiefly because the government failed to act in a large enough way.

Bernanke, Geithner, and other monetary theorists who are in charge of the financial system rely upon academic work that argues the operation of a currency system that each year prints money (historically an average of 7 percent for M3) and elicits a percent or two of consumer price inflation is inherently stable. This work also finds that a system, such as gold, that limits monetary growth would result in deflation, instability, and sub-optimal economic growth.

We have a centrally managed fiat currency by choice. It ensures a small, manageable amount of inflation, and isolates control of the quantity of money in the hands of a benevolent few who possess the highest degree of understanding of its operation. But there is a side effect: It presents an enticing one-way bet to profit from the use of debt. Known to all students of finance is the Capital Asset Pricing Model (CAPM), which states there is an optimal mixture of equity and debt in investment decisions. Although as a theory it holds appeal, in practice the lure of leverage, which exists even in monetary systems that are not established by fiat or lack central control, is powerful. The record shows that neither is there long-term correlation between interest rates and inflation, nor between interest rates and money supply growth. These are tremendously counterintuitive conclusions, but they are nonetheless true as will be shown in the figures that follow in this chapter. Instead, real growth is optimized when credit expands moderately, which historically occurred more often than not over a gold-reserved monetary base. Extremely low *or* high monetary growth is associated with an interventionist, centralized system, and it has shortchanged mankind with periods of low real economic expansion.

Federal Reserve System governors have a difficult task, and they know it. If things were simple, they would elect to let the money supply expand at a comfortable low single digit rate. They would let the chips fall where they may, immune from political fallout. Like the rider of a horse, they might hold the reins lightly but firmly, allowing a trot or canter, but not letting gallops persist or walking too much. However, money is no longer a stack of gold bars or a pile of currency. It is a made up of electrons coursing through the banking system, and these expand whenever a new loan is made or contract when one is repaid. The soundness of its overall value hinges upon the reserves of the banks that issue the loans, and ultimately from the government that can inject or remove base currency from the reserves of the banks that form the core of the system. The expansion of credit might be controlled some by those at the helm of the Fed, but the animal spirits of those who would lend and borrow are equally important, as was proven back in the times when there was no Fed and gold was the monetary base. If the horse has been run too hot (as it was in the 1920s), loosening the reins may not be enough to entice it to speed up again after the race is over. To borrow from an old saying, the Fed governors could not "push on a string."

Fiat money, electronic or paper currency that is not redeemable into a hard asset, has dominated the modern financial era. Cultural and political change has trended against prudent management of credit growth for nearly a century. As a consequence, outside a few doomsayers, libertarians, and boldly curious economists or money managers, most observers in our time have little more than a theoretical conception of why a fiat currency system could come under stress, and whether the current crisis might be handled effectively or deepen to the point that the political demand for an alternative form of money would emerge. U.S. fiscal policy will play a role, for the market's perception of the credit worthiness of the U.S. government ultimately determines whether its fiat currency is sound.

The world might be best served by a fiat currency whose growth is managed such that there is little or no inflation of credit. Milton Friedman suggested that the Fed might be replaced by a computer that would regulate the money supply, holding its growth to a low single-digit rate, originally 3 percent per year, in line with economic expansion. The modern orthodoxy has discredited that theoretical approach for a number of reasons. One pragmatically questions which money supply would be targeted. Another posits that interest rates or exchange rates would be overly volatile. Consequently, the modern way is to target the outcome rather than to focus on mechanistically committing to one tool that may be tremendously flawed. But the Fed's inflation-fighting ability is hampered by measurement difficulties and heavy reliance upon another singular tool, the federal funds rate, for affecting policy. Human instincts can interfere and generate waves of unwarranted optimism or pessimism, which can override or amplify central bank actions. The U.S. central bank may feel it has kept tight control over its monetary base, but increasingly intermediation takes place through securities firms' actions in the open market, and lax control over the fractional reserve mechanism has promoted the velocity of credit expansion. Inflationary signals have not been received by Fed governors, since they are watered down by hedonic, geometric, substitution, owners' equivalent rent, and bogus seasonal adjustments to the official yardstick, CPI-U, made by government bureaucrats. Some argue that measuring inflation might be as problematic as following a policy rule of predictable quantitative restraint.

But even if one conceded that inflation has been tame in recent times, the understanding embedded in the consensus of economists ignores an overwhelming underlying trend that prices would be declining. Productivity and the gravitational pull into the developed economic system of the 90 percent of Earth's population born into poverty who are willing to toil for $2 per hour account for the trend. Policymakers are so fixated upon the desirability of 0 percent inflation and so wary of deflation that they prescribe judicious printing that would maintain 1 to 2 percent inflation. But to achieve this end, money growth has approached double digits during expansions such as 2003-2007. Economists believe the world of prices should be flat, when instead it is naturally round, curving downward at a few percent per year. Besides the appeal to simple minds of the two-dimensional model, a not-so-intended side effect is that the monetary excess required to defy natural curvation automatically dumps into markets excluded from inflationary calculations. The excess might not inflate the price of apparel, tuna fish, or toys, but it blows up a bubble in investment assets such as corporate equities or real estate. This creates inequity, benefitting the super-rich who can borrow and extract cash tax-free from these appreciating assets or sell them and bear minimal tax rates associated with capital gains. Borrowing comes cheaply in a world of artificially suppressed interest rates caused by excessive monetary growth. Labor and small business remain taxed at ordinary rates that progressively rise as income spikes in an overheated economy. If money growth were left to organic means, the river of credit would meander gracefully across the plains, rather than be channeled directly to seas of derivatives and 30-year mortgages. The government subsidized homes and IRAs of the common man might be sensibly built only on high ground, not dependent upon engineers at the Fed to maintain levees and repair concrete containing the river in a straight direction. And when the once-in-a-generation storm hits, damage would be limited, lives saved, and the incursion of salt water stealing away wetlands of savings might cease. Rather than channeling the rich silt of gold to the seas, its bounty would be spread upon an expanding delta of permanent prosperity.

## Weighing the Evidence

A simple policy guideline known as the Taylor Rule (developed by Stanford's John B. Taylor), although not followed by the Fed, has gained accolades from the academic community in recent years. Taylor suggests raising the Fed funds rate by 1.5 percent for each 1 percent rise in inflation observed, but cutting it by 0.5 percent when real GDP falls 1 percent. By watching two outcomes, real growth and inflation, the central bank might pursue a flexible path that responds to market conditions, yet telegraphs to market participants that credit growth might be restrained within a friendly channel. Thus, in periods such as the 1960s when President Johnson pressured the Fed to monetize government spending for the war on poverty and the Vietnam conflict, the central bank might defend maintaining a prudent stance with this institutionalized formula.

But a larger theoretical question gnaws at the accepted convention of inflation targeting, even if it is improved through considering real growth as well. Is the primary outcome being targeted—inflation—really the underlying problem, or is it a symptom? Today in Zimbabwe or after the Great War in Europe inflation was the one-dimensional villain. But by the 1930s, and perhaps after the panic of 2008, the last stage of the disease of excessive leverage might be deflation, and inflation an intermediate condition, like syphilitic chancres that enter remission before severe systemic damage is done.

The freezing of the credit markets in 2008 throws an inconvenient monkey wrench into the inflation-targeting orthodoxy of the high priests of central banking. Inflation targeting is like a surfer's fancy maneuvers to optimize his ride on the crest of a building wave. It's great when he first catches it, and it is exhilarating to sustain a long ride. But it is extremely hard to do. As often as not, one can be smashed against the ocean floor with the fury of a heavy wave pressing down almost to the point of suffocation. Figure 4.1 reveals an interesting big picture. Extended periods of high *and* low money growth produce anemic real economic growth, and can be associated with deflation. The relationship appears to be robust with a curve fitted that explains 88 percent of the statistical variation (R-Squared = 88%).[1]

When credit growth is moderate, between 3 and 6 percent, real economic growth is solid. Remarkably, deflation isn't all that bad. Rapid economic expansion can happen when the consumer price level is falling, as the 1879 resumption to the gold standard induced in the 1870-1890 period. Or, under a fiat system such as 1940-1970, an inflation level above the comfort zone of today's inflation-targeting Fed governors might result. But it wouldn't necessarily restrain economic output. With credit held in check, the increase in money tends to flow to productive areas of the economy. There is no question that some speculative excess spills over into the equity and real estate markets in

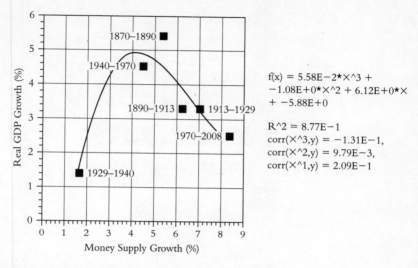

f(x) = 5.58E−2★X^3 +
−1.08E+0★X^2 + 6.12E+0★X
+ −5.88E+0

R^2 = 8.77E−1
corr(X^3,y) = −1.31E−1,
corr(X^2,y) = 9.79E−3,
corr(X^1,y) = 2.09E−1

**Figure 4.1  Money Supply & Real Economic Growth**
*Sources:* Historical Statistics of the United States; Federal Reserve System Data.

periods of moderate money growth. Consumer prices may rise some-what more than moderately, but the reason may be shortages caused by the business cycle, or in the case of 1940–1970, the rebuilding of Europe and the fiscal policy of the Johnson administration. Granted, this attribution is overly simple, and one might legitimately assert that the meltdown of the early 1970s would have been averted with better policies, both fiscal and monetary, than those in force during the 1960s. But it may also be said that Nixon's abrogation of gold settlement of international accounts in 1971 may have initiated a particularly delete-rious chain of events instead of what might have been a more normally shaped recession. Once the markets received a "coup de whiskey" with 14 percent-plus money expansion in 1971 and 1972—to borrow the 1928 phrase of Benjamin Strong—it was a whole different ball game. That period of the early 1970s might be kept in mind when noticing that the two top stretches of rapid money creation (shown in Figures 4.1 and 4.2) preceded the worst financial debacles felt since the Fed was established in 1913.

Turning to the one period of low money growth (1929–1940) at the bottom of Figure 4.1, we see the miserable economic performance of the Great Depression. During its first years, the banking system collapsed

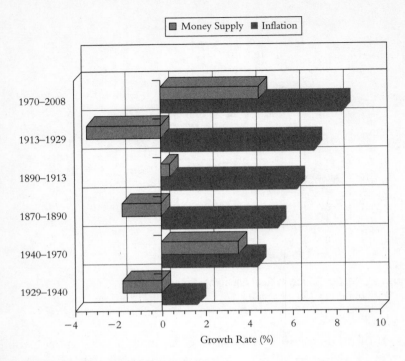

**Figure 4.2   Money Supply & Inflation**
*Sources:* Historical Statistics of the United States; Federal Reserve System Data.

to such an extent that devaluation of the dollar, substantial gold inflows from Europe, and expanding public sector debt and spending still could not cause the money supply to exceed its 1929 total until 1939.

Figure 4.2 displays these periods in the same rank order of money supply growth, but this time the resultant inflation is shown. The theoretical logic of inflation being caused by growth in the money supply is unassailable. However, there must be other factors at work because in three of the six long time periods shown, the directional movement is negative! Moreover, if inflation targeting through using the lever of the Fed funds rate is our intervention weapon of choice, the scatter plot in Figure 4.3 would indicate that there is not a very strong relationship between short-term interest rates and inflation.

In fact, the 19th century, which saw the creation of substantial bank money to augment specie, witnessed considerable economic growth in its first and second halves. Through 1850 consumer prices fell by nearly

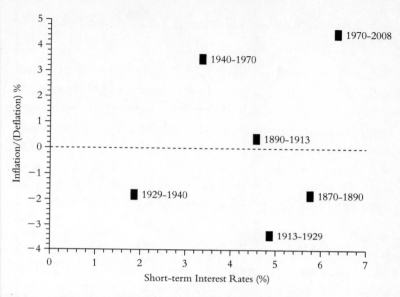

**Figure 4.3    Interest Rates & Inflation: No Long-Term Correlation**

*Source:* Commercial Paper Rates from Homer, Sidney, A History of Interest Rates; Federal Reserve Statistical Release, Historical Data, H.15 Selected Interest Rates. Inflation: Historical Statistics of the United States.

half. The Civil War brought the greenback, which restored prices to the post-Revolutionary War level. But they would fall from their own weight after the orgy of printing stopped, returning to their low pre-Civil War ebb by the time gold resumption occurred in 1879. If the blocks of data examined earlier showing how deflation and money supply growth are uncorrelated over long stretches of history are not convincing enough, then certainly the record of the entire 19th century shouts out the message loud and clear. During it, prices fell 50 percent and the money supply mushroomed from less than $100 million to $7 billion. Attachment to gold permitted necessary speculation episodically, but it did not allow inflation to roar out of control (the greenback episode being a hiatus). Still, the money supply could expand on top of its gold base and provide enough elasticity to encourage a pace of real business investment that has not been witnessed ever since.

During the late 1800s gold discoveries are thought to have considerably expanded the money supply. But instead, these were just adequate for gold to replace silver as a medium of exchange, as explained in the words of Laurence Laughlin in his tome, *The History of Bimetallism in the United States*:

> We find ourselves, in the period following 1850, confronted with an enormously increased production of gold. How enormous it was I do not think has been generally recognized in our monetary discussions, particularly of late in those dealing with the appreciation of gold. It seems almost incredible to say that, in the 25 years following 1850, as much gold was given forth by the mines as had been produced to that time since the discovery of America by Columbus. And yet it is literally true.[2]

In this contemporaneous text of Professor Laughlin set in 1885, we learn that by virtue of gold discoveries in California, Australia, and Russia the world's supply of gold—measured in dollars—finally approached the value of silver at hand in the mid-century. The silver that had been in circulation in Europe and the United States moved to India and Asian nations, so net-net there was not much if there was any increase in the monetary base of Europe or the United States.[3]

Short-term interest rates were extraordinarily high during the hard money Jacksonian era of the 1830s, averaging over 10 percent and topping 30 percent in 1836, 1837, and 1839.[4] In contrast, short rates averaged only 7.1 percent at the height of the greenback era of the 1860s, and were calm—averaging less than 8 percent in nine out of the 10 years of that decade. Under the gold standard to follow, they were only 4 to 5 percent. Although there was generally not a central bank in the 19th century, what seems apparent is that deflation and inflation can be very independent of money supply growth and of interest rates, as is shown in Figure 4.4. Deflation is probably better explained by productivity growth

### Table 4.1: Cumulative Global Precious Metals Mine Output

| Era | Gold | Silver |
| --- | --- | --- |
| 1493–1850 | $3,314,553,000 | $7,358,450,000 |
| 1851–1875 | $3,317,625,000 | $1,395,125,000 |

Note: The figures above are taken from Laurence Laughlin's "The History of Bimetallism in the United States," and reflect the value of gold and silver in 1885 dollars.

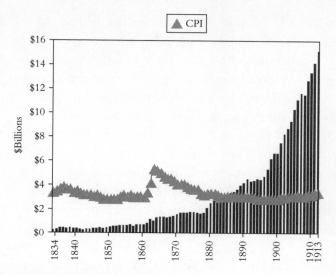

**Figure 4.4    19th Century Money Expansion**
*Sources:* Historical Statistics of the United States; Federal Reserve System Data.

and technological progress. Had some friendly low-single digit amount of inflation been targeted by all-knowing central bankers, quite a bit more money would have been printed, and the gold coin standards in place at various times would have been abandoned earlier. Speculative blow offs might have been more frenzied, and depressions may have caused massive unemployment rather than mere defaults of western land speculators and geographically spotty and infrequent reversions to subsistence agricultural activity.

Monetary incentives were dramatically altered with the founding of the Fed in 1913. This new regime ushered in a primary tendency for inflation that is not very detectible on a year-to-year basis, but has been extraordinarily high as its effects compound over time. The compounded annual average growth rate of consumer prices has been just 3.3 percent from the Fed's founding to 2007, but this means that a nickel in 1913 is worth more than a dollar today. In the 19th century there was some value to holding wealth in the form of money: On one hand money would buy *more* commodities over time due to deflation; on the other, one would receive several percentage points of real (and untaxed) return on investment from lending at the low-risk rates even in short-term maturities. The fiat money system of the 20th century would change the rules: Holding monetary wealth would be like bailing out a leaky boat. One might accrue 4 to 5 percent interest on prime short-term paper, but between inflation and taxation there would be no real earnings and perhaps even erosion of value. Is it any wonder that the savings rate is chronically low, debt has risen to record levels compared to income, and wealth has been compelled to reside in risky assets?

It may sound flippant, but the bedrock of today's monetary policy is the rapid expansion of monetary aggregates at *all* points in the business cycle. The broadest measure of money supply (M3) was over $14 trillion in the United States as of December 2008, at which point its year-over-year growth rate was almost 11 percent.[5] The power of compounding is remarkable. No one notices that prices in the United States increased 400 percent from 1940 to 1980. Disinflation reigned from the chairmanship of Paul Volcker on, but the price level of 2008 is over two and one-half times that which held when Reagan took office, and this is calculated with a CPI-U that is increasingly biased. M3, conveniently no longer reported by the Fed but estimated by others, began expanding in double digits beginning in December 2006, not the first time in this decade.

In theory the Fed only controls the monetary base. Broadly defined money does not always expand or contract evenly with income (a phenomenon measured as monetary "velocity"). Consequently the central bank has chosen to target the Federal Funds rate, the cost of money lent overnight by one bank to another to meet reserve requirements, thinking that controlling the price of this highly sensitive form of money puts its finger on the pulse of credit demand. But often, especially recently, this interest rate has been held very low while the broad money supply has grown in the high single digits or low double digits, which might be seen as fuel for the bubbles observed from the Greenspan era (1987-2006) through 2008. Nonetheless, Fed governors are on record saying that because velocity is not well correlated with income, it essentially does not even try to target monetary aggregates, even if these grow at unruly rates.[6] By having an academic justification for not targeting money supply growth, the Fed permitted one super credit cycle greater than those that punctuated the 19th century frequently. This necessitated years of tight targeting of the monetary base to be scrapped in lieu of a massive infusion of high-powered money in

2008, which may ultimately amount to a 50 to 100 percent expansion in one shot.

The overproduction of credit combined with the seeming assurance that it is properly meted out thanks to regulation has slowly caused a radical transformation, unrecognizable to the eyes of any one generation. Over the last hundred years there has been a role reversal: Banks used to compete on the basis of balance sheet strength and provided safekeeping. The U.S. government was financially weak and could not provide a refuge to investors, since it used to be constrained by constitutionally enumerated powers. Hard money is now soft; weak government has become strong thanks to its iron-clad grip on private property through unlimited power to tax. Attitudes about central banking completely reflect our culture. That in turn changes slowly, and it is still in the process of eroding long-held values. So for the pendulum to change course, a major economic or world political shock would be required. The collapse of the world equity markets begun in late 2008 may usher in just this change, but so far the response has been to solve the problem of excessive debt by using the power of central government to erase market signals as best we can. To solve the debt crisis we have issued more debt. To reverse the damage from reckless lending, we have showered money on risky banks, stunting competitive gains that would have been realized by smaller prudent institutions.

The academic and investment community has intellectually bought into theories of interest rate manipulation based upon signals gleaned from the quicksand of near-term economic statistics. Although proven by the scientific methods of economics, somehow the chain of desired short-term outcomes generated through this central planning has a side effect of producing long waves of debt accumulation.

While we were still in the long wave of debt accumulation relative to national income that stretched from the early 1950s to 2008, it was impossible for anyone to refute the case for such a system. Academic studies reinforced the view that inflationary money growth was beneficial and optimal, and importantly, they did not anticipate a financial meltdown. But the collapse of the stock market in September-October 2008, triggered by the fall of Lehman Brothers, would put academic theory to the test, for the media and politicians would invoke the dreaded analogy to the Great Depression.

Economists will never cease to debate what forces pulled the world into that lost decade of the 1930s, what lifted it out, and what improved policy making might have done. A great deal of academic literature exists, and the tone of the discussion has shifted ever since contemporaneous commentators began the debate over the causes and remedies. A brief review follows, but in advance two areas in particular might deserve increased attention going forward, forcing accepted explanations to be revised. One is the tendency of credit to grow excessively under a regulated centralized bank that targets inflation through interest rate setting. Another is why modern day floating exchange rates were unable to prevent the buildup of destabilizing trade and capital imbalances.

Economists have gained notoriety in recent decades for linking gold to the Depression's downturn and then crediting the revival of the late 1930s with the lessening of its use as a currency reserve, not necessarily by outright accusation but through its ability to transmit deflation globally. This being the case, the inability of today's floating exchange rates to block the transmission of credit contraction and the deflation of asset prices (and prospectively wages and consumer prices) is a glaring counterpoint to singling out adherence to gold as a cause of poor economic performance of certain nations during that era. The plethora of academic research published to date advocates the transmission thesis, yet upon careful examination these papers have established only a weak statistical case for it. Uniquely this chapter contains new research that demonstrates a more convincing correlation that the countries which experienced recovery of industrial production by 1935 had central banks which refrained from extreme efforts to violate the rules of the game necessary for the gold standard.

## A Short History of the Great Depression

It may be presumptuous to say there was a consensus about the Great Depression prior to the panic of 2008, with factions such as monetarists, Keynesians, Austrians, and various others weighing in on the debate. However, below is a condensed account of how it unfolded, after which some color of the times is presented, followed by some thoughts about how economists may change their perceptions of the 1930s and the present adversity.

Many explanations of the depression start by noting that consumer spending, which had shown signs of weakening, dropped suddenly due to the psychological impact of the stock market crash in October 1929. The Fed had tightened credit beginning in 1928, particularly in the "call market," which was used to assist purchases of publicly traded equities. President Hoover in particular echoed a sentiment that credit extension for this purpose was suspect and counterproductive to bank lending for tangible business investment. Those economists who start here categorize the drop in consumer spending as an "exogenous" shock—that is as if it magically appeared from outside the system. As the review of monetary policy in the previous chapter suggests, an interwar gold standard poisoned by heavy indebtedness and trade restrictions helped set the stage, a factor cited by some but not all commentators.

After the initial sharp downturn in business activity, the consensus is negative monetary forces took hold. This contribution to our understanding comes from the Nobel laureate Milton Friedman and Anna Schwartz, who showed that waves of banking panics beginning in the fall of 1930 and ending with the national banking holiday in March 1933 worsened what might have been merely a normal recession. The contraction of the money supply was mild at first, with M2 falling less than 2 percent in 1930. That year saw a stock market rally and active government and Fed intervention, with President Hoover claiming credit for engineering a recovery with a hat tip to the central bank in a speech before the American Bankers Association in October. However, the monetary contraction picked up steam in each year through 1933, ultimately shrinking bank money to $32.2 billion from $46.6 billion four years earlier. Stock market panics, bank runs, and business depressions were much more in the memory of individuals in that era than today. Probably by late 1931 the progression of events began to imbed fear and severely altered behavior, because hopes of merely replaying the comparatively shorter crises since the early 19th century were dashed by the severity of the decline in stock prices through the end of that year, over 74 percent as measured by the Cowles Commission data. In May 1931 the fall of Austria's largest Bank, Creditanstalt, triggered runs on European banks and central banks, which remained in weakened reserve situations that had never improved adequately after the depletion of resources caused by World War I. The most important situation was Britain, which seeing gold outflows, abandoned the gold standard that September after having returned to it six years earlier. This nation had been at the center of global finance, and it had been the driving force of the industrial revolution.

It is difficult for us today to relate to the psychological impact this must have had. In April 1931, stocks had held their head at the 50 percent loss mark for about half a year before the European crisis hit. Even two years later at the London Economic Conference in the summer of 1933 the delegates who represented 66 of the world's major countries clung to the orthodox view that the gold standard could be patched back together (but their hopes would be dashed by Roosevelt's bombshell message that America would devalue). Against a larger backdrop, the world had been in flux from the turn of the century. It was challenged by the destruction of Europe in world war, inflation, deflation, and the beginnings of fascism in Germany and Italy as a "third way" between laissez faire capitalism and communism (which had overtaken Russia). In science, the world had already been shaken by the breaking of Newtonian physics by relativity theory; in music, chromaticism seemingly took to an extreme the rejection of rhythm, melody, and harmony; in painting, perspective had been abandoned for cubism, expressionism, and other abstract forms. Rejecting gold for paper, even after the horrendous inflations of the 1920s, must have been heretical and dangerous in the opinions of many.

The tale of Major General Smedley Butler captures some of the passion that may have been felt by those whose wealth disintegrated in seemingly safe banks, and to whom the rise of Roosevelt would be an anathema:

> Major General Smedley D. Butler revealed today that he has been asked by a group of wealthy New York brokers to lead a Fascist movement to set up a dictatorship in the United States. General Butler, ranking major general of the Marine Corps up to his retirement three years ago, told his story today at a secret session of the Congressional Committee on Un-American Activities.[7]

The McCormack-Dickstein Committee agreed to listen to Butler's story in a secret executive session in New York City on November 20, 1934 ... Butler's testimony, developed in two hours of questions and answers, was recorded in full.[8]

The implausible account of how a few Wall Street financiers planned a fascist coup d'état in 1934 and attempted to recruit "old gimlet eye" is a true though little-told episode of American history. Butler had received Medals of Honor for bravery in Haiti and Mexico, saw action in the Boxer Rebellion, and commanded in World War I, so at that time he was quite well known and revered by veterans. In September 1932 he had spoken to the "Bonus Army" that had marched on Washington, D.C. to protest Congress' voting down a bill that would have awarded $2 billion to veterans payable in 1945, which President Hoover dispersed with fire and bayonets under the command of General Douglas MacArthur. The amount of this award was roughly 3 percent of the money supply at the time. An institutional bond salesman, Jerry Macguire, was tasked with recruiting Butler to lead the coup to replace Franklin Roosevelt by a top executive of a leading Wall Street brokerage house linked to the Morgan interests, Grayson Mallet-Prevost Murphy. But loyal to his country to the end, Butler passively played along with the conspirators until such point when there would be no turning back; he exposed the plot before the McCormack-Dickstein Committee. Portions of his testimony are so sensitive they were permanently expunged from the record. In all probability these implicated senior executives under the Morgan ambit.

No doubt because of this backing at the highest level of The New York financial community, the case has received little attention in history books compared to the treasons of Aaron Burr and Benedict Arnold. Besides wooing him with money and position, the conspirators sought his sway over veterans to achieve a guarantee of benefits payable with currency backed by gold. In 1933 they approached him about making a speech at the American Legion convention in Chicago, where he would urge the group "to adopt a resolution calling for the United States to return to the gold standard, so that when veterans were paid the bonus promised to them, the money they received would not be worthless paper."[9] He was supposed to travel to Chicago on a train with 200–300 veterans. These would be salted in among the crowd at the convention, awaiting Butler's appearance in the spectator's gallery, whereupon they would spring to their feet in wildly animated support of his speech.

In April 1933 Roosevelt declared by Executive Order (Number 6102) that "all persons are hereby required to deliver on or before May 1, 1933, to a Federal reserve bank or branch … all gold coin, gold bullion and gold certificates now owned by them." The catch was that the government would buy in the gold at $20.67 per ounce; later it would reset the price to $35. When the order produced $500 million less than demanded, the government required citizens to report to it what they did own, or be subject to a $10,000 fine or 10 years in jail, or both.[10] Another order added, "Your possession of these proscribed metals and/ or your maintenance of a safe deposit box to store them is known to the Government from bank and insurance records. Therefore, be advised that your vault box must remain sealed, and may only be opened in the presence of an agent of The Internal Revenue Service."[11]

In the face of such unashamed predation, is it natural that some citizens might sense that the government was not protecting their basic right to own property, thus justifying in their minds the path to resist? Clearly launching a Fascist coup is treasonous, and politically well beyond the pale, for other far more serious basic human (and Constitutional) rights were intended to be curtailed had the elites behind it assumed power. But interestingly, the conspirators were merely seeking to protect a constitutionally guaranteed freedom. Today most view such unbridled passion for gold as an oddity, even a perversion. But before World War I, gold was the official store of wealth, and the countries of the world cooperated in maintaining a gold standard. In 1913, some $834 million of specie and another $1,473 million of gold and silver certificates were in circulation in the United States (compared to a total money supply of $15.7 billion), and contracts often had a clause enabling at the lender's option payment in gold, a contractual element later abrogated in the Depression. Although many other countries had suspended the gold standard until about 1925, the United States continued to recognize it (with the exception of wartime constraints). While by 1933 specie's share of the money supply (M2) had dropped to 1.9 percent from 5.3 percent in 1913, when combined with gold or silver notes, overall hard-backed currency still comprised 58 percent of currency in circulation.[12] [13] In the context of competitive devaluations from other countries, Roosevelt's new U.S. peg may be understandable, but the government predation that occurred simultaneously is not.

The torch for hard money, long carried by the Democratic Party, completely burned out by the end of the interwar period. After World War II, the Bretton Woods system would stabilize exchange rates, but domestic money creation would become nearly completely elastic. The grand success of the Marshall Plan era contrasted pleasantly with the sudden boom-bust cycle that followed World War I. Many if not most current day economists look at the increase in money supply in the late 1930s, which stemmed mostly from the monetization of government debt issued to fund the New Deal, as the impetus of the economic recovery. This was a contributing factor, but additionally the private sector reduced debt by repaying it or defaulting.

There is considerable evidence of unique national economic experiences during the 1930s beyond the observation that the United States and France failed to recover much by the end of that decade, and that these were among the last countries to devalue. That finding should not be trivialized, the criticism written here notwithstanding. But just stepping back and forgetting which countries of the 10 largest was pegged to gold and when they devalued, a greater pattern emerges needing explanation. First is that the U.S. and German economies plummeted far more steeply than other nations at the opening of the Great Depression. Industrial production fell a whopping 47 percent in the United States and Germany from 1929 to 1932. The remaining eight of the top 10 free-world economies saw a less severe falloff: The worst, France, contracted 28 percent and most saw industrial production sink less than 20 percent. Germany suffered an almost unimaginable 42 percent contraction of commercial bank deposits from 1929 through 1931, partly in sympathy with Creditanstalt, but mainly because it followed the gold standard template of deflation, mandating that wages and prices of all sorts of public services be cut by over 10 percent (back to 1927 levels).

What is even more intriguing are the phenomenal recoveries of what would become the axis powers. Germany saw its unemployment fall rapidly from 6 million workers to 2.6 million between January 1933 and December 1934, mostly because of an ambitious scheme to expand and improve road and rail infrastructure. However, its exports would remain constrained, resting at only 69 percent of their 1929 peak as late as 1937.[14] But its index of industrial production would go on to rise at a 9.3 percent annual rate from 1935-1938, second only to its trading partner Finland (11.2%). Close behind in that three-year period after the dust had settled from devaluations were Sweden (7.6%) and Norway (6.4%); the other European nations were well behind. Japan did even better, seeing its industrial production rise 62 percent from the 1929 level by 1937. The combination of monetary expansion and fiscal spending was so powerful by 1936 that the Japanese finance minister protested that his country had reached a liftoff point when inflation might be threatening. He should have been more concerned about other things, because the military element that had taken over the controls of the state after a brief bout with deflation (gold was restored in 1930 but rejected by 1931) thought his stance was an impediment to rearmament. In that year he was murdered. Germany likewise pursued a policy of fiscal stimulus that was geared ultimately towards military ends. The erection of enormous trade barriers: quotas, tariffs, state-sanctioned international cartels, and exchange controls were not a proximate cause of Germany's and Japan's expansionism, but without colonies and with smaller blocs of trading influence, geographic conquest was appealing.

What may have accounted for the ability of Germany and Japan to stage a sharp recovery during the 1930s, besides the knee-jerk explanation of rearmament, is the role of debt. The United States suffered a loss by having a large receivable from the allies move into the nonperforming category. Japan never was in the debt triangle, so it could increase borrowing freely, which it did. Germany saw the rise of Hitler, with the Nationalsozialismus ideology enacted upon the 1933 election of his party. The strain of the Depression caused payments within the debt triangle to go into arrears, but the new nationalism essentially allowed Germany to act as if the burden was permanently lifted. Hitler's reestablishment of military power meant there was no chance for retaliation such as the occupation of the Ruhr in the early 1920s. With the middle class having been wiped out by the inflation of that former time and workers further impoverished by unsuccessful deflationary policies enacted in 1930, there was ready acceptance of being put back to work in a state-directed effort, and an industrial sector well furbished with capital equipment installed with the Dawes and Young plan largesse could be fed by raw materials through the new trade arrangements with neighbors to the north.

The United States eventually would see a recovery, but unemployment remained high through 1940 and industrial production would not touch its 1929 level until 1937. The Federal Reserve despite adding $1 billion of reserves was powerless to stop bank deposits from imploding at an 18 percent annual pace from 1931-1933, more than double the damage felt in any other of these countries, and neither could it prevent gold from fleeing. Although these phenomena might not have been independent of the Treasury's $20.67 peg to gold that lasted until September 1933, it is not clear that academic research could ever separate out that effect. Friedman and Schwartz have ensconced a view in the academic literature that the Fed stood by and did nothing. Until the Fisherian thesis of gold transmission was revived in the last few decades this monetarist solution to the riddle was the defining rule. During the late 1930s, Fisher and others thought that monetarist solutions had failed. With unemployment stuck at 15 percent by 1940 (still prior to gearing up for the war), the consensus was that the Depression was a permanent condition that the fiscal programs of the New Deal and the monetary actions of the Fed had not corrected more than partially, rather than having had a recovery that current day economists would link to one successful policy or the other.

Another popular notion is that World War II was directly responsible for the recovery, for it alone resolved the unemployment situation, which still saw about 15 percent of the workforce idle in 1940. A view quite distant from this mainstream one has been championed by scholars such as Robert Higgs, alleging the rise in employment of the war years really represented conscripted labor, and that the private sector rebounded only *after* World War II, once government agencies that intervened in private commercial activity were dismantled. At wartime in 1944, only half of the prices in the United States were market-based; a study by Hugh Rockoff, Milton Friedman, and Anna Schwartz tried to estimate economic activity based upon an estimation of actual prices, which showed that real consumer outlays fell from 1931 to 1943 (in contrast to official government statistics as depicted in Figure 4.5), and they did not return to the 1941 level until 1946.[15] [16]

Higgs states that the economy wallowed in the late 1930s up through the war and was plagued by very low levels of private investment, this being caused by the reservations concerning government intervention. A *Fortune* magazine survey of November 1941 asked about 1,000 businessmen to predict the political and business climate after the war, and the result characterizes the depth of this suspicion. Just 7 percent thought a system of free enterprise would emerge; the majority (52%) predicted there would be a system under which government would take over much but leave many opportunities to the private sector. However, 37 percent believed there would be a semi-socialized society with little room for the private economy, and 4 percent felt a fascist regime would emerge.[17] If one can't go so far to accuse the Roosevelt administration of advancing the cause of socialism, at the very least

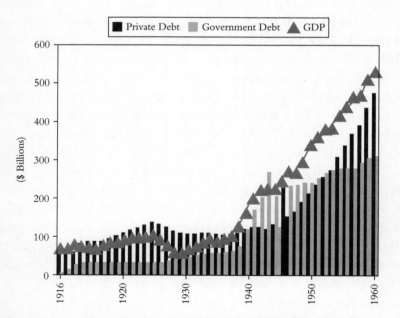

**Figure 4.5   Economic Output and Private & Government Debt (1916–1960)**
*Source:* Historical Statistics of the United States.

the government, being friendly to labor, had encouraged wages to rise 10 percent from 1929 to 1937 while prices of finished goods were 8 percent lower, a dyspeptic recipe for business.[18] It is little wonder why businessmen remained discouraged in 1940. The small rise in federal debt evident in Figure 4.5 anemically lifted GDP statistics, and did so mainly through the inclusion of "make work" expenditures in the Keynesian national accounting formula where GDP equals government spending alongside consumption, investment, and net exports.

While Higg's description may be revealing, modern day observers are likely to accept the notion that the defense sector is a component of the economy and that it indeed reduced unemployment and lifted GDP. Figure 4.5 shows the dramatic impact upon GDP of government debt-financed war expenditures. But clearly the evidence is that individuals and businesses did not begin to aggressively commit funds to rebuild capital investment until after the war. Only at that moment was there a sharp jump in the private sector's demand for credit—a break from its intense preference for less-risky uses for savings and the extinguishment of debt. Whatever the storyline, the experience of the United States is that the Great Depression earned its name not only from the depth to which the economy fell by 1932, but also because of its length.

While the observations of Higgs are trenchant, if one instead views the period through the simpler explanation of Fisher's debt deflation theory, the recovery from the Great Depression can be explained by economic actors having repaid debt or had debt extinguished through bankruptcy by 1942, making them feel freer to make use of low interest rates and exploit profitable business expansion. In 1942 total debt including federal, state, and household had fallen to less than 160 percent of GDP from a peak of 300 percent in 1932. That low level had not been seen since 1918, well before the roaring twenties. No econometric regression analysis could detect this sort of causation, because in the years leading up to the big turn in the economy decreasing leverage would be coincident with weakening consumer demand and increasing savings. Then all of the sudden decreasing leverage would act like a dry forest floor, ready to be ignited by the flames of rearmament. One could argue that the brief period of federal borrowing in Figure 4.5 was stimulative, but it might not have been so had it occurred in the early 1930s when the populace was highly indebted and excess capacity had not been flushed away. True there were powerful rebounds in the 1930s, but they were neither sustainable nor did they return business to normal profitability and put people back to work in a meaningful way.

This brings us to the record concerning other countries. The orthodox view is that carefully constructed regressions of economic activity against the trait of gold devaluation by nations reveals that remaining on the gold standard caused economies to implode, and releasing the central bank from this constraint reignited credit growth, spending, and income. Fed Chairman Bernanke among others has written of this, as echoed in his March 2004 speech, *Money Gold, and the Great Depression*: "The existence of the gold standard helps to explain why the world economic decline was both deep and broadly international ... The longer that a country remained committed to gold, the deeper its depression and the later its recovery. (After Roosevelt came into office) the gold standard constraint (was) removed and the banking system stabilized, (and) the money supply and the price level began to rise. Between Roosevelt's coming to power in 1933 and the recession of 1937-1938, the economy grew strongly."[19] However, many think the downturn of 1938 was the direct product of the Fed's having raised reserve requirements. Economic activity remained depressed through 1941 at the earliest and 1946 at the latest.

## The Academic Orthodoxy

There have been a series of papers dealing with the transmission of the Great Depression, like a disease, through the gold standard. What this orthodoxy does is downplay the true cause as identified by Irving Fisher, debt deflation theory. It is a bit like celebrating the genius of those who strung power lines instead of acknowledging Thomas Edison for inventing the light bulb, Anyos Jedlik the dynamo, or Michael Faraday the alternator. Although the transmission mechanism was also described by Fisher in the 1930s, the first economists to trumpet this new thesis in recent times were Ehsan Choudhri and Levis Kochin in their paper: *The Exchange Rate and the International Transmission of*

*Business Cycle Disturbances.*[20] In this article, regressions show what Bernanke states in his speech and has echoed in his academic work, that nations remaining on the gold standard were worse off, and those that recovered sooner had abandoned gold earlier. Regressions by scholars such as Choudhri, Kochin, and the parade of others who have reprocessed the data first observed by Fisher undeniably establish the case. But the argument oversimplifies and puts a microscope to a small part of the trend occurring at that time.

Gold had lost much of its importance by the 1920s, and central bankers had ceased to play by the rules of the game. Like steam cleaning an automobile engine before selling a used car, the frantic efforts of central bankers to dump foreign currency reserves and hoard gold in the 1930s were desperate measures to paper over the financial mess that had been made in World War I and its aftermath. (Efforts of the Fed to extend borrowed reserves to illiquid and insolvent banks in 2008 are similar, a point explored later.) The enormous debt manufactured in World War I was payable in other than home currencies, so it could not be inflated away despite monetary printing early on. By the mid-1920s nations were increasingly relying on foreign exchange as the reserve of their native money supply, pumping up a credit bubble. (Bordo and Eichengreen trace this to a beginning point in 1895 or 1900, noting foreign exchange reserves were less than 10 percent of reserves in 1880 but 21 percent by 1910.[21] A more accurate statement would be that in 1913 Britain, the United States, and France were 100 percent reserved, with Germany holding forex of 15 percent and the rest of the world 31 percent. Under the gold-exchange standard of the 1920s, France saw its sterling reserves swell to 51 percent of the total.)[22] When danger lurked in the 1930s, central banks decided other currencies were unsound (because pledges to maintain gold pegs were coming unglued after the United Kingdom devalued), so they sought to revert to actually using gold as the basis for money. The rapid reattachment was a rejection of the paper claims stacked on top of the only real reserve of value, but culturally this was excessively bitter medicine, quickly taken in a large dose.

Although the regressions regarding gold's transmission of deflation are not wrong, too many academics elevate this point to being the solution of the riddle of the depression, when it could be just masquerading as true causation. Some examination of the countries with the strong-est correlation is revealing. According to Choudhri and Kochin's work, "The centerpiece of our evidence is Spain" which "provides a strik-ing historical experiment on the insulation capabilities of the flexible exchange rate system." The case of Spain being an economy that with-stood the Great Depression on account of its being off the gold standard belies the fact that its economy had already been depressed, fraught with turmoil, and largely isolated. Spain's interest rates remained among the highest in the world during the depression, with a 5.4 percent dis-count rate from 1930-39, a phenomenon shared by Norway, whose discount rate averaged 4 percent compared to 2.5 percent for England at that time. Note that these two countries, which aggressively detached from gold, maintained high interest rates, a policy prescription that gets excoriated by academics today—usually in reference to the Fed's sharp rise in the discount rate in 1931. Sidney Homer describes the unusual conditions in Spain:

> In modern times, Spain continued to isolate herself economi-cally from neighboring economies. In the 1930's, after a long history of political instability, she developed an authoritarian form of government and a controlled economy. Therefore her interest rates lack the economic significance of interest rates in other countries. The Spanish discount rate was very high in the 1930's, almost the highest in this history. It came down steadily, however, from 6.41 annual average in 1932 to 4% in 1939. The Civil War did not seem to interrupt the decline. Nonetheless, the rate averaged more than twice the official discount rates then prevailing in England and the United States.[23]

While noticing that coming off the gold standard relieved the trans-mission of economic depression somewhat, it might be just as well said that the maintenance of *high* interest rates might have been equally important. In fact, under the classical gold standard countries that would experience gold outflows due to trade imbalances and their depressive effects on GNP were expected to raise interest rates. This would induce corrective deflation and lure gold back into the banking system, setting up an economic recovery.

Nonetheless, turning back to the example of Spain, economic statistics are hard to come by and must be regarded with suspicion. Other wide-ranging works, such as Lewis's *Economic History 1919-1939*, omit the country save for noting its leadership position in setting the highest tariffs in the world, both in 1913 (33%) and later in 1925 (44%), along with its joining a host of Third World nations in imposing import licenses and foreign exchange controls in the early 1930s.[24] Its political situation began to be deeply troubled during the Depression years, as detailed by Stanley Payne:

> The tenor of the new government was revealed within less than a month, on May 11, 1931, when mobs led by anarchists (and some Radical Socialists) sacked monarchist headquarters in Madrid and then proceeded to set fire or otherwise wreck more than a dozen churches in the capital ... Anarchists denounced the Republic as being worse than the monarchy. During 1931-1933 they carried out scores of strikes and terrorist attacks, culminating in the *tres ochos* of January 8, 1932, January 8, 1933, and December 8, 1933—small-scale pseudorevolutionary strikes and petty insurrections in scattered parts of the country, with the principal focus in Catalonia . . . The revolutionary insurrection of October 1934 in Asturias was entirely different. It was a revolt of Socialist workers, supported by the CNT and the Communists, that occupied the entire mining and industrial district . . . Altogether the year (1935) was one of frustration. Some aspects of the economic depression grew worse, and in certain sectors unemployment mounted . . . It was the Communists who gained the propaganda advantage from the 1934 insurrection on the left, falsely claiming for themselves the main role in that tragic drama . . . During the spring (of 1936), a wave of revolutionary strikes began whose object was not to win economic improvements but to break the Spanish economic structure. At one point in June a million workers were out on strike, roughly 25% of the labor force. During May and June a number of small and medium-sized businesses were forced into bankruptcy. Capital fled the country, the exchange balance and the peseta value declined, and it became increasingly difficult to fund the national debt.[25]

Spain may have been the epitome of stability from 1929 to 1932, magically holding output and pricing constant and proving to Choudhri and Kochin that its being on flexible exchange rates and not on the gold standard made it an island of tranquility amid the maelstrom the rest of the planet was experiencing. But at the very least its extremely high tariffs, high interest rates, and strict import licenses smacked more of autarky than laissez faire, and few capitalists other than arms dealers might have ventured there to do business.

Moving on to other nations comparatively less affected by the Depression in Choudhri and Kochin's study we find the Scandinavian countries. Their regression work shows that these countries (Denmark, Finland, and Norway), were dragged down by the world downturn in 1929-1930. Then after choosing to devalue by 31 percent in 1931 (to reach about 50% by 1934), they were rewarded by being somewhat decoupled from the spreading malaise during 1931-1932, an important period due to the Anstalt crisis and its domino effect. The gold devaluations of these countries were considerably greater than that of nearly every other developed industrial nation, and exceeded generally by Latin American countries, which also were less impacted by the Depression.

Probably the most important developments affecting the Scandinavian countries were the Oslo convention of 1930 and negotiations that followed the Ottawa agreement in 1933. Oslo was originally conceived by these small nations as a way to dismantle tariffs of the most powerful states that started up in the deeply suspicious postwar environment of the 1920s and which increased when protectionism took hold after the economic crisis hit in late 1929. The Oslo states (Norway, Denmark, Sweden, Belgium/Luxemburg, the Netherlands, and later Finland) formed a bloc rivaling France or Germany in size. This strengthened bargaining power initially produced little result, and the Ottawa Imperial Conference in 1932 placed *higher* tariffs on important Scandinavian exports such as farm products, steel, and paper. But Britain remained uncompetitive in its key coal & coke industry, with northern Europe underbidding it. Sweden, Denmark, and Norway then succeeded in obtaining markets for their timber and paper products as well as butter and bacon in exchange for agreeing to take nearly all of their imports of coke and coal from the United Kingdom. This was particularly beneficial to Finland, which had

barely been industrialized before this period. It went on to enjoy 7 percent GDP growth throughout the Great Depression, ending the period
as a modern industrial state. Further aiding Finland and the entire Nordic
region was secular growth for paper and timber necessary to fuel a
revival in housing that swept through Britain beginning in the 1930s.[26]
According to Arthur Lewis: "There is a housing boom in Britain about
once every 20 or 30 years, and it seems to occur whether prices and
interest rates are rising or falling, or whatever is happening to the terms of
trade. A boom was due some time in the 1920's, and was delayed, mainly
through the affects of rent control in keeping rents below costs. After the
fall in prices, this factor ceased to operate, and the boom probably would
have come about even if interest rates had not fallen."[27]

The next big impetus for Nordic outperformance of the world
economies was the quick return of Germany to health and its rearmament. It had been shut out of world markets since before World War I,
seeing its share of global exports tumble from 13.1 percent to 9.7 percent from 1913 to 1929. Lacking the former colonies, Hitler turned to
the resource rich-region across the Baltic and North Seas for supplies
and set up preferential bilateral agreements, payable in special types of
German currency reserved for that purpose. Sweden continued to supply the Nazis through the end of the World War II.[28]

Following up on Choudhri and Kochin's 1980 work, Barry
Eichengreen and Jeffrey Sachs add a formal econometric model and
attempt to describe the structural mechanisms linking exchange rates,
mainly comparative real wages. Their paper, *Exchange Rates and Economic
Recovery in the 1930s*, gracefully leaves out Spain, the centerpiece of
Choudhri and Kochin's work. Again, they present an interesting and
complete set of regressions that indeed demonstrate that when a country
devalues its currency it gets a boost in trade. A controversial and well-
noted point that the authors make is that even when only a few countries
devalue, besides being beneficial to the initiating countries, the impact on
the world system may not have been negative. Before their work, most
had equated the "beggar thy neighbor" effect of tariffs with devaluations.
They state that there should be a ". . . sharp analytical distinction between
protectionist measures (such as tariffs and quotas) and exchange rate management. Tariffs and devaluation are often spoken of as two sides of the
same coin, both being policies to shift demand from foreign countries

to the domestic economy. In fact, the general equilibrium implications of the two sets of policies are very different. Tariff changes inevitably create output price distortions, while a series of devaluations in many countries can leave relative output prices unchanged."[29]

Put in plain English, the key to understanding this is to know the operative phrase above is "many countries." What the authors are saying is that if countries are on a gold standard before and afterward and most of them devalue, then in essence what has happened is much less a movement to secure competitive advantage than it is a purposeful, coordinated effort to cause inflation—or to reverse deflation—which is how Roosevelt attempted to work through the Depression. By printing money, reducing its value relative to gold, and raising wages, U.S. policy effectively tried to devalue debt. (One could argue that the policy was unsuccessful, because the doubling of federal debt more than offset the private sector's reduction of loan balances through repayment and write-offs, and the economy remained weak throughout the 1930s. Also, prices failed to increase, crimping business profitability.) In contrast, an extremely aggressive monetization of the added government debt might have been successful. Alternatively, the 19th century solution of speedy liquidation and wage deflation might have cleared out the deadwood faster and returned leverage ratios to healthy levels rather than maintain them at dangerous levels for a prolonged period of time as the government's meddling did.

In Figure 4.6, one of the key regressions from Eichengreen and Sachs is reconstructed. Similar to the Choudhri and Kochin study, the establishment of the new trade bloc of Scandinavian countries with the United Kingdom and Germany might explain the relationship as much or more than the impact of gold devaluation does. In fact, the regression only establishes a weak statistical relationship. Statisticians attuned to the principal measure for this, known as R-squared, would notice a value of 0.56, whose compliment (44%) would be the percentage of variance seen in the data that remains unexplained. Given that there is a cluster of Scandinavian countries with the unique characteristic of having associated with each other for trade improvement that dominates the results, probably rerunning the study with that attribute isolated would change the slope and intercept that determines Eichengreen and Sach's conclusion regarding gold. No doubt it would

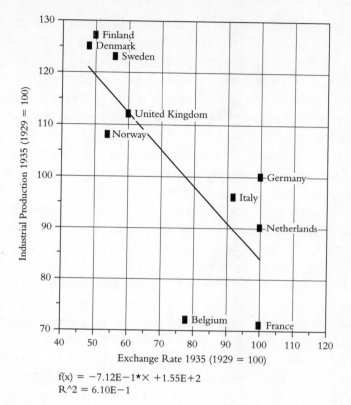

$$f(x) = -7.12E-1 \star X + 1.55E+2$$
$$R^2 = 6.10E-1$$

**Figure 4.6  Exchange Rates & Industrial Production**
*Source:* Replication of Eichengreen & Sachs regression analysis.
*Note:* Exchange rate is expressed as units of gold per unit of domestic currency. Original study equation was IP1935 = 153.9 − 0.69 ER1935 with R-Squared of 0.56.

flatten out the response that now tilts in favor of devaluation, and its inclusion might raise the percentage of variance explained by both variables, but it could also reduce the importance of gold devaluation.

Even among those countries that did not devalue and whose industrial production was mired at or below parity with 1929, Germany is a standout, maintaining economic output equal to 1929 rather than the value of 84.9 percent predicted by Eichengreen and Sach's regression equation. From eyeballing the data, Germany appears to receive about two standard deviations better economic performance (for those not familiar with statistics, this is a considerable amount), which might then be attributed mostly to the vigorous trade it established with its

new partners in Scandinavia. These smaller countries enjoyed essentially a new relationship with Germany, but they pretty much formally
renewed the good trading relationship extant with Britain prior to the
Depression. This would also be consistent with Britain not varying
from the predicted value of the equation while Germany is an outlier.

Another thing that jumps out from the data is that the two countries at the bottom of Figure 4.6, Belgium and France, by far were the
ones that chose to hoard gold during that period. The assumption is that
some of the other countries lost gold, and this happened because these
country's notes were presented for redemption. Countries that hoarded
probably found it profitable to present their overvalued notes for freshly
mined gold, as well as gold won on speculative attacks. Could it be that
the countries that were stockpiling gold reserves were seen as economically belligerent? Belgium saw its central bank gold climb from 5.9 billion to 12.5 billion Belgian francs, and France's jumped from 41.6 billion
to 82.1 billion French francs in the period from 1929 to 1934.[30]

It could very well be that the cause of the poor economic per-
formances early in the Depression in Belgium and France (and for that
matter the United States, which was excluded from Eichengreen and
Sach's study) was not exchange rate overvaluation per se, but the sudden
change in policy to simply hoard gold. In other words, exchange rates
undeniably have a powerful effect on all the mechanisms that these two
scholars document in their report, but perhaps that case is overstated and
the change in attitude towards balance sheet improvement was the para-
mount determinant of the direction of a country's economy. If insolvency was the primary concern of the primary actors of the gold block
countries, then nothing else much mattered. This fear might prompt
either hoarding or complete abandonment of gold. The hypothesis is
that during the period 1929-1935, countries taking extreme actions on
either end of the spectrum would be punished in the marketplace; those
that had moderate policies would be rewarded. What happens if one
tests this theory by comparing the improvement or deterioration of the
gold reserve ratio backing each country's central bank with industrial
production? The answer is that one gets a near complete explanation
of the behavior of industrial production, for a polynomial curve fit (i.e.,
one that shows declining utility to extreme actions on either end) has
an R-squared of 92 percent. (See Figure 4.7.)

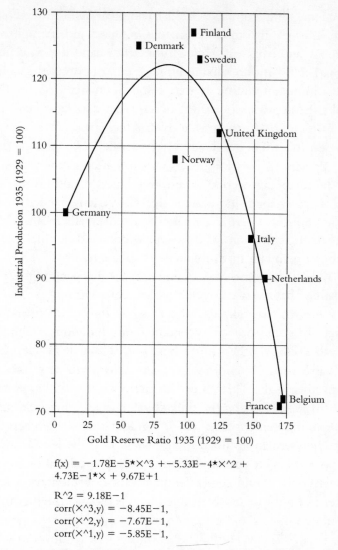

Figure 4.7 shown with equation below:

f(x) = −1.78E−5*x^3 +−5.33E−4*x^2 +
4.73E−1*x + 9.67E+1

R^2 = 9.18E−1
corr(X^3,y) = −8.45E−1,
corr(X^2,y) = −7.67E−1,
corr(X^1,y) = −5.85E−1,

**Figure 4.7   Sensible Gold Backing Improved Economic Growth: Extreme Measures Were Less Effective**
*Source:* Eichengreen & Sachs data; League of Nations.

What is even more remarkable about this hypothesis is that policy moderation might have been helpful during the depression in more than one way. An effort by central banks to slightly improve their central bank balance sheets through boosting gold backing by 10 to 30 percent (i.e., Sweden going from 29% gold backing to 32%) probably brightened the internal investment climate. On one hand it might discourage currency and bank runs, but on the other hand it would not spook capital markets by monopolizing limited state resources through hoarding. Even more interesting is that some countries such as Denmark could take the approach of dialing down what may have been excessive reserves (40% in 1929) to a more manageable ratio (25% in 1934), and be rewarded for it. The tendency of economic researchers to think linearly is a dangerous oversimplification. Gold, used in the proper dosage, may be the medicine needed to restore financial health. If too much or too little is prescribed, the patient suffers. What is needed is maturity and recognition of where the financial system needs to go, which is to have a dramatic reduction of debt and widespread popular support for how it might maintain that sublime state of affairs.

It may be that as the world contemplates deleveraging in the wake of the panic that began in 2008 policymakers might consider some unique solutions that take us back to some temperate financial status. One might be to restore some restrained and judicious backing of currency with gold. Another could be to assist the deleveraging process not by massive fiscal spending (Germany and Japan may have successfully done this in the 1930s, but U.S. actions actually depressed recovery), but through resetting the dollar's value to a higher gold price than is evident in the marketplace, which would actualize the proper reserve backing. The calculations for this are reviewed in the last chapter of this book about possible policy solutions. Large-scale monetization of government debt would be needed in advance of this activity, so the reattachment to gold would be critical to offset concerns that monetization would go too far or continue indefinitely—again the point would be to target a return to equilibrium, which by definition is moderate.

Eichengreen and Sachs show excitement for explaining 52 percent of what happened in the Depression, but like having an adolescent infatuation or an obsession with beauty over substance, less impulsive consideration would recognize the wisdom of retaining a permanent, immutable rule system to keep economic actors within bounds so they would not take actions that would injure or impoverish themselves. In a larger sense, the fixation the economics community has with fiat money and its blind spot for a commodity-reserved currency expresses our cultural shift to reject absolutes and self-discipline and to defer consequences, financial or otherwise—an adolescent mindset. Gold has its drawbacks and thus is less than ideal, but it may be a 92 percent solution that is capable of restraining bad behavior most of the time. Before we layered the massive debt of World War I upon its flourishing classical system and hollowed out its core by allowing foreign exchange holdings to impersonate reserves, gold was remarkably effective.

## Debt Among Nations

The debt created by World War I was catastrophic, as predicted by Lord Keynes in his classic, *The Economic Consequences of the Peace* (1919). With the triangle of having Germany owe the allies reparations, the allies needing to repay the United States for what they borrowed to engage war, and the United States being the marginal lender to Germany to restart its economy, there was a tornadic circle too overwhelming to be stopped. When the withdrawal of capital from Germany in 1928 occurred (to inflate the dollar and thus support Britain's gold resumption), the building clouds of consumer debt in the United States (as well as abroad) were seeded enough to unleash the exogenous shock to start the global deleveraging.

So what analogy might be drawn to the present period of economic stress? Using this country-specific model and knowledge of the debt situation, the countries most likely to be left holding the bag full of bad debt are China, Japan, and the Middle East oil producers. Chinese such as Gao Xiqing, who oversees an important tranche of China's $2 trillion in dollar holdings, have stated: "We know that by pulling out money, we're not serving anyone's good. Including ourselves. So we're trying to help, at least by not aggravating the problem."[31] But persistent rumors to the contrary have been aired on respectable media. The Bloomberg newswire relayed this November 19, 2008 missive: "China's central bank is considering increasing its gold reserves by 4,000 metric tons from 600 tons, *Guangzhou Daily* reported, citing unidentified industry people in Hong Kong. The move is designed to diversify the risk of holding massive foreign-exchange reserves, the newspaper reported today on its web site."[32] Four thousand metric tonnes amounts to one-half the gold reserves of the United States, and would make China the second-largest holder globally, edging out the IMF, Germany, and France. At the same time, Luo Ping, a director-general at the China Banking Regulatory Commission, puts forth the equivocal guidance that China must continue to buy U.S. Treasury securities, but asks perhaps not so rhetorically what else his country might hold, and answers, "Gold? You don't hold Japanese government bonds or U.K. bonds." He continues, "We hate you guys. Once you start issuing $1 trillion to $2 trillion . . . we know the dollar is going to depreciate, so we hate you guys but there is nothing much we can do."

Who benefits? Like Germany of the 1930s, the United States does, because being the operator of the world's reserve currency, even if the creditor nations pull out of the dollar or other perhaps equally inflated paper currencies, it can make one last withdrawal of seigniorage from its money supply by monetizing it. But the cost would be the loss of operating the world reserve currency. Gao Xiqing continues, "'If China has $2 trillion, Japan has almost $2 trillion, and Russia has some, and all the others, then—let's throw away the ideological differences and think about what's good for everyone.' We can get all the relevant people together and think up what people are calling the second Bretton Woods system, like the first Bretton Woods convention did."[33] The replacement might be gold-based, especially if China has a say in the matter, but the United States would be ill advised not to monetize its debt first, since there is nothing stopping it from doing so. It is also possible, but not desirable, that there would be a system such as between 1934 and 1971 (bracketing the Bretton Woods era) when international transactions occur in currency backed by gold, but paper dollars would continue to be used for legal tender domestically. But instead in the April 2009 G-20 meeting the idea was floated that a new reserve currency might be constructed using a basket of currencies including the ruble and the yuan. Such rumination again reflects complete misunderstanding of the credit crisis, for it would substitute one weak fiat currency with others that have experienced explosive money supply expansion based upon debt proliferation possible only in a fractional reserve banking order.

There is a silver lining for the Chinese. They have established trade patterns with the United States that should be lucrative; they simply need to facilitate importation of something, anything, made in the United States such that trade accounts would not remain painfully unbalanced. Africa and Latin America could possibly have winners, emerging as a supplier of raw materials to feed the machinery of China, much like the Scandinavian countries thrived in their relationship with Hitler's Germany, but there are countries in these continents with intractable political problems. Countries on the west coast of Africa such as Ghana, Mali, Cote d'Ivoire, or Burkina Faso that lie in the Birimian Trend could become the Saudi Arabia of a reinvigorated gold mining industry.

The above ruminations about how a country-centric formulation of scenarios might unfold is intriguing and useful, even if it contains much conjecture and isn't purely scientific. However, still unanswered is the question of whether great depressions are caused by the excessive buildup of debt, which is fostered by centralized control over money and the policy of inflation targeting, which inclines the money supply to expand faster than real economic activity. Considering that blaming gold for transmitting the depression globally is in vogue today, particularly among important central planners at the Fed, might not their explanation have been defended in order to take some of the heat off holding their predecessors accountable for mishaps as well as from those of more recent vintage, such as Alan Greenspan, once heralded as "the maestro?" Perhaps more importantly, wouldn't it also obstruct consideration of taking away some of the Fed's powers through adopting decentralized or gold-based approaches to managing the money supply? The panic of 2008 is challenging the very assumptions that belie the anti-gold thesis, for the financial world crumbled after having been freed from the barbarous relic for 37 years. Barry Eichengreen and Peter Temin, two renown economists, teamed up to author a paper titled *The Gold Standard and the Great Depression* in 1997, which begins by saying: "Recent scholarship has resulted in striking agreement on the reasons for the crisis; the modern literature can be regarded as having substantially solved the riddle of the Great Depression. The constraints of the gold-standard system hamstrung countries as they struggled to adapt during the 1920s to changes in the world economy. And the ideology, mentalité and rhetoric of the gold standard led policy makers to take actions that only accentuated economic distress in the 1930s.

Central bankers continued to kick the world economy while it was down until it lost consciousness."[34]

Having gained notoriety for helping to solve the riddle by being one of the several economists who jumped on the exchange rate transmission thesis bandwagon, in 2003 Eichengreen joined forces with another economist, Kris Mitchener, to pen *The Great Depression as a Credit Boom Gone Wrong*, which sets about to put to bed a competing thesis gaining attention in the wake of the bursting of the Internet bubble at the turn of the millennium. That thesis comes from the Austrian School, which instead squares the blame on the Depression and on the role of cheap (low-interest rate) money encouraging a massive credit bubble that would implode of its own weight. Rearranging regression variables as deftly as Martha Arguerich would play notes in a piano concerto, the duo vainly struggled to produce statistical significance that credit accumulation explicates the Depression, and at best conclude that "the point is evident in the fact that the credit boom indicator explains less than a third of the cross-country variation in the post-1929 slump in economic activity."[35] Case closed: A managed money system beats gold.

The work is masterful at describing how cultural norms were changing, having made it impossible for central bankers to adhere to the rules of the game of the gold standard since the 1920s, and setting up the disaster of the 1930s. They catalogue the voices of numerous adherents to gold, who nonetheless had succumbed to political pressures and sterilized gold movements such that wages would not adjust after postwar inflation. The most loyal adherents were the French, which had suffered inflation that had wiped out savings in the 1920s, giving them strong political cover. To them, "disregard for the gold standard led to financial excesses, economic chaos, and social turmoil," and was thus dangerous. Likewise, before abandoning gold even the British thought leader Lord Keynes "was willing to try anything—a tariff, quotas, a national treaty on wages, profits and rents, foreign lending restrictions—anything except suspending the gold standard, which was too drastic to contemplate." In the United States, "when there was a threat to the U.S. commitment to gold in 1931, the Fed responded by raising interest rates sharply and driving the country deeper into depression." In the authors' words, there was a mentalité, and indeed it turned out to be self-destructive.[36] Perhaps they use the diacritic form of the word to buttress their case that a discussion of using gold to back currency is like taking a trip to the museum to see evidence of some ancient fetish—one that might have harmed the tribe but was believed and practiced to the death. But in the modern world, as explained by William Greider in his opus *Secrets of the Temple*, the Fed governors behave like ancient priests, withholding knowledge of certain actions and speaking in enchanting twists of language, working to instill confidence in money that has no backing.[37] What is the more powerful fetish: gold or infinitively expandable paper cum electrons? What is more legitimate: mentality or mentalité? The Austrian view is demeaned by being called barbarous, marginalized to a dustbin of history by being just a mentalité in a world where modernity triumphs; the new mentality is scientific and true, and the old is a quaint superstition.

Nonetheless in the work there is a hint that the Austrian viewpoint might have some validity. Eichengreen and Mitchener go on to test whether economies had wilder swings in gold standard rather than non-gold standard business cycles, but with the twist that the interwar period is left out. What they find is "any evidence that credit booms were more pronounced under the gold standard than other monetary regimes, in other words, is attributable to the 1920s experience that is the subject of this paper." So their overall conclusion is "the gold standard was neither the cause nor the solution to the credit boom problem; the effects depended importantly on how that gold standard was structured and managed."[38] While their case against gold remains seemingly fortified by their regressions, suddenly there is a crack in the rampart deep within their paper, obfuscated from Fed governors or others who might read only the article's abstract.

Historically gold has been adopted as a monetary base after there has been large-scale cleansing of debt, which can occur either through deflation or inflation. Because the continental dollar was inflated to near worthlessness, the states ratified the U.S. Constitution with a clause demanding that money be gold or silver coin based (Article I, Section 10, Clause 1). When the cultural preference permitted deflation, that mechanism reset the system effectively in the early 19th century. Arguably the deflation associated with the depression of 1839-1843 was difficult, but the nation's economic progress was not impeded for long despite the prior reckless public spending of states such as Pennsylvania.

The tremendous inflation of the greenback era begat the Resumption Act of 1875, which ushered in the classical gold standard era.

The linear regression research of the academe, while interesting, really may be masking a deeper phenomenon. In the world of finance, relationships are unstable over time and there is a plentitude of cross-currents. To the extent that countries could periodically maintain a terms of trade advantage through devaluation or they valiantly pro-tected an overvalued currency, GDP dutifully responded. But all this may prove is that competitive devaluations or trade arrangements might yield short-term effects, and these would not be unmet by oth-ers feeling the ripple when it washed ashore on their borders. From the eyes of one less enamored with impressive econometrics, some other items not included in the regressions that blame gold for spread-ing the Depression also suggest correlation (and may even be responsi-ble for some causation). The Nobel Prize-winning economist Robert Mundell is known for having a nuanced view that up until Nixon's complete severance with gold in 1971 the world operated a less than perfect gold-exchange standard whose weakest point was having a price that was improperly set. Specifically, in the 1920s the dollar may have been overvalued by as much as 35 to 40 percent, thus validating Roosevelt's devaluation.[39] Gold has been marginalized since 1971, but it may be making a comeback in the private sector, where price dis-covery was unleashed and a new system of "free metallism" might be unfolding.

Economists are trained to act scientifically, and the emphasis over the last 50 years has been to rely on regression analysis to establish proof for theories. In the 1970s and 1980s, it was difficult to find courses in economic history or business cycles, even at Ivy League institutions. So while the qualitative side of the discipline has been wanting, the quan-titative rigor is heavily reliant upon a technique that emphasizes lin-earity, the normal distribution, and parsing of data covering truncated stretches of time divided into equal units. This has its benefits: One can be quite definitive about establishing a relationship between two or more variables. But it may not hold up over time. No serious insti-tutional portfolio manager or trader would base a decision rule upon the limited data contained in most regressions in the anti-gold models, because they are intimately familiar with the tendency for relationships to change over time. Ned Davis Research, an authoritative source of cataloging financial market relationships, monitors hundreds of correlations and readily acknowledges the best of these have a tendency to deteriorate, either suddenly or over time. This firm's researchers, who are tasked to make money rather than to win Nobel Prizes, would be unlikely to bet heavily on a correlation that cannot explain nearly half of a model's outcome. Foolishly, those running the Fed would not hesitate to do so even though the wealth of America and the world is put at great risk.

Moreover, the first thing statistics students are taught is that correlation does not necessarily mean causation. The stock market may rise when old NFL franchises win the Super Bowl and fall otherwise; it is inexplicable why this is so, and clearly there is no cause and effect. After having solved the riddle of the Great Depression, to leave the back door open by saying that this is so except for the experience of the 1920s and 1930s seems odd. And it is especially suspect now that in a world of freely floating currencies the freezing up of credit markets caused the stock market to crash in a mere subset of months within 2008.

The assumptions of linearity and normally distributed outcomes are perhaps the most worrisome and limiting of thought, particularly because in the discipline of finance it has been almost unquestionably shown that six sigma events are happening with all too much regularity to be assumed random. (Two sigmas denote that in 95 percent of outcomes results will be within a stated boundary. A six sigma event is extremely rare; normally it would occur just 3.4 times in a million instances). The principals of Long-Term Capital Management, who had PhDs in economics, assumed away the possibility of rare outcomes with ruinous results for their investors. Nassim Nicholas Taleb has gained notoriety for reminding the investment community of this uncomfortable point. Linearity is another problem. As Einstein's work in the area of physics revealed, the human preference to regard the world in terms of three dimensions restricts comprehension. The existence of another dimension explained how the universe and time actually folded back over on itself. Would it not be unreasonable to expect that the economy, the shape of which is determined through the interaction of humans with biomechanical brains, might not react to stimuli in equally divided increments of time always with proportionately the same force or effect? If economists are unable to find that sequential patterns of small, equal bites of time are predictive or explanatory of credit meltdowns after there has been a large credit buildup, yet they are able to conclude that fixed exchange rates (particularly when based on gold) were significant factors in taking the Depression to painful depths, then maybe they should question the carte blanche usage of regression analysis.

Consider the opinions of no less than Michael Bordo and Anna Schwartz. Bordo is a monetarist who is of the view that a gold exchange standard is flawed because there is a "tendency for such a system to amplify and propagate the effects of unstable policies in the reserve-currency countries."[40] Schwartz partnered with Milton Friedman on his groundbreaking monetary explanation of the Depression. Although they seem to vigorously support freely floating exchange rates, they conclude in a 1988 paper looking at the economic volatility from the end of Bretton Woods (1971) that "floating rates may not provide the degree of insulation once believed," debunking the thesis that "transmission that occurred under fixed exchange rates ...was mostly prevented when exchange rates floated."[41] Their disparagement of the work of other economists studying the field of fixed and floating exchange rates and their degree of stability to the world economic system is illuminating, for it highlights the inadequacy of econometric capability: "The exercises in model building that have occupied specialists in international economics seem designed to impress readers with the ingenuity of the effort rather than the value of the analytical contribution. The theoretical predictions in many cases conflict because they are model specific. Similarly, the empirical evidence on channels of transmission based on these theories has not yet resulted in a consensus. This suggests that policy advice, particularly with respect to support for exchange market intervention and policy coordination, should be forsworn."[42]

The Depression contemporary Irving Fisher, whom Milton Friedman referred to as "the greatest economist of the twentieth century," proclaimed in September 1929 that "stock prices are not too high and Wall Street will not experience anything in the nature of the crash."[43] He continued to be optimistic through 1930 and 1931, having invested his wife's and sister-in-law's fortunes in stocks.[44] But by January 1932, with the evidence mounting that something greater was at work, he developed a thesis that overindebtedness, challenged by a shock such as a stock market selloff, might set off a self-reinforcing deflationary spiral characterized by forced liquidation. Liquidity became a focus of his attention, particularly in the mid-1930s, after it was apparent that one third of the "cheque-book money" had been destroyed by the waves of bank failures culminating in the bank holiday of 1933. He advised Roosevelt to scrap the gold standard and was an advocate of reflation as a way of cleansing the debt overhang and restoring the growth of credit.[45]

Fisher and Keynes enthusiastically endorsed experiments for reviving consumption and the velocity of money such as the distribution of "stamped money," which had a requirement to be spent before an expiration date, and was tested in Howarden, Iowa, in 1932. Fisher also endorsed the Goldsborough bill (HR 10517), which sailed through the House of Representatives in May 1932 by a vote of 289-60. This bill proposed the payment of printed money of $5 per month to each American, the intent of which was to restore prices to 1926 levels. The larger systemic and utopian aim of an obscure cult led by Major C.H. Douglas (1879-1952) and Louis Even (1885-1974), who invented and proselytized the concept of "social credit," respectively, was to establish money that once distributed to consumers would then be retrieved through a discount taken from retailers that would sterilize inflationary issuance and stabilize prices. Part and parcel to the concept was that such a monetary system would be debt free. Although strongly supported by farm interests, fierce opposition by Senator Carter Glass and the eventual passage of the Agricultural Adjustment Act in 1934 would be enough to placate that interest group.[46] [47] [48] It may be that these radical ideas led Fisher to eventually propose doing away with fractional reserve banking, publishing articles and pushing for "the 100% money project." The logic was that if there were 100 percent reserve-backed banking, the printing function of the Fed could have a one-for-one effect, whereas the public's unpredictable demand for credit might in some instances cause inflation or in others not be responsive to monetary stimulus as was the case in the Depression.[49]

The evolution in Fisher's thinking is a microcosm of behavior at an inflection point, a phenomenon portrayed early on in this book. At first, it was unthinkable that the prosperity of the 1920s would end, and then the downturn was a correction as opposed to a systemic unraveling. The mentalité of those who could not imagine an end to the gold standard and obstinately clung to the need to liquidate excessive investment and reduce wages, so closely rendered by Eichengreen and Temin, parallels Fisher's early experience. The obstinance of those who did not feel the tremors of the tectonic shift away from gold is merely par for the course at such an important inflection point in the world's cultural and monetary history, for there is a human tendency to think linearly and extrapolate. But Fisher then became a leading indicator of the intellectual mood of the 1930s. He quickly grasped reflation as a way out of the liquidity trap and, out of self-interest, his personal dilemma. Fisher helped construct a new orthodoxy that likewise has calcified academia around support for floating exchange rates, elastic currency, and the uselessness of commodity-backed currency.

If the world, as Einstein proved, is circular and contains an unseen dimension, then why might not also the riddles of finance be? As we shall see in the following chapter, "Spitting into the Wind," the Federal Reserve governors have clung to the prevailing attitudes of the Fisherian and Friedmanist school of thought. Cleansing debt through outright monetization began in 2009, but a question remains whether the Fed's remediation will be in the correct proportion to the overindebtedness of the United States, much less the world's. If half the $53 trillion of private and public debt in the United States needs to be expunged, then printing a trillion dollars or two might just be a drop in the bucket.

Although the riddle of the Great Depression was apparently solved, one might be impolite and point out some big picture observations that may not have been adequately addressed in the mainstream economics literature. The most glaring of course is unfolding as we speak: a multigenerational credit meltdown that has been transmitted across borders despite the banishment of gold from the temple decades, if not close to a century, ago. In 2008, industrial production eased just 8 percent from its peak to year-end—not horrific by comparison to past recessions. Whether Fed easing and a $1 trillion fiscal stimulus package contemplated by the Obama administration can avert a deep recession will impact to what extent economic theory would need revision. It is hard to imagine 2008 or 2009 fitting in neatly with the predicted outcomes of econometric models built with *either* postwar or Depression era data. Instead, one more look at the economic record of countries during the Great Depression may reveal important policy clues for use in the present.

The riddle of the Great Depression may never be completely solved. Some of its many causes will inevitably be elevated by observers over time, and others will be demoted. The new data unfolding in the crisis begun in 2008 already has called to the fore interest in the Austrian School of economics, which emphasizes the role of debt and its abnormal creation through deposit lending. Mises and his apostle Rothbard articulate the virtues of laissez faire and destigmatize the potential salutary role deflation might play in assuring a rapid recovery after generational credit booms go awry. But we know from the record in Germany, Japan, and to a lesser degree in the United States that when the people of a nation are faced with that bitter pill, they cough it up in political disgust, whether or not it might be curative. The outcome can be fascism or militarism. Although not well known, the tale of Smedly Butler attests to the closeness of that possibility for the United States in the early 1930s.

Instead the Great Depression opened the door for experimentation with numerous socialistic remedies, with economists such as Fisher and Keynes on board. With a new administration having taken the helm in 2009 in the United States, inflation may be the course chosen to purge the debt built up in the boom years presided over by Maestro Greenspan. While it would be immoral to erase the savings of the most prudent among us, the actions of the Fed since 1913 have beaten the proverbial swords of thrift and risk aversion into a plowshare of leverage and speculation, sowing the seed of economic destruction among the weed patch of socialism that has been crowding out capitalism for decades since the Roosevelt era. Can we not blame the new debtor class for welcoming the soaking rains of inflation rather than the draught of deflation? Would not a just and caring lord of the people thus absolve and undo the sins of debtors it so wickedly enticed, and recognizing the folly of it all, resolve to restore the ideals of earlier, wiser generations?

# Chapter 5

# Spitting into the Wind

*There may be an equilibrium which, though stable, is so delicately poised that, after departure from it beyond certain limits, instability ensues ... such a disaster is somewhat like the "capsizing" of a ship which, after ordinary conditions, is always near stable equilibrium but which, after being tipped beyond a certain angle, has no longer this tendency to return to equilibrium, but, instead, a tendency to depart further from it.[1]*

FISHER, IRVING, *THE DEBT DEFLATION THEORY OF GREAT DEPRESSIONS,* "ECONOMETRICA" (MARCH 1933)

This chapter focuses upon the tumultuous unraveling of the financial market that occurred mostly in 2008, and continued on into early 2009. Many began to argue in March and April 2009 that this period was a mere cyclical bottom that would be left behind in an ensuing recovery engineered by effective government intervention, but it may instead be an inflection point marking the end of a great excess. Policy actions were directed at solving an illiquidity crisis, but these scantly acknowledged insolvency, a distinction highlighted in the analysis that follows. Like placing a penny in a fuse box, the injection of credit to solve a problem caused by having extended too much credit before the crisis may ultimately cause our financial circuitry to blow in greater magnitude, just later. Debt itself is a mechanism for deferring financial consequences, and its use may dodge them entirely if the printing of money is so excessive that it inflates away the real value of principal owed. That our primary institution that produces the coin of our realm would facilitate too much accumulation of debt leading up to the present and then choose to defer the consequences with massive infusions of more debt is entirely consistent with the debased culture that has evolved over the last century, a subject explored in more detail in Part 6 of this book.

## Making Sure "It" Doesn't Happen Here

Nearly four years before Ben Bernanke assumed the mantle of Fed Chairman in early 2006, he made a speech titled *Deflation: Making Sure "It" Doesn't Happen Here* at the National Economists Club in Washington, D.C. His remarks extensively tell us how, when faced with a systemic collapse of the banking sector (an outcome usually synonymous with deflation), he would use Federal Reserve System powers to reflate the credit market. It is thus a template with which to monitor his actions in 2008 and 2009. In the speech he makes mention of Milton Friedman's quip about making a helicopter drop of money into the banking system, for which Bernanke earned the sobriquet "Helicopter Ben."[2]

The speech was given in October 2002, almost at the exact moment that the stock market bottomed out after the Internet bubble. Both the technology-heavy NASDAQ Composite and the S&P 500 hit a low at this time, the former having dropped over 75 percent. The National Bureau of Economic Research (NBER) would peg the end of the economic recession at about one year earlier.

Bernanke feared deflation in that recession. With the emergence of systemic risk on three occasions in 2008 (Bear Stearns, GSEs, AIG/ Lehman), he feared it again. His approach is to recognize that the fiat money system he operates can "always" induce growth in prices and higher spending in the economy. A famous quotation from the speech is, ". . . the U.S. government has a technology, called the printing press (or, today, its electronic equivalent), that allows it to produce as many

U.S. dollars as it wishes at essentially no cost."[3] Indeed, he is right about this, but perhaps only in nominal terms and when measuring things from an aggregate perspective—that is, when looking at the wealth of the government combined with that of its people. If the Fed prints too much money through direct purchases of government obligations, it transfers wealth to the government—by taxing the value of savings—a concept known as seigniorage. During normal times, it would print through fractional reserve lending, which would transfer wealth to borrowers. Moreover, this latter form of credit inflation is a windfall for those wealthy enough that their net worth is primarily affected by asset appreciation, as opposed to through the accumulation of ordinary income after taxes.

Bernanke for one has been a believer that it would be easy to clean up after a financial mess (but hard to foresee it coming). Bernanke explained in the 2002 speech, "First, the Fed cannot reliably identify bubbles in asset prices. Second, even if it could identify bubbles, monetary policy is far too blunt a tool for effective use against them." Years later during the crisis he admits to *New Yorker* reporter John Cassidy, "I and others were mistaken early on in saying that the subprime crisis would be contained. The causal relationship between the housing problem and the broad financial system was very complex and difficult to predict."[4]

It would only be hard to predict if one required a regression model that could be fed bites of data from short time periods chopped into months or weeks, then spit out an answer with two sigmas of accuracy that a bubble was underway or a collapse imminent. Knowing that a leverage problem develops over a long stretch of time and that it involves human psychology, the reality is that such a regression will never exist. In fact, it's impossible, for if it did, all humans would be machines that never strayed far from a straight line, and there would neither have been business cycles nor hyperinflation and great depressions. Interestingly, the logic that flows from this is that under a monetary system anchored firmly by gold, man's weaknesses are counteracted. Oddly, the scientific method so honored by economists is the enabler of outrageous and risky behavior. Entranced by mathematics and caught in the headlights of the coming credit implosion, Bernanke believed that papering over a debt problem with more loans and guarantees would be effective. According to Cassidy, he told a visitor to his office in August, and maintained through Labor Day, "A lot can still go wrong, but at least I can see a path that will bring us out of this entire episode relatively intact."[5]

In the speech, he posits a parable wherein a modern alchemist invents a way to produce unlimited amounts of gold at no cost. This fellow announces that he will begin manufacturing it in a few days, but then in reaction the price of the yellow metal plummets before he can even get started. The conclusion is nonsense, because aggregate wealth would remain unchanged, but the alchemist's share of it would increase unless he produced so much that the world would elect to switch to another store of value, such as paper or silver. Of course either way the purchasing power of the yellow metal would erode, but this is the mechanism that would transfer the wealth to his greater share of the enlarged pool of gold. When the Romans mined Spain and the Spaniards exploited the gold and silver of Central America, these empires became outrageously wealthy.

In 2009, the Fed and the U.S. government conspired to print a quantity of money roughly equal to one year's collection of income taxes through direct monetization of debt. In this way interest groups in cahoots with the government have expropriated assets held by others in the private sector, just as the alchemist would become rich. While some benefit would trickle up, the spending would largely go to the nontax-paying element of society, which would spend its newly acquired wealth on discretionary items like trips to Disneyworld or Las Vegas if home equity lines or credit card accounts were encouraged to grow.

The majority of Americans have little stored wealth to protect. In 2008 it was largely this bloc of voters which elected liberal candidates into the executive and legislative branches by a wide margin. And why not? They have everything to gain from redistributing income and erasing the value of assets accumulated by the affluent and pools of capital managed by faceless institutions that may even hold retirement investments for these very same voters. Such a policy would also rescue failing financial institutions and further consolidate the financial industry, as well as eventually bail out homeowners. The Fed and the mortgage agencies in this context may be seen as supplementary organs of government (such as the Supreme Court), which are moving to compliment the axis of dependency and the modern technocratic state.

There was a great debate among market observers as the credit crunch became virulent in late 2008 between whether there would be deflation or inflation, assuming away the base case of muddling through for the moment. Those who rooted for the deflationist camp looked to the depression years and saw a consumer heavily laden with debt and a highly leveraged banking system wherein over half of its loans relate to real estate.[6] They saw interest rates at generational lows already, with the Fed discount rate near zero by year-end 2008. With loan demand sated and a need for banks and consumers to deleverage, they saw any Fed action to inject reserves into the monetary system as "pushing on a string," to use the phrase invented by the monetarist Friedman in his analysis of the Great Depression.

From within the Fed in the days that the policy of quantitative easing became official, Philadelphia Federal Reserve Bank President Plosser alerted us that "(recent economic statistics) prompted some commentators to suggest that the United States is facing a threat of sustained deflation, as we did in the Great Depression or as Japan faced for a decade. I do not believe this is a serious threat ... (but) the Fed must credibly commit to preventing sustained deflation from becoming widely anticipated, just as it must prevent sustained inflation from becoming widely anticipated."[7] All this is well and good. But between the lines one gets the feeling that Plosser and much of the Fed want to be inflation hawks and are maybe a little bit irritated that they have to stop and do something so radical as print money just like in the olden days of the Continental Congress, the French National Assembly, or the Weimar Reichsbank, as if the current circumstance had nothing to do with their having presided over a doubling of the broad money supply from $7 trillion to $14 trillion in the eight years ending in 2008. Up until now Fed governors felt very effective, having seen strong income and employment growth, yet inflation was subdued. In the eight years through 2008, the CPI-U increased at an annual rate of just 2.9 percent, well below the 4.6 percent average of 1971–2007 or the 3.3 percent felt from 1913 to 2007. But so much focus on the targeting of inflation has permitted robust credit expansion to stowaway on the economic ship, lifting total commercial bank credit ($10 trillion) to 77 percent of GDP from 45 percent of GDP in 2000, and seeing debt in aggregate rise to 360 percent of GDP, twice the level touched in 1929.[8]

The policy Bernanke advocated is a departure from the boring old central bank remedies of slashing the discount rate and moderate buying of Treasuries from banks. In deflation, he says it must "expand the scale" of its asset purchases or "expand the menu" of assets it buys. If its overnight rate to banks hits zero, then it would try to stimulate spending by lowering rates further out along the Treasury yield structure, or commit to holding the overnight rate at zero for an extended period of time, perhaps two years. Going further, it could announce a ceiling for rates on long-term government debt, by committing to make unlimited purchases over a period of time. It could also buy agency mortgages directly. By 2009, he would do just that. He cites an episode of bond price pegging in the years before the Federal Reserve-Treasury Accord of 1952, when the Fed maintained a ceiling of 2.5 percent on long Treasury bonds for nearly a decade to help extinguish debt needed to fund World War II. From 1941 to 1951, the CPI-U clocked an over 75 percent rise, thus having the dollar lose 43 percent of its purchasing power.

Bernanke also added in the possibility that the Fed could become involved in the foreign exchange market, noting that the 40 percent devaluation of the dollar against gold in 1933–34 enforced by Franklin Roosevelt had been effective in ending deflation. Prior to this, the government had outlawed private ownership of gold before resetting its price to $35, in effect taxing private savings and eliminating this refuge from bank runs. Like his statements about the alchemist, this is also nonsensical, because now there is no link to gold.

## A Penny In the Fuse Box

In 2008 Federal Reserve governors more than doubled the central bank's balance sheet, pumping roughly $1 trillion of credit into member banks and securities markets, and importantly other central banks globally. This action has one parallel historically, when Fed reserves mushroomed from $1.85 billion in February 1932 to $2.51 billion at the end of that year. This injection, which was partly made to accommodate a federal government budget deficit of $3 billion, failed to discourage the destruction of some $3.2 billion of deposits, and a similar contraction of the money supply to $65 billion.

In 2008, the Fed would explicitly espouse a "too big to fail" policy, having been blamed for causing the crisis by not saving Lehman Brothers. Although Bear Stearns was "saved" and Lehman Brothers was not, in reality the Fed's reserve injections were widely disbursed, and later would be augmented by direct Treasury assistance through the Troubled Asset Relief Program (TARP). Internally, Fed officers called this the "finger in the dyke" strategy, implying that the 100-year flood of bad credit might magically recede in a reasonable period of time. During the year, the financial community's perception of the crisis would change. Initially problems were thought to be contained in the subprime sector or within specific institutions. Once the equity market collapsed beginning in September, bank deposits took flight, some money market funds had failed, and it became clear a systemic meltdown had occurred.

As of March 31, 2008, only $170 billion of what the IMF and others projected as likely losses of nearly $1 trillion on subprime assets had been recognized. The perception of the extent of the credit crisis steadily worsened through the year. In early March 2008, Standard & Poor's pegged total losses at only $285 billion; later in that month Goldman Sachs economists bumped this to $400 billion and then $500 billion.[9] By August 2008, Bloomberg reported that U.S. bank losses from the credit crunch crossed the $500 billion mark, but this had been offset somewhat by the raising of $358 billion of capital. Should liquidity contract systemically, the value of other debts such as home equity lines and credit card receivables would erode substantially, too, a point that caused New York University's Nouriel Roubini to jump to the head of the doomsayers' pack at mid-year with a $2 trillion loss estimate.[10] Two months later, he would up the ante to $3 trillion.[11] When using data available at year-end 2008 there was scant evidence that consumer price deflation had occurred. But during the crash the capital markets discounted this possibility, perhaps looking ahead to the first zero percent monthly CPI on record for at least 50 years from December 2008 to February 2009, or even to the negative year-over-year readings that began to show up in March and April 2009.

If solvency and not illiquidity was the underlying problem, then the Fed's actions look less like sticking a finger in the dyke and more like placing a penny in a fuse box. Before homes used circuit breakers, they were protected by round, screw-in fuses. If no spares were around when they blew, in a pinch a penny could be inserted. It was apt to work for a while, but it would not address the underlying condition of an overload of electricity on the system. Eventually the excess current will find the next weakest point in the wiring at an unpredictable location within the house, and with no protection, possibly the entire edifice could burn down. If the problem persists (and wasn't caused by a fluke overload from a storm, for example), fewer appliances should be loaded onto the circuit or the house should be rewired. We all know instinctively that there is something wrong with using the penny, which simply overrides the protection of the circuit breaker. But if we insert a penny anyway, we nonetheless cheer when the lights go back on, because we can go back to what we were doing before we were unexpectedly interrupted. When in October the stock market followed the credit market into the abyss, the lights flickered off.

Despite unparalleled intervention, well into 2009 there remains a huge standoff between borrowers and lenders, and an inability for most market participants to comprehend why market prices for fixed income securities could sink below rationally computed values. The U.S. economy is creaking under the weight of public and private debt that reached 364 percent of GDP in 2008, up from 267 percent 10 years earlier and 188 percent 25 years previously. This is well above levels for the last century, including the Depression-era when the denominator, economic output, collapsed. Should there be a reversion to the mean underway, it would imply deflation, reduced economic activity, and an even higher ratio of debt to GDP, just as was the case in the Great Depression. From 1929 to 1933, debt increased by over 100 percentage points because the denominator fell. Should that happen through the year 2012, debt could ascend to four or five times GDP, implying a larger default rate than in the 1930s.

In previous crises, the Fed would reliquify the entire banking system by dropping interest rates, allowing institutions to earn their way back to health. And it might prop up a few by injecting cash into them in a swap for good but illiquid collateral. But both tactics failed in 2008, so it opted to take actions that confirmed systemic insolvency was at hand. It makes complete sense that the Fed would take remedial action that is the reverse of what it and other central banks would do historically. If it insisted upon good collateral, this would signal that the system was primarily suffering from an absence of liquidity. It would also show the Fed had confidence that the institutions it was rescuing possessed relatively sound assets and had set aside substantial reserves that had provided a first line of defense. Today's fix of excising bad assets proves that risk taking reached new heights, was widespread, and that there was barely the thinnest skin of protection available for the depositors and account holders at these institutions.

The actions of the Fed reinforce moral hazard as do the ongoing practices of the government's mortgage agencies. In late 2008, depositors flocked to banks based upon their size rather than upon the health of their balance sheets. Banks which managed their credit risk more prudently (for example those with fewer Tier 3 assets) began to lose deposits in the second half of 2008 to these weaker, but larger institutions. John Allison, CEO of BB&T, wrote a letter to legislators in Congress complaining about the bailout as proposed, alleging its prime beneficiaries were Goldman Sachs and Morgan Stanley, saying that the U.S. Treasury is "totally dominated by Wall Street investment bankers and cannot be relied on to objectively assess all the implications of government policy on all financial intermediaries." The government aided a rescue plan for Wachovia Bank by Citibank, which was followed by a competing offer from Wells Fargo, both of which would rely upon government purchases of failed mortgages. Eventually Wells Fargo would receive an additional $5 billion of direct funding from the October 13, 2008, intervention. Had Wachovia gone under (and its depositors compensated by the FDIC), BB&T would have likely seen a dramatic market share gain.[12] In 2009 FHA loans were available with only 3 percent down and even this is more than refundable thanks to an $8,000 tax credit. Outside that niche market, mortgage interest rates remain heavily subsidized both through Fed intervention in the trading of mortgage securities and because of the government guarantee of credit risk.

So what sort of penny has the Fed been placing in the fuse box? There is a dizzying array of programs. Some simply offer credit at rockbottom rates to banks and now brokerage firms. A few, such as the Term Securities Lending Facility, swap the Fed's U.S. Treasuries for riskier mortgage collateral. By far the largest ($620 billion at year-end 2008) is vaguely referred to as "Other Assets" in Fed balance sheet reporting, which is footnoted with the message, "Includes assets denominated in foreign currencies and any exchange-translation assets, which are revalued daily at market exchange rates." The largest component, "Reciprocal Currency Arrangements," usually called simply "swaps," is an exchange of dollars from the Fed to other central banks, which in turn post collateral of their native currency.

In theory these dollars get lent to foreign private banks, relieving pressures on busted money market investments but there is an interesting opinion from the financial blogosphere that suspects these foreign central banks have actually been commissioned to use the large leverage inherent in the derivatives market to actually bet these loaned funds in *support* of the U.S. dollar in forex futures. Anecdotally the foreign exchange holdings reports of the New York Fed and the U.S. Treasury also suggest a pro-dollar bias. A $62 billion short position showed up starting in May 2008 in the U.S. Treasury's regular reporting of its international reserve position (www.treas.gov/press/releases). Likewise, the New York Fed, in its ongoing reporting of foreign currency holdings, stated that it had concentrated its swaps in euros and yen by year-end 2008, these two occupying $436 billion or 75 percent of all swap lines. From the beginning of its intervention to year-end the dollar strengthened, and the Fed disclosed it had substantial unrealized gains from both positions as well as in a variety of smaller currencies.

In the media the descriptive has been that the Fed provided dollars that were crucially needed by ailing foreign banks, who would obtain such loans from the central bank of their native country. But that would imply the Fed was in possession of foreign exchange received for its dollars. If that were the case, it would have suffered a loss during the second half of 2008, not the profit it reported. In official documents, Fed descriptions of the swap arrangements have been noticeably terse, whereas significant, granular disclosure has been made of small, irrelevant programs such as the individual Maiden Lane SIVs. The conspiracy theorists believe that since sums can be leveraged through derivatives or guarantees, these U.S. portfolios could be a template for the order of magnitude larger activity that may be occurring inside this vaguely disclosed "Other Assets" account.

No doubt the conspiracy theorists are barking up the wrong tree.
On one hand we know that European banks are weak because risk-
adjusted capital rules permitted them to lever up to buy supposedly safe
AAA-rated U.S. mortgages, and it is logical that the Fed might cooperate
to ease that burden. On the other hand, probably an even bigger head-
ache may be the mortgages they granted to Eastern European homeowners, who are struggling to earn incomes in depressed local currencies
that must be converted into euros or surprisingly, yen—the currencies in
which these loans are denominated. It is logical that the swaps have been
put in place to somehow plug that latter black hole.

The Fed's response is adolescent in the sense that it has permitted
major damage by allowing the credit boom to happen. Right under
its nose, the broad money supply (M3) doubled in the last eight years,
from $7 trillion to $14 trillion, but it is trying to fool the market into
thinking this statistic is irrelevant because it was vigilant and never
allowed inflation to surface. Can one really double the money supply,
produce a few percentage points of inflation and GDP growth, and not
have this prodigious sum of cash not produce some tremendous effect?
If the answer is truly "no," then why not double it again? In reality,
this ballooning quantity of reserve currency dollars was a base upon
which other countries could pyramid loans, repeating the pattern seen
when the classical gold standard was liberalized under the tutelage of
Kemmerer and Conant, morphing into the gold exchange standard.
Then and now this caused prices of equities and real estate to surge
globally. In 2008 it also triggered a spike in commodities, sending oil to
$140 per barrel, but strangely it evoked tame inflation for most com-
monplace items monitored in the United States' CPI gauge, including
importantly, wages. Suppose that we were using the same yardsticks to
evaluate the hyperinflation of late 18th century France. In that period,
the real wages of the peasantry did not rise at all, but there was sudden spontaneous wealth in all of Paris and some in medium and small
urban centers, where more than a few astute individuals abandoned
farming for finance. Yes, there was great inflation for items like bread,
but all in all the lowest rungs of society stood still while wealth was
transferred to speculators. By using newly issued U.S. government debt
to print dollars to be swapped out for bad credit, the Treasury and the
Fed wished to reset the clock back eight years by undoing much of

the damage done to the system from real estate. However, M3 is not reset back to $7 trillion; it remains at today's greatly expanded $14 trillion figure.

As will be detailed in Part 3, individuals in the upper-middle class have high incomes but experience difficulty in accumulating assets due to confiscatory tax rates. Savings are also penalized by the constant erosion of purchasing power of the dollar. Until the current crisis, economists used to explain away the chronically low savings rate by reminding us there was substantial unrealized value locked in residential real estate. The Fed's suppression of interest rates at artificial, Japanese-style lows combined with the heightened availability of home equity loans and exotic mortgages provided upper-middle class homeowners an opportunity to assemble—and spend or invest—a mountain of cash. Normally remittance of such income would be shackled by a requirement to simultaneously mail back to the federal and state governments a check for 50 percent of the proceeds, which would be the case had such individuals instead worked longer hours or taken a new risk to grow sales in a small business, if they owned one. Can we blame today's peasantry for wanting in on the action, pressuring their congressmen to make it possible through pressuring banks to lend without documentation or down payment via coercive programs such as the Community Reinvestment Act (CRA), and then borrowing to the hilt? Is the Fed beyond reproach for this mess, as its pathetic struggle to posture as a stalwart inflation fighter beholds?

With our culture not having changed as a result of the crisis (yet), the attitude across the board has been that deleveraging might happen to others, or be done later. Nowhere is this more evident than in government policy. The Fed, the Treasury, and the Congress have decided to address the two monetary problems of our age, excessive debt, and moral hazard, by *increasing* debt and bailing out large, risky banks to the detriment of their better managed but smaller competitors. Even the solution for Freddie Mac and Fannie Mae followed the pattern: They will be deleveraged in 18 months, but to get through this rough period, their balance sheets will *temporarily* grow now that they are owned by the federal government.

Certainly the bold action to prevent Armageddon was welcomed by most observers close to the scene. But Main Street saw this, and more especially the injection of money to troubled entities under Congress's TARP facility, as something that it would be expected to pay for eventually through higher taxes. Since these guarantees could pay off nearly the total mortgage principal of all U.S. citizens, the public rightly asked why it should help bail out Wall Street when repairing finances closer to home would solve the problem. The nub is that either option requires taxpayer funds, which at best is like paying oneself and at worst robs Paul to pay Peter, which could be good or bad depending upon one's end of the bargain. A consensus developed by mid-2009 that the vast amount of credit the Fed has injected into the banking system might produce inflation, and perhaps even hyperinflation. However, without massive, direct injection of cash into the hands of borrowers, pressure on asset and securities prices would remain. Financial institutions may have been temporarily saved, but individuals have not.

## Forced Lending: To Print or Not to Print?

The Fed's swapping out good assets for bad is the first step outlined in Bernanke's 2002 speech, and it is clever in that it simply resets the clock for banks as if they had not made bad loans in the first place. When this remedy was applied in early 2008, the monetary base did not rise initially as a result, although it was hoped that the stimulation might catch on and expand money creation in banks and in the fixed income securities market.

The crux of the problem can be seen clearly from the perspective of the financial institutions being rescued. To allude to the freezing pond allegory sketched out in the beginning of this book, the credit markets may have been melted loose by the Fed's pouring salt on the ice, but the overall weather conditions remain the same. True, they can keep adding salt, but if it remains cold outside, there is a much more fundamental problem going unaddressed. The Fed can crow all it wants to about having done something, and it can jawbone bank executives about the need to make more loans to get the economy moving again. The government can mail out moderate stimulus checks or even cough up a $1 trillion ditch-digging program and a middle-class tax cut, but as long as consumers, businesses, and financial institutions remain highly leveraged, they will prefer to use their incremental cash flow to reduce what they owe.

Imagine you are a bank CEO, and you were leveraged 15-to-1 before the crisis. Over half of bank loans are real estate related, and that asset class has fallen about 25 percent from the peak. The Fed extends a guarantee, swap, or loan to your bank, so now you may be liquid. But from the perspective of the marketplace, you remain insolvent—that is if your depositors pull out, you will be left holding the bag as long as the Fed expects to see this money extended from its temporary facilities back someday. So you don't make any more loans, and your customers wouldn't want to borrow more, even if you did press them to do so.

What does this mean? It means that the underlying problem is not *illiquidity*. (But the drying up of funds is a very important intermediate mechanism of a marketplace that is trying to sort out problems by forcing liquidation.) It really indicates that *insolvency* is the problem, and it was caused by both the private and the public sectors borrowing too much relative to their income. What if you say their equity seemed adequate at the top? Indeed it was, if everyone in the world could have transacted assets at that price and deleveraged at precisely that moment, an impossible and totally theoretical feat. In reality asset prices were pumped up by a credit boom, so the income those assets generated to justify their dear prices was dependent upon ever-increasing waves of lending to produce growth, or a perpetual excess of demand over supply, however you want to look at it.

After not being successful at stimulating the economy through the injection of nearly $1 trillion of bank reserves during late 2008, the Fed began to acknowledge Wall Street's concerns of a possible deep and prolonged recession in its December 15-16, of 2008, Federal Open Market Committee (FOMC) meeting. It reiterated statements made by Chairman Bernanke a few weeks earlier that it would "need to focus on other tools to impart additional monetary stimulus." Most significantly it indicated that "the Committee stands ready to expand purchases of agency debt and agency mortgage-backed securities, and that it is evaluating the benefits of purchasing longer-term Treasury securities. . . . By the end of the second quarter of next year, the Desk is expected to purchase up to $100 billion in housing related GSE debt and up to $500 billion in agency-guaranteed MBS."[13] In March 2009 the Fed announced it would buy $1 trillion of mortgage securities and Treasuries. Almost immediately the consensus that deflation would occur, which was prevalent in October 2008, melted away into an inflationary scenario when monetization of federal debt headlined in the news.

By early 2009 the Fed would target 2 to 3 percent inflation, explicitly stating it would intervene in the open market to buy Treasuries, hoping that recipients of federal spending would deposit freshly printed funds at banks, stimulating lending. These more aggressive moments of market intervention would epitomize the gearing up of the printing press technology to which Bernanke refers. It might lead to nominal growth in the economy, but it remains to be seen if real growth or wealth creation would ensue.

However, in the momentous meeting in which quantitative easing was ratified, FOMC members thought that this extraordinary measure could be undone. Meeting notes declare: "as economic activity recovered and financial conditions normalized, the use of certain policy tools would need to be scaled back, the size of the balance sheet and level of excess reserves would need to be reduced, and the Committee's policy framework would return to focus on the level of the federal funds rate."

But to a banker or a borrower whose balance sheet is weak, having this sword of Damocles hanging over his head would communicate the message that any economic activity sparked by the injection of freshly printed money had better be directed at debt pay down rather than spending or long-term private investment, because the mopping up operation is likely to rekindle deflation fears. If a bank, business, or individual's balance sheet remained stretched but the economy recovered for four or five quarters (or even worse—an inflationary recession began), the Fed has telegraphed that it would pull the rug out from under everyone. On the other hand, through the TARP facility, the U.S. Treasury made a declaration that it will backstop risk. Its recipients may say they have modified their attitudes about credit, but in practice their newly cleaned up assets and liabilities would not change much from a ratio analysis point of view compared to how things looked in the years before the crisis hit.[14] Confidence in the government as a backstop for risk would be that much greater, so the logical outcome would be for the worst players to continue to operate on the edge once again, still able to be connected to the government's iron lung at will.

In 1933 Irving Fisher correctly diagnosed the cause of financial meltdowns in his book *Booms and Depressions*, which was followed by an essay, *The Debt Deflation Theory of Great Depressions*. In the essay he said: "I have, at present, a strong conviction that these two economic maladies, the debt disease and the price-level disease (or dollar disease), are, in the great booms and depressions, more important causes than all others put together ... Thus over-investment and over-speculation are often important; but they would have far less serious results were they not conducted with borrowed money. That is over-indebtedness may lend importance to over-investment or to over-speculation. The same is true as to over-confidence. I fancy that over-confidence seldom does any great harm except when, as, and if, it beguiles its victims into debt."[15]

Unfortunately, there are only two ways to get rid of the debt that periodically gets built up: inflation or deflation. Both can happen in either a fiat currency or a gold-backed currency, provided there is a fractional reserve banking system, although clearly the magnitude of credit booms have been their greatest without gold as an underpinning. Neither the moderate steps resolved by the FOMC in its December 2008 meeting nor the swapping out of bad debt with Fed credit are likely to overcome the fears associated with what may be something like $20 trillion of excess debt being carried in the financial system relative to the low points of leverage experienced, such as the 1950s. About the only positive from not printing the massive amount of money needed to truly stabilize the system is that the gigantic moral hazard of wiping out savings might not happen. But, even without such printing, wealth will be redistributed from savers to nonsavers through crony capitalism to government contractors or whoever else would benefit from fiscal spending likely to be authorized, including or above the $1 trillion signed into law in February 2009. These dollars will be circulated soon, but the Treasury bonds and notes needed to be repaid would most certainly crimp taxpayer pocketbooks now or in subsequent generations unless so many were circulated that a great deal of consumer price inflation would result.

What this suggests is that the Fed will tinker with monetization
in 2009, but consistently undershoot. Like a space capsule that must
time its reentry within seconds and achieve a precise angle of approach
into the atmosphere, the Fed must not miss its window of opportunity
or it might share the fate of the original "lost cosmonaut," whose tiny
capsule has been sailing away from the Earth at 18,000 mph for the
last 45 years; it just kept on going. If it acts with restraint, that is manufacturing a quantity well below total excess debt, borrowing would
remain unserviceable with income, triggering a collapse in the money
supply. Like Andrew Mellon who admonished liquidation was healthy,
Austrian economists would prefer this quick, effective, but hardly pain-
less solution.

Although NASA never lost an astronaut during reentry, the Soviet
Union is rumored to have several times. In the early 1960s, two young
men in Italy who had a keen interest in radio transmission developed
hardware that enabled them to intercept communications of Russian
cosmonauts as they were in low level orbit above them. Reprinted
courtesy of the *Fortean Times* from its July 2008 issue, their conversation
with one just before her death is a reminder of how exacting the angle
of approach can be for those who return to earth:

> Midnight, 19 May 1961. A crisp frost had descended on Turin's
> city centre which was deserted and deathly silent. Well, almost.
> Two brothers, aged 20 and 23, raced through the grid-like
> streets (that would later be made famous by the film *The Italian
> Job*) in a tiny Fiat 600, which screamed in protest as they bounced
> across one cobbled piazza after another at top speed.

> The Fiat was loaded with dozens of iron pipes and aluminum
> sheets which poked out of windows and were strapped to the
> roof. The car screeched to a halt outside the city's tallest block
> of flats. Grabbing their assorted pipes, along with a large tool-
> box, the two brothers ran up the stairs to the rooftop. Moments
> later . . .

> The brothers finished setting up, grabbed their head-sets, twid-
> dled the knobs on their portable receivers, hit the record but-
> ton and listened . . .

'Come in . . . come in . . . come in . . . Listen! Come in! Talk to me! I am hot! I am hot! Come in! What? Forty-five? What? Fifty? Yes, yes, yes, breathing. Oxygen, oxygen . . . I am hot. Isn't this dangerous?' The brothers looked nervously at one another. They only fully understood the Russian later when their sister translated for them, but the desperation in the woman's voice was clear."[16]

## Bernanke: Going Down in History

No Fed chairman wants to go down in history as the one that inflated away half the nation's $52 trillion of public and private debt, which if done would still not bring leverage down to that of a 1950s-era balance sheet. The public image of the Federal Reserve is that it steadfastly fights inflation and stands ready to act when financial institutions collapse, either individually or systemically. On the surface, this is so. Officially reported inflation has largely been under control ever since the early 1980s, and even in the case of Lehman Brothers, it stepped in to arrest the ill effects upon collaterally damaged institutions. Moreover, its august management, largely bankers and economists, is regarded as pro-business and supportive of capitalism. However, it also has a broader mandate, which was established by the Humphrey-Hawkins Full Employment and Balanced Growth Act of 1978, brought into law under President Carter during a time of high inflation and unemployment that was occurring despite expansion. With jobs being lost rapidly in the wake of the financial meltdown of 2008-2009, members of Congress are apt to pressure the Fed to be ever more expansionary, so long as economic recovery remains elusive. U.S. Treasury Secretary Timothy Geithner telegraphed this in a televised interview in March 2009 on *This Week With George Stephanopoulos*: "You know, the big mistake governments make in recessions is they put the brakes on too early . . . we're not going to do that."

By allowing rotten credit to substitute as backing for more than half of the nation's bank reserves, the Fed delayed the time when it would need to replenish high-powered money through government support, which would effectively internalize to its core the dramatic growth in money that has been taking place in the outer orbit of its system. Culture, politics, and economic matters are always intertwined. The rise of relativism, secularism, and socialism will continue to shape the attitudes of central bankers, whether or not they as individuals subscribe to these modern liberal doctrines. Pedigreed from the large institutions that they protect and manage, and ultimately exposed to a media that is also very influenced by shifting cultural values, tolerances for pain of any kind are so reduced that support for moving to any other system of money is nil. Moreover, trading off some added inflation for maintaining high employment is a political winner, so hopes for heightened consideration of controlling monetary aggregates look dim. Indeed, it took double digit readings in the CPI-U before Fed Chairman Volcker, appointed in August 1979, took strong action and abandoned interest rate targeting despite political attacks and protests such as the blockading of the Eccles building on C Street by indebted farmers. In fact, as undersecretary of the Treasury for international monetary affairs, Volcker had played an important role in suspending gold convertibility in 1971.

There is a human and moral problem with operating a faulty system and legitimizing it at every turn with academic studies that embolden market participants to invest their life savings, only to see these vaporized either through a collapse of asset prices, inflation, or even more dangerously, through putting in place a cure that accomplishes both in sequence. It is like imposing slavery—after the fact, because a life's worth of labor is lost. Inflation of the money supply is the electricity of relativism and this modern brand of socialist capitalism, for it courses through our circuitry and transfers the energy of producers and savers to consumers and borrowers, lights the darkness of business depressions, sparks bubbles and purportedly economic growth also, discounts looming entitlement liabilities through sleight-of-hand CPI measurement, and negates the theism of rewarding prudent institutions and citizens. To move away from fiat currency is to reject socialism. Like the mighty Mississippi River, which periodically through nature's wrath breaks free of government's dykes and levies, once again gold, the natural money of the millennium, might freely meander through commerce and stop the erosion of the rich delta soil lost each year to corrosive incursion of the salt water of socialism.

# Chapter 6

# Moral Hazard

*A bank of the United States is in many respects convenient for the government and useful to the people. Entertaining this opinion, and deeply impressed with the belief that some of the powers and privileges possessed by the existing bank are unauthorized by the Constitution, subversive of the rights of the states, and dangerous to the liberties of the people, I felt it my duty at an early period of my administration to call the attention of Congress to the practicability of organizing an institution combining all its advantages and obviating these objections. I sincerely regret that in the act before me I can perceive none of these modifications of the bank charter which are necessary, in my opinion, to make it compatible with justice, with sound policy, or with the Constitution of our country.*
PRESIDENT ANDREW JACKSON; VETO MESSAGE, JULY 10, 1832

**M**oral hazard is a term with specific meaning in the financial community. Originally the phrase was mainly used to describe a phenomenon within the insurance industry related to the uncertainty about the honesty of those insured. Premium writers have at times noticed that a few who buy insurance lose any incentive to minimize risk, correctly thinking this has been laid off on the company writing their policy. Insured lives sometimes commit suicide but leave no notes. Warehouses burn down more often when filled with hard-to-sell

inventory. Auto owners sometimes fail to lock their cars if they are behind on their lease payments. Expensive jewelry gets misplaced when its
holders come under financial pressure.

This phrase now is more often used to describe components of systemic financial system risk that have sprung up in the financial crisis
that began in 2008. The odd marriage of Wall Street and government
has produced two enormous moral hazards: the securitized mortgage,
as well as its cousin, the credit default swap, which together brought
down the financial system in 2008. It has begotten conflicted market
structures, such as the government mortgage agencies that promote
home ownership through weakening standards, but at the same time
implicitly guarantee these loans. Large brokerage firms and banks fear-
lessly extended credit knowing they had the Federal Reserve standing
by to slash the cost of funds and repair their balance sheets. Depositors
readily handed over their savings to them, because the FDIC guaranteed against loss. Other strange beasts have evolved over time: Ratings
agencies are paid handsomely by issuers, particularly for high margin,
complex derivative securities. For years many feared a conflict between
commercial banking and brokerage, but this separation was irrelevant in
the current crisis, as proven by the better performance of institutions
in Canada and other countries. No one objects that investment banks
give away purportedly objective research that happens to compliment
high-margin corporate finance activity and proprietary trading operations, a structural flaw that damages the competitiveness of those who
would author reports on investments with an independent perspective.

While these financial hazards have gained attention, the largest by
far gets no recognition at all. The operation of a fiat currency encourages the accumulation of debt, which in turn pumps up the value of
assets including stocks. After generations so much can be amassed that
a mega-collapse can ensue, one far greater than if gold backed the currency and also bank reserves. Gold acts as a brake on reckless expansion
because the threat of conversion of paper back to gold is always a possibility. In fact it is likely whenever pyramiding of national currencies
or bank loans is uncomfortably high.

The danger of fiat currency is invisible to the public, professional
investors, and political commentators, who are oblivious of its mechanism. Thought to be a "normal" element of finance ever since we

moved off direct specie systems shortly after the Constitution was ratified, its inherent flaw has remained concealed despite the meltdown of the financial system in 2008. Since it is likely to remain unknown, it provides the ideal vector for transmitting the disease of socialism throughout the economic corpus. The collapse of the economy permitted the majority-controlled Congress in conjunction with the new administration to authorize an unprecedented quantity of government spending, which will be funded in part by some $1 trillion of freshly minted fiat currency. There can be no question that this is a seizure of wealth roughly equivalent to one year's collection of income tax, yet there is more outcry over making a trivial increase in the topmost bracket from 35 percent to 39.6 percent.

The conditions for vulnerability to this virus are ideal, for the window for fiat money growth through bank loan expansion, which would normally accrue to the private sector, was closed once the public discovered it could no longer tolerate debt levels at over three times national income. As the adage goes, when one door closes another opens; money creation can only be done now through flat-out printing, and this solely flows through a pipeline directly into the U.S. Treasury. The historical record is such that helicopter dumps of cash through the monetization of debt enliven an economy temporarily, like the flash of burning magnesium. So it is likely that another downleg could follow, which would require repeated doses of the same inefficacious medicine. The effect is to exhaust the wealth from savers and investors and dispense it to the lowest income brackets of society through entitlements such as expanded health care. Thus, in addition to spreading socialism through changing the tax code, the new administration will be able to utilize the interlocking system of fiat currency and fiscal spending to redistribute far more wealth quickly than ever was collected and redirected by the IRS. Commentators on Wall Street greeted the first salvo of the economic recovery strategy by cheering on a massive stock market rally that began in March 2009, while talk radio focused only on the spending and taxation angle of the stimulus, completely missing the point that none of this could have been accomplished without facilitation from the Fed.

The pages that follow will begin by touching on the linkage between the financial industry and the government, and the evolution of this system. The peculiar microeconomic distortion of mortgage incentives will be explored. Then, in a broader sweep, the harmful effect of central bank sponsorship of fractional reserve lending will be touched upon, because the excess creation of credit eventually lures wealth into high-risk investments and away from low-yielding ones. With these moral hazards established, next the discussion will turn to the inherent conflict within democracy. The chapter ends by returning to the theme of fiat currency's destructive tendency, and how the leading conservative commentators of our time have yet to even embrace the concept. Interestingly, the most trenchant analysis of the rot created by operating within a debt-based currency expansion comes from liberals, who have authored books such as *The Trillion Dollar Meltdown* by Charles R. Morris (Perseus Books Group, 2008) and *Bad Money* by Kevin Phillips (Penguin Group, 2008), or articles such as Simon Johnson's "The Quiet Coup" (*The Atlantic*, May 2009). Yet they also blissfully ignore the role of fiat currency, forsaking true Democratic Party roots planted by Andrew Jackson, and instead they advocate the case for ever more onerous regulation. They begin history with Reagan, as if the orgiastic affair with debt that began in 1914 and restarted in the late 1930s had no pregnancy.

## The Great Bank Robbery

When the going got tough on Wall Street, the nation's largest institutions went hat in hand to the U.S. Treasury for a bailout, and they extracted over a trillion dollars in credit from the Federal Reserve System. On its face, there is something wrong with this. If the government had any responsibility to mend these banks, it would have been solely to depositors and account holders, and it should not have enriched those who financed them as business ventures. The private sector would have gladly capitalized small- and medium-sized institutions that had been less wanton in their participation in the excesses of the last few decades, for dramatically increased market share would have been their reward. And it would have done so even if structural and regulatory changes that would limit the financial industry's profitability going forward had been imposed.

Who oversees the financial markets ultimately? The answer is the Senate Banking Committee, currently led by Senator Chris Dodd from

Connecticut, and the House Financial Services Committee, whose chairman in 2009 is Congressman Barney Frank of Massachusetts. Dodd received favorable mortgage terms on his homes in Washington, D.C. and Connecticut from Countrywide through a VIP program known informally as "friends of Angelo" (Angelo Mozilo having been the CEO of Countrywide Financial). Several chapters later the role of political donations is reviewed in detail, but for now in brief Dodd's judgment may also be compromised by having been the leading recipient of donations from the insurance industry and Fannie Mae and Freddie Mac. Bank of America, which bought Countrywide and Merrill Lynch, has only paid more to Barack Obama than Dodd. Bernard Madoff and Allen Stanford were huge donors to those with responsibility over them.

Congressman Frank likewise has been a recipient of sizeable campaign donations from the financial industry, and he has been criticized for blocking increased regulation and scrutiny of the government mortgage agencies, particularly when this issue came to a head in 2003 during the congressional hearing of OFHEO's investigation of Fannie Mae and Freddie Mac. One of the most replayed political videos, with over 3 million hits on YouTube.com, during the 2008 election cycle was of OFHEO's lead regulator Armando Falcon being roundly criticized by a parade of hostile Democratic congressmen including Frank and Maxine Waters, and Republicans repeating the severity of the unfolding problems at Fannie and Freddie.[1]

So besides voting $750 billion in aid through the TARP facility and standing by when the Fed pumped $1 trillion into the system, what did Congress do? In June 2008, Congress saw fit to investigate the exercise of judgment by investors of capital—often large, high-profile pensions and endowments—to devote a considerable allocation of assets to the commodities markets. Hedge funds make up an increasing allocation of institutional funds. Certain of their brokers secured special regulations that unfairly advantaged large customers, many of which manipulated commodity prices. Their use of short selling was heavily directed against the financial sector itself, and by July 2008 Congress looked into the matter, triggering the SEC to ban "naked" short selling of the common stocks of 19 banks and brokers. By generating such a list, the government favored some companies over others, socialistically guiding where dollars may and may not flow, to the detriment of others not privileged enough to make the list. In September, the list was expanded to cover 799 financial firms for which no short selling would be permitted, even when it would be done with borrowed shares.[2]

The Congressional hearings are reminiscent of the government's scrutiny of capital pools in the early 1930s. Stock market operators had been free to collude, spread rumors, and use considerable leverage to make their impact ever more potent. But such behavior is just as reprehensible on the upside as it is on the downside. In the last decade or more, these issues are subject to regulations, and these apply equally to short-sellers and buyers. One can argue whether the restrictions placed on these activities is adequate or excessive, or for that matter, if they effectively serve the public good. But what is far more relevant is the SEC's tacit allowance of naked short selling through what became known as the "Madoff Rule," which exempted market makers from the same requirements to deliver stock after stock sales. This essentially provided broker-dealers with the ability to legally counterfeit securities, and to rent this resource out to hedge fund clients. Patrick Byrne, CEO of Overstock.com, a company victimized by relentless naked short selling, worked with reporter Mark Mitchell to reveal the extent of the naked short-selling problem through his web site www.deep-capture.com. Clearly this activity has been pernicious to the equity of some companies. However, it did not cause the downfall of the global economy or of the stock market. Excessive leverage was the culprit. If economic actors had been relatively debt free, they would have been strong enough to intercede in capital markets and take advantage of economic opportunities presented by illegitimately pummeled stock prices, somewhat akin to the soaking up of stock through corporate repurchases in the aftermath of the 1987 crash.

Politicians demonize the hedging of risk with commodities and even the legitimate deployment of short selling, but the quasi-government entities they have chartered—the Fed and the mortgage agencies—have fostered the overexpansion of credit that is debasing the coin of the realm and brought us to the edge of systemic failure. Only a socialist government would single out those seeking to flee and penalize them as perpetrators.

Wall Street knows where its bread is buttered. Goldman Sachs has had deep ties to both Democratic and Republican administrations through figures such as Henry Paulson (Treasury Secretary to George W. Bush) and Robert Rubin (Treasury Secretary to Bill Clinton). In April 2009 it hired Michael Pease, a top staffer for Barney Frank, to be its director of government affairs, replacing a former Tom Daschle intimate, Mark Patterson. Throughout the crisis to that point, Goldman has been regarded as one of the financially strongest firms on Wall Street, but it has accepted TARP funds. However, like many other broker-dealers, its leverage ratio swelled to near 30-to-1, which means that failure of any large derivatives on (or off) its books could have wiped out its equity. Goldman purportedly had a large credit default swap it had entered into with the failed insurance giant AIG, which the government fulfilled as part of its bailout of that firm. In addition, Goldman has stated that it had hedged its exposure to AIG, perhaps through a short position in AIG equity or derivatives of the same, so it in essence may have collected twice on its loss. While this is hardly illegal, it seems unnecessary given the firm has also received substantial taxpayer funds. Moreover, unlike AIG, which has been criticized for paying large bonuses to its employees (enabled through a provision inserted into legislation by Senator Dodd), Goldman has quietly supplied multimillion-dollar loans to selected employees to support capital calls they needed to meet for private partnerships made available to them through their positions at Goldman. Little publicity of this possible use of taxpayer funds has been aired by comparison.

In the historical analysis of this book, the point is made that banks 100 years ago were strong and the government was very weak, a direct consequence of the protection of private property through the granting of limited powers of taxation and regulation in the original U.S. Constitution. The banks even had to bail out the U.S. Treasury upon occasion in the 19th century. Moreover, later this book will review how individual character was honored as a virtue in Victorian era times, and how this has been supplanted by reliance upon the state or through passing on blame to other societal groups. The moral hazard this shift exhibits is echoed by the voices of modern day gurus of Wall Street such as television personality Jim Cramer and Bill Gross, the most renowned bond manager of the largest fixed-income management company in the world, PIMCO.

Today's most popular financial guru, Jim Cramer, host of *Mad Money* and a founder of TheStreet.com, was bullish on the banking sector during most of 2008. Being a better trader than investor,[3] he managed to be on the correct side of the market in the short term by saving his powder to weigh in with bullish comments at moments when the group was heavily oversold, such as January and July of 2008. His vision originally was based upon the old saw that big cuts in interest rates by the Fed lead to a rally in the group.

With rates so low they might not be cut much more, he made a bullish forecast on a new premise, this one even more reliant upon government largesse. On July 30, 2008, he told the audience on TheStreet.com's video program, *Wall Street Confidential*, that the Foreclosure Prevention Act of 2008 (H.R. 3221) was crafted in such a way to help Bank of America especially over other financial services companies, since it was the largest direct owner and servicer of mortgages (it does not cover complex pools of mortgages such as CDOs that are more common in the securities industry). Essentially H.R. 3221 enables such banks to take a large portion of their balance sheet comprised of mortgages valued in the marketplace at 20 to 50 cents on the dollar and lay them off to the FHA at a valuation of 85 cents on the dollar. His observation: "If you look at it with a (*sic*) cynical way I look at things, this was a win for Bank of America; I can make a lot of money that is a loss for the taxpayers; I am not a political guy."

Cramer and most other Wall Street gurus have repeatedly encouraged the government to intervene through the Fed or directly to aid the banking sector or the economy, not so much to help people as to support the stock market. Cramer's position at the time was intriguing, and like the proverbial stopped clock, he will be right eventually, especially if the "green shoots" rally of early 2009 persists. However, Bank of America's stock price collapsed from $34 on July 30, 2008, to $4 by the end of February 2009. Wall Street's leaning upon the taxpayer for support is unsettling. Cramer's view epitomizes the cultural weakness of today's hybrid capitalist-socialist economy, which taps government favoritism of selected large corporations over middle-class taxpayers and small business, two overlapping political factions increasingly being disenfranchised.

Cramer may be the most publicly visible of the bailout crowd, but he has plenty of company and many admirers. The largest bond fund in the country, the PIMCO Total Return Fund, holds over $130 billion of assets, much of this invested in mortgage-backed securities issued by Freddie Mac and Fannie Mae. Its manager, Bill Gross, has been an outspoken cheerleader for intervention. It should be no surprise that his fund was highlighted as one of the biggest winners the day the GSE rescue was announced, which caused spreads between Treasuries and agency bonds to tighten. It should also be no surprise that he was first to volunteer PIMCO's fixed income management services for the new TARP facility, and is one of a chosen few to fund the Public-Private Investment Program (PIPP) unveiled in March 2009. Fellow Democrat Paulson, who placed a caveat that his decisions on running the TARP fund "may not be reviewed by any court of law or any administrative agency" would then be free to choose the fund's manger. PIMCO offered its services for free, but fund companies have a habit of waiving fees initially and then raising them later. Paulson had carte blanche to accommodate PIMCO. Managing TARP side-by-side with private assets is a horrendously conflicted position, perhaps another factor why Gross would want to be an insider to what may soon be the world's largest fixed-income market maker.

In his September 2008 Investment Outlook, Gross opened with three paragraphs full of gushing praise for Cramer. He warned, quite rightly, that "if we are to prevent a continuing asset and debt liquidation of near historic proportions, we will require policies that open up the balance sheet of the U.S. Treasury—not only to Freddie and Fannie but to Mom and Pop on Main Street U.S.A., via subsidized home loans issued by the FHA and other government institutions."[4]

There is one small problem with this. The balance sheet of the federal government has already been opened up—to the tune of over $500,000 for every household in the United States, if liabilities were measured by generally accepted accounting principles. This in a nation where median household income is south of one-tenth said liability. The problem is that Mom and Pop already own the balance sheet of the United States; the nation's credit is the people's credit. Worse, thanks to socialism, we would push this debt onto the top brackets only. Placed solely upon the top four (everyone above the 15% bracket), it creates a debt per household of over $2 million. So Gross unsuspectingly is an advocate of socialism, and from a financial perspective, quite an advanced stage of it at that. Just like Al Gore, who demands that

further discussion of whether global warming exists should cease, those
in the financial community who seek to hide under the skirt of government instinctively don't want to discuss this elephant in the room.
They would prefer to shut down debate or shout down opponents. In a
twisted denial of the inflationary implications of "opening up the balance sheet of the United States," Paul McCulley, managing director of
PIMCO, chimed in alongside colleague Bill Gross in September 2008,
by adding:

> Policy makers, and even more so academics, just don't seem to
> collectively "get it" when it comes to understanding what is
> unfolding in the capital markets right now, and the implication
> for a whole array of policies, not just monetary policy . . .

> The hawks scream that the Fed must tighten sooner rather than
> later, so as to burnish the Fed's anti-inflation credibility, but to
> do so without any discussion whatsoever of the monetary pol-
> icy transmission mechanism; they simply look at the negative
> prevailing real Fed funds rate and say it's too damn low and
> should be raised.

> Really, that is essentially their entire story. The only good thing
> about their story is that it is so easy to refute using standard
> macroeconomic and finance theory. But unfortunately, not
> even that seems to get them to shut up."[5]

Shut up? Maybe the hitch is that standard economic theory needs
to be freshened up a little by the clean sea breeze of the centuries. As a
fixed-income manager operating at a moment when interest rates are
at generational lows and the credit of the U.S. government is deemed
to be risk-free, maybe a little perspective might be in order. Inflation
will not be the friend of this manager. Even though it was sent away
for a while, relentless leaning against the Federal Reserve System and
U.S. Treasury balance sheets might be precisely the yeast that would
make it rise again. To use another analogy, expanding credit might be
like leaving filet mignon on your back patio and hoping the varmints
don't catch a whiff of it. If it isn't standard economic theory, then it's
plain old common sense. To claim that it simply doesn't exist in the

textbooks is to admit you are intentionally blind, for to see it would be to point the finger at those who are truly to blame for this mess. In the immortal words of the originator of the comic strip *Pogo*, Walt Kelly, "We have met the enemy . . . and he is us."

Wall Streeters who clamor for government intervention are like vultures eating at the financial carcass, but they would have us believe they are doctors trying to resuscitate the patient. The sharp difference on expected outcomes crafted by socialists and conservatives is attributable to how each estimates the behavioral aspects of the problem of moral hazard. The former ignore this effect, thus enhancing the chance of systemic destruction; the latter attempt to stave off disaster through strongly incentivizing market participants to be risk-proof. It may well be that the last stone in the foundation of the construction of the modern socialist state will be laid by the financial community, as it thinks nothing of surrendering its dominion to the government in a time of crisis. The call for a comprehensive government solution to the credit crisis is the ultimate temptation of moral hazard, for the certainty that unsuccessful financial ventures will always be healed by the public treasury creates a nation of financial participants who can pursue upside without the fear of financial ruin.

Following Karl Marx's observation that capitalists would hang themselves with their own rope, Cramer camouflages his desire to profit at the hand of government by declaring that he eschews politics. (However, he is likely quite left leaning, since the cofounder of TheStreet.com, Martin Peretz, is the editor-in-chief and chairman of *New Republic*, and the company's board of directors includes others who have been published in that same magazine.)[6] Content to be a bottom feeder in the socialist pond, he becomes no different from those who gladly accept the dole in lieu of earning a private-sector wage. He seeks profit that is garnered from someone else's wealth, but feels morally justified, since he did not ask for it (but he did indirectly by encouraging government help in front of millions of investors for months on end). Rather than avow to be apolitical, he might have told us he is immoral as well. This is the state of our culture. Cramer portrays a character on the plasma screen that is raw, brutally honest, and decisive, earning himself the mantle of the modern capitalist. By protesting political neutrality too much, to draw a parallel with Queen

Gertrude's famous quip in Hamlet, he reveals a buried inner compass that he himself does not know where it points. The rise of secularism has released the businessman from overlaying morality upon his decisions. Using government to make a fortune through the taking of little bits of the hard earned wealth dispersed among others is no longer a concern, and it is more a sure thing to boot, like finding a dollar laying on the pavement.

## The Socialist Incentive

The only antidote to the call to socialize credit risk is a change in attitudes about debt. To achieve this, the middle class must rethink the fundamental case for saving rather than extracting free money from credit. Much like an alcoholic coming to admit his addiction, such a rearrangement of inner values could not be possible through everyday thinking. It requires catharsis. Simply put, it is a better deal for a debt-laden middle-class homeowner to reduce his monthly payment and save for a down payment by walking away from his house and renting instead. It sounds unthinkable, but the few who are beginning to do this will be better off than those who reach out for the government lifeline, prolonging high payments for 30 years. The outcome would be a shorter recession, for the housing market would quickly readjust rather than suffer from the agonizing slow-motion erosion in prices and perpetually high inventories that are occurring today. Socialism's solution to the housing crisis is reminiscent of the Japanese perpetual recession, where a bear market in equities has run 19 years and counting.

The moral hazard that has been built into the nation's mortgage market is a function of the structure of the system, something that the liberal Keynesian economist Paul Krugman drives home in his nostalgic plea to return to a simpler, 1950s-style banking system. While this is true, it demotes the importance of Democrat-inspired programs that tilted the playing field to incentivize origination of mortgages on behalf of those with poor credit, and it also ignores the role of wrapping a government guarantee around this compromised product. When all is said and done, securitization and lack of regulation will be blamed for much of the trouble in the real estate market and the credit market in general. It is easy to see why. A putative cause of the credit melt-down was subprime lending, which was extended with abandon to low-income households. Conservatives are howling that this was done because of the Community Reinvestment Act (CRA), a program in existence for more than 30 years that suddenly exploded in size after reforms were put in place in 1995 during the Clinton administration. Indeed, one can see a direct link between the giant bank mergers of 1998, 2004, and 2008 and spikes in CRA commitments of approxi-mately $1 trillion or more in each of those years. Loans aggregated in securities, both those conforming to government standards for guaran-tee by Freddie and Fannie and those that did not, included low-income lending that would not pass muster in times when lending practices were more rational. The logic of calling for more regulation rests upon the desire to control the irrational behavior of borrowers and lenders that reached a crescendo in the years prior to the meltdown.

Who could not be struck by this archetypical case in affluent Irvine, CA, where in 2005 a family purchased a Mediterranean-style home for $1.1 million in a nearly 100 percent financed transaction, and later took down nearly a half-million dollars on a home equity line? Now upside down, the family seeks to forestall foreclosure, and it elicits sympathy from those who might bail it out.[7] Or take the even more politically charged case involving ACORN worker Donna Hanks. Her associates at ACORN helped her break into her home at 315 South Ellwood Avenue adjacent to Patterson Park in Baltimore while cam-eras for local television stations relayed the story to the city that the bank had arbitrarily raised her mortgage by $300, triggering foreclos-ure. Michelle Malkin scratched beneath the surface and found that Ms. Hanks had bought the house for $87,000 in 2001 and then refi-nanced it for $270,000 in the ensuing years, as reported on her web site www.michellemalkin.com in a story entitled *Document Drop: The Truth About ACORN's Foreclosure Poster Child*, posted on February 23, 2009. Hanks defaulted on her loans, but in September 2006 she negoti-ated a $340 monthly payment for arrears recognized in her bankruptcy filing, which she failed to subsequently make, leading to foreclosure in February 2008. So by the time of the break-in, the home had been sold to another individual, William Lane. The television coverage of the event made no mention of the background, but it featured interviews with the ACORN official, Louis Beverly, who says Hanks was a "victim of predatory lending," and that their break-in was an act of civil disobedience. He continues, "Legally homesteading is the only means left she has left to stay into her house, and we feel as though this is the right thing to do at this particular time to save this family." What about the $270,000 she extracted from the bank as a tax-free cash flow?

The traditional banking remedy is to recycle homes to other willing buyers, albeit at more rational prices, and condemn such risk-takers to the rental market. But with bankruptcy laws being watered down and other alternatives to it becoming widespread (see www.youwalkaway. com), where is the justice to savers and investors? When what would appear to be a bankruptcy in the Irvine situation is really a restructuring, doesn't this once again shift consequences to banks and taxpayers rather than those who walk away? How about in the case of Ms. Hanks' foreclosure, where ultimately depositors and taxpayers foot the bill? Unlike the Irvine family, taxpayers did not access nearly one-half-million dollars of tax-free money to spend from a home equity loan. And citizens who paid their mortgages also paid income taxes, while Ms. Hanks got to extract income from her property tax free. Why did Republicans join Democrats to vote for a solution that instantly attempts to shield such homeowners from the recapture of taxes? Moral hazard is not just a concept for economists; it involves real money. It not only transfers money from those who use it judiciously to those who are wanton, it orders holders of wealth to henceforth protect their capital by withdrawing it from countries that are stripping rationality from the investment market, to exchange it for gold, to short equities, and take other protective measures. What could be more damaging than creating the unpredictable circumstance where investors in short-term interest-bearing funds cannot be certain whether these will break the buck as liquidity is withdrawn?

*Bloomberg Magazine* authors Seth Lubove and Daniel Taub presciently depicted the regional corruption of credit in their portrayal of practices in southern California in an article titled "Subprime Fiasco Exposes Manipulation by Mortgage Brokers"dated May 30, 2007. They begin by relating the sudden transformation of a 27-year-old employee at Target, impressed by cars, girls, and cash being bandied about by his mortgage broker friend, who joins Secured Funding, one of several subprime originators based in California that collectively wrote 40 percent of the nation's subprime loans for several years. Before the bubble burst, some 600,000 brokers had been extending mortgages to people with lousy credit, touting how they could extract cash up front or consolidate loans and reduce monthly payments. The system would not work without being able to upstream the mortgages into securities that would be guaranteed by government-sponsored entities or held by large banks compelled to satisfy CRA regulations. Ignoring that CRA regulations and intervention caused the problem, most observers conclude that better regulation would have averted the problem. They would prohibit low-doc or no-doc loans, known as "liar's loans." However, they would probably see no ill in continuing the redistributive aims of the CRA, which dilute qualification hurdles for low incomes.

Substantial funds for community activist groups were included in the bailout signed into law in February 2009, signaling increased emphasis on low-income lending and subsidization through regulation. In response to the crisis, voters chose to sweep the transgressions of Fannie Mae and Freddie Mac under the rug, believing the public good would be served by preserving these entities and also by the redistribution of wealth implicit in the CRA mandate. Their footprint in the marketplace would be expanded forcefully through the crisis. What was left of the good credit of the federal government was used to undercut private lending with government-subsidized mortgages, leaving a bifurcated market of readily available 4 percent loans for borrowers seeking these loans, while jumbo mortgages became hard to get at 8 percent. Moreover, shortly after year-end 2008 the banking system was poised to be nationalized, which likewise might promote wealth distribution through differentiating interest rates and credit requirements according to need rather than ability to pay.

In reality the structure of securitization proved to be toxic because it separated the role of credit gatherers and investors. One might argue that had banks been forced to eat their own cooking, they would not have relied on bucket shops in Irvine, California to originate mortgages. Yet banks owned the paper that rolled up these loans, and they also owned subprime assets. So there was an element of speculation at fault that simultaneously infected borrowers and lenders, which can only be attributed to an out-of-control monetary system in general, where the central authority watching over monetary expansion was politically unable to reduce growth in broad money from double-digit rates to low single-digit growth where it belongs. Moreover, academically they steadfastly believe that controlling money supply expansion is imprudent, preferring to inflation target instead. Fixing the system with additional regulation and encouraging more credit to be soaked up through the banking sector is fatally flawed. Securitization per se was a contributing factor, but not the primary cause of the meltdown.

## Forced to Accept Risk

Even before the financial crisis of 2008 arose, there were signs that the operation of a centrally managed fiat currency system was creating stress. Consider the dilemma of retirement. On one hand, many might not have saved much, because throughout life government had stepped in to take care of every need from health care, elder care, child care, tuition, or even to make unaffordable mortgages affordable. With fallbacks like these where is the incentive to spend within one's means? But putting aside these and other reasons why one might have saved only a few percent of income annually (as is the national average), what circumstance were baby boomers in by the turn of the last century? Someone with a salary of $100,000 might have saved $1,000 each year early on, rising to perhaps $10,000 annually or more near retirement. With compounding, that might have produced a nest egg worth $200,000, assuming no taxes (FV30 of $1,000 at 7% equals $94,000). What would one have done with this upon retiring? Investing in safe CDs would provide only $10,000 of annual income at 5 percent. But then twice in the last decade the central bank has dropped interest rates to nearly zero. Bonds would yield only a little bit more.

So without much income, stocks would have been the best alternative, because studies of long-term total return suggested 10 percent was obtainable. However, the first decade of the new century is likely to close with having provided a negative return, regardless of whether the consensus opinion that economic recovery would lift the equity market in 2009 or 2010 pans out. Moreover, there is inflation to consider. The persistent printing of money, which averaged about 7 percent since the founding of the Fed nearly 100 years ago, accelerated to over 8 percent since Nixon went off gold in 1971. Besides converting what would have been organic deflation into manufactured inflation of roughly 4.5 percent on average from 1971 to 2008, generally this increase in bank money has pumped up the value of assets, especially real estate and equities. Moreover, the value of stocks was pushed higher by expanding the presence of the financial sector within the S&P 500 to nearly 40 percent of earnings, clearly an unnatural phenomenon. The expansion of credit to unheard of levels tended to inflate earnings per share through putting the economy on steroids and from machinations such as share buybacks. Looking at a longer time frame, equity investors were cautious after a similar debt bubble was pricked by the end of the 1930s, demanding dividend yields in excess of long dated bonds in the early 1950s. By the turn of the century, yields were down to near 1 percent.

The bottom line for those who might retire is that manipulation of the money supply first drives the populace (and the pensions held by investment managers) to not hold cash due to taxes and inflation. Then it presents an unappetizing alternative of low-yielding bonds that similarly are ravaged by these two factors. Finally it pushes everyone into equities in desperation. Excessive money supply growth distorts the earnings the underlying corporations achieve and puffs up the valuation of those same earnings, a double whammy that magnifies risk. The aftermath is now ugly, with nest eggs reduced, taxes increasing, inflation probable, and the risk of a generational depression palpable but now downplayed by a financial community whose forecasting and analysis blows with the latest breeze.

Consider the risk that no one wishes to discuss, which is the failure of the U.S. government. Today the only safe haven is investing in debt obligations of the U.S. Treasury, which define the risk-free rate. This solidarity has been unquestioned since the passage of the Sixteenth Amendment in 1913, which granted the Treasury Department unlimited power to confiscate the private property of its citizens. The next chapter, "Faux Class Warfare," will argue that taxation may have reached its upper limit of productivity in the United States, just as it has in other socialist regimes. With $2 million of government GAAP liability per household to be borne by the few brackets held responsible for generating the nation's tax revenue, the government itself may have reached the end of its ability to pick up the tab for the products of the moral hazard it has encouraged.

The fiat era was successful as long as government had capacity remaining in its credit line. When the Great Depression hit in the 1930s, government would quench an ailing economy's need for liquidity as easily as if it were filling an empty glass with a bottle of Coca-Cola. After the go-go years of the 1960s and the increased spending for the Vietnam War and Johnson-era programs, it could pour the soda into a half-filled glass. The high tax rates of the 1970s similarly would not bankrupt the system yet, because growing into unused debt capacity produced inflationary gains for holders of assets, which would be deferred of taxation. After the Internet bubble, pouring in the Coca-Cola produced much fizz and displaced little emptiness. Today, correcting the failure of a second or third tier investment bank is a tedious exercise of trying to finish filling the cup to the brim without causing a mess all over the table. Bear Stearns and Lehman were large, but not dominant forces in 2008. Their failure at any other time would have been easily contained. Some 38 percent of total deposits nationwide of $7 trillion were uninsured because they exceed the $100,000 limit, yet less than 15 years ago only 23 percent were.[8] With the passage of TARP, the ceiling was reset at $250,000, but this leaves 27 percent of depositor funds unprotected.[9] With money market funds losing assets, it is possible that new deposits above the limit could enter the banking system.

Since the Great Depression, credit grew relative to GDP by an order of magnitude. Private debt was just 57 percent of GDP in 1944, with only 14 percent of this being mortgages. By 1954 it would be 71 percent, with 28 percent of this financing residential dwellings. These statistics would not skip a beat in the 1970s, despite a shakeout in the stock market, because inflation would be raging. By 1984, private debt rose to 140 percent of the economy; you could trend-line it right up to over 300 percent by 2007. If during the 25-year or so final blow-off stage one decided to bet against the house, figuratively or literally, one would lose. If one plunged in to buy real estate at any time during the upswing, chances are he would feel pretty good about his investment. Anyone with a sense of caution would have kicked themselves for having delayed a purchase of this essential building block of life (See Figure 6.1).

Although so far this example deals with real estate, partly because it is so vital to everyday living, the same could be said for stocks; during the great bull market any delays to buy were fatal errors. You would be told to buy on dips, to dollar cost average. Academics ranging from Roger Ibbotson to Jeremy Siegel would assure you that over the long run, stocks would outperform every other asset; the mean annual return of large company equities was over 10 percent from 1925 to 2007, with a standard deviation of just 20 percent. Small company returns were even plumper, but there was more risk.[10]

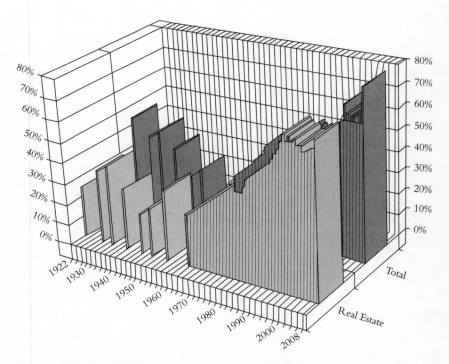

**Figure 6.1    Rising Private Sector Leverage: Loan Balance as a Percentage of Collateral Value**
*Source:* Historical Statistics of the United States: National Wealth by type of Asset 1850-1956 (Series F 197-221) and Net Public and Private Debt, by Major Sectors: 1916-1957; 1900-1958. Federal Reserve, Flow of Funds Accounts of the United States: 1955-1964, Annual Releases.

What changed over the last century? One hundred years ago government was small, money was hard, and leverage could be found and used, but it was costly in real terms since there was deflation most times. Then came the Fed: Money was cheap. Although there were slumps, asset values, unlike trees, actually did grow to the sky. In the 19th century you might not be a loser if you waited to buy a house, horse, or commodity. In the 20th century, if you didn't buy it fast, and even use debt to do it, your relative position weakened. In the former, one was free. In the latter one was forced to act, or else. At some point the buildup of credit would bring on a complete, utter collapse. It happened in the early 1930s, causing misery after debt rose to 185 percent of GDP by 1929 (to be increased by government borrowing to finance a recovery that wasn't). In 2008, debt hit 364 percent of GDP. Might not the practice of having an expansive central bank be like loading up one round in a revolver's cylinder, say one with 50 or so holes, and pulling the trigger once per year while pointing it to the cranium of the banking system? Eventually too much debt will wreak havoc, whether or not inflation is evident in the years close to the day of reckoning. (In fact, there was deflation in the 1920s.) And like the legendarily lethal game of chance played by Russian soldiers or their prisoners, fatality would be inevitable.

Although the Austrian view of credit explains the above perfectly, it does little to address the moral shortcoming of having imposed such a system upon the entire population, and especially the baby boomers who accumulated their life savings only to see them wiped out as they enter retirement age. True, everyone should have seen this coming and refused to leverage up their balance sheet. But most instead took out mortgages on the right hand side and accumulated mutual funds on the left hand side, assuming they would save at all with the complimentary moral hazard of reliance upon state services from Medicare to Social Security. Extremely strong and persistent incentives were codified into law that undermined any attempt by the citizenry to avoid debt, stocks, or real estate. The result is that out of a sense of equity we now find ourselves in the messy predicament of engaging in wholesale printing of money directly and outside the banking sector, which favors statist interests over the private sector, and further erodes any wealth left in the upper-middle class among those who were prudent in the face of central bank seduction. Contrary to the Austrian orthodoxy, it may be necessary to favor debtors over creditors slightly in acknowledgement of the perversity imposed on the American people, which was perpetuated through economic ignorance. But ultimately the entire system must be dismantled and replaced with a gold-backed currency, because two wrongs do not make a right. Otherwise, the heavy handed actions of the Fed and the Treasury in this cycle will send a clear message that reckless financial institutions and borrowers alike will never have cause to avoid risk.

## Fiat Currency—Not Yet a Mainstream Conservative Issue

Unfortunately, the conservative community is largely unaware that the extraordinary debasement of our currency through pyramiding credit upon a baseless reserve was the principal driver of the multigenerational meltdown that began in 2008. When the money markets seized up after AIG and Lehman went under in September 2008, the possibility that the whole financial system could implode seemed even more real than it did after the Bear Stearns rescue or the nationalization of the GSEs. At that moment conservative thinkers such as Rush Limbaugh had to confront the fundamental nature of the problem, but they came to the wrong conclusion. One problem is that they are by and large unschooled in monetary policy and in the ways of fiat currency in particular. It's hardly unusual; most Americans are equally unaware. The curricula of top-tier business schools or undergraduate economics departments typically do not include any discussion of the theoretical underpinnings of fiat currencies compared to metal-backed money. Such thinking was drummed out of mainstream academia generations ago, reserved for scorn to be heaped upon it by Nobel laureates. In his September 25, 2008 monologue Rush recounted, "Snerdley (one of the program's producers) came in today and said, "I have never worked harder in my life trying to understand this financial thing. I've been spending more time this past week working on trying to understand this. 'Cause this is all Greek, all this lingo jingo they use, talking about these derivatives and the credit swaps.'"[12]

Another problem is that they are surveying the opinions of knowledgeable Wall Streeters. As described in the first chapter of the book,

these people view the world through the lens of evidence-based observation, which focuses them on the post-war experience of recessions
and monetary stimulation rather than upon the systemic change that
has gradually occurred after a century of socializing credit and fiscal
policy simultaneously. Reports Limbaugh in his program:

> Now, in looking into the financial mess, as I said at the begin-
> ning of the program, who do you trust here? It's simply too
> massive and there are too many opinions. I mean, you can go
> certain places and you can find a conservative and say, "I've
> been talking to the smartest people in the room, and they tell
> me, you know, we gotta do this and we gotta do that now and
> if we don't do it we're in big trouble." And other people saying,
> "Well, you know I've been talking to the smartest people in the
> room and they say this is a disaster waiting to happen, and if we
> do this we're going to be paying for the rest of our lives and
> we're going to end up with socialized, nationalized everything,"
> and other people are saying, "I've talked to the smartest people
> in the room about this, and one thing I have understood, yeah,
> we gotta be conservatives and we gotta be conservatives first,
> but this trumps conservatism." And that's the one that got me
> because, for me, nothing trumps conservatism." There are ways
> of dealing with this that do not have to include total socializa-
> tion of the market process or the nationalization of the mort-
> gage industry.[13]

It is simply human nature that these observers will extrapolate
recent experience rather than look at the fundamental underpinnings
of the problem. Who could blame them? Their fathers and grandfathers
lived under this system, and it has worked until now when the amount
of leverage and taxation has been stretched to a breaking point. Sure,
while there is room for more government spending and layering on of
additional leverage, the solution is to expand it more.

Limbaugh's instinct is, as usual, dead-on in that there should be a
conservative solution that does not involve massive nationalization of
the mortgage industry and the financial sector in general. But already the
trade has hit the tape. The GSEs *are* nationalized, the large investment
banks have abandoned their business model and are trying to become

commercial banks, and the U.S. Treasury and the Fed are set to give everybody a mulligan. The top 19 commercial banks are now explicitly backstopped from failure. Many if not most may still be nationalized should the crisis worsen beyond the assumptions of the not-so-stressful "stress test" regulators conducted in early 2009. Here is where Limbaugh veers away from conservatism: He quotes former hedge fund manager and Morgan Stanley semiconductor analyst Andy Kessler, who projects that the U.S. government will *profit* by as much as $2.2 trillion from its ownership of mortgages and derivatives obtained through the GSEs and the TARP bailout facility. Kessler may indeed be correct, and he hints that this would happen because ". . . the Treasury and the Federal Reserve get to cheat . . . with lots of levers (they) can and will pump capital into the U.S. economy to get it moving again. Future heads of Treasury and the Federal Reserve will be growth advocates—in effect, 'talking their book.' While normally this creates a threat of inflation and a run on the dollar, and we may see dollar exchange rates turn south near term, don't expect it to last."[14]

Kessler also describes how institutions were highly leveraged and owned speculative derivatives at the bottom of the seniority ladder. He laments this permitted hedge funds to opportunistically capitalize upon this weakness (shorting bank stocks), because FASB Rule 157 would demand that the banks mark these assets to market values, even in a liquidity-starved environment. Limbaugh falls into the trap of thinking that an accounting change combined with a raid by short-sellers brought down the financial system, and recommended that we go back to the historical cost accounting—which would prevent recognition of impaired value. But it would not unwind the decades of layering more and more debt onto the private and public sectors. Limbaugh says: "So rather than being able to peg asset value down the road, you have to peg it to asset value today. And that's why some of these firms are going under, because the value of what they hold is so little, that their stock prices plummeted, nobody wants to invest in them—simply because of an accounting change! That's another thing that's gotta be done away with. Go back to the old … accounting rules, get rid of mark-to-market."[15] By March 2009 market valuation would be abandoned, permitting banks to claim profitability had been restored, despite rising defaults and delinquencies.

What Kessler envisions is simply a repeat of what has happened after each great buildup in debt that has occurred in the past. But each of these events has been associated with the financing of a war, and back then there was ample debt and taxation capacity backing the government's effort to reflate. This time the leverage has been slowly accumulated and compounded over time because of cultural changes that have encouraged reckless lending and borrowing, and likewise the government sector cannot control spending or refrain from intruding upon the free market.

Inserting a newer, shinier penny into the fuse box might resume the inflation of assets, reward moral hazard, and reset the government spending pump, but success would require unlimited tolerance for taking on debt among the populace. As with any economic model, the logic of it may be enchanting, but the assumptions from which it was constructed are what make or break it. The assumption has been that a long-term rise in credit is sustainable or irrelevant (since it has had no effect for decades). Now that the panic of 2008 may have taught us that it may be extremely germane, we must ask this: What is the best course of escape from a policymaker's perspective? Moreover, would whatever option chosen be fair and likely to promote healthy economic behavior over time?

The solution was unknown or beyond the bounds of discussion to conservatives such as Limbaugh before the crisis. It remains theoretical, poorly understood, and hardly agreed upon. Imposing a flawed gold standard upon the world as in the interwar era could be devastating, for initially it could peg currencies at distortive foreign exchange rates or embody excessive leverage if nations use the dollar as their central bank reserve instead of gold. It could lull theoreticians into believing a solution is at hand while an essential reparative measure such as ending monopoly control over the money supply, free metallism, or free banking might have provided more beneficial effects. Free banking as advocated by the likes of economist George Selgin does not necessarily require precious metal as the basis for reserves. Instead, it stresses the decentralization of loan making and the role of imperiling shareholder's capital at banks that issue too many notes. Selgin appears agnostic about a reserve medium, but reading between the lines, perhaps concluding too hastily, gold would be the most congruent with his free market ideology.

To think that somehow we can maintain the structure of socialized money, taxation, and government spending and have the Fed cure our problems by putting a penny in the fuse box may be to ignore the rot in the entire structure, and whether it is capable of holding up under another wave of socialism. The panic that began in 2008 may continue to produce results outside the statistical boundaries established in recent decades, providing evidence-based thinkers with new data with which they can extrapolate the future. The historical trend of cruising forward painlessly under a managed fiat currency system would be decisively broken. At some point those who are both conservatives and "the smartest guys in the room" are likely to notice a new pattern and bring into the political sphere the possibility of altering the present monetary system.

The danger is that the mainstream opinion leaders, including the media, look at the new evidence and conclude that capitalism is broken and more socialism is needed. It is the task of conservatives like Limbaugh and his sidekick Snerdley to feel the fresh breeze of the centuries blowing our way and articulate an element of the conservative message that has been repressed since the Great Depression at best, rather than permitting the babble of a roomful of smart conservatives to maintain a splintered, incoherent message while socialists give the financial system a bear hug.

Limbaugh may be correct nearly 100 percent of the time as he boasts, but espousing economic views such as Kessler's might put a ding in his track record. He and others such as Sean Hannity may be right to criticize Democrats for fanning economic fears for political gain. But the market is bigger than even its mightiest participants, much less radio talk show hosts, and its direction will be determined by the movement of the aggregation of tens of trillions of dollars, euros, and other stores of wealth, an inherently unpredictable organism. In the meantime, there are signs that some in the conservative community are keying in on the systemic nature of our financial problems, and how the ideology of socialism and cultural change have ushered in the present instability. Mark Levin, the "Great One," had been spot on for months before the crisis, but even he has (perhaps wisely) avoided prognosticating about solutions, the great choice being between deflation or reflation. In mid-December, Rush Limbaugh devoted much of his initial two hours of a broadcast to the phenomenon of credit and money, which elicited a cry for relief from the dismal science of economics via listener email that implored him to move on to the more entertaining discussion of Caroline Kennedy's senatorial aspirations.[16] To his credit, Rush mused about the effect of excessive debt and briefly wondered whether another monetary system, perhaps even one involving gold, might be preferred. On December 26, 2008, another conservative talk show host, Bob Grant, startled the Mark Levin Show's audience, which is accustomed to hearing disparagement of Ron Paul, when as a guest host he told a caller, "I apologize to Ron Paul ... I did not recognize along with everybody else, I did not recognize during the heat of the primary campaign, that Ron Paul was correct. He was the only one who warned about what was going to happen."

Meanwhile, the GOP, which lost its bearings and presented a presidential candidate in 2008 who espoused a grab bag of conservative and liberal ideals, continues to fall for the trap of detaching more middle-income households from the necessity of paying taxes to woo votes. In the bid to regain earth scorched in the 2008 election cycle, Republican economic strategist Cesar Conda, Dick Cheney's former chief domestic advisor, proclaimed: " . . . instead of calling for a flat tax or a retail sales tax, which will never happen in our lifetimes, how about cutting the middle-income tax bracket from 25 percent to 15 percent, which means most people would pay a flat 15 percent tax? . . . Or how about treating investments in human capital the same as investments in physical capital by allowing taxpayers to deduct all educational expenses? Our party can't simply rehash the Reagan 1980s; we need a future-oriented economic agenda."[17]

Such thinking comes from the same template that not only caused Republicans to veer from principles, it hollowed out the middle class by placing nearly all of the burden of paying for the government upon an entrepreneurial minority, something that did not even occur under Franklin Roosevelt.

It may simply be possible that we muddle through the financial crisis and that placing the penny in the fuse box averts disaster. But on the other hand, it is far more likely that history is being made. The great conservative voices of our time can choose to weigh in on the topic or be curiously absent and spoken over by the voices of the left, as if they were having a bad day as a guest on *Hardball* or some other one-on-one political TV segment.

Although by and large today's most visible conservative thought leaders articulate the dangers of socialism well, their failure to concentrate upon the need to dismantle the technocratic state as well as their rudimentary understanding of the monetary system and its history is an Achilles heel. Worse, knowing full well the unreliability of economic forecasting, in the period leading up to the 2008 election they became whiners about the press highlighting deteriorating business conditions and they acted as cheerleaders for economic recovery, only to reverse this posturing once Obama was elected. Moreover, they have chastised those who raised concerns about the stability of the financial system. Now that the evidence of a new financial disorder is accumulating, they will remain ideologically lost unless they come to understand the true implications of complimenting big government with big central banking. Sadly for conservatives, cheerleading walks into the trap set by the liberals. Recessions do happen. They are not always contemporaneous with the policies of administrations or Fed governors. Like their brothers in the financial arena, conservative political pundits' understanding of monetary and fiscal policy is clouded by the mist of soft recessions and the slow debasement of capital by the inadequately restrained credit that is possible with fiat currency.

Some liberal political observers use evidence of pricked bubbles as fodder for Bush-hating rhetoric and to promote the change Obama has promised. But bubbles are good, say most free marketers. Even noted contributor to the liberal magazine *Slate*, Daniel Gross, chimed in last year with a book entitled *Pop! Why Bubbles are Good for the Economy*, perhaps pandering to the Silicon Valley wing of the Democratic party. Out of ignorance, both the left and right can agree they like the false wealth of fiat currency, and at the same time the populace can find electable a candidate who ostensibly is against bubbles, but illogically promises to cure their ill effect through fiscal expansion, accommodative extension of credit, and socialization of risk. Great leadership has a habit of appearing at our darkest moments. Unfortunately, neither may have happened yet.

# Part Three

# FAUX CLASS WARFARE

In recent times economists and media observers have used income statistics to make the case that there is a widening gap between rich and poor. Statistics, as the saying goes, can be tortured and they will say anything. There is no doubt that income inequality has developed to some extent since the 1950s. It may be attributed to the rising returns on human effort aided by education combined with technology or by opportunities created by the "tournament effect," as described by Nassim Taleb. But income inequality might mainly be attributable to fiat currencies having spawned massive profitability to those involved in the financial markets, which by 2007 accounted for nearly 40 percent of the operating earnings of the S&P 500. Meanwhile, the bottom rungs of wage earners have seen their earnings held in check. A wave of immigration that has once again lifted the foreign born to a double digit percentage of the population, a phenomena not seen since nearly a century ago, creating competition for menial jobs. Also, inner cities with concentrations of African American population have decayed. In part this is due to cultural influences such as susceptibility to crime and drugs, but also these areas have been "surprisingly" unresponsive to the infusion of government assistance that began under Johnson's Great Society. Their public schools have failed to graduate students with basic skill sets, and dropout rates approach 50 percent in these areas.

Regardless of the reasons, the rising gap has provided political advantage to those who favor socialism, and it has played a broad role in moving the political needle to the left in recent years, even within the Republican political party. This part of the book, "Faux Class Warfare," takes an alternative perspective to this classic debate by making the case that the centrally managed fiat currency system has interacted with a tax code that confiscates earned income rather than wealth, potentially producing a knockout punch to entrepreneurship, our society, and our national destiny as envisioned by the founders. The combination explains the emergence of a disturbing trend of ensconcing a powerful, lightly taxed elite at the top, which like the aristocracy of Rome did, supports an agenda that places the maximal burden upon not the middle class, but the upper-middle class, the biggest threat to its hegemony. This elite poses as a champion of the downtrodden and often leans left in the political spectrum. Make no mistake: This posturing is not done out of egalitarianism. In support of this thesis some of the first chapter of Part 3 probes the role of the fiat currency system in enriching the elite largely free of taxation, and it closes with an accounting showing nearly half its ranks then choose to wield their influence upon liberal politicians.

The second chapter analyzes how inflation has affected tax brackets since Roosevelt's time, tracing the burden to the present in cost of living adjusted terms. Today the typical upper-middle class professional couple gets captured by the topmost income tax bracket. Remarkably, during the punitive tax structure imposed in the Great Depression, which by design was installed to soak the rich, the burden on such a couple would have only been 17 percent. This income strata is further examined on an all-in basis to reflect other taxes, which by death causes its estates to be liquidated with a fraction of their accumulated lifetime income actually passed on to the next generation. Hence, that chapter is aptly named "Sharecroppers." In this exercise, a conclusive case is made that these socialist policies have tapped out the wealth of the upper-middle class, a group that is solely capable of funding our bloated government and its entitlement promises. However, its ability to pay is exceeded to such an extent that the U.S. government is bankrupt by any rational calculation.

# Chapter 7

# The Rich are Different from You and Me

*"Let me tell you about the very rich. They are different from you and me. They possess and enjoy early, and it does something to them, makes them soft, where we are hard, cynical where we are trustful, in a way that, unless you were born rich, is very difficult to understand.*

F. SCOTT FITZGERALD, *THE RICH BOY*, 1926.[1]

I f you were a billionaire, what sort of system would you want? Suppose you could, through a fiat currency system, ensure that your assets nearly always increased in value gently. You could borrow against companies or assets you own, taking advantage of artificially low interest rates set by the central bank and extract cash without having to declare taxable dividends or realize capital gains from stock sales. Or you could lever up within your corporations or partnerships to make use of tax deductibility, depending upon what is best for you. While there is an interest expense, it nearly always is exceeded by a rise in the value of your assets, which is driven by rigorous monetary production inherent in the fractional reserve banking system. At the same time, the risk of using leverage could be reduced by using derivatives to hedge the underlying cash flows of your business backing the loans. The only things stopping you are your confidence level in the correlation between these hedges with their underlying asset and the potential counterparty risk from those taking the opposite side of your derivatives. You could use this sophisticated ATM machine to buy your estates in the Hamptons, private islands, or castles in the Alps. You would pay almost no income tax, save that your corporations pay to the extent they are not leveraged and hedged. Even that can be attenuated through the use of offshore havens. Then you would loudly sing support for the common man by calling upon government to raise the individual income tax, and you would magnanimously call for more bread and circuses for the masses. Another key part of the PR campaign would be to project a philanthropic image through several high-profile donations. In this way you would replicate the behavior of the senatorial class in ancient Rome, which also paid no taxes but was expected to contribute to the public good by building the occasional wall or aqueduct, which would be sure to impress the citizenry and prove one's worth in the patronage system.

What is your nightmare? The revolt of the upper-middle class, an assemblage like that which became the origin of modern representative government: the nobles in 1215 who forced King John to sign the Magna Charta Libertatum—literally the "Great Charter of Freedoms." This distributed some monarchical power to a band of barons, but more importantly it limited the king's abuse of scutage, which he had transformed almost entirely into a tax. Another nightmare is that the moral hazard created by the socialization of money inherent in a fiat currency system might, upon a crisis, require the printing of new credit to more than replace what has turned sour, including the ability of the government to make good on its debt. For no longer would there be a gentle wind pushing your assets ever higher, and low interest rates against which you would be charged to extract cash from the system. This outcome would be a nightmare for many. Would it be poignant enough to the nobles who might go calling upon King Obama or his successors to demand an end to the tax manipulation possible through a fiat system by tethering it to gold?

In some ways the socialism of the Western World resembles the monarchical systems that predated the mercantile era. But instead of a king, there is a loose oligarchy of ideologue politicians who bestow favors to and receive funding from a thin layer of elites. Part of the bargain is to institutionalize the stripping away of the estates of the lesser nobility (the upper-middle class). If these lesser nobles were allowed to gain power, they would surely restore republican rule, with a small "r," which would rock the boat of vested interests. They would shrink big government. Without taxation and regulation, they would ruthlessly and industriously build and create enterprises that might muscle aside big businesses. They would let bloated financial institutions fail (but depositors might be spared) and allow smaller institutions that eschewed risk to gain market share. As for the peasants in the lower class, the legislators of today, both Democrat and Republican, appease them by requiring only a token amount of taxes and returning many times these funds in the form of government largesse. Call it democracy, call it progressive, call it liberal, call it just, but today we dare not call it anything save what it is: socialism.

## Never Realize a Gain

The most interesting thing about the fiat money system is that if culture does not corrupt it, it provides a gentle wind to lift asset prices. If one has accumulated massive wealth, one can use the fiat credit system to borrow against it and not trigger taxes much the same way that the middle class extracted wealth from their rising home values through home equity loans during the real estate bubble. Billionaires don't usually have much W-2 income. If they need cash for lavish lifestyles, they can borrow against the assets they own, and it is better yet if the Fed accommodates this with easy credit. They even get a tax deduction for the interest expense if it's done within a corporate structure. They can lever up nowadays by quite a bit, because the risk that the assets backing the loan to them decline can be laid off in derivatives contracts. Why should they do this? The capital gains tax rate may be low (15 percent in 2008 and an increase being debated), but if the cost basis of the business you founded 30 years ago is near zero, even 15 percent or 20 percent can be a lot of dollars. Why not see this basis get written up upon death and avoid the gains tax entirely? There is a whole industry that exists to facilitate such tax avoidance. Consider the services of one Sidley Austin LLP, a law firm with large offices in New York and Chicago, but really so spread around the world that on its web site there is no mention of one headquarters anywhere attributable to any of its 16 global locations:

> Our lawyers advise clients in structuring and implementing various types of complex derivative financial instruments and products in the most efficient manner as a means of providing alternative economic investments, *monetizing existing financial positions, providing leverage, hedging economic and business exposure risk* and otherwise fulfilling their clients' particular business, economic and investment needs. These derivative financial instruments and products include swaps, options, warrants, futures contracts, short sale strategies, notional principal contracts, structured notes, debt instruments, and numerous other innovative financial products that are linked to (and derive their value from) various equities, currencies, commodities, interest rates, indicies, debt instruments, credit exposures, weather patterns, and other properties, economic conditions, and risks.[2]

It just so happens that this law firm was where Michelle Obama met Bernadine Dorn, a founder of the Weatherman group, which bombed federal buildings and police stations in the 1970s. Dorn worked there from 1984 to 1988, and was hired by Howard Trienans, head of the firm at that time, who reportedly said, "We often hire friends."[3] It is also where Barack Obama met Michelle. On their first date they saw a Spike Lee movie, "Do the Right Thing."

Lest one wonder how often these contracts are used, there are over $500 trillion of them in force in this private market whose precise size is hard to estimate.[4] This is quite a bit larger than the estimated value of world GDP ($30 trillion), or world real estate ($50 trillion).[5] The pros at Goldman Sachs or J.P. Morgan will monitor the effectiveness of the hedging through tracking covariance of the hedge with the underlying asset, and calculating "value-at-risk," a statistical measure that uses standard deviation to bracket the range of normally expected outcomes—based upon historical data, which is derived from markets that have behaved well at least up until recent times. The average Joe doesn't participate in the derivatives market, and he has little idea that the billionaires at the top use it for tax avoidance. Sadly, he will lash out at the upper-middle class and demand higher taxes on ordinary income, almost none of which will touch the super wealthy.

President Obama and many Democrats propose to eliminate the preferential capital gains tax rate, but in 2009 they instead moved to raise this and the top income bracket by roughly 5 percent. Ordinary income would be more heavily taxed, at 39.6 percent compared to 20 percent for capital gains and dividends. At first glance there indeed appears to be some inequity caused by this; within the 138 million households filing taxes, there is an elite of some 41,000 households whose income of over $5 million comes as much from capital gains as it does ordinary income. Obviously the farther above the $357,700 threshold of the top ordinary income bracket one gets, the less ordinary income is a factor for this group. It is probably safe to assume that this set is not made up of day traders, and that the turnover of their holdings is held low due to a high representation of direct corporate ownership. (Much of their wealth resides in private companies or real estate.) So the capital gains realized are probably low in proportion to unrealized annual gains. This structural underpinning is what gives this group the flexibility to defer taking gains or to borrow within corporate structures (which is deductible) or outside of them (which is not). They may also pay dividends, which would be subject to 20 percent as well, but that rate is seen as a companion to the capital gains rate should there be any tax legislation.

Raising the capital gains tax in an effort to instill equity or generate tax revenue would be about as effective as swatting a fly with a bare hand. If the top bracket paid taxes evenly at 39.6 percent, its average rate would rise by 10 percent, yielding approximately $135 billion to the U.S. Treasury. But in reality the structural flexibility to defer gains implies that few if any dollars would be raised by the IRS if the capital gains preference were eliminated. In a fiat system of gentle inflation, most profits are never realized. They can be monetized through borrowing and derivatives, thus never having any tax rate applied to payouts. In fact, the incentive to extract capital through the tax-free mechanism of borrowing would become greater with a higher tax bite. Indeed, the unexpected inflows of tax revenue seen when Bush 43 *lowered* the capital gains tax rate, which was predicted by supply-side economists, tapped in to the desire to exchange assets and rebalance portfolios in this select group of ultrawealthy, as well as in the greater population. In 1995, the Treasury collected $14.2 billion of capital gains tax, and the maximum rate was 28 percent. By 2000, a peak year for the stock market, it only collected $1 billion. After tax reform kicked in, collections soared to $33 billion in 2003 (near the bottom of a bear market) and $55 billion the year after.

The bottom line is that raising the capital gains tax would hurt the upper-middle class, which might need to sell publicly traded stock from time to time, but billionaires would opt to cease making transactions other than tax-free exchanges, often facilitated by derivatives. For this reason, a wealth tax might be the only fair tax system possible. It would fail if it were not inclusive of all pools of wealth, especially those that enjoy freedom from taxation today, because that status has been overextended. Moreover, all other taxes would need to be abolished. Another weak point is that money might evade it by moving offshore (depending how it is legislated). But rightfully a government should only be able to tax that which rests inside its domain anyway. If those funds can earn a higher return elsewhere, so be it. Most likely, there would be massive capital *inflows* to the United States if a small wealth tax of say 1 percent replaced the income tax, because the marginal rate of taxation on income would fall to zero here, which compares very favorably to regular rates elsewhere. If the average pretax rate of return on capital employed is north of 20 percent generally, then a 1 percent tax rate would be the equivalent to a 5 percent income tax.

Double taxation still exists. It is essential to appreciate that those who pay capital gains are doing so on money that is residual to the prior application of corporate or individual tax rates—unless that individual hails from the über-rich and can make use of borrowing or derivatives or perhaps even a foreign tax haven. To enjoy the low capital gains tax rate, such assets typically exist in a structure such as a domestic C-corporation or a commercial real estate direct investment or partnership. The former is taxed at a 35 percent rate pretty much across the board, and the latter would generate rental income subject to the regular tax table. There are many who are not part of the super wealthy who have small businesses or a small plot of second tier commercial real estate that might need to be sold, perhaps due to divorce, a change in financial condition, or use for another investment, or to simply spend and enjoy. They will be the ones who will be swatted by the bare hand of the IRS at the higher rate should it be placed into effect, because such sales by supposition are unavoidable. The income from these assets would have been taxed annually at the individual tax rate in the years preceding their sale.

## Income Tax: A Billionaire's Best Friend

A sickening twist to the income and wealth distinction is the political manipulation of the debate commonly seen from the liberal über-wealthy elite. Some, such as Silicon Valley executives Jerry Yang (Yahoo), Steve Jobs (Apple), Larry Page (Google), and Sergey Brin (Google), pay themselves just $1 of W-2 income, but each year they may accrue millions or even billions of dollars of unrealized capital gain. Once a certain threshold of wealth is achieved, taxpayers have some latitude in structuring when and where income originates, reclassifying it in such a way as to minimize and defer taxation.

Tycoons such as Soros and Buffett can call for higher taxation of *income*. This is a very cynical and downright mendacious strategy, for they know full well this burden would fall primarily upon members of the upper-middle class, who have not yet achieved the threshold that would permit them to shift income to tax-minimizing structures. Rubbing salt into the wound is their rhetoric that such appeals improve fairness, and their accusations that payers in the upper bracket are unjustly rich and are therefore deserving of funding the brunt of increased government. Buffett is also a particularly vocal proponent of the death tax, and his company (Berkshire Hathaway) is one of the largest buyers of family businesses that wind up on the auction block when founders die and the heirs choose to sell to fund the tax.[6]

Commercial real estate possesses special characteristics that enable its owners to pit the taxation system against the policies of the Federal Reserve System and avoid massive amounts of taxation. An important component historically to commercial real estate investment returns has been appreciation of value. This component can be magnified many times over through the use of debt, and the interest expense from the debt can be used to shield rental income, since it is deductible. Returns on stock investments also tend to come from appreciation, but the government imposes margin requirements that severely restrict lending and require marks-to-market to occur daily.

Thus, the subsidization of commercial real estate through the interaction of tax policy and a fiat currency system shifts income out of the ordinary fully taxed bucket into the perpetually deferred category. Usually, commercial property owners choose to extract cash by rolling over mortgages and adding to the debt balance. This is a much more sensible alternative than the selling of fractional ownership in properties (as a C-corporation owner would sell shares) or permitting deleveraging to expose rental revenue. But wait, like the infomercial that surprises viewers with another incredible offer long after providing a convincing pitch, the tax code saves what may be its most important payoff element for last. Upon one's death, the negative basis created through the repeated cashing out through boosting the mortgage gets erased, offsetting much of the burden of the punitive death tax rate.

Quite a bit of wealth escapes taxation entirely, either from the use of offshore havens or from illegal activities that are cash oriented. The OECD estimates that between $5 trillion and $7 trillion, or 6 to 8 percent of total global assets under management (AUM) resides in tax havens, with $1.4 trillion of this in the Cayman Islands alone. The Tax Justice Network suggests that tax revenue lost to tax havens is about one-quarter trillion dollars annually, with about $100 billion of this being in avoidance of taxes in the United States. By comparison, the total taxes collected from the roughly one million returns filed by households in the top tax bracket were $345 billion in 2006. Assuming the poor don't fly to Liechtenstein, Andorra, or the Caymans to open accounts or to deposit cash, there appears to be considerable leakage from top bracket U.S. taxpayers seeking to avoid the government's 70 percent take by the time of death, or perhaps they simply wish to launder illicit funds. Many assume that tax compliance is the norm and that few of means would dare to risk prison sentences to save a portion of their fortunes. Anecdotal evidence of evasion surfaced once again recently when in July 2008 UBS announced that accounts for 20,000 U.S. clients opened through its private bankers in Switzerland would need to be closed amid investigations by the United States.[7] Considering that only an estimated 250,000 households earn greater than $500,000 per year, might one generalize that the border fence in place to discourage capital flight looks like, ahem, Swiss cheese? Given that this is for one bank and one highly visible tax haven, does it not take much imagination to conjure up hundreds of thousands of such accounts?

In February 2009, UBS entered into a $780 million settlement agreement with the U.S. Department of Justice. Although billed as a massive victory for the U.S. government, in reality UBS has agreed to name a mere 250 clients, and perhaps as many as 400 among the 20,000. These are probably individuals whose identities the Swiss Financial Markets Supervisory Authority had already planned to reveal in earlier negotiations, because they were also persona non grata in Switzerland for having violated tax laws of that country. The Swiss government is also unlikely to turn over for extradition Raoul Weil, the former head of wealth management for UBS. So the 20,000 clients and senior management are likely to come away fairly clean in the deferred prosecution agreement (DPA) that was reached. The IRS is asking the 20,000 to come forward, but they are being advised by counsel not to do so because of the protection afforded in the DPA, and since it is unlikely the IRS would ask them to do so if they knew their identity.

Indeed, the rich are different, because the utility of money changes when one has more of it than is useful for even somewhat conspicuous consumption such as a large house, a second home, or fancy cars and vacations. This divide is what separates the upper-middle class from the über-rich. The utility and purpose of money changes even more when control over it passes not to another generation, but to foundations, which over time can be hijacked by professional trustees. Grover Norquist, who heads Americans for Tax Reform, separates the political world into two halves, the "takings" and the "leave us alone" coalitions. But floating on the very top is a powerful concentration of wealth in two groups. One is locked behind foundations and controlled by trustees unrelated to or generations away from their founders. The other is the über-rich, who in time will see their wealth transferred beyond family control just as it was from those who preceded them.

The majority of Americans oppose the death tax when polled on the topic; few stridently support it. Those who favor its retention at today's absurdly punitive federal and state rates oddly hail from the very top as well as from those with the obvious self-interest of having no wealth to protect. Warren Buffett is perhaps the most vocal adherent. Besides being perhaps the largest buyer of family businesses from estates, he and others at the very top favor the death tax because they would carve out large philanthropic gifts anyway, just as the great scions of the Gilded Age did over 100 years ago, and just as Bill Gates, Ted Turner, and George Soros have done today. Big business loves the death tax. It is an effective weapon for smiting pesky upstart competitors, and it produces a steady deal stream from estates from which managements can cherry pick a feast of reasonably priced hors d'oeuvres that might be bolted on to rejuvenate tired and mature franchises.

Often the super-rich fear their offspring might be corrupted by fantastic wealth, and they know their kids could easily live with tens or hundreds of millions rather than billions. These dangers were poignantly portrayed in the movie "Born Rich" (later an HBO series), in which 10 heirs to vast fortunes, such as Ivanka Trump and Georgina Bloomberg, discussed their lifestyles. Many of the "idle rich," whom Buffett characterizes as members of the "lucky sperm club," fall prey to drug abuse or lack any ambition to develop their abilities or careers. The movie's backer, Jamie Johnson, heir to the drug company fortune bearing the same name, films members of his own family whiling away their days playing croquet in a sequel.[8] Indeed this is an issue for parents who might have not passed along moral values to their children and a society that has rejected traditional morals and replaced these with values of tolerance—specifically anything goes. Think this is over the top? Why is Paris Hilton so mainstream that she gets her own television reality show on Fox, *The Simple Life*, in which she lives with a wholesome farm family in Arkansas whose fresh-faced 19-year-old boy she tempts into a threesome frolic?[9] Would not the amateur blue movie that catapulted her career have been a private matter and not celebrated or commercially exploited? While unlimited financial resources might fan the fires of hedonism and self-destructive behavior, it may not necessarily follow that removal of wealth would teach offspring much about morality. However, it might keep them busy with the task of providing for the families they might have had if they were not busy vying for coverage on page six of the *New York Post*.

## Ignoble Pyramids

F. Scott Fitzgerald hobnobbed with the sons and daughters of the very rich when he began his literary career as a Princeton undergraduate. As he says, the "born rich" may be soft but their parents may not be, and in many cases they have larger-than-life egos, for they engage the world on a global scale. Here they interact with politically correct world leaders, and their every action is watched by the left-of-center world media. Soros has said that the "main obstacle to a stable and just world is the United States." Ted Turner supported his vision of one world by promising the donation of $1 billion to the United Nations in 1998. The über-rich have a strong urge to make eye-popping gifts, and the motivation is purely egotistical. In this life they can be admired for their generosity; after passing away their names can be immortalized. Foundations are to today's billionaires what the pyramids were to the Pharaohs.

What is remarkable is that over time the clearly defined intentions of the entrepreneurs who set up foundations have been in many if not most cases completely subverted and replaced by a highly leftist agenda. With the influence of full-time professional trustees, the foundations are often wrested away from the descendants, or if the descendants are left-leaning, the mission set by their forebears is summarily altered. Since the American tax system leaves only 20 to 30 percent of a lifetime of income to heirs after individual income, death, and other taxes, all the great wealth contained in the capitalist system must pass through this funnel which redirects the vast majority of it to either the government or foundations.[10]

Thanks to public relations, the public perception of the good works of foundations is positive, yet their actions not infrequently cloak political intentions that are shockingly anti-American and morally depraved. In his 2007 book *Foundations of Betrayal: How the Liberal Super Rich Undermine America* (Zoe Publications), author Phil Kent profiles many major foundations, and the following recounts his treatment of four majors: Pew, Ford, Rockefeller, and Carnegie. It may seem alarmist, but after joining author Kent in his deep dive through countless federal Form 990 tax filings, his conclusion is well supported. A quick spin through some of the most prominent of the roughly $500 billion

held in some 1.5 million tax exempt 501(c)(3) and 501(c)(4) organizations (excluding churches) shows they are dominated by big government collectivists, globalists, and radical leftists. Many leave the ranks
of foundations and become public charities, qualifying them to spend
5 percent of their disbursements for grassroots lobbying in Washington,
DC., a threshold that is almost never scrutinized and often surpassed in
practice at least indirectly.

The largest, the Pew Charitable Trusts, had $4.1 billion of assets in
2003 filings, an amount comparable to the shareholders equity of the
world's largest financial institutions (before they melted down). Howard
Pew formed the trusts in 1957 to educate Americans on "the values
of the free market" and "the paralyzing effects of government controls
on the lives and activities of people." Marvin Olasky wrote an essay
titled "Philanthropic Correctness" in the publication *Hederodoxy* in 1992
that revealed the president of the Council on Foundations, a group
involving members totaling $74 billion of assets, urged foundations to
bring on liberal and progressive trustees and staff to replace conservative
members. According to Olesky, leaders of the Council on Foundations,
through its publication the *Foundation News*, praised the Pew trusts for
having "eliminated almost all their right-wing grantmaking" and
for appointing as its executive director Rebecca Rimel, approvingly
describing her as an "activist" and "socially liberal," and moreover
celebrating her disregard of the intent of the Pew's Christian founders.[11]

What makes the actions of foundations like the Pew trusts difficult to trace without the help of analytical resources like Discover the
Networks is that they in turn give to other organizations whose purpose is politically directed, thus working around the 5 percent limitation
to which charities would be held. In 2002, the Center for the Defense
of Free Enterprise petitioned the IRS to remove the tax-exempt status of the Environmental Working Group, which had received a grant
of more than $1.6 million from the Joyce Foundation for "work on
the 2002 farm bill." The Environmental Working Group is also heavily
funded by the Pew trusts as well as the Turner Foundation and the Ford
Foundation.[12]

The Ford Foundation weighs in with grant awarding that is 15
times that of the three largest politically conservative foundations combined. It was funded with about 90 percent of the family's holdings of

Ford Motor Company stock, thus averting outright sale of these shares to pay off the death tax or the donation of the same directly to charities. Just a few years after the death of conservative patriarch Henry Ford in 1947 (who outlived his son Edsel by four years), the heirs turned over the operation of the trust to its trustees, who appointed a committee headed by leftist lawyer Rowan Gaither to study a new direction for the trust. After two years of deliberation, "world peace" became the foundation's preferred object of grant making, which pleased officers Paul Hoffman and Robert Hutchins. By 1954 this duo would be sent packing when their sympathy to communist causes was suspected. Among other things, they had favored support for the American Friends Service Committee, a pacifist group that wanted to reconcile with Red China. Feeling the heat of the red scare, these two officers established the Fund for the Republic with $15 million from the Ford Foundation, immediately hiring the former head of the U.S. Communist Party as a consultant. It would also fund the activities of the National Lawyers Guild, which was closely associated with the Communist Party.[13]

The Ford Foundation went on to advocate nationalization of companies in significant industries such as oil and gas production in 1972. By 1977 Henry Ford II, grandson of the patriarch, would resign in total disgust, lamenting that his family name graced the organization. After that, it would continue to generously reward radical, anti-capitalist, and anti-American causes.[14] It would seek to radicalize law school clinics and it heavily financed the ACLU, providing it with its largest single gift ever in 1999. Not content there, it spent more than $400 million to influence public radio and television with programming overseen by liberal consultant Fred Friendly.

Eventually its radical bias would land it in hot water after disbursing some $35 million to Arab and Palestinian groups after the attacks of September 11, 2001. Prior to this terrorist attack, substantial funds were given to the Palestinian Committee for the Protection of Human Rights, a group which became the object of a corruption probe. Records that might prove or disprove whether Ford monies supported terrorism have been sealed by the Ford Foundation for 10 years, but it insists it has not, despite debate so hot to the contrary that the ACLU saw fit to return funds and refuse aid from Ford. It has also targeted corporate America through funding environmental propaganda and lawsuits.[15]

The Rockefeller and Carnegie Foundations follow a pattern similar to the Ford and Pew entities, having had their conservative founders' missions similarly hijacked by radically leftward trustees and staff. For over 80 years, these two foundations have endeavored to sway the institutions of higher learning, providing two-thirds of their total endowment funding in the first third of the 20th century. Carnegie Corporation funded a project in the 1930s that British socialist Howard Laski termed "an educational program for a socialist America." Continual grants have been provided to Communist-leaning professors such as Columbia University's Robert Brady, author of *Business as a System of Power*, a book that concludes, "… capitalistic economic power constitutes a direct, continuous, and fundamental threat to the whole structure of democratic authority everywhere and always." Rockefeller along with Carnegie funded textbooks promoting socialist John Dewey's educational concepts, such as the controversial "Building America" that was rejected by the California legislature.[16]

Rockefeller would go on to fund the academic research of Alfred C. Kinsey, whose conclusions about human sexuality were cited as gospel for years until a column by Col. Ronald Ray in *The New American* in 1998 revealed that he "… was a sadomasochistic homosexual on a perverted mission. Trolling through homosexual bars and nightclubs, Kinsey gathered the subjects for his research, drawing disproportionately from those participating in sexual perversions and other criminal acts. Those acts were then portrayed by Kinsey as both commonplace and natural."[17]

Most discussions of whether the tax code is fair begin to look at issues from a point that starts *after* the great wealth of the über-rich has already been run through the complex machinery of estate and income tax avoidance. But the foundations of the über-rich systemically capture an estimated 40 percent of the wealth created through the capitalist system. Since control over these organizations will essentially slip into the hands of anti-capitalist forces, will this not lead to subversion of the very system that generated our nation's wealth and economic strength, if it hasn't already?

But what of the new money—that of the super-rich who have succeeded in amassing wealth during their tenure as sharecroppers on the government plantation? Would not one think that these would be fiercely conservative, exerting their influence to the maximum to cast off the yoke of taxation? Certainly many do. But consider the modern Fortune 500 CEOs. Their wealth may have been accumulated from running large, previously established multinational corporations. They may, in the corporate interest, prefer to rub elbows with politically correct leaders of foreign states, for example ingratiating themselves with leaders of Communist China in order to gain access to these huge emerging markets or to exploit low-wage manufacturing.

In Roman times, the elite aristocracy paid no taxes but was expected to build walls, aqueducts, or other public works periodically, while the populace was mercilessly taxed. What is the difference between the modern structure wherein foundations are a tax dodge, and the taxes of small businessmen are higher than they otherwise would be to subsidize the deification of the über-rich through monuments to their generosity, or worse, their political ideals, especially when these are anti-American? Why should not the upper-middle class be livid? Certainly the richest of society should be praised for philanthropy. But to accomplish this through shifting economic resources away from the middle class is demoralizing and destructive to our economic fabric. To push the concept to the max by calling for higher marginal tax rates, whose full effect is felt by small businessmen, and insisting they are advocates of social justice is a shameless deception. F. Scott Fitzgerald was right that the rich are different from you and me, but he could have added that the difference is not softness but arrogance, for they can manipulate the strings of government to their benefit just as their Roman counterparts did nearly two millennia ago.

## Charity or Syndicate?

WYSIWYG is an acronym for "what you see is what you get." The average Joe thinks of charity as something that helps the needy and accordingly is granted tax exemption by the IRS. But charities are now just one part of what the government has designated as non-profit organizations. No longer is this substantial subsidy, which is a burden to bear for those Americans who pay taxes, something that is generally agreed by them to be for the betterment of humanity. Instead, it is pointedly directed at outcomes that might be abhorrent to at least some of them. WYSIWYG no longer applies. Most of the American public, too busy with earning a paycheck and paying the mortgage, don't have time to think about the politicization of charities. But in reality, there are strident voices that do. One who does is George Soros, and he has been willing to put billions of his fortune to work for political causes. It's a free country, and anyone should be able to do so, rich or poor. Unfortunately, Mr. Soros has figured out that the line between charity and political activism can be blurred. Funds he donates to charity can be used to reduce his taxable income, and the income such charities receive is not taxed. But it should be if it resembles revenue for services performed more than it does contributions for charitable ends. Many organizations in this grey area have silos of activity standing side-by-side, one ostensibly a charity, another a politically active arm, both branded under one name. Legitimate charities should be very concerned, for the corruption of the mission of giving makes a radical solution to this problem more appealing as this corruption grows: rescinding the tax deduction for all charities and foundations.

Much of the Rockefeller's, Carnegie's, Pew's and the rest of America's old money resides in the traditional foundation structure. But why should today's new variety of billionaires be constrained by the limit this places upon political activism? Perhaps inspired by the Ford crossover into non-profit status and the rough and tumble tactics of Jesse Jackson's Rainbow/PUSH Coalition, George Soros has redefined the non-profit vehicle by "funding pressure groups and foundations he misleadingly characterizes as promoting 'civil society' and 'democracy,'" as described in an exposé in *Investor's Business Daily (IBD)*. Soros has given away $5 billion of an estimated total net worth of $9 billion through The Open Society Institute, of which he is the founder and chairman.[18] The Open Society Institute and related foundations in turn donate to MoveOn.org and other radical groups such as Americans Coming Together (ACT), the Association of Community Organizations for Reform Now (ACORN), and the Tides Foundation. The Federal Election Commission sanctioned ACT and ACORN. ACT illegally funneled $70 million set aside for voter registrations to Democratic candidates. ACORN has been accused of voter fraud in 13 states since 2004 and for falsifying voter registration drive signatures in July 2007. Since 2003, tearing down the "fascist" tyranny of the United States, as he has put it, is "the central focus of my life."[19]

IBD, Fox News Bill O'Reilly, and Phil Kent have accused Soros of indirectly funding Media Matters, a group dedicated to "correcting conservative misinformation in the U.S. Media," which in turn was influential in blocking Senator Joe Lieberman's primary bid for office in Connecticut. There he was challenged by Ned Lamont, whose great-grandfather was Corliss Lamont, the legendary socialist and director of the American Civil Liberties Union (ACLU). O'Reilly stated that "the Tides Foundation donated over $1 million to *MediaMatters* in 2005," and then "just by coincidence Soros' Open Society Institute (OSI) donated more than a million dollars to Tides in 2005 ... Figure it out." Kent added that "the Open Society Institute has given over $17 million to the Tides Foundation between 2001 and 2005. Tides then shamelessly turns around and grants Media Matters $3.3 million between 2003 and 2005." Media Matters has attempted to correct the record, but in so doing it seems to corroborate the case against Soros. It insists OSI only approved grants to Tides of $13.2 million, and that "every dollar OSI granted to Tides from 2001 to 2005 was earmarked for specific Tides-related programs and entities, and that *MediaMatters* was not included on the list."[20]

The parsing of the publicly available data by Media Matters technically may absolve it of the lie that Soros directed funds to it. But does it not reveal more about the highly legalistic and complex framework behind which today's billionaires can wash their hands of directly influencing elections? Just as mob chieftains might order a hit without leaving their own fingerprints, does the resulting opacity leave the community feeling safer or more vulnerable to powerful, organized ringleaders? Like a once-removed Citizen Kane, Soros is free to yield maximal political influence, enjoy tax exemption, and through McCain-Feingold legislation reduce the ability of others to donate directly to the candidates of their choice. If Hollywood had much conservative firepower, it might try a remake of that 1941 classic with Soros, not Hearst, as the model for its central character.[21]

The 2008 Democratic Party platform included a proposal to create a "Social Investment Fund Network" that would set up a government office to provide funds through grants to "social entrepreneurs and lead-ing nonprofit organizations [that] are assisting schools, lifting families out of poverty, filling health care gaps, and inspiring others to lead change in their own communities."[22] Given the influence Soros has said to have had over the hard left, which has come to dominate the Democratic Party, is it any wonder that he would seek to potentially divert tens of billions of taxpayer dollars directly into the coffers of his politically influential left-wing organizations? Would this not be the ultimate, most exquisite corruption of the U.S. government imaginable?

Howard Wolfson, communications director for both Charles Schumer and Hillary Clinton's first Senate campaigns and one of Hillary's three major consultants during the 2008 presidential pri-mary, said during an interview with Bill O'Reilly that MoveOn.org, with over 3 million members, is the primary Internet fund raiser for the Obama campaign.[23] By clicking on a spot on the main page of MoveOn.org, one could make donations and get campaign buttons for free, $2, or $20. The landing page was clearly marked as belonging to MoveOn.org, and there was a notice at the bottom of the page indi-cating one could subscribe to MoveOn.org to receive ongoing news about the Obama campaign.[24]

Campaign finance reform (specifically the Bipartisan Campaign Reform Act of 2002, or the McCain Feingold Bill) has redefined the political landscape by drastically restricting donations given directly to candidates to $2,000. 527 groups like MoveOn.org, which are not supposed to directly advocate the election or defeat of specific candi-dates (unless they choose to file reports), can nonetheless make political statements that lean as far left or right as they wish. They frequently have 501(c)(4) affiliates which permit large tax-deductible donations, but they must restrict themselves to advocating causes such as combat-ing global warming that are deemed not to influence elections directly. The waters are muddy among these various versions of advocacy groups enumerated in Table 7.1 on the following page.

For example, the top three types of advocacy organizations may raise non-federal funds, which can mobilize voters and advertise just before an election in a not-so-subtle attempt to influence the outcome of elec-tions of specific candidates. Who are the arbiters of whether 501 (c)(4) activities are "primarily" non-political? Perchance the politicians who

**Table 7.1: Tax-Exempt Advocacy Groups**

| Category | Purpose | Constraints |
|---|---|---|
| 501(c)(3) Groups | Religious, charitable, scientific, or educational typically | Some voter registration permitted, but not supposed to be political. |
| 501(c)(4) Groups | Social welfare organizations | May engage in political activity as long as this is not their "primary purpose." |
| 527 Group | Political | Political issues only. However if they file disclosure reports, they can advocate election or defeat of specific candidates. |
| Non-Federal Group | Political. For raising unlimited contributions called "soft money" | Voter "mobilization." Criticize or tout candidate's record just before election. Importantly, the prior categories (501(c) & 527) can raise non-federal money. |
| Political Action Committee | Usually business associated. For raising "hard money" | Can give directly to candidates, but very tight limits are set: $5,000 per candidate and $15,000 per party. Donations to PACS limited to $5,000. |

Source: The Center for Responsive Politics.

benefit from this largesse and its opacity? Once the government itself begins to provide funds to these quasi-political organizations when it establishes the "social investment fund network," won't voters be completely removed from the election process, because government would be funding the reelection of those who make the laws of the land in a closed loop? If this sounds alarmist, look at which groups are active in the new system: ACORN, which is charged with voter fraud on multiple occasions, and the Democratic Party, which proposes the network to strengthen and expand the new system.

Transparency is a major problem. On one hand the categorization of political activity allows for inconsistency, such that those who challenge the tax-exempt status of Rainbow/PUSH, for example, get no traction. On another hand, if one fits into one of the advantaged categories, donations are invisible. Karl Rove, knowing that the Republican base is behind the curve in the new fund-raising paradigm, now is encouraging donors to use the groups that might work as adjuncts to his party, such as Freedom's Watch or the National Right to Life Committee. Why? As Jeff Birnbaum of the *Washington Times* says: "because they often can remain anonymous and because the groups' expenditures are not disclosed until after they are made, if at all."[25] Yet there is granular visibility to regular donations to candidates that the average Joe makes.

## Invisible Money

Three things jump out if one tries to analyze the data of giving to advocacy groups and campaigns. First, the effect of being able to donate money to various nonreporting entities in the categories above masks ultra-large donations. Second, George Soros has emerged as a dominant figure in political giving, and he is having an effect on many other wealthy liberal elites. As a group America's richest are blocked from making meaningful donations directly to candidates, so they have embraced the world of 527s wholeheartedly. Third, even in direct-to-candidate donations liberals and conservatives weigh in almost equally, something one would never think possible given the class envy rhetoric of our time. It may be that the über-rich are giving to left-leaning candidates out of the goodness of their hearts. But it is far more likely that they are doing so out of self-interest.

527 groups have become an essential part of the election funding landscape. However, due to the opacity of giving directed towards the various types of 501(c) groups and their blended aims of serving charity and politics, money used to affect elections is not traceable. For example, a privately commissioned study by the author that the Center for Responsive Politics undertook for more than two months failed to turn up much activity from the Fortune 100 wealthiest billionaires. Although George Soros was on the list, his donations were catalogued at just $4.7 million in 2008 and $32.1 million for all of 2003 to 2008. Yet the press revealed donations of $5 billion overall and $400 million annually on an ongoing basis by Soros.[26] When CRP was asked why these

funds were not evident in the commissioned study, the answer was that there were different types of tax-deductible vehicles, and that Soros had probably used one that was not reported into its database (See Table 7.1). How many more billions are not observable? As reported by John Fund in the *Wall Street Journal*, "in 2005, billionaire investor George Soros convened a group of 70 super-rich liberal donors in Phoenix to evaluate why their efforts to defeat President Bush had failed. One conclusion was that they needed to step up their long-term efforts to dominate key battleground states. The donors formed a group called Democracy Alliance to make grants in four areas: media, ideas, leadership and civic engagement. Since then, Democracy Alliance partners have donated over $100 million to key progressive organizations."[27]

ACORN is a very significant group, whose aim it is to make a difference at a local level rather than nationally. ACORN has 120,000 dues-paying members, chapters in 700 poor neighborhoods in 50 cities, and 30 years' experience."[28] Its political arm is technically segregated from its non-partisan voter registration and mobilization, but its political involvement is so strident that one wonders if it might not be intentionally blurring the lines. A total of $440 million was given to the top 20 federally focused and state-focused 527 groups in the 2004 election cycle, with nearly 70 percent going to Democrat-leaning organizations and 30 percent to Republican-oriented ones. In the 2006 cycle, Democrat associated 527s claimed over 70 percent of fund raising.[29]

The 527 data above reflect the money spent, but there is not transparency as to where it came from, as the Soros disconnect in the Center for Responsive Politics tabulation proved. Nonetheless, an author-commissioned study of the period 2003-2008 turned up some $35 million of gifts from the Fortune 100 wealthiest billionaires to Democrat-leaning 527 groups, an amount that is more than double what billionaires sent to Republican-leaning 527s. However, if the full $5 billion Soros donation reported in the media were included, the percentage of 527 funds coming from the left would be an astonishing 99.7 percent of the total.[30] ACORN's significant influence over legislators became apparent when the TARP bailout bill endorsed by then Treasury Secretary Hank Paulson apparently included a provision that it would devote $100 million of funding for housing entitlements, some of which would flow through ACORN.[31] This was stricken from the bill in response to public outcry, but legislation hastily passed during the bailout of Fannie Mae and Freddie Mac a month earlier set aside funds that could be directed to community housing activist groups, which might naturally include ACORN. The funding comes from a $420 fee per each $100,000 mortgage value of GSE mortgages, disclosed in a line item as a carve-out for affordable housing.[32]

When the data is retrieved for donations directly to candidates, we see that 87 out of the 100, or nearly all, of the top billionaires gave to candidates of one party or the other in 2007. As an illustration of how incomplete and opaque the 527 giving audit trail is, this same group for the five-year stretch from 2003 to 2008 saw only a 24 percent participation rate. Moreover, for the year 2008—in the heat of the election—we only saw 10 out of 100 donors to 527s. It is hard to imagine that the same people who were active on the political front with candidates who could only accept trivial amounts of money would not have seen fit to make their influence felt more palpably in the 527 sphere. It is quite hard not to miss the almost daily deluge of mail from 527s one gets if he has ever written a political check or lives in an affluent neighborhood. And if one is a billionaire, it is even that much harder not to have been approached for money by numerous causes, particularly the advocacy groups, especially if your public record of giving for regular political campaigns is there for all to see right on the Internet.

An interesting exercise is the examination of which candidates received the greatest donations from employees of the country's biggest and most troubled financial and mortgage giants. The public perception is that Wall Street is responsible for the mess, and Democrats fan this myth by claiming that deregulation of the financial sector caused it to spin out of control. Ergo, tighter regulation should be promulgated and capitalism restrained. However, the linkage to Bill Clinton and Walter Mondale of Fannie Mae CEOs Franklin Raines and James Johnson (as well as Vice Chairman Jamie Gorelick) shows the tightest connection between failing institutions and the Democratic side of the aisle. Table 7.2 shows a strong preference for Obama in campaign donations.

According to the Center for Responsive Politics, individuals and PACs from the investment industry contributed $146 million to federal campaigns in the 2008 cycle. Christopher Dodd, chairman of the Senate Banking Committee, and Barney Frank, chairman of the

Table 7.2: Political Donations from Troubled Financial Institutions
(2008 Presidential Campaign, $ Thousands)

| Institution | Obama | McCain | Ratio |
|---|---|---|---|
| Bear Stearns | 51 | 88 | 0.6:1 |
| Fannie Mae | 80 | 7 | 11.4:1 |
| Freddie Mac | 19 | 9 | 2.1:1 |
| Wachovia | 152 | 113 | 1.3:1 |
| Lehman Brothers | 255 | 104 | 2.5:1 |
| AIG | 76 | 39 | 1.9:1 |
| Merrill Lynch | 173 | 300 | 0.6:1 |
| Washington Mutual | 17 | 1 | 17.0:1 |
| Morgan Stanley | 301 | 217 | 1.4:1 |

Sources: Federal Election Commission; Center for Responsive Politics; CQ
Moneyline; McElhatton, Jim & Haberkorn, Jennifer, "Failed Firms Directed
Millions to Politicians." *Washington Times*, September 22, 2008, p. 10.

House Financial Services Committee, each saw four out of their top
five donors hail from the financial industry. Among the companies represented were flagging enterprises Royal Bank of Scotland, American
International Group, and Bank of America.

In this modern world of Internet transparency, unaided by reporting from the mainstream media, eventually the citizenry of the United
States might discover that the Democratic Party is a party heavily influenced by the super rich and the financial institutions that most deeply
embraced moral hazard.

# Chapter 8

# Sharecroppers

The American Dream, a phrase coined in 1931 by author James Truslow Adams, is to aspire to a successful life, particularly one with an improved economic status compared to one's parents. Consider this: Two upwardly mobile upper-middle class citizens marry and start a business or rise in their professions to earn a combined $360,000 annually, which places them in the top 5 percent of earners. The marginal federal tax rate this household would pay is 35 percent. Much of the U.S. population resides in high-tax states, which would extract 5 to 10 percent additional tax (this has been deductible, but a 28 percent ceiling was recently introduced). Then, payroll, property tax, and excise taxes might take more than 10 percent, leaving just 45 percent in residual. If they have accumulated an estate, the death tax levied would leave their heirs just 20 to 30 percent of what was originally earned (assuming the use of a deduction).[1]

As a presidential candidate, Obama contemplated boosting the top federal rate to about 40 percent and placing a 10 percent surcharge on high incomes for Social Security. He favored returning the federal portion of the death tax to 55 percent, which would cut the residual calculated above from 20 to 30 percent to just 9 to 13 cents on the dollar. If an estate were left to three children, each would get just three to five *pennies* for each *dollar* his parents earned.[2]

Could it not be fair to say that the private property of this household was in reality owned by the government? This successful couple merely had a rental claim on less than half of their possessions while alive, and had only that just as long as they worked themselves to the bone. In contrast, most Americans pay little to no taxes. Median household income in 2006 was $48,000,[3] which generates federal tax of about 8 percent.[4] As citizens, our choice is either to live the life of the average American household or aspire to an American Dream, where unless we are George Soros or Warren Buffett, we have relinquished our claim to the private property we accumulate—nearly in totality.

If this is not considered socialism, then at what percentage retention of a citizen's assets would this amount of confiscation be aptly described as socialism—maybe something a tad lower, say 15 to 20 percent, or perhaps the roughly 10 percent proposed as "fair" by Obama while he sought our vote in 2008? The only difference between living in the United States and the former communist regimes is that at least a highly productive U.S. citizen gets to sharecrop his property from his master during his lifetime. As for his children, they are essentially booted off the plantation.

## How (not) to Repay $1 Trillion

We have been living in a fantasy in which our country is so rich that it may raise spending indefinitely, that the bottommost 50 percent of taxpayers may be nearly excluded from the burden of paying for this, that the upper echelons can afford to underwrite it, and that the capital markets accept the deferral of any payment through granting the nation an unlimited credit line. The truth is that we are flat broke. Each household or individual filing taxes would owe about $80,000 to extinguish the federal debt, and it is on the hook for a total of $520,000 including future entitlements. In the pages to follow, the effect of shifting this burden to specific subgroups of tax payers quickly escalates the per household obligation to ludicrous heights. The picture does not look much better if we spread the pain to the bottom half as we used to decades ago. Concentrating the burden upon the very richest Americans is equally shaky.

If sharecropping has not sapped the vibrancy of the American Dream compared to the 19th century, then surely the next wave of socialism will. Most voters in the 2008 presidential cycle believed there would be a small adjustment to taxes that only affects the highest brackets under Obama's plans for fiscal expansion. Although Bush is credited for undoing the Clinton tax increases, in reality he continued a precedent of buying votes by essentially phasing out the taxation of income for the lowest tax brackets. It is a testimony to the nation's ability to sell Treasury debt at historically low interest rates and to the tsunami of credit in the 2000s that the economy expanded and tax revenue increased, narrowing the budget deficit. Accustoming the lower half of income earners to the nonpayment of taxes forces any incremental burden upon the upper brackets. This small group at the top is now the swing supplier of revenue to the government, so the slightest imbalance in funding will potentially cause politicians to claim a tremendously greater slice of its income.

The political trend of the last few decades has been to segregate the population politically by eliminating the tax burden on nearly half of it, and forcing this obligation upon a group that can be shrunken to a minority incapable of voicing opposition under democracy. The analysis that follows may seem to be a *reductio ad absurdum*. However, the recent surge in debt, upper bracket tax rate increases, and stealth tax transfers through the use of credits, deductions, and limitations or phase-outs of the same makes it abundantly clear the trend to segregate the population and target the upper-middle class is accelerating at precisely the moment our national financial health is deteriorating under the pressure of unwinding excessive leverage.

Unfortunately, this is not a worry merely destined to haunt a later generation or pressure us in 10 to 20 years when the weight of entitlements might crush the unified budget. In the current financial crisis, $1 trillion of obligations could suddenly arise from nowhere, because the economy may be overleveraged by a factor of two or more, implying some $50 trillion of private debt and public entitlements could be worthless. In fact, even before adding the debt the government just assumed from its takeover of Fannie Mae and Freddie Mac, federal debt had climbed by 11 percent in fiscal 2008 to $10 trillion. By calendar year-end 2008, it had surged to $10.7 trillion.[5] However, the analysis in this chapter uses the 2007 figures (because of delays in IRS reporting), thus understating the problem by about 10 percent for now, and by as much as 30 percent prospectively if projections of $12 trillion to $13 trillion of federal debt by the end of 2009 come about.

In fiscal 2008 the U.S. government budget deficit climbed to $455 billion, which included $168 billion of checks mailed to households not in the top brackets.[6] This combined with the pressures of funding bailouts (but not including Federal Reserve actions, which are sizeable) are now assumed to take the deficit to $1.75 trillion in fiscal 2009. During his campaign, Obama proposed tax changes that would redistribute wealth, but little in the way of large new program expenditures, perhaps because playing that hand would have opened his platform to criticism. Now that there is a bona fide economic crisis, he has carte blanche consent for such spending, which is proposed to be $250 billion annually for the next four years. It would also open the door to tax increases beyond the $1 trillion of redistribution evident in the Obama-Biden *Blueprint for Change*, which already includes automatic boosts for top brackets that were lowered under Bush. With the political mood being to rebate funds to the low end, clearly increasing taxes for that segment is off the table.

A call for new taxes on the top layers has been workable historically when small amounts of new spending are required, but if a crisis such as a war or the default of government-backed banks or mortgages triggers a massive need for funding, someone astute might notice that the socialist scheme to confine the new burden upon just the rich might fail. It would not fail because a sleepwalking Congress did or did not act; rather it would fail simply because the numbers don't add up, regardless of which bipartisan solution might be contrived to achieve an incremental fix.

If just the debt that the government owes were to be assigned to certain top brackets, here is how it would look: The top three tax brackets capture some 6.6 million households and individuals, so spreading $9.2 trillion among them would burden them with $1.4 million each. If the one million filers in the topmost 35 percent bracket were to assume all the liability, there would be a $9.2 million debt due for each of them (See Table 8.1).

Table 8.1: Federal Government Debt Impact on Middle & Upper Tax Brackets

| Bracket | Minimum Income (a) | Cum. No. Returns (mil.) | Debt Per Household Return | | $1 Trillion Reduction |
| --- | --- | --- | --- | --- | --- |
| | | | GAAP (b) | US Debt (c) | |
| 10% | $0 | 96.0 | $625,000 | $96,000 | $10,000 |
| 15% | 16,050 | 70.2 | 854,000 | 131,000 | 14,000 |
| 25% | 63,700 | 28.9 | 2.1 mil | 318,000 | 34,000 |
| 28% | 128,500 | 6.6 | 9.1 mil | 1.4 mil | 151,000 |
| 33% | 195,850 | 2.6 | 23.2 mil | 3.6 mil | 386,000 |
| 35% | 349,700 | 1.0 | 59.9 mil | 9.2 mil | 998,000 |

Sources: IRS data for 2006 except where noted, excludes capital gains income and non-taxable returns. U.S. Census data.
(a) Brackets for 2008.
(b) GAAP Liability for the U.S. of approximately $60 trillion as of 2007 Y/E.
(c) U.S. Debt of $9.2 trillion (is prior to consolidating GSE debt of approximately $5 trillion) as of FYE 2007.

If we used GAAP accounting to recognize the promises the government has made (mostly for Medicare and also to fund Social Security), the liability per household would be phenomenally large. For the top three brackets, the liability assumed would be $9.1 million each! If the top bracket only were required to pay off the GAAP liability, each filer in that bracket would absorb a debt of $59.9 million, a ridiculous amount that would take 44 years worth of their pretax income to repay.

Even zeroing in on the über-rich doesn't work: They would owe $28 million each for the debt portion, or $180 million each if all entitlements were included. The estimated household income for this small subsegment of the 35 percent bracket is $4 million annually so even these well-heeled households would need seven years to work the debt down to zero and more than the balance of their lifetimes to fund entitlements—this assuming they accede to being slaves who retain no income for personal use at all.

If we were examining the credit worthiness of the U.S. government as a business or as a nonreserve currency nation, a helpful exercise would be to stress test it to see if its income producers could comfortably shoulder repayment of a small fraction of its loans, let's say $1 trillion to pick a round number. Let's examine five options for demanding $1 trillion from various combinations of upper income filers.

## Option 1: Wide Dispersion—Include the Top Four Brackets

In the 25 percent bracket and up, there are 28.9 million households (or individuals). These paid almost 82 percent of all income taxes in 2006. The 25 percent bracket started at $63,700 of income in 2007. For the 25 percent layer alone, average income is $90,000, which generates a moderate ongoing tax obligation of $11,000. However, no part of this analysis addresses Social Security, which once one goes down to the 25 percent bracket becomes important. That claim on income is $13,000 for each individual, double this for working couples.

If all 28.9 million in the 25 percent bracket and up were to equally share the burden of a $1 trillion surcharge, $34,000 of taxes would be due per filer. Of course, in reality much of the $1 trillion would be progressively distributed, but as we examine the other options that focus upon taxing fewer brackets, it becomes obvious that as one restricts the denominator, the tax surcharge becomes extremely heavy. If one made an assumption that half of the burden could be upstreamed progressively, still the remaining $17,000 of tax due in the 25 percent bracket would be onerous on top of the Social Security and ongoing income tax levies.

## Option 2: Somewhat Wide Dispersion—Include the Top Three Brackets

The number of households that made over $128,500 in 2007 was only 6.6 million. Politically they would make a better target, but even Obama as a candidate was unwilling to include this large a group in his plan to raise taxes, which was reserved for only those whose income exceeded $250,000. That plan would only cover a portion of the uppermost bracket. Thus, the details of the Obama plan have an order of magnitude of internal inconsistency, something that not even one reporter or John McCain noticed during the presidential campaign. There are fewer than one million returns where income exceeded $250,000 in 2007. As a percentage of total filers, that group would be about 1 percent of the total, whereas Obama promised to tax the top 5 percent.

If we take Obama at his word, then his new taxes would actually dip into the 28 percent bracket, probably capturing those who make $175,000 and up. How heavy a burden would be placed on the 28 percent bracket if it and all persons in the brackets above it were expected to pay an additional $1 trillion of taxes? This group already pays more than 56 percent of all income tax. Spreading the pain there as well would create an average burden of $151,000, which would be added to ongoing tax liability of $87,000. This compares with average income for this group of nearly $390,000 (but only $159,000 solely in the 28 percent bracket).

## Option 3: Just Tax the Top Two Brackets

This option most closely resembles one proposed by the Obama administration in February 2009. It captures 2.6 million households in the 33 percent and 35 percent brackets, representing about 4 percent of all returns, which remit 44 percent of all taxes. To meet a $1 trillion surcharge, these 2.6 million would be taxed to the tune of $386,000 per household. One would need to make assumptions about how this might be spread between these two brackets, because if the $1 trillion surcharge were divided equally, this liability would exceed the average annual income of the 33 percent bracket filer, which is only $321,000. Bear in mind this filer would need to continue to pay his ongoing income tax bill, which averages $65,000. The 35 percent bracket is a mixture of billionaires and couples just edging over the $349,700 minimum income qualification, so any discussion of "average" burdens would yield similarly punitive results for a great deal of the filers in that category. Even so, if one went back to the hypothetical case of making the top two brackets pay the $1 trillion surcharge, the "average" household in this group would be quite stressed. The tab comes to $386,000, or 53 percent of one year's average income in this group of $724,000. When combined with their ongoing tax bill of $174,000 per return, 77 percent of their income would be wiped out.

## Option 4: Just Tax the Top Bracket

This bracket is quite distorted, because it is open ended and includes many who make just $350,000 per couple, an amount two middle-aged professionals in New York City might typically pull in, as well as billionaires. Moreover, the region in which such a couple live is also burdened with extraordinary housing costs, taxes, and cost of living, so they would hardly feel rich. Due to this distortion, option #5 is presented in an attempt to separate out the super-wealthy as a separate case. Nonetheless, the straight numbers on the 35 percent bracket indicate that it would need to pay about $1 million for each filer, an amount that is more than double its average income and probably triple its median income.

## Option 5: Just Tax the Super Rich

Let's take a look at what would happen should our politicians decide to just tax the "really rich"—thinking this might solve all of our problems. Suppose we create another tax bracket with a minimum income cutoff of $500,000. There is no way to know for sure, but let's assume that 25 percent of the over one million households or individuals who file in the 35 percent bracket earn 75 percent of the adjusted gross income of the bracket. It is not a bad assumption, because if one sets this ratio at another level, say 80%/20%, then fallout statistics such as average income for those left in the 35 percent bracket begin to migrate out of the bounds of common sense expectations. The results are shown in Table 8.2. Note that this display assumes all of the $1 trillion needed for debt reduction (or columns for GAAP and U.S. Debt) are divided by only those in each bracket, not the cumulative filers (as was the case when working one's way through the brackets above). This is because in this hypothetical case debt per household is spread only between these two new brackets. Also, in this case it is being spread by income, that is—25 percent to the old 35 percent bracket and 75 percent to the new 50 percent filers.

So, lets assume the über-rich get tagged for 75 percent of the tab (in line with their assumed income), and only 25 percent were payable by those who would remain in the old 35 percent bracket. The result would be that instead of a $1 million payment required per household or filer for every $1 trillion of debt the government would pay down in the old 35 percent bracket, in the new 35 percent bracket only $333,000 would be required for each $1 trillion of debt that the government

**Table 8.2: Hypothetical Case: A New 50% Tax Bracket and Complete Burden Placed Upon Only 35% Bracket and Higher**

| Bracket | Minimum Income | No. Returns (mil.) (a) | Debt Per Household Return (d) | | $1 Trillion Reduction |
|---------|----------------|------------------------|-------------------|-----------------|------------------------|
| | | | GAAP (b) | U.S. Debt (c) | |
| 35% | $349,700 | 0.75 | $19.7 mil | $3.1 mil | $333,000 |
| 50% | 500,000 | 0.25 | 179.6 mil | 27.5 mil | 2,994,000 |

Sources: IRS data for 2006 except where noted, excludes capital gains income. U.S. Census data.
Author assumptions about 75/25 split for the new tax bracket.
(a) Assumes 75% of the 1.0 million of the 35% bracket remain there, and 25% are eligible for the new
    50% bracket.
(b) GAAP Liability for the United States of approximately $60 trillion as of 2007 Y/E.
(c) U.S. Debt of $9.2 trillion (is prior to consolidating GSE debt of approximately $5 trillion) as of
    FYE 2007.
(d) Assumes 75% is borne by the 35% bracket, 25% by the new 50% bracket.

would choose to extinguish. This is still an untenable requirement, for the average adjusted gross income of the new 35 percent bracket would be about $450,000 per household. The new 50 percent bracket members would owe about $3 million for every $1 trillion the government would pay down.

If solely the über-rich were saddled with the $1 trillion surcharge (not shown in Table 8.2 above), they would each owe $4 million of taxes. Assuming they earned 75 percent of the old 35 percent bracket's income, this equates to one year of earnings. If they were required to extinguish the entire $9 trillion the U.S. government owes, they would write a check for nearly $37 million each. To prepay all government liabilities, a $240 million garnishment per household would ensue. So, despite how sweet liberals would think setting up a new category just for the über-rich might be, the sad reality is that our government has spent and promised so much that the outcome would be very damaging to the economy, further aggravating the collapse in the stock market, banking, and commercial real estate sectors that began in 2008.

Many might dismiss all of the above analysis as being hypothetical, because after all the government never pays down its debt. This may be the case, but that statement is only valid in the last century, a time when we have changed our culture considerably. It was not the situation in the first 130 years of the U.S. republic. Rather than pay down $1 trillion (any tax increase would probably be committed to new spending the instant it became law), each year we have attached a looming liability of at least half this to the upper tax brackets. This amount approaches half a year of their members' income, which in practice probably could never be collected in addition to the taxes they already remit. Beginning in 2009, we will add at least $1.75 trillion of debt, and probably more in entitlements!

Presently the government is hooked on debt and does not feel its pinch due to generationally low interest rates. Legislators maintain high spending to maintain voter support from the left. As socialization spreads to the mainstream, spending increasingly helps the lower-middle class, which might vote conservative otherwise. Government can essentially operate a Ponzi scheme, fooling buyers of Treasury bonds into believing that other dupes, be they taxpayers or other bond buyers, will be there to make good on the next coupons as they are presented for payment. We have operated this way for decades, causing layer upon layer of debt to be added, but in the Bush presidency the problem became intractable due to the math of compounding, despite generally having had manageable deficits as a percentage of GDP. Can there be any question that we might be broke? When might our trading partners and government bond investors discern this fact?

## $1 Million Just Isn't What It Used to Be

The analogy between the Obama and Roosevelt administrations has become so mainstream that *TIME* magazine ran a Photoshopped cover picture on November 24, 2008, with Obama riding in a vintage open-air sedan decked out in a crumpled fedora, temple-free spectacles, and an elongated cigarette holder clenched by teeth frozen in a grin. Although many scoff at "depressionistas" who harp on the negative message that we might be headed for another period like the 1930s, the indebtedness of the private sector is even greater now, and indeed that is the main cause for our economic instability. But interestingly, if one examines tax brackets now and then, there is a world of difference.

The top individual income tax rate in 1931 had been 25 percent for incomes over $100,000. In 1932 brackets were expanded with the

highest set at $1 million of income, taxing dollars earned above this
at 63 percent, a level not seen save for briefly during World War I. It
is essential to consider the effect of inflation over time when assessing
the impact of Rooseveltian tax schemes vis-à-vis the super-rich and the
upper-middle class. The middle class has become heavily taxed over
the past 90 years, while the über-rich have seen a lessened burden. A
household in the 35 percent bracket today would have paid a maximum 17 percent rate under Roosevelt; Warren Buffett pays 17 percent
today, but he would have paid 63 percent early in the Great Depression
and 79 percent midway through it.

One million dollars in 1932 would be equivalent to $16 million in
2007 purchasing power. Even Roosevelt's embrace of Keynesian economics and progressive socialist ideas would only lead him to tax what
qualifies for today's highest bracket—just shy of $350,000 of income—
at just a 16 percent marginal rate when converted into 1932 inflation-
adjusted dollars. At the beginning of the depression, annual income
approaching $16 million in 2007 value dollars was thus considered rich;
by today's era, at least as far as politicians and the IRS are concerned,
two married professionals earning $175,000 each receive the most
punitive rate of 35 percent. Moreover, the phenomenon of states developing voracious budgets, particularly on America's urban coastlines, has
led to an approximate doubling of the burden of state income taxation nationwide, despite there being many states that are free of income
tax, bringing total income tax to roughly 45 percent in locales holding
concentrations of the population. In 2006, the U.S. Treasury recognized
state income tax deductions of $246 billion (from individual filers who
itemized), which was 29 percent of all federal individual income tax
paid.[7]

Figure 8.1 helps to show what the tax burden is when adjusted for
inflation. In it, the marginal tax rate is plotted against inflation-adjusted
income levels measured in 2007 dollars at various breakpoints from
$25,000, which is below the poverty line for most households, all the
way up to $1 million. While Roosevelt did his best to tax the rich, he
actually reserved the sting of the taxman for the über-rich. Nonetheless
he pushed the limit in expanding government, thus continuing the cir-
cumvention of a constitutionally limited federal sector begun under
Woodrow Wilson.

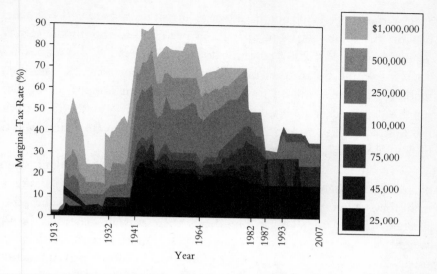

**Figure 8.1    Marginal Tax Brackets of Various Inflation-Adjusted Incomes (1913–2007)**

However, near-confiscatory tax rates did not make the scene until the advent of World War II, and in inflation-adjusted terms these remained in effect until the presidency of Ronald Reagan. The mountainous formation of this era dominates the center of the chart, and makes it hard to appreciate how upper-middle class tax rates remained higher than in the Roosevelt era even after the Reagan revolution occurred. Figure 8.1 thus reveals that the era of the 1930s looks little different from the post-Reagan/Bush years (which include Clinton and a Congress inspired by the Contract with America). In fact when the effect of state taxation is rolled in, the burden upon the middle class was considerably less onerous!

What is puzzling is that some conservative commentators worried that the huge shift to filibuster-proof Congressional majority in 2009 would lead to socialism. While that may indeed be the case, in reality redistributive tax rates have been part of the landscape ever since the highest marginal rate was set at 67 percent in 1917 under Wilson. A slight respite occurred from 1925 through 1931, when the top federal rate was chopped to 25 percent, but in essence we have never looked back. Socialist spending got its biggest push in the 1930s under President Roosevelt. Roosevelt certainly conducted class warfare against the super-rich, but its effect is invisible in Figure 8.1. This is because the figure zeroes in on regions pertinent to the middle classes, up to $1 million of 2007 constant dollars, and does not show tax rates for what would be an ultra-high bracket structure today that stratified income in the $1 million to $16 million per year zone. The tax rate on the top bracket increased from 25 percent in 1931 to 63 percent the following year, and to 79 percent by 1936. When financing WWII became necessary, it rose to 94 percent!

Two other observations about federal taxation become evident when examined through this lens of inflation adjustment and a broad sweep of history. One jumps out from Figure 8.1, which is that from the postwar era through the Reagan presidency there was an extremely heavy weight of taxes upon the American people. If one agrees with those of today's liberals who would fail to concede that Roosevelt was in practice a socialist, even if he did not call himself such, the case of not admitting that the United States eventually drifted into socialism would be almost impossible to make after 1942, when the top bracket was raised to 88 percent! Whether or not Roosevelt or Wilson could be labeled big government collectivists may not be relevant; both of them did their best to lay the stones in the foundation for institutionalizing socialism for the nearly half century that separates Reagan from the depression, as is clearly evident from the bulge at the center of the chart.

The second observation is invisible on Figure 8.1, and so being, is all the more insidious. Many conservative commentators remind us that most Americans pay little to no taxes. The bottom 40 percent of all earners in aggregate receive a small credit and pay no income tax at all, and the next 20 percent pay just 7 percent of all the nation's income tax.[8] Overall, the burden of the bottom half of all earners has nearly been cut in half since 1990, with this group's share of the income tax dropping from 5.8 percent in 1990 to 3.5 percent in 2002.[9] The view from the top is quite different. For the tax year 2005, the top 1 percent of filers fund over 39 percent of the federal government's cash inflow. Nearly 60 percent of the government's receipts come from the top 5 percent, and the percentages coming from the top 10 percent and 25 percent are 70 percent and 86 percent, respectively.[10]

Median household income in 2006 was $48,000,[11] which generates federal tax of about 8 percent.[12] Note that this is well below the marginal rate indicated on the chart for 2007 of 15 percent, which applies to all married households up to just over $65,000. A small part of the difference stems from a rate of only 10 percent being applied to the first 16,000 or so of income; by far the lion's share comes from Congress having passed credits and deductions favoring the bottom half of earners. The stripe at the bottom of Figure 8.1 used to be a potent determinant of take home pay for the American worker for much of the postwar era, but today it is a paper tiger, and might even get airbrushed out of the picture to be accurate. Yet one other pictorial adjustment is needed. The seemingly low top rate is quite understated, because states have built massive government structures that dwarf those of the early 20th century. So for most in the urban coasts, the top rate is closer to 45 percent and in some cases it exceeds this. What has happened is that in response to the lowering of rates Reagan accomplished, states rushed in to fill the vacuum by raising taxes. Having a culture that cannot comprehend the moral hazard of redistributing wealth, is it any surprise that conservative policies enacted nationally would be counteracted on a state level?

Reagan attempted to flatten tax rates by chopping the top percentage considerably and reducing the number of brackets to essentially three by 1988, but at the same time deductions and exclusions for the upper brackets were eliminated or constrained by the AMT. The bracket structure was promptly expanded again under Clinton to five in 1993 when the top rate rose to 39.6 percent from its low of 28 percent in 1990. (George H. W. Bush initially bumped it to 31 percent in the Omnibus Budget Reconciliation Act of 1990, hypocritically breaking his pledge of "Read my lips: no new taxes.") Bush the younger reversed half of the Clinton increase (to 35 percent) in 2003. Essentially there has been a game of ping-pong for the last two decades, whose latest volley restored the Clinton top rate.

Great damage was done by the strategy of absolving taxation for half the nation. Welfare reform was one of the great successes of Republicans and one of the few accomplishments of the Contract with America, which Clinton wisely incorporated into his centrist platform. Returning the lowest of society to work was a great moral accomplishment, much less a political one. Now tax credits are being extended liberally to the bottom, in effect restoring the dole outright through IRS transfers. Even worse, at the least prick of pain supposed conservatives led by George W. Bush volunteered roughly $500 in the form of a one-time tax rebate to taxpayers below the upper-middle class strata (up to $600 for unmarried individuals, twice this for married households plus child credits for up to two children at $300 each). Obama has promised further tax credits, including those who pay no taxes. Even without a Democrat running the country, legislators obliged the Republican Bush with Medicare Part D drug benefits for all elderly persons payable beginning in 2006. In the following year they proposed increases in the State Children's Health Insurance Program (SCHIP) that would have widened eligibility of free insurance to "children" up to age 25 in "poor" families of four earning up to $82,600, a level well ahead of median income. In her run for president in the 2008 primary, Hillary Clinton said, "I have a million ideas. The country can't afford them all."[13]

The landscape has now permanently changed, such that there is a massive group in the bottom half that pays little to no taxes, an upper-middle class that feels the full impact of any need to fund ever-expanding government, and an über-class that has fit through the eye of the needle, no longer depending upon wages and able to at least on the margin protect itself somewhat and buy influence at the highest levels of the Democratic and Republican parties. While a flat, fair, or consumption tax might resolve these problems, it would not without repeal of the Sixteenth Amendment, for to not do so would preserve *two* large-scale systems. Repeal would require an even stronger consensus than Reagan mustered, a doubtful outcome in this generation. The more likely near-term scenario is more ping-pong resulting in ever more punitive taxation near the top and a greater dole for the bottom. However, with the public and private balance sheets leveraged as never before, economic catastrophe could force both political parties to acknowledge the failure of socialism and unchecked credit growth if collections fall under the strain of higher rates and increased progressivity.

Pointing out inconsistencies such as those raised by the commercial real estate industry raises the question of whether America should adopt a fair or flat tax. Unfortunately, the mechanics of overriding a Constitutional amendment are prohibitive, so this eventuality has seemed doomed for years, but it did gain some public exposure through the presidential candidacies of Mike Huckabee and Ron Paul, and more than a decade ago with Steve Forbes, who received 11 percent of the Republican primary vote in his 1996 bid. Exposing unfairness lucidly may only arm the liberal political contingency with targets for "closing loopholes" and thereby extracting even more tax from the upper-middle class, such as the raising of income limits on Social Security contributions or AMT reform that would only apply to incomes below the top bracket or two. Not to be left out of the fairness discussion are pools of wealth that receive tax-free status. Foundations, labor unions, and groups such as MoveOn.org Civic Action (structured as a 501(c)(4) affiliate) should be subject to taxation; they would always be free to minimize their exposure by putting their not inconsiderable sums to worthy causes, but contributions to them from left-wing billionaires would no longer be deductible. Rather than being entities focused upon their own growth or survival, they might actually self-liquidate and distribute a torrent of cash to worthy causes. Think of the good works and economic stimulation this would yield, much less the rooting out of tax havens for society's most radical elements.

While flat or fair taxes may improve upon progressive taxes, a more fundamental question needs to be asked. Have the less than 100-year-old experiments with income taxation and centrally managed fiat currencies begun to produce a situation that might alter society by causing catastrophic economic depression? At its last instance, the 1930s, socialism resulted as measured by income and estate taxes, which only temporarily abated under Reagan. And in fact on inflation-adjusted terms, the upper-middle class was not anywhere near as penalized in the Great Depression as it has grown to be over the decades that followed. During the 1930s, the super rich were singled out for taxation. In contrast, in the downturn that begun in 2008 the unintended consequence might be punitive confiscation of wealth held by the upper-middle and middle classes, and the entrenchment of the super rich, who can operate partly outside the conventional income tax mechanism and wield heavy political influence through 527 groups, while the populace is restricted in the political process.

Flat income taxes cannot address the inequity of permitting a very select elite group to accumulate its wealth largely outside the grasp of ordinary income taxation, aided by inflation, leverage, and derivatives, while those who aspire to the same lifestyle are incessantly restrained in good times and held responsible for cleaning up the toxic mess that inflation, leverage, and derivatives inevitably produce. Only a flat tax on wealth itself could fairly bridge this divide. Sadly, a century of centrally managed fiat currency and progressive taxation of income has incubated a pernicious sentiment of class warfare that has pitted the lowest half of society against the upper-middle class. An objective stress test of the progressive tax code placed upon a population that has borrowed heavily in response to the inexorable inflation of investible assets stimulated by fiat currency shows that the casualty of this class warfare is the financial security of a generation and perhaps another to follow. But it is faux class warfare, for its natural endpoint is the mutual impoverishment of nearly all citizens through the languishment of incentives and the ascendance of a ruling plutocracy.

# Part Four

# ASSUMING POWER

*Among many other evils they endured also that of tyranny; for when, on the populace violently clamoring for an abolition of debts, and a division of the lands of the rich, the subject was long discussed in the senate, and no settlement of it was devised, they at last sought assistance against the commons, who were grown riotous by too long idleness . . . they had recourse to Clearchus, whom they themselves had exiled; such being the urgency of their distresses, that they recalled to the guardianship of his country him whom they had forbidden to enter his country. . . The people, induced by (his) fair speeches, conferred on him the supreme authority, and, while they were incensed at the power of the senate, surrendered themselves, with their wives and children, as slaves to the power of a single tyrant. Clearchus then apprehended sixty senators (the rest had taken flight), and threw them into prison. The people rejoiced that the senate was overthrown, and especially that it had fallen by means of a leader among the senators, and that, by a reverse of fortune, their support was turned to their destruction . . . Returning into the city, he threw same into prison, stretched others on the rack, and put others to death; and not a place in the city was unvisited by the tyrant's cruelty. Arrogance was added to severity, insolence to inhumanity. From a course of continued good fortune, he sometimes forgot that he was a man, sometimes called himself the son of Jupiter. When he appeared in public, a golden eagle, as taken of his parentage, was carried before him; he wore a purple robe, buskins like kings in tragedies, and a crown of gold.*

MARCUS JUNIANUS JUSTINUS, *EPITOME OF THE PHILIPPIC HISTORY OF POMPEIUS TROGUS*[1]

205

T he financial collapse that began in 2008 had many causes, but the excessive use of credit ties them all together. At the heart of the credit system are mortgages, and from these emanated nearly all the problems. Mortgages were taken by homeowners who could not afford payments, financed by banks whose thin reed of equity could not withstand the slightest downturn, and encouraged all along by the innovation of government-sponsored entities that enabled securitization with a federal guarantee. True, innovation enabled securities to be sliced and diced, and derivatives of all sorts fostered a perception that risk had been reduced or borne by someone else. These moral hazards might have been contained through regulation. However, financial regulators failed to spot the most basic fraud schemes even though they nearly doubled their budgets in the decade prior to the meltdown. It is doubtful they could conceptualize even to this day the invitation to excess that government guarantees provide. In 2009, the United States government continues to subsidize mortgage interest rates through the use of its AAA credit rating. In some cases it is providing tax credits in excess of required homeowner equity, and is intervening to prop up the mortgage securities market through direct purchases.

Part 4 of this book begins by recapping the plight of the government sponsored agencies and their role in the crisis, which inevitably leads us into the politics of their role from their humble beginnings in the 1930s to the expansion of the Community Reinvestment Act in the Clinton years that set the stage for the boom and bust that began under Fed Chairman Alan Greenspan. Politics play a sweeping role in the drama that would unfold from the Depression forward. In the chapter "A Return to Malaise" the focus is upon the latter half of the 20th century, wherein the pattern of rising government spending and continuous printing of fiat currency combined to unify both political parties behind the buying of votes with the provision of entitlements. At work here is what economist Sowell terms the "open-ended fallacy." When subjective rather than objective criteria are used to determine government policy, there is no comeback to repeated demands for more of a good thing. Greater health, retirement, housing, education, or transportation benefits are always desirable.

Eventually this takes us to the point where a young and charismatic Barack Obama becomes president at precisely the moment when the financial system melts down. His response is a staggeringly large expansion of government and debt and a redistributionist taxation policy. He followed the Keynesian template and acceded to Fed Chairman Bernanke's printing of dollars to monetize the debt that would be used to pay for the spending. By mid-2009 it appears that a revival of economic activity and financial market speculation has erupted without much solid evidence of a true recovery, but the structural problems of the public and private sector remain gargantuan by historical standards. For this reason the question is asked: Will these bold strokes bring a return to malaise, a phrase immortalized by President Jimmy Carter, a politician who likewise took the helm during America's darkest times since the Great Depression? The final chapter of Part 4 asks an even larger question: whether democracy itself might be a fatal condition that would make republics succumb to the wishes of the mob.

So entrenched is the modern socialistic and technocratic state that political strategies that buck the trend and advocate restraint of government expenditures have been barred from consideration since prior to the crash of 1929. Even notable conservatives who shared power with a liberal Congress or executive branch, such as Ronald Reagan or Newt Gingrich, respectively, were unable to restrain the growth of government, much less undo the empowerment extended beyond its original constitutionally enumerated powers.

# Chapter 9

# The Heart of the Financial System

H ousing is probably the most heavily subsidized industry in the United States. Mortgages are tax deductible, and $5 trillion of them piggyback upon the full faith and credit of the U.S. government, providing an interest rate subsidy to homeowners in addition to the tax savings[1]. By promoting home ownership so forcefully, might the demand for housing have been overly stimulated to the point that we now face a systemic financial crisis? Might the banking sector have been crowded out of the bread-and-butter section of the market and concentrated its bet upon jumbo mortgages, home equity loans, interest-only loans and other mortgages that did not compete directly with the government agencies? Over 50 percent of loans made are real estate related, including commercial real estate.[2]

The cottage industry of doom-and-gloom prognosticators has long predicted the end, but a more humble opinion might be that in this cycle we may be institutionalizing socialization of assets and debts as a priority, and that its cost will be less control over dilution of currency value (inflation), greater seigniorage (a tax that degrades incentives and therefore erodes capitalistic growth), and the concentration of risk into large institutions that are "too big to fail," producing de-facto nationalization of banking. With the unanimous prescription of even greater regulation

209

and oversight, our largest banking institutions may have become quasi-government entities well before the federal government made a direct investment in the nation's nine largest banks in October 2008.

In early July 2008, the equity market value of Fannie Mae and Freddie Mac, the government-sponsored entities (GSEs) that control half the residential mortgage market, declined precipitously. Among the issues coming to light at that moment was a Financial Accounting Standards Board proposal (FAS 140) to require financial services firms to consolidate off-balance sheet securitizations into their balance sheets. To do so would require an estimated haircut to book equity of some $46 billion for Fannie Mae and $29 billion for Freddie Mac. This compares with stated equity in March 2008 of just $39 billion for Fannie Mae and $16 billion at Freddie Mac. Since during 2008 these stocks traded at discounts to their book value, the dilution to existing shareholders needed to clean up this mess would have been massive, even assuming that further deterioration of the firm's assets would not occur. However, knowing what we know now, it is unlikely enough equity could have been raised to offset losses at Fannie and Freddie. Just two months later, AIG and Lehman Brothers collapsed, and these entities controlled some $2 trillion of assets, a large number compared to M3, the broadest measure of the money supply, which stood at an estimated $14 trillion by September 2008.

At the beginning of that year, the government mortgage agencies, which profit from the implicit backing of the federal government, were given a green light to buy in more assets despite their decayed and razor thin capital ratios. Consequently their already massive share of the mortgage credit business became dominant. (They own or guarantee almost half the $12 trillion of U.S. home loans). By September 8, 2008, they were backstopped by the U.S. Treasury, theoretically nationalized through December 2009 using a process known as conservatorship, wherein they would be nursed back to health. On October 13, 2008, the CEOs of the nation's nine largest banks were summoned to Washington, D.C. and handed a term sheet detailing how the government would buy $125 billion of preferred stock in their companies. "They weren't allowed to negotiate" wrote the Wall Street Journal, "... Just weeks earlier, (Treasury Secretary Paulson) had said that injecting capital directly into banks would appear to be a sign of 'failure.'"[3]

By February 2009 the share prices of Bank of America and Citicorp reached $3, emboldening analysts of the consensus-oriented large Wall Street brokerages to raise the question of whether these institutions might be imminently nationalized. When therefore if not then is it not obvious that credit risk is no longer borne by the private sector, but passed to the taxpayer? Still, the newly appointed Treasury Secretary Tim Geithner and President Obama, wary of spooking already unsettled markets, were quick to suggest that nationalization might only be "temporary"—along the lines of the Swedish model of the early 1990s—which stripped out bad assets and quickly auctioned the revitalized core operations back into the marketplace.

But with a systemic crisis possibly still unfolding, a large healthy global market no longer exists to absorb a small exceptional pocket of weakness as was the case in Sweden nearly twenty years ago. A silver bullet that might clean up the mess may be a pipedream. This is not to say that healing might not occur. It could after the super-sized debt ratios of the global economy recede by an order of magnitude, something that neither socialization nor piecemeal quasi-free market solutions might hope to achieve. Or paradoxically, the forced injection of fresh government credit could unfreeze markets, but it would increase systemic leverage and make us more vulnerable.

## A Canary in the Coal Mine

For some time observers have warned of problems at these entities. The crisis was presaged in an unusual source—*The New York Times*—back in September 1999, which cited Peter Wallison of the American Enterprise Institute warning that the July 1999 proposal by the Department of Housing and Urban Development to require half of Fannie Mae's and Freddie Mac's loan portfolio to be made up of loans from low- and moderate-income borrowers would "not pose any difficulties during flush times," but would "prompt a government rescue similar to that of the savings and loan industry in the 1980's." Wallison edited a book published in July 2001 titled *Serving Two Masters, Yet Out of Control* (AEI Press 2001), which laid out the irreconcilable posture of the GSEs, who maximized profit and market share at the expense of the private sector, yet laid off all their risk upon taxpayers. He published numerous articles sounding the alarm. In *The Fundamental Problem With Fannie Mae and Freddie Mac* (AEI: December 1, 2000), he concludes, "From time to time, supporters of Fannie and Freddie have argued that these companies represent the perfect form of organization—a combination of private sector efficiency and government financial power. The record shows, however, that the opposite is true. By combining the government's exemption from market discipline with the aggressiveness of private sector management, Congress has created a financial monster." In January of 2000 Wallison and coauthor Charles Calomiris are troubled: "Not only do the GSEs distort the allocation of credit by funneling financing to politically favored sectors of the economy, but once they have entered an area of financial activity the GSEs' implicit government backing allows them to drive out private sector competitors and achieve dominance in their markets. In addition, because they can provide financing at subsidized rates, the GSEs are able to muster substantial political support from the favored groups, which over time insulates them from Congressional oversight and could make them invulnerable to Congressional control."

Steve Sailer, publisher of the popular blog www.isteve.blogspot. com, posted an analysis of dollars committed to low-income mortgage lending triggered by the Community Reinvestment Act (CRA), which showed that $4.2 trillion of CRA loans had been placed from 1992 to 2005. Within this total, there were notable spikes in activity, such as roughly $1 trillion committed in 1998 and about $1.6 trillion in 2004. The teeth in the CRA legislation come from the requirement that federal regulators consider "community needs" when banks request approval to merge, so this pattern is not surprising. 1998 was the year of the Bank of America merger with NationsBank, and 2004 contained that bank's purchase of Fleet as well as JP Morgan Chase's acquisition of Bank One. In 2008, Bank of America pledged $1.5 trillion of CRA loans to be made when it sought permission to buy Countrywide Financial. The CRA commitments do not include promises that the government-sponsored entities made to purchase mortgages originated by these and other banks in the securities market, an amount estimated by Sailer to be in the trillions of dollars. With the government standing by to provide liquidity and manipulate the actions of bankers to affect public policy goals, a giant moral hazard was created. Bankers no longer cared about the financial soundness of their underwriting, for they would be given carte blanche to expand market share through consolidation in exchange for looking the other way. And they would not be expected to hold all the risk, for it could be laid off to taxpayer-subsidized quasi-government corporate entities.

So-called progressive policies advanced by groups with ties to Democrats like the Association of Community Organizations for Reform Now (ACORN) lobbied to get regulators to relax lending standards. These changes were institutionalized within the lending system through the government-sponsored entities, Fannie and Freddie, making the problem systemic in nature. But this cause and effect is still not understood by Obama policymakers, who are expanding government subsidization and risking an even more catastrophic outcome for the capital markets. Progressive groups pushed the idea of ending "redlining," the practice of not granting mortgages in low-income, mainly black neighborhoods that was prevalent before the savings and loan crisis wiped out that industry. Before that time, S&Ls had interest rate ceilings above which they could not issue loans, so they naturally avoided lending to anyone with high risk of nonrepayment, since a premium for that bad outcome could not be built into the loan price. Despite this being confined to the dustbin of history, in 1989 ACORN got sympathetic members of Congress to amend the Home Mortgage Disclosure Act to force banks to collect racial data. This was used in a flawed study by the Boston Fed (disproved by Stan Liebowitz and Walter Williams, among others) wherein it recommended that mortgage lenders not use "arbitrary or outdated criteria that effectively disqualify many urban or lower-income minority applicants." These outdated criteria included "the size of the mortgage payment relative to income, credit history, savings history and income verification. Instead, the Boston Fed ruled that *participation in a credit counseling program* should be taken as evidence of an applicant's ability to manage debt," according to Liebowitz.[4]

Selected abrogation of mortgage contracts or the insertion of the state between borrowers and lenders may be a rolling stone already set in motion upon the plank of the Democrats in the 2008 presidential election. Judicial powers to rewrite mortgage contracts were contemplated under the TARP fund, and in 2009 these are likely to become reality in a backroom deal now that the government owns stakes in banks. Such reform would cause private sources of lending to demand higher interest rates, were it not for the government guarantee of conforming mortgages, or it would provoke greater than historical loss ratios. Even without this, if much of the $790 billion passed through into securities by companies such as Countrywide went into prime-rated paper (the exact amount is unknown), then default risk could be higher than expected for conforming loans. In a conference call in mid-2007 Countrywide's chief risk officer patiently explained to seasoned Wall Street analysts that indeed prime-rated paper originated by the company with a FICO score of 620 did contain bad credits that were blended in.[5]

## Shooting the Messenger

Freddie and Fannie were at the center of the brewing maelstrom, and in exchange for their unabashed promotion of unsound lending in the noble mission to expand home ownership, they were afforded protection from the scrutiny of regulators, save for one small agency, the Office of Federal Housing Enterprise Oversight (OFHEO), whose powers over them were substantially restricted. Undaunted, OFHEO director Armando Falcon began an investigation of Fannie Mae in July 2003. The company had increased its earnings like clockwork at 15 percent on the nose for years, which probably looked suspicious to OFHEO when it surmised that the company had taken significant interest rate risk when rates fell in 2002, causing billions of dollars of economic, but not accounting, losses.[6] This was not the first time, for "in the late 1970s and early 1980s, Fannie Mae made a bet on interest rate trends that left the institution technically insolvent as its net worth briefly turned negative, raising fears of a financial collapse."[7]

The publishing of OFHEO's findings in September 2004 revealed management had significant problems with its accounting for amortization of premiums and discounts on securities and loans (FAS 91) as well as for its derivatives and hedges (FAS 133). Furthermore, management (in particular CEO Frank Raines and CFO Tim Howard) was severely criticized. (During the 2008 election cycle, Jim Johnson was an economic advisor to Obama, who himself was the second largest recipient of GSE political donations, but Raines' role as an advisor to Obama was denied by his campaign.)[8] A few words from the report are eye-opening:

> The highest levels of senior management wanted Fannie Mae to be viewed as "one of the lowest risk institutions in the world" and as "best in class" in terms of risk management, financial reporting, corporate governance, and internal control ... The image of Fannie Mae communicated by Mr. Raines and his inner circle and promoted by the Enterprise's corporate culture was false. In the words of one current member of Fannie Mae's Board of Directors, the picture of the Enterprise as a "best-in-class" financial institution was a "façade." To maintain that façade, senior executives worked strenuously to hide Fannie Mae's operational deficiencies and significant risk exposures from outside observers—the Board of Directors, its external auditor, OFHEO, the Congress, and the public. The illusory nature of the Enterprise's public image and senior management's efforts at concealment were the two essential features of the Enterprise's corporate culture.[9]

Chillingly, a House of Representatives committee review of OFHEO's findings was chock full of Democrats condemnations of OFHEO having ever brought up issues of mismanagement in the mortgage agencies, and staunch attestations that there was no financial problem brewing within them. The review is punctuated by repeated pleas by Republican congressmen to further empower OFHEO (which had little regulatory power) to examine and clean up the situation—all this before the hyperbolic layering on of mortgages that occurred in 2005 and 2006. A video of the proceedings is available on YouTube.[10]

If accounting had been the only issue as things stood in the precarious market conditions that emerged in 2008, a fix could have been made and cash flow would have remained unchanged at presumably healthy levels. If management had been the problem, executive housecleaning would have sufficed. However, the underlying proposition of why the entities exist, whether they are achieving their mission, and most important, whether they are counterproductive are the questions that must be asked and resolved. Ronald Reagan quipped in his first inaugural address (1981) that "Government is not the solution to our problem. Government is the problem."[11] The record shows that Fannie Mae and Freddie Mac follow in the footsteps of previous failures. As Ronald Utt writes, "... federally sponsored financial institutions, including those that the federal government closely regulates and insures, have a knack of frequently exploding in hugely horrific and costly ways. Since the mid-1980s, massive losses have occurred in the federal Farm Credit System, the Federal Deposit Insurance Corporation, and the Federal Savings and Loan Insurance Corporation. Worse, the heavily regulated and supposedly closely supervised savings and loan industry collapsed more than a decade ago, and repairing the residual damage cost the U.S. taxpayers $130 billion."[12]

## More is Always Better

The original mission of Fannie Mae when it was created in 1938 was to stabilize the badly battered home mortgage market of the Depression with a focus on first-time homebuyers. The idea was that banks could create loans and sell them to Fannie Mae, freeing up balance sheet capacity. Like many government programs, initially success may be evident, but as in the "open-ended fallacy" that economist Thomas Sowell exposes, monstrous results can emerge as momentum for more subsidization builds. Yes, the new agency's presence created more loans. But the cash had to come from somewhere, and that somewhere was the federal government and its tax revenue, which under Roosevelt saw income tax rates raised overall and sharply boosted for high brackets.[13] The combined result would be smaller private sector consumption and expanded government take, and a more indebted consumer. After the economy emerged from the Depression era, this and the tax deductibility of interest continued to increase leverage and homeownership. Home ownership increased as the innovation of the long-term fixed-rate mortgage caught on in the postwar housing boom, which was partly kick-started by the release of accumulated savings of soldiers returning from the battlefront (and reduced down payment requirements). From 1940 to 1965, homeownership expanded from 44 to 63 percent. Note that its good intentions were hardly felt in the 1930s when the effect was needed, but its ill effects have now reverberated generations later.

Since the secular trend towards the democratization of credit began decades before the depression, it is arguable whether Fannie Mae was necessary for continuance of the trend. However, even if that is assumed to be so, what occurred after Fannie Mae was privatized in 1969 and Freddie Mac was chartered a year later, to provide competition, is instructive. The new face of Fannie Mae and its clone turbocharged growth. These institutions enjoyed the access to capital from the public equity market, but their special status (line of credit with the government, no SEC oversight, and a government guarantee that gave these entities a lower cost of funds than their private market rivals) was preserved. Armed with these advantages, GSEs increased their book of business from $13 billion in 1965 to $1 trillion by 1990 and $3.4 trillion in 2003. Once the great real estate bubble had concluded by year-end 2007, Freddie and Fannie combined had purchased $4.9 trillion of mortgages, repackaging 70 percent of these into guaranteed securities for the secondary market. This (along with Ginnie Mae) gave the GSEs roughly half of the $11 trillion mortgage market, but their share of new originations has become near dominant. Many sources peg this at 70 percent, but an interesting take from *TIME* magazine business and economics columnist Justin Fox takes into account the impact of refinancings into GSE-backed loans. Juxtaposing GSE total volume ($539 billion) against new originations ($313 billion), GSE market share was 172 percent for the first quarter of 2008.[14]

Just as in the depression, the GSEs are stimulating the creation of credit and indebting homebuyers at the expense of the highest-income-earning taxpayers. Homeownership topped out at 69 percent in 2004 and stood at 68.4 percent in September 2007, not having increased much from its 63 percent level nearly 50 years ago when the government restructured the agencies to promote their growth. Citizens know that owning real estate in an environment when credit expansion under a fiat currency has devalued the purchasing power of the dollar by over 60 percent since 1980 has made real estate an enticing investment, particularly if it can be leveraged 4:1 with low interest rate fixed debt. The increase in primary mortgage credit, rather than promoting homeownership, wound up escalating prices beyond the reach of many of the first-time homebuyers it was intended to subsidize.

Moreover, the credit availability made itself felt through higher loan-to-value ratios and diversion into consumption. When house prices ran up sharply between 2001 and 2007, homeowners extracted a staggering $8 trillion of equity from their homes, all a tax-free stream of cash, which is now quite material relative to the overall value of residential real estate ($20 trillion). $8 trillion is a lot, more than half a year's GDP, and it distorted signals to businesses, which expanded and repurchased shares. Individuals saw the rising fortunes and bullishly invested in the stock market. Sadly this withdrawal closes the gap between financing and the now reduced value of properties. As of 2008 it left some one-third of all homes with negative equity. A report issued by Harvard University's Joint Center for Housing Studies in July 2008 documented that even if interest rates fell by 1 percent, the median home price in 18 major metro areas would need to fall another 25 percent to return affordability to 2003 levels.[15] Interestingly, the problem is not as acute for flyover country, because if rates fell that much nationwide, only a 2 percent adjustment in price would be necessary.

The government bailout of the GSEs might restore confidence, but it may be a superficial fix. By long-term historical standards the entities would remain incredibly leveraged. The government would inject some $170 billion into them, but this is still a drop in the bucket. For example, Fannie Mae had a GAAP carrying value of its common shareholder's equity of just $19.5 billion as of June 30, 2008, just 2.2 percent of total assets. And bear in mind that its guarantee applies to nearly $2.4 trillion of mortgage-backed and other securities that are not on its balance sheet. With these factored in, equity was a mere 0.6 percent of assets. This is based upon historical costs, including charge-offs and provisions. In its footnote disclosing the impact of fair market value, the firm's common equity would be *negative* $5.4 billion! In case one feels more comfortable with this scientifically determined amount, the adjustment to get to it is only $24.9 billion, or 0.8 percent of the total book of business. Over the last year the value of America's real estate has declined by more than this each month. This has been the case despite the government, through these agencies, and the Federal Reserve having shoveled money into real estate financing to keep it propped up with artificially low mortgage rates. Taking the government at its word, in December 2009 this activity would come to an end through the GSEs at least. If one had capital with which to invest in real estate, would it be smart to buy now, when the government is spraying money through a fire hose to buyers that need government subsidized borrowing to come up with the funds to close a transaction, or to wait until it can no longer or will no longer do so? Isn't this December 2009 deadline a bit like telling al Qaeda that you intend to pull out of Iraq by a certain date?

According to the bailout plan, each GSE would see its portfolio of mortgages rise, but neither could hold more than $850 billion of mortgages directly. This implies an injection of $144 billion compared to a total of $1,556 billion in their portfolios as of July 2008. But more might follow, and the December 2009 deadline for cleaning up the companies might need to be extended if the real estate market remains in oversupply. The real estate market had dropped about 25 percent through year-end 2008, and the thesis popular in mid-2009 that the economy had bottomed out is highly dependent upon no further decrease in value.

## The New Rent Control

What is missed by most observers is that interest rates outside the government-subsidized market have risen sharply and may continue to remain high for two reasons. The mortgage rate seen earlier in this decade was at a generational low, in part because of Fed policy. Additionally, this cycle is the first in the postwar era that has exhibited falling prices, and as a result credit quality has become an issue. Rates on jumbo loans, which are not guaranteed by the GSEs, climbed to nearly 8 percent by year-end 2008, thus standing some 3 to 4 percent above the subsidized rate. The socialization of credit has caused a tremendous bifurcation in the market unseen before. It is reminiscent of other dysfunctional markets, such as the New York City housing market, where rent controls created artificial shortages, discouraged investment, repair, and rehabilitation, and led to oddities such as millionaires over the age of 50 living for decades in subsidized one-bedroom apartments while 20-somethings and young families were priced out of the market or paid well over 50 percent of their income for rent. By linking mortgage rates implicitly to income brackets, the GSEs now supplement the progressive tax rate mechanism of the IRS. Like rent stabilization in New York City, it separates homeowners as much by geography as it does income, because the cost of living on the coasts and in different cites varies considerably.

Unprecedented government intervention has occurred in response to the credit meltdown. In 2008 the government mortgage agencies were essentially nationalized, and through the TARP program, nearly $1 trillion was made available to recapitalize commercial banks. That same year the Fed injected roughly $1 trillion of credit into the financial system, and by early 2009 it promised to buy mortgages and Treasury notes and bonds with another $1 trillion of freshly printed money, plus provide additional credit facilities also in the trillions of dollars. At the center of the meltdown was real estate, which has approximated half of commercial lending. These unprecedented steps showed signs of unlocking the credit markets by spring of 2009, forestalling the withdrawal of deposits over $250,000 in size from the banking system. But there are consequences: The money supply has increased, diluting saved wealth, and national indebtedness has soared. Much more taxation than the 5 to 10 percent proposed through the top bracket hike and raising caps on taxable Social Security income would be needed to counteract a fraction of the money spent to defend the system, a conclusion meticulously calculated in the previous chapter.

In May 2008 the Obama team floated a trial balloon of imposing a VAT tax, which would probably claim a mid-single digit percentage of nationwide retail sales value, adding to the potential burden of the massive proposed carbon tax. Together these could sink an already weak economy in a way reminiscent of the Smoot-Hawley tariff made law in 1930. Knowing the horrific results of having gradually nationalized real estate finance since the 1930s, what might lie in store from large-scale intervention into the banking business itself? In a not-so-subtle way, that also has been happening slowly through the Federal Reserve System, which has pumped $1 trillion annually into the money supply through fractional reserve lending each year since the Internet bubble topped out, a continuation of 8 percent M3 growth since Nixon completely ended gold convertibility. The distortion of the government agencies took 70 years to gestate into a monster. How much longer will it be before the culmination of manufacturing vast amounts of credit-based money yields equally tragic results?

# Chapter 10

# A Return to Malaise

*The symptoms of this crisis of the American spirit are all around us. For the first time in the history of our country a majority of our people believe that the next five years will be worse than the past five years. Two-thirds of our people do not even vote. The productivity of American workers is actually dropping, and the willingness of Americans to save for the future has fallen below that of all other people in the Western world.*

JIMMY CARTER, CRISIS OF CONFIDENCE SPEECH, JULY 15, 1979

G overnment receipts as a percentage of GDP have averaged 18 percent since World War II, but spending has grown nine times faster than median income since 1965, the advent of the Great Society under President Johnson. (Median income grew 35 percent, but spending jumped from $628 billion to $2.7 trillion, increasing indebtedness.) Spending has grown regardless of Congressional leadership, which confirms the thesis of this book that in practice conservatism has been dormant since nearly a century ago.

Many Republicans wear the badge of conservatism, but once elected—either because they are outnumbered or become swept up in the rush of power—they abandon conservative principles. Spending has grown despite the winding down of military spending, both before and after the peace dividend enjoyed in the Bush 41 and Clinton years. The burden of protecting our nation as a percentage of GDP fell from above 6 percent in the early 1980s to roughly 3 percent late in the Clinton years and still manageably rested at just under 4 percent in the Iraq War years.

## Going Deeper into Debt

Debt has grown even faster than spending, from $628 million in 1965 to $9.5 trillion as of the end of the 2008 fiscal year. By October 2008 total debt had reached $10.5 trillion.[1] It is likely to grow by well over $1 trillion in the 2009 fiscal year from bailouts alone, and the trend in existing programs could produce nearly another trillion dollars of debt. Many note that over $6 trillion of the $10.5 trillion of federal debt is held inter-governmentally (mainly for Social Security), and that in either case it appears controllable compared to a Gross Domestic Product of some $13 trillion. However, by 2016 Social Security benefits will exceed withholding taxes, triggering liquidation of these securities. Moreover, the debt that financed some $5.2 trillion of GSE mortgages could be consolidated onto the federal balance sheet now that effectively they have been nationalized (but this will remain off the books). With the total debt measured at over $90,000 for each household in the United States a threshold may have been reached that is reminiscent of accumulations that resulted after the great wars of our nation: Revolutionary, 1812, Civil, or both World Wars. In most cases these were associated with periods when the government chose to debase the currency, and in some cases to raise taxes dramatically. Remarkably, from the founding of the Federal Reserve System in 1913 to Nixon's severance of gold convertibility, federal debt has grown at a 9 percent rate. Prior to 1913, a year that might be pegged as the turning point from conservatism to socialism, debt vacillated between $2.8 billion at the peak of the Civil War to a low of $1.5 billion in 1891 and back again.

## The E-Bomb: Entitlements

Even more worrisome is that using GAAP accounting, total government obligations were $60 trillion at the end of fiscal year 2007, a near doubling from the $35 trillion of just five years before. The $60 trillion is 24 times annual federal tax income (both are inclusive of Social Security and Medicare). (David Walker, the former U.S. comptroller general, refused to certify or render an opinion on the GAAP statements, because the government's ability to generate GAAP accounts is unreliable for significant portions of its operations. Nonetheless, this basis of accounting is far less subject to misstatement than conventional reporting of deficits.)

In Western Europe, the situation is similar. Public financial debt, under the auspices of the EU central bank, appears carefully controlled at less than one times GDP for most nations. However, when public pension liabilities are layered in, large socialistic nations such as Italy, Finland, Belgium, and France have future liabilities that are between four and five times GDP. Outliers such as Spain and Greece are eight to nine times GDP.[2] This excludes health care programs. Having aging populations, these socialistic systems are sure to feel the same or greater strains that are on course to beset the United States in about a decade.

While today the United States is at war with Islamic fundamentalist terrorists, most notably on two fronts in Iraq and Afghanistan, this cost has been far lower in dollars and in loss of life than even minor conflicts such as Vietnam. Never have we entered a major conflict already burdened with so much debt, yet this adversary appears poised to have nuclear and someday intercontinental ballistic capability. At the same time, although China is our largest trading partner, it has stolen military secrets from us, and it displays an uncomfortable amount of nationalistic fervor. To engage either or both sometime in the next two decades would be more challenging than ever historically, even with our brave troops who have proven themselves in the Middle East twice in the last two decades and with our mighty and innovative defense industry.

Entitlements are the heart and soul of the socialist state, since they ensnare voters for life. And sadly, to operate the entitlement system and the rest of the bureaucracy the recruitment of millions of government workers is required, capturing souls that might otherwise become part of the private sector and advance new technologies or processes that would improve our lot in life. The Democratic Party knows that entitlements and growing public sector employment are its lifeblood, so it has worked hard to deliver on sweeping expansions to benefits, the next being universal health care. Already the government pays for 47 percent of all medical costs in the United States, dominating certain areas that are in the domain of the elderly, such as oxygen therapy. The argument goes that moving to a single-payer system would save 25 percent off the top and rationalize inefficiencies, such as the indigent seeking treatment for routine sickness in a hospital emergency department. But when this has been tried, it results in long wait lines, a diminished quality of care, and the denial of life-saving treatments (see www.biggovhealth.org). Within the spending mix, mandatory spending has steadily gained share, standing at 53 percent of the $2.7 trillion budget in 2007. Nearly all of this is for Social Security, Medicare, and Medicaid.

These three entitlements summed to about 8.5 percent of GDP last year, but demographic changes and rising health care costs would take this to 11 percent by 2020 and over 14 percent by 2030, without a nationalized healthcare system. Like the tiresome warning that the wolf is at the door, the populace is inured to the possibility that the promises made would come due. But in less than a decade the era of surplus payments into the system from contemporaneous workers that started in the late 1960s will come to a close. The unified budget deficit will see hundreds of billions of dollars added every year, necessitating tax hikes and compromises in medical care.

The largest discretionary spending item is for the military, which constitutes 53 percent of the expenditures not deemed to be off limits. Although only about 15 percent of our active duty troops are deployed in the Iraq and Afghani theatres, there is intense pressure on reservists. Manning a conflict even a fraction of the size of World War II would require massive expenditure. More military restructuring might be done under a Democratic administration, but at 20 percent of total spending, it is hard to see how further force reductions would be material. The next largest discretionary categories are education and transportation, which are each well under $100 billion.

So, without much room for military reduction, spending as a percentage of GDP was on course to break out above the level it settled into after rising from the establishment of the technocratic state under Wilson and its expansion under Franklin Roosevelt. Under Obama, mandatory spending will reach an even higher level. In reality, health care is moving toward nationalization, discretionary spending would be sharply raised, and higher taxes might shed jobs and exacerbate the credit crunch, further pressuring the budget on both sides. Without Fed purchases of Treasuries artificially depressing bond and note yields, interest costs would rise substantially, increasing the cost of capital for both the government and private industry. The money printed out of thin air to manipulate that market most certainly will impact the nation's financial health.

Republicans under Bush needed a brush-up on economics by focusing on the budget deficit rather than on spending (or in particular spending as a percentage of GDP), which permitted government to expand at a faster rate than even under the two Clinton terms in the 1990s. Consequently, in matters of both fiscal and monetary policy, Republicans have been unfriendly to capital formation (despite success in slightly lowering taxes), because it has been off limits to engage in the debate over whether government should shrink or tax rates should be flat. Through the clarity of the panoramic view of income tax rates reviewed earlier in this book, the reduction of tax rates at the top achieved through ping-pong with the Democrats was minor, and it restructured the expectations of the lower half of all taxpayers, bringing them closer to being on the dole outright.

## Devil-May-Care Budgeting

The largest challenge likely to the new Obama administration could be a sharp decline in tax revenue despite the increases in the top two brackets proposed in February 2009. When sworn in January 2009, the Congressional Budget Office projected a $1.2 trillion deficit, which incorporated a 6.6 percent decrease in revenue from the $2.5 trillion of taxes the government collected in 2008. Individual income taxes ($1.1 trillion) and Social Security and Medicare ($0.9 trillion) are sensitive to employment; corporate taxes ($0.3 trillion) had already begun to decline sharply in 2008. The 11th U.S. Congress passed a $1 trillion stimulus package in February 2009, which was signed into law and would add some $250 billion annually to the deficit.

By the end of February, Obama released a 134-page outline of his budget, which projected a $1.75 trillion deficit for fiscal 2009. With weaker tax revenue than thought by the consensus, even this jaw-dropping figure could be surpassed. What should come as no surprise is that the details include many elements from what Obama as a candidate had proposed as of the final weeks of his campaign that deal with structural changes to taxes that go well beyond tinkering with rates assigned to brackets. Few appreciate what precisely was contemplated in his plank, which if reworked is likely to reemerge on a grander scale as the Obama presidency unfolds over the next four or eight years. The consequence will be a dramatic transfer of wealth and sharply reduced incentives for business to invest capital, particularly small business.

Nearly all the details of Obama's intentions to establish a major transfer of wealth from the topmost income brackets to the bottom 50 percent and to increase taxes to all Americans to fund an expansive new vision of a much larger government sector, including socialized health care, were evident within his *Blueprint for Change* campaign document circulated during the campaign. Oddly enough his opponent, Senator John McCain, was unfamiliar with the details when he faced Obama in a debate held just before the election on October 15, 2008. He accused Obama of having $1 trillion of new spending planned, a charge that was easily deflected because in actuality his bold plans did not so much encompass traditional fiscal spending. Instead, it contained material changes within the tax code that would leave brackets largely untouched, but transfer vast sums of money from the wealthy and corporations to the bottom 50 percent, Obama's electorate. Moreover, diehard Obama supporters such as Warren Buffett and Jim Cramer would be surprised by January when it became clear Obama would not choose to govern in the centrist way Bill Clinton did in the 1990s. Both would publicly question Obama's policies, especially the layering on of $1 trillion of spending to revive the economy, which was not revealed in the blueprint booklet.

As analyzed by the left-center Center for a Responsible Budget, Obama's plank as envisioned in 2008 did not contemplate new spending, save for a $108 billion boost in Medicare coverage. Almost everything involved a tax change, with the largest increases being a cap-and-trade carbon tax ($100 billion over four years), closing loopholes ($75 billion), and increased income, capital gains, and estate taxes ($120 billion). The increases go to fund tax credits for "Making

Work Pay" ($72 billion), tax rebates ($85 billion), and reducing the Alternative Minimum Tax for those not in the top brackets ($106 billion). Interesting in the CFRB report for its petite contribution is a savings item nestled in a long list of tweaks dubbed "Reform Government Spending," $17 billion over four years, just between 0.001 and 0.002 percent of government outlays.[3]

The pattern established in the 2008 plank was evident in the actual 2009 budget, except in the American Recovery and Reinvestment Act of 2009 copious spending for stimulus ($590 billion) is now included, and $210 billion is stimulated through transferring cash to citizens through tax credits and transfers. To this end, the baseline projected of current policy shows deterioration of the budget to a $1.5 trillion deficit in 2009, which upticks to the aforementioned $1.75 trillion by virtue of adding a $250 billion placeholder for added financial stabilization efforts. Administration projections reduce the stimulus spending to a trivial amount by 2012, at which point tax increases would be in full swing.

It is hard to compare the new budget with the analysis of the campaign plank, because in recognition of the deep recession, much of the tax increases purportedly won't fully be implemented for three years. But once they kick in, on an annualized basis Obama projects tax cuts for families would be almost $100 billion annually, almost entirely from an $800 credit per household for "Making Work Pay." The budget projections show that by 2012 annual tax revenue would be raised through phasing out deductions for the top two brackets (~ $40 billion) and the new cap-and-trade carbon tax (~ $80 billion). Savings would include exiting Iraq (~ $140 billion) and increased Medicare efficiency—primarily competitive bidding for Medicare Advantage (~ $40 billion).

From a 10-year perspective, the largest concepts are funding near-universal health care and the tax credits for the non-rich. The cost of expanding Medicare above its already planned growth is projected at about $650 billion, and it would be funded mainly through the deduction phase out on the upper brackets and savings from competitive bidding. The tax credits ($770 billion over 10 years) would be mainly financed by cap-and-trade. This is self-defeating, because energy costs would be expected to rise as utilities and energy companies pass the new tax through to the very same consumers who would enjoy the credits. Another notable distortion would be the detrimental impact upon high-tax rate states, whose wealthy citizens would lose some 30 percent of the deduction of state taxes against federal income.

## Redistribution or Bust!

So if the detailed study of Obama's plan shows that it is mostly about wealth redistribution, why would that message have resonated with the American people during the 2008 election cycle? A 2001 study by professors Daniel John Zizzo and Andrew Oswald holds a clue. In a carefully controlled setting, they tested 116 subjects through 29 separate interactions to see if these people would be willing to give up some of their own cash to see the money of others eliminated. Indeed, they did, and their willingness to do so was triggered by "whether another person deserves the money he has." Moreover, this preference was highest among participants cast in a "disadvantaged" role. Interestingly, taxation does not reduce the desire of participants to burn the money of the most well off in the study. In the original experiment, a 25 percent tax was imposed, with no effect on the outcome.[4]

What is likely to result from this vast allocation of $1 trillion of spending offset by $1 trillion of savings (again, if we are to accept these proposals at face value) is at best a Keynesian and at worst a Marxist sizeable redistribution of wealth. Those at the bottom would likely spend everything given to them; those at the top would liquidate investments, cut jobs if they operate small businesses, or reduce personal or corporate spending to make ends meet. Moral hazard is all about incentives. The Obama plan would tilt them even more toward dissaving. The engorged $1.75 trillion federal deficit now projected was already poised to expand over the medium term due to promised entitlements whose present value is five times as large as our current debt. There will be pressure to maintain rather than eliminate the new stimulus spending, which is to be in the hundreds of billions per year through 2010. Incentives to earn in the highest brackets have been reduced not just through changes to bracket rates, but from Social Security and fewer deductions. With deleveraging occurring, tax revenues are likely to fall, because income and employment may decline in a longer than expected recession. Furthermore, the inability of citizens to accumulate the savings they desire, which is necessary for deleveraging, will be exacerbated by the need to pay higher taxes. Desired savings will be reduced systemically because growth in government spending will far outstrip whatever the private sector might salt away.

We are opting to solve the two problems of our time—excessive debt and moral hazard—with more debt and insulation from risk. Realistically, with an accommodative and successful Democratic-controlled Congress, we might move from an all-in state, federal, and FICA 60-plus percent rate to something far higher. Proposals such as a bill before the Senate ("Global Poverty Act" S2433) authored by Obama when he was in the Senate that seeks to dedicate 0.7 percent of U.S. GDP annually to foreign aid might become law. Still, mega-rich liberals such as Buffett and Soros might continue to see nearly all of their income be subject to something less than half this, since neither tycoon derives much if anything from W-2s or ordinary income like regular Americans do.[5, 6]

Even if the credit crisis fades, two terms of socialism might pass, only to be in hailing distance of IOUs from Social Security and Medicare being taken out of the vault and presented to the U.S. Treasury for payment. The 2009 Trustees Report projected this would occur in 2016, a year earlier than in their report issued in 2008. So the fiction that the budget is only mildly out of balance permitted by the "Unified Federal Budget" (instituted by President Johnson in 1969 that offset Social Security inflows against deficit spending) would become exposed once and for all when demographics force a direct call upon taxpayers.

The most crushing blow to the economy would be through the devastation of the engine of job creation: small business, whose entrepreneurial owners constitute two-thirds of the top bracket and also create the same proportion of jobs to the economy as a whole. Given the near-perilous amount of leverage in the mortgage market, the unemployment caused by the sharp rise in taxation of sub-S companies (which flow through to individual income) would roil the conventional mortgage sector, and it would deliver a body blow to the jumbo mortgage portion. Also, consider the effect of a tax increase from the perspective of spouses in households in the top few brackets. If they live in a large urban center, they pay state and local taxes approaching 50 percent upon their salary, which might be $50,000 to $75,000. To go to work they must drive or commute, and child care might be additive to this. So those with marginal retention rates of this added income of only 30 percent or so after related expenses might decide, after a tax hike, that it simply does not pay to keep up a career. Finally, the resetting of the already confiscatory death tax to its Clinton-era level of 55 percent, contemplated by Democrats but not yet proposed, would be exacerbated by previous actions of states, many of which opportunistically tacked on as much as 16 percent in tandem with the 10 percent federal reductions begun in 2001. So the death tax could rise to be two-thirds or three-fourths of the value of an estate.

## Malaise

Raising taxes in the middle of what may become the most severe recession since the 1930s could create a deepening malaise last seen under President Jimmy Carter, when the top bracket was 70 percent, to which state taxes were additive. That brief span, poignantly described by that president as a "crisis of confidence" that "strikes at the very heart and souls and spirit of our national will" leading to "the erosion of our confidence in the future" and "threatening to destroy the social and political fabric of America" may be the mood required to shake free the conviction of liberals behind policies that enfeeble the private sector and widen the reach of the vine of socialism.[7]

Carter was clueless about why the malaise had occurred, and he could not have anticipated the quick turnaround in confidence that began when Reagan took office. Seeing only an energy crisis, he proposed import quotas on foreign oil; massive government investment in alternative energy (both directly and through subsidies); gasoline rationing; increased public transportation; and conservation through speed limit and thermostat controls. As all of this involved "the most massive peacetime commitment in funds" we might have seen, plus an even higher tax rate than what was in force then. That would have been a remarkable feat, since when combined with state levies, tax rates were at a breaking point that could not possibly have fostered any incentive for small businessmen, who then kept barely a quarter of the next dollar they might earn. And might not the tremors felt throughout the land have been from the debasement of the currency caused by the fiat money system, especially once it was completely cut free from gold by Nixon in 1971, as well as the socialist regime of 70 percent marginal tax rates?

Amnesia of this low point in American history runs deep, even in one of its most renowned actors, former Fed Chairman Paul Volcker. Volcker is lauded by the financial community for having stopped inflation in its tracks through switching the emphasis of Fed policy to the control of monetary aggregates and ratcheting interest rates to hitherto unseen heights. He must have remembered the extent of the malaise. Yet in a speech delivered to the Economic Club of New York in April 2008, this lifelong Democrat says that surveys taken every year going back to when he was newly minted as president of the Federal Reserve Bank of New York (prior to being Fed Chairman) showed that at a minimum 70 percent of the American public thought government could be trusted to do the right thing most of the time, but that under Bush this confidence has collapsed. So his rationale for endorsing Obama in 2008 was that he was the only candidate capable of changing the partisan political climate and bringing into being solutions to foreign policy, global warming, Medicare, soaring medical expenses, or something as "simple" as solving Social Security.[8] Can there be no question that Obama would cure all these ills with heightened spending and taxation? And in so doing would that not be a return to the Carter malaise?

# Chapter 11

# Democracy: The Achilles' Heel of Capitalism?

*It is quite plain that your government will never be able to restrain a distressed and discontented majority. For with you the majority is the government, and has the rich, who are always a minority, absolutely at its mercy . . . Is it possible to doubt what sort of a legislature will be chosen? On one side is a statesman preaching patience, respect for vested rights, strict observance of public faith. On the other is a demagogue ranting about the tyranny of capitalists and usurers, and asking why anybody should be permitted to drink Champagne and to ride in a carriage, while thousands of honest folks are in want of necessities.*

LORD THOMAS BABINGTON MACAULAY, 1857[1]

With a goal of establishing a majority of the electorate that pays no income taxes at all, the new economic overlords may have inadvertently harnessed democracy to strike a fatal blow to capitalism. How could the country, and for that matter most of the western world, have gotten stuck in this blind alley? The answer may lie in a fault of democracy itself. In the mid-19th century the British Lord Macaulay wrote the above as part of a curious letter to the most prominent biographer of Thomas Jefferson, which sadly may be prophetic.

One may guffaw at the sweeping nature of such an unrealistic prognostication. But remember Britain relinquished its empire and then began to embrace socialism in earnest when it booted out Winston Churchill, because its populace preferred socialized medicine over honoring the continued leadership of its greatest hero of modern times.

Another intriguing theory is raised by talk show host and former law clerk to Clarence Thomas, Laura Ingraham, who points out that we no longer have representative government:

> . . . the Constitution provides that the number of representatives shall not exceed one in 30,000 persons . . . The Founders thought that in a representative government, each member of the House should represent roughly one small town's worth of constituents (by today's standards). Things have changed since 1787. To have a 1 to 30,000 ratio today, we would need approximately 10,000 members in the House . . . Instead, today, each member of the House represents almost 700,000 people . . . there are only one hundred senators and only one president. How "representative" can such a government be? Not very.[2]

## Shades of Juan Peron

Lord Macaulay thought that in times of economic stress the people would opt to use the machinery of democracy to successfully wage a class-based revolution and alter the American political system. Conceptually Lord Macauley did correctly anticipate that the Great Depression would sweep socialists into power. But he did not anticipate that after decades of gestation, the public would increasingly turn to fiscal and monetary socialism in conjunction with a long spoliation of cultural values. That voters would coalesce to wage class warfare through candidates Obama and Clinton in 2008 when the economy, for all its signs of wear, still had achieved unparalleled prosperity for all levels of society is remarkable. How could he imagine that conservatives—in the persona of Bush 43 and the Republicans serving in Congress—would be generous spenders and commit us to remarkable socialistic achievements such as "No Child Left Behind" and Medicare drug coverage legislation?

The lack of fiscal restraint, the growth in federal debt and future promised benefits, and accommodation of these policies through the doubling of broadly measured money (M3) to an estimated excess of $14 trillion over the last seven years may have brought us to a breaking point. Consider the following description of the Argentinian experience in the post–World War II era:

> The economy used to grow while being pushed by demand-driven policies (fiscal and monetary) as imports followed GDP growth, implying an increase in the balance of trade deficit. This deficit, when it reached a point of financial unsustainability, was resolved through a huge devaluation that caused higher inflation in tradable goods, which resulted in a fall in real wages and real money balances. The economy was then put in a recession because aggregate demand had fallen, but the improved balance of trade set the stage for recovery.[3]

Of course, there are major structural differences between the United States and Argentina that would cause business cycles to behave differently, the most often acknowledged being our having the world's reserve currency. For some time the latter country pursued autarkic policies (restraining imports in particular), and these complimented labor-friendly laws that resulted in rigidly high real wages that exacerbated hyperinflationary tendencies. But by explaining away the differences, we excuse the very behavior that causes economic order to decompose into a less productive state.

Similarly the United States appears to have a structural trade deficit and ballooning federal debt and future liabilities. Key factor inputs to the modern U.S. economy now exhibit grave rigidity. Oil drilling is severely restricted; corn must be unprofitably converted into gasoline; construction of new coal-fired and nuclear electric power generation plants is effectively banned; new oil refineries and LNG receiving terminals cannot be built; payment for medical services is bifurcated into commercial rates that rise 20 percent annually and Medicare, which is free and often incorporates downward pressure in reimbursement; education is heavily if not completely subsidized, contributing to a bimodal tuition structure that is either free or sold at highly inflated tuition rates; and open trade agreements promote importation but fail to stimulate exports (often due to abuse of intellectual property rights).

Each year more government regulation is imposed upon the economy. According to a 2005 study for the Small Business Administration, the cost of all rules on the books is $1.1 trillion, about the same amount that Americans paid in federal income taxes in 2007.[4] Despite rhetoric by regulation advocacy groups that the Bush administration has weakened protective standards, regulations have increased with major rule changes being only marginally lower in number under Bush compared to Clinton, according to the U.S. GAO. A surge in new rules is expected under Obama, with carbon dioxide constraints being the most costly.

Moreover, the Obama administration has worked behind the scenes to use the partial nationalization of banks to demote secured creditors and transfer private property to unions when financial pressures opportunistically erupted. In connection with the bankruptcy of Chrysler, the U.S. Treasury demanded that the auto company's assets be stripped away from the coverage of senior lender's liens, which violates private property rights and a host of prior court rulings. During prebankruptcy negotiations, banks that are heavily dependent upon TARP funding from the government laid the groundwork for this expropriation of fixed income collateral by accepting roughly 20 cents on the dollar, thus enabling the United Auto Workers to own 55 percent of the company's stock (and Fiat 20 percent). A similar fate awaits General Motors. Ironically this tactic is straight out of the Juan Peron playbook, which used bank nationalization to transfer ownership of Argentinean corporations to unions. Moreover, if card check legislation passes, unionization of labor might flourish like it does in that country.

## History Repeats Itself

If Argentina seems like a stretch, consider this lucid description from Bill Bonner's article in *'The Daily Reckoning'* of how fiscal and monetary policy (along with cultural rot) pulled under the once great

Roman Empire:

> Eventually, Roman expansion reached its limits under Trajan. Then, the military machine gradually changed from a profit-making institution manned by Romans, to an expensive peace keeping force staffed largely by barbarians. Worse, the clattering of chains was no more to be heard in the Delian slave market. Now the problems really began. The government had begun distributing free bread, in order to keep the urban mobs quiet, a program similar to today's Tax Rebate checks. Already, under Augustus, one in five people in Rome depended on the "dole." Then, Rome's balance of trade grew increasingly negative. This gave rise to something else that will be familiar to us: inflation. Nero took 10 percent of the silver out of the denarius. Then, under Marcus Aurelius, it was down to 75 percent. Finally, by the third century, the denarius was made of brass, with a silver coating. Consumer prices soared. Diocletian's solution was very similar to what Richard Nixon would do many years later—The Edict of Prices, a system of price controls.[5]

What Bonner is getting at is that the transformation from a vibrant republic to a disintegrating bureaucracy takes place over a long period of time. It occurs at the behest of the common man who forms a dependency upon demagogues who will always promise more in an attempt to maintain authority. While Bonner cites the example of Rome, he might just as well have retold the tale of the Heracleans used as the excerpt at the beginning of Part 4. The story is apt to be repeated for centuries to come, for in the short term at least, wealth is as easily gained through the taking as the making. Bonner's view uses the analogy to Roman times to remind us that when socialism is unified with currency debasement it takes on its most destructive form, potent enough to bring down empires. Make no mistake. Capitalism has been under attack by socialism for nearly a century, and fiscal policy has become an engine of redistribution, creating debt and obligations for future administrations and generations that may imperil the very democracy that has enabled the greatest prosperity seen anywhere on Earth. As our culture loses respect for long-held axioms of morality, such as private property, the sanctity of contracts, and the direct meaning of words written in the Constitution, what follows is a fiscal embodiment of a return to rule by tribalism and the rejection of trade and monetary systems.

# Part Five

# SOCIALISM—ROMAN STYLE!

*When wealth was once considered an honor, and glory, authority, and power attended on it, virtue lost her influence, poverty was thought a disgrace, and a life of innocence was regarded as a life of ill-nature. From the influence of riches, accordingly, luxury, avarice, and pride prevailed among the youth; they grew at once rapacious and prodigal; they undervalued what was their own, and coveted what was another's; they set at naught modesty and continence; they lost all distinction between sacred and profane, and threw off all consideration and self-restraint. It furnishes much matter for reflection, after viewing our modern mansions and villas extended to the size of cities, to contemplate the temples which our ancestors, a most devout race of men, erected to the Gods.*

GAIUS SALLUSTIUS CRISPUS, *CONSPIRACY OF CATILINE*[1]

The fall the Roman civilization is a complex subject. Some might argue as to Rome's preeminence among the great empires, but by the scope of its influence, geography, and persistence over time combined with its providing a foundation for the most advanced societies of today, it has rightfully earned benchmark status for all great political enterprises since. This being the case, it will forever invite comparison with each of these, even the relatively young but highly prosperous and successful United States of America. The question that looms over those who are in awe of man's greatest collective achievements is why did it fall apart, and what does this say about the tendencies for even the best of governmental systems to self-destruct? Perhaps the questions of why Rome fell and what does this imply for America are not precise enough. Might we ask: Why did their republic and ours give way to unmanageable government?

To obtain answers to these questions, Part 5 explores many topics, and these bring to the surface several uncomfortable threads. One is that the evolution of both these great societies began with capitalist states that became regimes with a sparse super-rich elite that would be lightly taxed and wield tremendous political power. The estates of Rome's middle classes were eroded by governmental action, mostly the suppression of consumer price inflation through food price controls and repression of wages through competition for labor by slavery. The emergence of populist politicians such as the Gracchus brothers in the first century BC introduced land reform and welfare, and the Roman populace shifted to embrace a socialist framework of rewarding idleness with bread and circuses.

The role of money in credit crises is carefully examined. The recurrence of credit panics on the surface seems incongruent with the discipline of hard money developed in the Republic. But as a reserve, silver expanded geometrically, acting as a rudimentary version of today's fiat backing, and its production was under complete government control in state-owned mines. Once the mines were depleted, emperors would resort to clipping and other forms of currency debasement. Under pressure from the populist Assembly, the government repeatedly accommodated overextended debtors as a group, and windfalls of new money were introduced to the system when conquests were made, pulling a rabbit out of the hat often in times of extreme asset price deflation. For the record, some other popular notions are explored, such as the depravity of the Empire, the extension of military power, and the role of religion in each era. But the role inflating the currency reserve played in stimulating the offering and use of excessive credit to fund real estate investment cannot be understated. When combined with government policies that repressed consumer price inflation and eventually led to an expanded welfare state, respect for private property would diminish and incentives for economic growth would completely disappear. Eventually serfdom and autarky would take its place.

The economic deterioration of the Roman Empire set in during the second century, well after its most prosperous time, which in fact arose out of the Republic that began to fade away starting with Julius Caesar's consolidation of power. The Founding Fathers of the United States were acutely aware of the fragility of political systems such as the early Roman Republic, and in fact the standard good education of their day was grounded upon the classics. Washington was compared to Cincinnatus, the farmer of a few acres outside Rome who was chosen to lead his republic in battle, and likewise when offered kingship, refused it to return to his land. A massive marble statue of Washington was made a few decades after his death and stands in the entryway of the Smithsonian, depicting him as casting aside his sword as Cincinnatus would. Cullen Murphy, author of *Are We Rome: The Fall of an Empire and the Fate of America*, wryly notes that the crowds who walk past it today would miss the reference to his Roman counterpart, instead thinking he "looks more like a man in a sauna, asking for a towel."[2]

Washington and the leaders of his era prized duty as a limited, patriotic offering of the self, dignity, and virtue—a direct reference to the early Roman triad of familia, virtus, and dignitas. Washington, Franklin, Jefferson, and others who convened the constitutional convention of 1787 knew full well that the Roman republic was short lived and replaced by an imperial state. Democracy had rarely been tried nor had it achieved sustained success through history on a large geographic scale, and their vision was to maintain its advantages through creating tension between the executive and legislative branches, with impartial arbiters of constitutionality weighing in from time to time from the judiciary. An important but now diluted concept they cherished was that of representative government, wherein each Congressman would be tied to a small number of citizens, thus avoiding the development of a powerful oligarchy beside the executive as was the case beneath the emperor in the middle years of Rome's ascendency. The judicial branch was seen by Madison to be the least likely to inveigh supreme power, despite the name of its highest court, for judges were expected to be readers of statutes and not writers of new legislation. Little did they know that this characteristic, that is being impartial technicians who are best able to interpret the intentions of legislators, became the rationale for the unconstitutional delegation of power by Congress to politically unaccountable bureaucrats started under Woodrow Wilson's leadership.

The story of why Rome disintegrated in its final 200 years attracts those who would draw analogies to the tenets of governmental systems they would favor in the current day. Great questions are debated over decades and sometimes centuries. The chief debate of our era in the Western World is between socialists and capitalists. One would think that with the unqualified collapse of the Soviet Union, the transformation of China into a quasi-capitalist state, and the pitiful condition of satellites such as North Korea and Cuba, there would be little intellectual justification for any system reliant upon centralized planning of resources or the redistribution of income. Yet that is not the case, for there is a strong human instinct for tribal culture, wherein the group is revered over the individual.

# Chapter 12

# From the Golden Era to Totalitarianism

*That the human race eventually was able to occupy most of the earth as densely as it has done, enabling it to maintain large numbers even in regions where hardly any necessities of life can be produced locally, is the result of mankind's having learnt, like a single colossal body stretching itself, to extend to the remotest corners and pluck from each area different ingredients needed to nourish the whole ...*

*These individual traders and hosts rarely know (as their predecessors rarely knew) all that much about the particular individual needs they serve. Nor do they need such knowledge. Many of these needs will indeed not even arise until a time so far in the future that nobody can foresee even its general outlines. The more one learns about economic history, the more misleading then seems the belief that the achievement of a highly organized state constituted the culmination of the early development of civilization. The role of governments is greatly exaggerated in historical accounts because we necessarily know so much more about what organized government did than about the spontaneous coordination of individual efforts accomplished.*[3]

        HAYEK, F.A., *THE FATAL CONCEIT: THE ERRORS OF SOCIALISM*

C apitalism is a system that has been built over the millennia, beginning with specialization of labor and trade from one community to another. More and more over time, the fruits of one might benefit another in a far-off place, and knowledge of profits gained and price signals exploited by intermediaries would become so complex, distributed, and subject to uncertainty that no central state authority endeavoring to improve upon the overall mechanism could do so without distorting market signals and impoverishing peoples. The historical background of the evolution of capitalism is well described by Hayek.

The archaeological accounting of shipwrecks near Italy, France, and Spain reveals an intriguing picture of the emergent period of commerce, and its subsequent decline. A study conducted by Dr. A. J. Parker in 1980 catalogs 545 dated sea wrecks, which shows that there was a slight rise in this activity before 400 BC, when 25 shipwrecks have been found and dated. In the period between 400 BC and 200 BC, the activity doubles to about 50 shipwrecks. What is interesting is that the number of shipwrecks jumps to 160 during the two centuries that precede the birth of Jesus Christ.[4]

During this time, numismatic analysis reveals a similar picture of blossoming of trade and prosperity hitherto unknown. Roman silver coins in circulation are estimated by Michael Crawford's *catalogue raisonné, Roman Republican Coinage*, which shows the volume of coins minted each year in the Roman Empire. Although coinage circulation was evident since 700 BC in the eastern Mediterranean, in about 269 BC the establishment of a mint for silver in the temple of Juno Moneta initiated widespread usage. The peak years of minting were 119-80 BC, when 14 million denarii were struck containing 50 tonnes of silver (mostly from Spanish mines), which is half the volume that Europe extracted from the New World in the 16th century. The supply of money increased maybe ten-fold in the last century of the Roman Republic as modeled by Keith Hopkins using the Crawford data.[5] This geometric increase under the supervision of state-owned production facilities contrasts with the experience of metal-backed currencies of the near-modern era, whose rate of increase has been in the low single-digit percentages.

Coinage was the invention that enabled people to exchange the fruits of their labor, and more importantly, store wealth produced from income. This was necessary, because production was not uniform, either across regions or at different periods of time. Rainfall was uneven at different places around the Mediterranean. Considering the better climate North Africa enjoyed compared to today, there was much opportunity for agricultural variety throughout the year. Specialization developed. "Terracotta lamps made by Fortis, in northern Italy, with the name stamped on them, have been found all over Europe and even in Britain ... A mixing tank of ten thousand gallons' capacity was used in the pottery works at Arretium ... When the technique of glass-blowing was discovered, prices fell so that a glass cup and saucer could be bought for a cent, and window glass became available."[6] Pliney says every peasant's wife "wears amber trinkets, and every servant girl has a silver mirror." Hayek's description of a lightly governed society giving birth to a money economy that could exploit the specialization of labor and production is very consistent with the early Roman experience.[7]

## Building Wealth

The profession of deposit banking was evident in Rome as early as 310-318 BC. The Roman senatorial and equine aristocratic classes would supplement their land patrimony with lending at interest, sometimes being silent business partners of bankers, because they were barred from profiting directly from foreign trade. Bankers who took deposits segregated these between sealed bags of coins (regular deposits) that were not to be lent, and sums that would be invested at interest. Most were in major ports, which greatly facilitated the work of traders, peddlers, and the elite alike to not need to transport money between cities. The scholar Jean Andreau (among others) makes the distinction between the activities of the elites and the professional bankers. The latter ascended from marketplace storefronts. Occasionally their progeny might climb in social status, but they would need to eschew the profession of their fathers. Andreau quantified funerary inscriptions and concluded that banking activity of the *argentarii* expanded from the end of the third century BC to the time of Caesar and the second triumvirate (43-33 BC), noting a pickup in activity after the Second Punic War (218-201 BC). However, the *argentarii* did not circulate negotiable bills or endorsable checks, and loans were generally short-term. Money changing was another distinct profession, whose members were known as *numerarii*. This was an important function for trade given the variety of coins circulating, and it appears to have been as interesting a profit opportunity as deposit taking.[8]

The inscriptions Andreau enumerates confirm Parker's shipwreck data, for he reports:

> In the course of the first two centuries A.D. …various signs indicate that Italy was sinking into financial decline, and Rome in particular … The number of bankers known from inscriptions decreases sharply. Not one is attested after the first century A.D. outside Rome and the major ports (Ostia, Portus, and Aquileia) … From the second century onward, in Italy, much less credit was provided in auction sales by the *argentarii* and the *coactores argentarii*, and it disappeared altogether during the second half of the third century A.D. There are other signs which are just as telling, such as the disappearance or decline of the *Janus medius*, the disappearance of the negotiators, and also of the great companies of tax-collectors.[9]

Coinage also changed the nature of taxation. Rather than needing to transport wheat or some other bulky good in payment, coins permitted Rome to collect funds from afar more easily without having a costly infrastructure to administer the system. Taxes in these early days were still derived from the output of citizens, so they would rise and fall with income, and of course be higher for those who produced and saved than for those who were not productive. They are believed to have been quite low, perhaps 0.1 percent to 0.3 percent in the beginning of the Republic, and then with the unification of Italy in 272 BC became a tithe on communities, still at these trivial percentages.[10]

At the unification of Italy in 264 BC the Republic was the size of Ohio and Kentucky. By the birth of Christ it had expanded to the equivalent of the United States east of the Mississippi. Defense and military conquest had profound effects. "Money, command of the Mediterranean, plunder from the provinces, slavery, and contact with the luxuries and philosophies of the East were to combine to transform Roman character as well as to create a new world."[11] The wealth of the aristocracy increased greatly, and the usage of slave labor undercut wages and the potential for income generation of small farms. Farmers would be called upon for military service, which would leave their parcels consumed by weeds and outfitted with dilapidated implements. Needing loans to rebuild and faced with competition of free slave labor, bankruptcy might follow, which created a pool of urban unemployed. Moreover, government intervention ruined the wheat market. Whereas prices used to fluctuate to the occasional benefit of Sicily, the "Kansas" of Italy, a policy of purchasing foreign wheat and reselling it at low, fixed prices was designed to insulate the public from the ill effect of war shortages. Recognizing the plight of the small farmer, the brothers Gracchus pushed through reforms that resettled urban unemployed back to farms, including legislation that limited the use of public lands to 300 acres, reviving Licinian laws once placed in force in 352 BC. The younger brother, Gaius Gracchus, set up sales of wheat at below market prices to the urban poor. A hundred years later, 500,000 families would be resettled, over six times the households Tiberius Gracchus moved. The dole expanded to 320,000 by the time of Julius Caesar, amounting to two pounds of bread daily plus regular distribution of some pork, olive oil, and salt.

The emperor Augustus, who ruled from 27 BC to 14 AD, changed the system of taxation from a percentage of income to 1 percent of wealth plus a flat poll tax. He believed that low, flat taxes would foster the prosperity of a bourgeoisie and be good for the empire, and indeed they were. Interestingly, this system stimulated economic growth, because the rate imposed on marginal income was thus 0 percent. His early administration benefitted by the infusion of money brought to Rome from the capture of the Egyptian treasury in the naval victory at Actium in 31 BC. He also ended a system known as "tax farming," wherein the wealthy would bid on and prepay for the right to collect taxes in their regions, which fostered uneven taxation. Great surpluses were had, which enabled Augustus to repair all the roads of Italy and Rome and construct a great many public buildings and temples. It is said when he came to Rome it was a city of brick; when he left it was a city of marble. The story of shipwrecks indicates continued prosperity, but there were setbacks.

## Credit with Wings of Silver

Originally debt crises were infrequent and linked to the financing of wars. The Romans had phrases to describe them: *Inopia nummorum* referred to times when there was a deficiency of coins; a period of *nummorum caritas* was when money would appreciate in value substantially relative to land. In 352 BC, after a century of trade disruption due to wars, Rome was conquered by Gauls, who exacted a heavy ransom in gold. Licinius Stolo, a tribune, led an effort to clear off a vast amount of debt through government actions. Later, in 300 BC after the first Carthaginian war the standard currency, one pound of bronze, was reduced by five-sixths, wiping out public debt. At the second Carthaginian war, bronze currency would be cut in half again. But wild inflation would not occur until the third century AD, when the public sector would become significant and currency would be debased rather than diluted through prodigious mine output or added to from the capture of accumulated savings of vanquished territories.[12]

Increased production of silver stemmed from discoveries in Spain originally exploited by Carthaginians under Hannibal's father, Hamilcar Barca, in the mid-third century BC. Further substantial increases in output there were made by the Romans. In his 1980 analysis, Keith Hopkins analyzes that data of the numismaticist Michael Crawford to estimate there was a ten-fold increase in the Roman money supply during the late Republic (from 157 BC to 50 BC), thanks to annual additions of 14 million denarii in the peak years (119 BC to 80 BC), which compares to a base of merely 35 million denarii in 158 BC.[13] (A denarius contained nearly 4 grams of silver, which would remain constant until Nero). Eventually under Augustus several new mints were established in Spain. In addition to these, large-scale coin factories were introduced in Lyons and Rome.[14]

With the reserve for its monetary system growing by leaps and bounds, from the consumers' point of view inflationary pressures might have erupted. However, productivity gains and the integration of trade across the Mediterranean, aided by Pompey's sweeping pirates from the seas, kept the rate of increase at bay. Moreover, government policy would restrain the cost of living. The rise of populism traces its roots from the famous Twelve Tables of 451 BC, the Licenian Laws of 367 BC, and the Hortensian Law of 287 BC. Approximately 100 years before the birth of Christ, the resentment of small farmers weary of fighting in military campaigns that enriched the aristocracy and introduced competition from slave labor swelled. The Gracchus brothers were the liberal politicians of their time, putting in place a two-tiered wheat pricing system and land reform. H.J. Haskell, in his 1939 book *The New Deal in Old Rome*, catalogs the surprising parallels between Roman legislation and Depression-era reforms in the United States. Wheat was initially offered without a means test to those willing to queue up at warehouses at half the market price, which over time would be reduced to being free of charge.

Rome came to resemble Manhattan, a hub populated by rich who received income from their great country estates and a magnet for the poor from all over. The cost of dwelling in modest housing was remarkably low, surmised by Haskell to have been only $190 per month in rent (2008 constant dollars) for the young Sulla, who was frugal, but bachelors seeking flashy digs might pay $1,900 per month (2008 constant dollars). Fires would rage through the slums, but in the affluent part of town real estate speculation took hold. "With the growth of the city, real-estate values increased and apartment houses sprang up, some of them so sleazily built that they collapsed. Augustus was forced to set a limit of six to seven storeys on the height of buildings."[15] Silver inflation and government intervention produced effects then that are similar to current times. The excess liquidity would spill directly into the business of housing, but it was cordoned off from inflating the price of consumer items such as food and entertainment.

Roman monetary history is one of rapidly increasing money supply punctuated by the explosion of credit bubbles that led to varying degrees of debt forgiveness. Deposit lending was significant, but the loans of the elite were probably as important to economic growth or more so. Overextension of credit became routine. The moral hazard inherent in silver inflation invited constant speculation in real estate, which would begin to build as soon as the last crisis had ended. The panic of 86 BC occurred during civil wars and when Mithradates VI of Pontus invaded Roman possessions in Asia Minor, causing the suspension of dividends from tax collection corporations. The government, led by popularly elected officials in the Assembly, scaled back debt by 75 percent.[16] But real estate speculation would resume, leading to the rise of Catiline, who sought election to the Assembly proposing a policy of *tabulae novae*, or widespread debt cancellation. Fear of his solution caused gold to flee and asset prices to collapse. The extension of 0 percent credit by Q. Considius, a super-rich financier, helped stem the crisis, but it was not really resolved until the return of Pompey to Rome with huge sums of gold from Asian conquest. Catiline epitomizes the cultural decay that occurred from reckless credit and get rich quick schemes typical in the late years of the Republic, and the zeal to redistribute wealth through its abrogation. Consider the account of Gaius Sallustius Crispus:

> But the love of irregular gratification, open debauchery, and all kinds of luxury, had spread abroad with no less force. Men forgot their sex; women threw off all the restraints of modesty… In so populous and so corrupt a city, Catiline, as it was very easy to do, kept about him, like a body-guard, crowds of the unprincipled and desperate. For all those shameless, libertine, and profligate characters, who had dissipated their patrimonies by gaming, luxury, and sensuality; all who had contracted heavy debts, to purchase immunity for their crimes or offences … were the associates and intimate friends of Catiline. And if any one, as yet of unblemished character, fell into his society, he was presently rendered, by daily intercourse and temptation, similar and equal to the rest. But it was the young whose acquaintance he chiefly courted; as their minds, ductile and unsettled from their age, were easily ensnared by his stratagems. For as the passions of each, according to his years, appeared excited, he furnished mistresses to some, bought horses and dogs for others, and spared, in a word, neither his purse nor his character, if he could but make them his devoted and trustworthy supporters.[17]

The return of Julius Caesar from Gaul frightened the aristocracy, who thought he would institute land reform like the Gracchus brothers had. Julius Caesar previously as consul had been able to secure land for veterans by using questionable political maneuvers. His crossing the Rubicon with an army (in defiance of a Senatorial order to disband it) induced a financial panic, which he resolved in part by allowing debts to be repaid using collateral priced with pre-crisis values. He also slashed the dole by over 50 percent and required one-third of all farm workers to be free men. The short reign of Julius Caesar was followed by the ascendance of Augustus, who infused with the Egyptian treasury taken at Actium, ushered in a long inflationary boom that would perhaps be the pinnacle of Roman economic achievement. Interest rates fell from 12 percent to 4 percent, and prices rose during his rule.

But shortly after his reign the wheels began to fall off. The great mines of Spain ran out. As the treasure of Egypt spread through the economy, it had pushed up real estate values considerably, inviting speculation. The result for Tiberius, who followed Augustus, was deflation and high interest rates. He ended the building spree and hoarded money collected from taxes so much that there was a shortage of coins; he then lent it out at 0 percent interest in large blocks, probably tens of millions of today's dollars, in an action suggestive of the first federal use of credit on a large scale akin to what the Federal Reserve System did in response to the financial crisis that began in 2008.[18]

## Squandering Wealth

The welfare experiments of the Graccus brothers had been embraced and reduced in cycles, but by the middle of the first century AD they had become ingrained. Eventually the tendency blossomed into socialism. Rather than welfare being accommodated by mine production and conquests, it was enabled through currency debasement. Paralleling the modern compulsion to redistribute wealth through big government fiscal programs, the Romans expanded public sector investment to such an extent that it drained the private sector:

> The upholding of the Roman standard of culture meant huge amounts had to be spent to provide an adequate supply of the amenities that were considered essential to the full life of a Roman citizen. There was the cost of building, repairing and maintaining the numerous temples, public baths, municipal buildings, gymnasia, town halls, wrestling schools, market places, triumphal columns and amphitheatres (the list goes on). Civic sacrifices, religious processions, feasts and the games also drained huge amounts from the financial reserves of the empire. The cost of the dole weakened the empire's finances. Originally this was passed out once a month but under Marcus

Aurelius there was a daily distribution of pork, oil and bread to the proletariat. The alimenta (farming subsidies), put in place by Nerva also cost the empire dearly. The adverse balance of trade which grew at this time proved to be very costly.[19]

By the time of Nero (who reigned from 54 AD to 68 AD), government became more highly developed and discovered a new way to obtain revenue. Taxes would not be raised for at least another century, but this emperor began the practice of seigniorage, wherein the silver content of coinage was reduced. Nero clipped coins by 10 percent. At first this produced immediate wealth for the emperor, but it began to backfire, and a long line of successors would blame rising prices upon the behavior of businessmen, not understanding the fundamental role of money. Importation of wheat for the masses contributed to a trade imbalance, and the consumption of luxury goods by the aristocracy led to the outflow of gold to the east. Central planning became difficult, with a geographic reach stretched thinly by military conquest and the populace having lost incentives to improve crafts or agricultural production.

Trajan (98 AD–117 AD) upped seigniorage to 15 percent, Marcus Aurelius (161 AD–180 AD) made it 25 percent, and Septimus Severus (193 AD–201 AD) debased by 50 percent. This amounted to a tax on cash holdings or savings, which could be substantial. It also probably caused an even greater effect on the money supply, as people would not circulate pure silver coins and only used bad ones, causing a contraction of "real" silver in circulation.[15] Consequently, the wonderful experience of the two centuries before Christ became frayed around the edges. Despite an increase in population, shipwrecks downticked slightly in the first two centuries AD to about the 130 level. Civil wars began in 180 AD, lasting for a century, wherein 25 of 27 emperors or would-be emperors would meet a violent death.[20]

But by late into the second century, according to Julian Fenner, most Romans "lacked the incentive to master their work and they also had little consuming power so there was a shallow internal market as a result." Fenner continues by saying:

> By the time of Antoninus Pius (AD 138-161), the Roman bureaucracy was as all embracing as that of modern times. This tendency sowed the seeds for the tyranny of the third century.

The historian "Trever" says of the situation …"the relentless system of taxation, requisition, and compulsory labour was administered by an army of military bureaucrats … Everywhere were the ubiquitous personal agents of the emperors to spy out the remotest case of attempted … evasion of taxes." Under Hadrian we also see the development of a system of secret police and informers. This system functioned in much the same way as the Gestapo and kept going until it was changed by Diocletian … By the third century the burden was so heavy that it began to consume the capital resources of the empire. However, this increase in taxation did not increase production, in fact increases in tax seemed to coincide with a decrease in manpower and production.[21]

Hadrian began an orgy of spending, expanding civil services and organizing them on a salary basis. By the reign of Pertinax (192 AD–193 AD) the treasury would be empty, proving that excessive taxation had reduced government revenue. Not learning their lesson, Rome's emperors would continue to debase the currency such that it would not even be accepted as a means of interprovincial trade by the mid-third century, when the denarius's silver content was only 5 percent. Also, starting in the civil war era, emperors would raise taxes on the wealthy and the senatorial class, in an effort to exterminate anyone who might challenge their authority, which by now began to solely rest with the army under their command. This extermination of the upper-middle class actually had begun nearly a century earlier: Domitian (81 AD–96 AD) would trump-up charges to confiscate estates of the rich on a targeted basis.[22] Shipwrecks plunged to fewer than 80 in the 200 years after Pertinax, and half again this in the next 200.

Punitive taxation and seigniorage eventually ended money-based exchange by the middle of the third century. What emerged was a government that was purely totalitarian and thoroughly dysfunctional, based almost solely upon barter, regressing back in this respect to the early Iron Age. There remained a thin strata of the senatorial and equine classes, which consolidated landholdings and would benefit from obtaining provincial lands at auction, from which they could lucratively extract taxes and rents. According to Murphy, "Rome's senatorial aristocracy, constituted by one estimate two thousands of one percent of the population; then came the equestrian class, with perhaps a tenth of a percent. Collectively these people owned almost everything."[23] The Roman system was steeped in patronage and influence, so such generosity might be rewarded with an inside track to foreign lands or government contracts. Everyone else would be subject to a vast apparatus imposed to collect taxes, for which it would enjoy certain amenities that characterized the Roman lifestyle. Under their administration, the burden of taxation fell heavily upon the mass of the population that was under them. Diocletian (284-286 AD) and Constantine (306-312 AD) restored central control; the former even put in place price controls.

The effect upon the people was to create a subsistence underclass. The population of Rome and other cities declined as their inhabitants left to obtain food through working at large estates. Think of these as giant collectives, within which Romans would be conscripted workers, much like under communism but with a few powerful individuals with skin in the game controlling each one. Rather than pay taxes, the few elites would occasionally provide for the community, usually in a flashy way that calls to mind the bridges, public buildings, and highways named Byrd in West Virginia. Like the slaves of the American Deep South, the underclass might seek to escape but would have nowhere to go save another collective. In fact, much farmland began to lay fallow. Individual farmers, bankrupted by taxes, would even give up their citizenship and become slaves to lords running these estates, and with this never be obliged to pay taxes again. Constantine tried to stop this by declaring that the capitation tax for these individuals would be owed by their lord, but the system had degraded to such an extent that the economic drain continued. Fifty years after Diocletian, taxes would be doubled. Clearly by the fourth century the empire had disintegrated, and it is no wonder it fell prey to invaders.

## Coping with Collectivism

Interestingly, even the socialist Douglas Smyth acknowledges the ignorance of Roman emperors presiding over its decline, admitting they had no concept of how markets worked. The myth may be that modern socialists do, but his description of the meddlesome Roman government is a grotesque example of central authority attempting to cope inventively with the economic disaster their misguided collectivist policies wrought:

> Markets, to the extent that they were allowed to operate at all, were significantly interfered with by the government: the dole was a major government intervention that massively skewed the production of food and its transport, and caused the government to create whole categories of state servants bound to their functions and status by birth: to give examples only from the dole complex: sea captains and sailors responsible for delivering the grain shipments and millers, bakers and butchers responsible for providing the food to the citizens.

> Not only were none allowed to desert their posts (although many did when they got the chance) but the Emperors were continually attempting to devise new ways to recruit workers to these despised positions: the daughter of a baker, for example, could marry someone who was not a baker, but then her husband would be required to become one.

> Another intervention: Emperors issued decrees stating that sea captains would suffer dire punishments for delaying delivery of their shipments, but since the decrees were repeated, and later punishments listed were even more dire, clearly the practice of dallying at port after port continued: "Every shipmaster shall know that within two years he shall either deliver the receipt for the cargo which he has accepted, or he shall prove the vicissitudes of his perils."

> After all there were no economic incentives for delivering the grain in a timely fashion; the prices were set by the state. I suspect that shipmasters were dilatory in delivering their cargoes, however, because they were probably selling them elsewhere. Shipmasters were given equestrian rank, so they were supposedly among the honored members of society.

There was no understanding of markets at all in the fifth century, at least among government circles. Blackmarketeers probably did have an inkling about how markets worked, but decree after decree by Emperors begins from the simple assumption that the government can simply declare economic policy and it will be followed. "... shipmasters shall be compelled to build their ships according to the requisite and constituted size ..." "If their fleet should collapse from neglect or from age, it shall be restored by the praetorian prefecture ..."[24]

Socialists such as Smyth probably would argue that the statist machinery of Europe or Canada is a well-oiled machine compared to the one operated by the incompetent Romans, who by ruthless abuse of human rights distinguished themselves as being the only people to maintain governance over the whole of Europe for more than a brief window of time. But one need not look far from the United States to see the disturbing parallel with one of the most cherished aims of today's enlightened progressives, the socialization of health care. Like the husband of the baker's daughter, in Canada young men and women from other nations are induced to train to be doctors (with tuitions far below American rates for all university studies). Although the status of doctors is equestrian by Roman standards, these recruits are so underpaid by government reimbursement for services that many opt to flee to practice in the United States or back in the nations of their birth. Unlike the sea captains, they cannot make up for below-market remuneration with outside work, for that is illegal. And unlike the suitor of the baker's daughter, they may divorce their relationship with the state (many Romans did this also). So who would marry the baker's daughter, but one truly in love with her or her assigned line of work, to be willing to put up with serfdom?

The sick of Canada must endure rationing, and in elections they plead for more and tastier bread. Waiting lists for procedures are months in length, but politicians reassuringly promise that if one is sicker than most, he will be shown to the front of the line, an echo of the Roman system of sycophantic patronage. Certain procedures are often deemed unnecessary, such as MRI imaging, which is among the very few medical services that Canada's people may purchase from their own pocket from a private clinic. Almost all else that is withheld to save the fiscal strain is illegal to buy in Canada, making the seeking of treatment outside the system a criminal act. Yet thousands who can afford to do so populate the first-rate clinics of the United States on medical vacations. (And, in another distortion, when Americans are not eligible for procedures at Medicare-mandated below-market prices (due to age, for example), they visit Third World countries in search of savings on these expensive procedures. They might even travel in search of treatments banned by regulators at the FDA.)

Those who stay behind in Canada must sit in waiting rooms for an hour or more when they show up for their scheduled appointments. When they do see the doctor, there is a sign to remind them to ask for treatment or diagnosis of only one ailment at a time, because that is all the government will reimburse. Socialism would hold itself out to be more efficient and less costly, promising ubiquitous care. It instead offers equal care for all for free, and to do so it must put in place wasteful impediments that cause its citizens to ration care themselves. The inefficiency reminds one of the ships filled with Roman wheat waiting in line to move up the Tigris, their shipmasters admonished to do their conscripted duty at least every other year. Their fleets routinely fell into disrepair due to the inadequate payment under a system of reimbursement for their cargoes that was well below the level a freely operating market would provide them.

Eventually the lower classes of the Roman Empire were so eager to cast off the yoke of taxation that they welcomed the barbarians: "By the time the Persians and Barbarians invaded, the Roman world was in a state of disarray and all that was required from them was a gentle push ... The attitude of the lower classes towards the Barbarians was by no means always one of fear and hostility. They were often met with feelings of relief and the desire to co-operate especially amongst the poorer men who were unendurably burdened by taxation."[25]

The collapse of the Roman Empire was not a sudden fall (Odoacer petitioned Constantinople to recognize his legitimacy). Instead it was a protracted slide that lasted hundreds of years. Rome's entrepreneurial middle class would prosper at the apex of imperial prosperity, but its success would prove to be overly alluring to Rome's rulers. Thinking they were immune from political upheaval if a broad underclass could be pleased by bread and circuses, they crafted fiscal and monetary policies in such a way that they would plunder the most dynamic element within their society and cause a nearly modern civilization to regress for a millennia.

# Chapter 13

# Other Perspectives

This chapter is a potpourri of noneconomic explanations used to explain the decline of Rome. Variety abounds: Decadence is a popular attribution, but it offers little substance. Slavery, on the other hand, explains much of the weakness of the Republic and its drift into imperial socialism. Historians periodically have emphasized pressures from outside the Empire. Socialists and sophisticated media elites blame Rome's downfall on capitalism, hoping to draw a parallel to the present. Hand-in-hand with this reasoning is to blame the downfall of both Rome and the United States on the excessive allocation of resources to the military. If that is not enough, then religion can be blamed for distracting rulers from the real business of running an empire. These are all easily dispensed with, and ultimately the most compelling reasoning rests with the inherent problems of big government and anticapitalist policies that sap the lifeblood of the entrepreneurial upper-middle class.

## Slavery

The institution of slavery could be pinpointed as the trigger for the initiation of socialist policies. Wealthy aristocrats of the Republic period used slaves on large estates and achieved food production costs that undercut the microeconomics of maintaining small farms. This combined with government price controls on wheat did in the middle class, producing a listless mob within Rome that became dependent upon free bread and entertainment. Its vote for Assembly offices was thus sold to the highest bidder, a moral hazard of the democratic welfare state. This united the idle poor with the idle rich in a conspiracy to maintain both by the work of the masses. Appian wrote that Rome's welfare attracted "the lazy, the beggars, and the vagrants of all Italy." Although slavery became limited from the beginning of the Augustan peace onwards, the economic destruction of the middle class was advancing and resulting in a highly developed form of socialism that would drift into a police state controlled by a succession of dictators. Paralleling the experience near the end of the 20th century, former areas of expertise such as lamp making, chinaware manufacturing, and glass blowing would be bettered by foreign industrial entities in Germany, Gaul, and North Africa. Large estates would be tilled by tenants who would mine the soil until its fertility collapsed. Many tenants would flee, eventually inspiring Diocletian to bind persons to the soil, creating the institution of serfdom. Government would also take over businesses abandoned by their owners, evoking the modern era when the United States out of necessity took over the automobile and financial sectors. The military, always a sought-after career, was even more desirable with others no longer lucrative. But the army became a destructive force, for troops were allowed to loot districts through which they marched, and townsmen were expected to house and provide for soldiers' needs, including transportation.

## Decadence

The popular attribution of the collapse of the once great Roman power rests, in many ways quite deservedly, upon the decadence of its culture. A republic originally founded upon the sanctity of the familia, virtus, and dignitas, it developed into an imperial state by 31 BC. Through military victory and empire building, it became fabulously wealthy. The second emperor, Tiberius, ruled during the time of Jesus Christ, and was known for morbid sexual perversions such as the enjoyment of snapping the necks of boys with his bare hands. Caligula, who succeeded him, was a psychopath who replaced his head for that of roman gods on statues, ran a private brothel, had sex with his three sisters, and raped the wives of his senators. Life and morality back then was clearly quite different from what the acceptance of modern Judeo-Christian values produced later in the evolving Western culture. Despite a growing conversion of its citizens to Christianity, the perverse pagan culture persisted. The popularity of orgies increased, and guests ate and drank to such excess that legend, although disputed, has it vomiting was common.[1] The Coliseum, completed in 80 AD, hosted before a potential audience of 50,000 blood fests of gladiators and animals for centuries. The obsession with blood sports seems to parallel the modern era of violent video games (*Grand Theft Auto, Mortal Kombat*) and films (67 receive a maximum rating of "10" at www.kids-in-mind.com). Another parallel development is the expanded interest in oriental religions in later Roman times and the growth of New Age philosophy that has gained popularity in recent times.[2]

Cultural decadence seems present at the pinnacle of empires and their later slides to ruination, but rarely during their rise to preeminence. Whether cause or symptom, other factors are always at work, too. For Rome, the certification of more substantive causes than decadence for the downfall likewise is an open matter: the extensive use of barbarians within the army, Christianity, taxation, slavery, co-emperors in two capitals, the great influx of Huns from Eastern Asia. One historian cataloged 210 theories.[3] Through the lens of economics, events such as Odoacer's deposition of Romulus Augustus in 476 AD (the official end of the Roman Empire), or the sackings of Rome such as by the Vandals (455 AD) and the Visigoths (410 AD) are merely a coda.

The deviant behavior of Rome, no matter how appalling it was, may not have much statistical correlation with its political time line (as if measurable data exist today to test this). But the decaying culture inwardly focused upon consumption, pleasure, and the maintenance of power may hold a mirror to government and political behavior that favored purveying to a crowd what it wants and severing its constituents from the incentive to produce. Somehow the most productive of the Roman citizenship ceased to contribute to the economy, weakening the power of the state so much that it became not merely vulnerable, but infiltrated with foreign elements complete with alternative cultures that eventually plunged the world into feudalism, an echo of the tribal existence that preceded the empire. What actually happened can be decisively linked to economic policy changes that parallel America's shift from republican government to technocratic socialism. Pro-growth tax and spending policies of the Roman Republic and its first emperors combined with sound money practices produced prosperity. Increasingly this was undermined by waves of socialism and currency debasement in the centuries to follow.

## Fat, Happy, and Defeated!

Another economic view, recently articulated by Peter Heather in *The Fall of the Roman Empire: A New History of Rome and the Barbarians*, turns the focus back to attributing the fall of Rome to external factors, a point of view evidently popular prior to the publishing of the monumental work of Edward Gibbon in the late 18th century. Heather argues that there was pressure to expand the military from the 230s onward to face challenges from the Sassanid Empire, which was the second Persian Empire. It enjoyed three major victories over the Roman army, spanned from Northern Egypt to Pakistan, and lasted roughly four centuries until falling to Muslim conquest. Oddly he explains away Roman hyperinflation of the third century by saying economic growth linked to expansion of the military sector outstripped the supply of silver. However, unequivocally when economic output expands and the supply of hard currency remains constant, *deflation* occurs, because goods and services provided have increased in number while money has remained constant. That Rome chose to debase its currency through seigniorage is another matter, and it belies the inability of commerce (as proven through shipwrecks) to increase Gross Imperial Product (GIP) and have adequate taxes accrue to the government for military defense.[4] Hopkins reminds us that "the mid-third century was almost certainly a period of economic depression … In provincial towns, the number of charitable foundations and of incised tombstones dropped; so too did the number of new public buildings, except for defensive town-walls."[5]

Heather raises the intriguing new methodology for analyzing pottery fragments in the western part of the empire, which has permitted a conclusion that the number of Roman settlements grew through the fourth century and that agricultural activity entered a period of maximal output. He therefore claims that "it is no longer possible to explain fifth-century political collapse in terms of preceding economic crisis." Yet this raises questions about whether or how GIP might have increased when trade between regions nosedived and banking vanished. There is evidence that the rights of citizens were diluted by the aristocracy, and that the Roman people essentially became serfs beholden to large, autarkic estates. Taxation was harshly metered upon the underclass, such that there would be an incentive to bury silver (where it might be lost over time) or to convert it into another tradable asset that might be inconvenient for tax collectors to transport—pottery!

Even if this theory is bunk, the wholesale conversion of an active community of trade and mercantile pursuits into subsistence living does not immediately point to an improved standard of living. Africa has over 900 million people today, having seen a steady increase from roughly 230 million in 1950, and probably just millions or tens of millions a millennia or two earlier. With agricultural activity still predominant, does this population growth indicate prosperity? Archaeologists some day may come upon flatware in Zimbabwe, where 25 million live today, and conclude that since this country's population has more than doubled since 1950, the regime change to the socialist rule of Robert Mugabe has been a boon. Later they might ascribe its political collapse to "exogenous" forces, the scapegoat Heather blames for Rome's collapse. Although Zimbabwe officially outlawed inflation in 2007, it hit 11.2 million percent in August 2008.[6] As for the Roman experience, real per capita income probably came under considerable pressure after 200 AD, especially relative to the era of trade from the Roman Republic to the end of the first century.[7]

## The Private Sector Did It!

To explain the decline of Rome, socialists would point to the impoverishment of the Roman peasant class and their rule by an aristocratic clique, drawing a parallel to today's greedy CEOs and a trend for concentration of wealth among the top 1 percent of Americans.[8] What this misses is that in all of world history chronicled at least for as far back as ancient Egypt there were rich and poor. But not all systems of government allowed the middle class to flourish. Uneven accumulation of wealth resulted from capitalism, and capitalism has enabled man to progress beyond a tribal existence. However, the danger for the United States and any other democratic capitalist state is that an overlay of socialist policies would further concentrate wealth and cut the middle class off at its knees.

Many on the mainstream left of today's political spectrum advocate socialist ideas, but they are not doctrinal enough to attach this label on themselves. Sometimes this is out of political expediency, but it is often because they somehow think there is a difference between confiscating 85 percent of middle-class wealth through a combination of income and death taxes compared to the way other self-described socialist countries accomplish the same thing. When liberals of this ilk explain the progression of the Roman Empire into the Dark Ages and the subsequent reemergence centuries later, they blame the private sector for plunging western humanity into ignorance and penury. They may also even blame the rise of Christianity, as detailed later; yet the church was a sanctuary for intellectuals, promoted scientific discovery, and maintained literacy and important written records of history.

For example, Cullen Murphy devotes considerable discussion to the role of privatization as a factor that weakened the Roman Empire. He recounts the compelling tale of the betrayal of the city of Lepcis in 363 AD by Count Romanus, and then infers that such corruption was widespread (which it likely was). Briefly, Romanus demanded payment of 4,000 camels for hunting down mischievous Berber tribesmen who were assaulting the city and taking hostages (reminiscent of al Qaeda actions in Iraq in 2006). The elders of the city dispatched an envoy to the Emperor Valentinian to redress the matter, for it was Romanus's duty to defend the city. In response, a fact-seeking mission led by the Emperor's aide, Palladius, turned up no controverting evidence, because Romanus blackmailed him using allegations that this aide had embezzled some of the imperial funds sent to pay troops that might go after the Berbers. The accusers were executed and some had their tongues cut out. Ten years later the situation deteriorated in Lepcis so much that Roman forces from the Germanic border were diverted there, opening up a breach in that frontier as well. Ultimately Romanus's lie to the Emperor was proven and punished, but the damage to the empire was considerable.[9] Because imperial officials saw government service as an opportunity for personal enrichment, Murphy makes a string of connections damning private enterprise. (As a matter of strategy, consider what might have happened had the United States withdrawn from Iraq in 2006 when al Qaeda was successfully conducting raids in Baghdad. Left to ascend to power, al Qaeda might have established a stronghold. Great numbers of American forces might have been needed to be diverted back to Iraq from other areas of importance to national security, similar to the Roman's leaving themselves exposed on the German frontier.)

Privatization is equated with corruption and blamed for bringing down the Roman Empire, since incidents such as the betrayal of Lepcis were replicated elsewhere militarily and throughout the government. From there, civilization slipped into the Dark Ages, where the autarkic estates that became the preeminent economic unit of the third century naturally rose to literally become fiefdoms owing little if anything to larger states. To Murphy, they embody privatization, for the lord became his own state, levying taxes and offering protection. Murphy posits that we lurched out of the Middle Ages only when this seizure of government by wealthy individuals ended. At that point the community interest was served through the formation of governments that would hold a more beneficent social contract with the people, rather than be a private enterprise that would exploit them. He goes so far to say that most observers agree on this, and that to achieve modernity and progress we would follow a natural tendency for power to gravitate to the state and be taken away from those who hold private property. With privatization reemerging in the late 20th century, affecting prisons, security forces, port administration, Medicare drug plans, universities (funding crowded out by endowments), and soon public schools (vouchers) or social security, he laments that this favorable trend began to reverse decades ago.[10]

The folly of this view is that privatization and big government are bedfellows. Once government gets to the size that it is involved in nearly every industry and aspect of our lives, people are naturally going to engage with it to shape outcomes. Tobacco companies agreeing to large settlements are going to have a say in how their future proceeds, namely that competition would be banned. Government will not craft a policy that kills the goose that lays eggs of taxation. Ditto for the oil industry. Bill Gross, the famous fixed-income manager at Pimco will write public letters to Obama encouraging him to run a $1 trillion deficit, because *some* inflation is friendlier to lenders of capital than writing off huge losses from bad credit granted. The financial industry has self-regulatory agencies, which are used by large players to drive out small competitors. Likewise, the mainstream media will lobby for a Fairness Act to silence talk radio, a small but threatening upstart. The über-rich will cordon off their wealth into foundations rather than pay the estate tax, preferring to direct its usage as they see fit, not where the government might spend it. Big government can be corrupted by big wealth, and the two will conspire to drive out competition from pesky entrepreneurs in the middle class. The societal deterioration into a wealthy caste that subjugated the common man arose because the Roman governmental system proved to be antithetical to capitalism, and in reality emulated socialism. When the market, like a storm drain, gets clogged with taxes, regulations, and yes, private entities behaving in ways blind of the signals flashed by consumers and producers, sewage will pour out into the streets when the next tempest strikes. Those who live on a hill won't care if it does.

Before even the modern socialist and communist states of the 20th century were established and generally proven to be failures, the fallacy of centralized planning was pointed out in the 18th century by Adam Smith, who in his *Theory of Moral Sentiments* said:

> The man of system, on the contrary, is apt to be very wise in his own conceit; and is often so enamored with the supposed beauty of his own ideal plan of government, that he cannot suffer the smallest deviation from any part of it. He goes on to establish it completely and in all its parts, without any regard either to the great interests, or to the strong prejudices which may oppose it. He seems to imagine that he can arrange the different members of a great society with as much ease as the hand arranges the different pieces upon a chess-board. He does not consider that the pieces upon the chess-board have

no other principle of motion besides that which the hand impresses upon them; but that, in the great chess-board of human society, every piece has a principle motion of its own, altogether different from that which the legislature might choose to impress upon it. If those two principles coincide and act in the same direction, the game of human society will go on easily and harmoniously, and is very likely to be happy and successful. If they are opposite or different, the game will go on miserably, and the society must be at all times in the highest degree of disorder.

Unfortunately, the tendency for the socialist is to insist that his system of experimentation is superior to the trial-and-error, organic development of capitalism. The flaw of this argument is that it does not contain feedback from error. In capitalism, a misconceived business is promptly destroyed, and in its place rises a successful venture. In socialism, the notion is to keep tinkering, which sends a signal to those who might produce that there is "no reliable framework of expectations, since they have no way of knowing what will happen next in an atmosphere if unending experimentation."[11]

To explain why the Roman economy collapsed, one must do more than simply point to a greedy ruling elite and claim that the rich were at fault. Instead, the root cause of dysfunctional systems is their governments' weakening of incentives for individuals broadly to produce and engage each other in trade. This may take two forms: one is punitive taxation; the other is redistribution. Both concepts are variants of disrespect for private property. By the third century, Rome had a highly *regressive* tax system; in the United States it is highly *progressive*. Both are exploitative and distortive of incentives, and they cloud market signals.

## The Unessential Army

Another parallel that liberal observers have drawn between America and the Roman Empire concerns the military services. Liberals, ever wishing to allocate tax revenue to domestic social programs rather than national defense, like to assert that if we do not cut back our military, we might

succumb to economic pressure such as what Rome must surely have felt
from manning its army. The argument intriguingly begins by comparing the global infrastructure of the U.S to that of Rome. Rome was the
first empire to build a large network of roads for the projection of power,
eventually 370 highways of 53,000 miles, a length rivaling the U.S. interstate system. Then, stationed in the provinces were the legions, about 25
in number during the best years of the regime, for a total force of about
500,000. Diocletian (284–305 AD) may have doubled or tripled the size
of the Roman army. Training and proper outfitting was emphasized, so
the legions would be vastly superior to their foes and capable of rapid,
forceful victory, just as America witnessed in the two Arab Gulf campaigns. In fact, as the parallel goes, for nearly two millennia the world
would not see such a large, complex, well-managed fighting force.[12]

Before dissecting the similarities and dissimilarities, what if one
simply accepts the proposition that military commitments so drained
the Roman treasury that it eventually caused the empire's fall? It may
be true, especially considering the buildup that Diocletian ordered in
the last years of the third century. Keith Hopkins makes a fascinating effort to estimate Gross Imperial Product around 70 AD, which
he pegs at some 8.2 billion sestertium (a measure roughly equal to 36
ounces of silver, denoted by "HS"), from which the government took
one-tenth, or about 820 HS. Military spending is estimated at 400 million HS.[13] But in practical terms the cost of the Roman military was far
more than this, because troops were fed and transported by people living in the regions through which they travelled. Moreover, they had a
license to plunder any estates save a few considered off limits politically
or which were able to project power locally. There were more than one
million people living in Rome. During various regimes the dole varied
from 200,000 to 350,000 persons in the capital, and in the later years
of the empire it was also available in other cities. The government also
provided public works, games, and so on and had a bureaucracy to support. Compared with 300,000 to 500,000 soldiers enlisted in the army
before the time of Diocletian, it is plausible that Hopkins' estimates of
the military being about half of the Roman budget are in the ballpark.
So it does not follow that for the United States, with defense outlays
being *less than 4 percent of GDP*, that the military is the root cause of
anything financial, especially when compared to Rome.[14]

The U.S. military is spread around the world in nearly 7,000 locations in 135 countries, with 114 large installations, as defined as having a plant replacement value exceeding $1.64 billion.[15] Total military personnel number nearly 1.4 million, but fewer than 300,000 are stationed abroad, and another 200,000 are deployed in Iraq.[16] The liberal argument concludes that since Rome's military was both bloated and stretched thinly, it became a financial sinkhole and eventually broke down to a state wherein cities built walls of defense and the legions roamed the empire like antibodies responding to foreign invasions.[17]

Although undeniably both Rome and America stationed troops across the world of their times, the comparison begins to strain when one realizes that the United States is not seeking to occupy land, subjugate peoples, or drain economic booty. Moreover, the importance of the military was far greater to the Roman economy than it is in the United States. There was industry of sorts in ancient times, for example in the mining, cutting, and transport of marble for Rome, but generally nearly all economic activity up through the early 20th century was agricultural. We cannot know reliably what weight military expenditure carried in the Roman economy, but it must have been significant. Cullen Murphy tells us: "The Romans didn't have Henry Ford-style mass production, but they did have factories and they did have a military-industrial complex. Three dozen *fabricae* were located strategically throughout the empire to provide the legions with armaments; some of them were general suppliers of swords and shields. Others were more specialized."[18]

We know that living conditions for those who were not part of the 600 senators and 30,000 equestrians (so named because they were entitled to a public horse) were so subsistence-like that they generally could not afford to use gold coins for commerce, using silver or copper instead. Moreover, the vast majority of the population within the Roman Empire's border were not citizens; a Claudian census of 47 AD counted seven million Romans, so it might be safe to assume that on average the balance of noncitizens might have had annual incomes similar to those who lived in the underdeveloped nations decades or centuries ago, before there were any modern inventions, where a living was scratched off the land with primitive implements. (Note that women were not counted as citizens.) Estimates by Branko Milanovic, the lead economist in the World Bank's research department, peg 85 percent of the citizen, noncitizen, and slave populations of the Roman Empire at having an income of merely 234 HS annually, with this wage coming from a subsistence farming existence.[19]

While the absolute number of troops in the U.S. forces are a bit more than double the standing Roman army, the U.S. population that we draw from is five to eight times as large, and these are all citizens. If the Milanovic numbers of one million in 14 AD are used, the present day U.S. forces are about the same size as the Roman army. Looking more broadly, the population figures within Roman borders contained people who might rebel. While in later centuries Rome increasingly manned its legions with barbarians, the inclusion of all persons under the emperor's rule in the denominator would be an apples-to-oranges comparison. We wouldn't recruit German citizens for our army, for instance (but they might assist in a NATO exercise). With this logic one might hypothetically look at Europe, Japan, Taiwan, and other areas under protection through treaty with United States as the noncitizens within the Roman borders. Compared only to the nearly one billion people we defend in just the three identified regions mentioned, U.S. forces of less than 1.4 million are miniscule. By comparison, NATO resolved in 1999 "to give the EU the means and capabilities to assume its responsibilities regarding a common European policy on security and defence ... (establishing a headline goal by 2003 to be able to) deploy and sustain for at least one year military forces of up to 60,000 troops."[20]

## Into the Furnace

The socialist view has strained to draw a parallel between the religious upheaval of the later years of the Roman Empire to the rise of the evangelical movement in America's 20th century (inferring a connection with weakness or decay). About the only thing in common between these two periods is that fundamentalist Christianity was on an upswing. But this observation is a strain, for at its founding the United States had a population that was mainly Christian, particularly in the sense that these individuals actively studied and practiced biblical teachings, whereas now it is largely secular if defined by this yardstick. Roman culture, in contrast, ended in acceptance of Christianity, and the bulk of the conversion occurred well after its glory years had passed. Economic ruin has hardly begun in the United States, despite wars, punitive taxation, and the weakened purchasing power of the dollar over time. Almost any objective measure of prosperity in this country has shown great progress. Not that there is not great danger of a collapse; encroaching big government socialism, currency debasement, and cultural depravity are worrisome road signs common to Rome and other fallen societies. Religion doesn't make the list.

From Lenin to Stalin to Mao to Castro, Christianity and Judaism have been movements that could only interfere with the workings of the socialist state. Whole books detail the vilification of it by the left, such as David Limbaugh's *Persecution: How Liberals Are Waging War Against Christianity*. The socialist sees the Calvinist protestant beliefs that were prominent at the time of America's origin as an ideology that reinforces class dominance. Some such as Smyth separate conservative from liberal churches, paralleling the rift within today's Episcopalian church. In his view, those who truly follow the teachings of Christ from his Sermon on the Mount give of themselves in soup kitchens, tolerate homosexuals, promote women to high liturgical office, and permit their abortions. The view of Christ as a socialist seems supported in the Bible (Acts 4:32-5:11 "The whole group of those who believed were of one heart and soul, and no one claimed private ownership of any possessions, but everything they owned was held in common"). He also maintains that the conservative religious wing supports policies that reward wealth, saying it comes from moral rectitude and hard work. This sets up a system of reinforcement wherein the rich have proof of their own high morality. His paranoia goes even farther when he alleges they would convert the U.S. into a religious state.

However, this cartoonish view breaks down on many accounts. For starters, the rich are not widely religious, and if they do attend services, they are not usually of the evangelical sort. And if one is to enjoy wealth, self-restraint through following each of the Ten Commandments rather than picking and choosing those that suit one's circumstance seems unlikely. Joining a fundamentalist sect, be it Christinan, orthodox Jewish, or Morman, may require tithing of income and a considerable time commitment whereby one comes in direct contact with the needy, spreads the word, or devotes oneself to reflection and learning periodi-cally. The conservative churches that are not fundamentalist, such as the high Episcopal order, follow a rigid progression within their services that allows little leeway for inserting justification for pursuit of wealth, and it provides ample opportunity to pray for the sorry state of the world.

For the socialist who might not have an aversion to religion, the Sermon on the Mount is seen as a justification of collectivist dogma, with the symbolic sharing of bread and fish among the multitude. His small band of followers might have lived communally, but they did not advocate the establishment of a government to enforce this life-style. Christ wanted little of the organized powers of man, be they the Roman authorities or the high priests of Judaism, and advocated per-sonal commitment instead. Rather, he taught that the meek would inherit the Earth spiritually. The rich, he argued, might make no time for matters of the spirit, which is often true today and reinforces the view that a selfish, all-powerful aristocracy would be unlikely to favor any church, conservative or liberal. The power of his message, however, would be strong enough to penetrate the senatorial class, reaching the Emperor Constantine (306–337 AD).

Christ, who lived under the Roman rule of Tiberius at a time of its great power and expansion, knew the empire was a pagan culture evolving with a system that eventually concentrated political power in the senatorial aristocracy, and the disenfranchisement of the inde-pendent farmer had begun in earnest with the end of the republic decades before. Rather than rant against wealth and power embodied in this unfortunate state of governmental affairs, most think he chose not to be a political revolutionary (which socialists do), rendering unto Caesar what was Caesar's. However, the biblical scholar Marcus Borg finds that Jesus' entrance into Jerusalem was a subversive act of political theater, arriving on a donkey coming from the east and mocking the annual Roman march from the west from the coastal base at Caesarea Maritima to reinforce the garrison during Passover. If Borg is correct, it would indicate that Jesus was against statism, and that his entrance legitimately provoked the authorities questioning him about being the King of the Jews. But in his interaction with tax collectors, he sought their souls, not what they had collected. We know the names of only two: Matthew and Zacchaeus. The first was an apostle and evangelist.

The other we know because Jesus ate in his home; he gave half his wealth to the poor. He did not advocate that Caesar should alter his highly regressive tax code and make it progressive, taxing the senators who were nearly exempt, and distribute tax remittances to the poor. Nor did he rage against the changes in law that allowed encroachments and ultimately the confiscation of lands of many within Italy that got rolled up into giant estates, and likewise in provinces such as Judea where lands were sold on favorable terms to equines and aristocrats seeking fortunes. Indeed these distributed seats of power carried certain rights of taxation that enabled considerable fortunes to be amassed. Eventually, though, at least to the privileged poor of Italy, the dole of wheat, oil, and pork did become a daily entitlement.

While Jesus tolerated Caesar's call for taxes, he presents to his followers a choice to accept a higher calling, recognizing that others here on Earth will always reject the notion of God and choose to lead lives that diverge from his teachings, such as the Ten Commandments. The Old Testament, which is honored by Christians alongside the New Testament, provides evidence supportive of Jesus's instruction that things made by man will be designed out of hubris and without morality in mind, wherein deceit or raw power can create misery for others. According to the book of Genesis, the Babylonian leader Nimrod sought to prove that his people could accomplish greatness without God by building a city and a great tower that could touch the heavens. The city and tower were constructed with clay bricks over the course of 43 years, occupying the time of the citizens to manufacture bricks and lay them. Nimrod was thought of as a tyrant. His name in Hebrew translates as "he said get down," meaning that all under his domain were to be subservient to him and the state, and not God. In the modern context, his actions suggest socialism and totalitarianism. The bricks Nimrod commanded his subjects to make are identical, and are metaphorical to his kingdom's subjects being thought of as undifferentiated and cogs within a centrally commanded enterprise. This brings to mind the uniforms Mao Tse-Tung required in communist China. Mao similarly required his citizens to manufacture steel in backyard furnaces during the Great Leap Forward. In that modern effort, initially production rose, but the centralized plan led to economic disaster and the death of 30 million people.

There is a symbol in the Bible for whenever force is applied against people, and it is the furnace. Almost nothing can stand up against its intense heat. Nimrod used to have a neck charm that was in the shape of a furnace, to remind his people of his approach of governing. Abraham challenged him by believing in God instead, and for this Nimrod threw him into a furnace to do away with him. Another famous biblical reference to bricks and furnaces is in Exodus, where the Pharaoh enslaves the Hebrews. Bricks are formed by man and exhibit sameness, whereas stones are made by the creator and are each unique. The stories of Nimrod and the Pharaoh are in the Bible to warn that it is dangerous to become dependent upon sustenance from the state, for it will condemn us to barren lives where we are unconnected to each other through family and charity and are vulnerable to tyranny. Bricks and furnaces are symbolic clues.[21]

The Babylonians and the tower of Babel receive their name from God's having dispersed the residents of the city before their work was done through making them cease to be able to communicate with each other by replacing their language with many tongues, which scatters them throughout the Earth. Perhaps instead starvation from unwisely slaving away at an unproductive socialist industrial goal led them to seek food elsewhere, where they would need to adopt the language and customs of their new habitats or resume old loyalties. With this rich Biblical lesson not long forgotten in ancient times, it is doubtful that Jesus would offend his heavenly father and advocate socialism.

## The Weight of Leveling

This brings us to the essence of what is wrong with socialism, and how it lures the American people into false hopes for a more perfect existence fashioned by man and certainly not by God. Today's progressive tax system targets the upper-middle class with a vengeance, attempting to have them "get down" in Nimrodian fashion to a sameness of income with everyone else. To an extent it exempts the senatorial class of Buffett and Soros. It leaves no mark at all on those who would assemble financial empires within the tax havens of Lichtenstein, Andorra, or Monaco, or behind the walls of foundations such as the Ford, Carnegie,

Pew, or Rockefeller. Ever since Keynes told us we might stimulate the economy through spending and assist the process through redirecting income through progressive taxation and credits to those among us with the highest "propensity to spend" (and least inclination to save), a moral desire to balance the budget was forever undermined and delegitimized. Like the rules that transferred the title of lands belonging to industrious republican farmers like Cincinnatus through encroachment and confiscation, the death tax ensures that the lesser nobles of the upper-middle class leave their heirs pennies on the dollar, with their estates purchased at fire-sale prices to buttress the investment portfolio of the Warren Buffetts of this world.

Fiat currency, like the repeatedly clipped denarius or the dilutively minted anoninianus, has made a penny a quickly browning token no longer worth bending over for, even by the gutter poor, whereas one century ago a nickel would purchase more bread and fish than today's dollar. It is a construct of man that has a history of complete failure dating back to the early 18th century and even eighth century China. The U.S. money supply (M3) ballooned from $1 trillion when Nixon abandoned gold to $14 trillion in 2008, and this severely diluted the value of cash relative to assets or ownership claims on businesses, with the benefit accruing to those who borrowed heavily early on to accumulate such things, or to large financial institutions that would enjoy an outsized claim on the blood coursing through the economic body. Eventually it would mean the financial sector would account for nearly 40 percent of S&P profits, a bloated percentage unseen before, when 5 percent was the norm. The Old Testament, warning of the tendency for those in power to alter money for the good of government but not its people, repeatedly refers to the immorality of using "false weights and measures." Accounts of this appear in Deuteronomy, Leviticus, Isaiah, and Proverbs: "You shall do no wrong in judgment, in measure of weight, or capacity. You shall have just balances and just weights" (Leviticus 19:35-37); "Diverse and deceitful weights are shamefully vile and abhorrent to the Lord, and false scales are not good" (Proverbs 20: 23); Thy silver has become dross, thy wine is watered down. Thy princes are faithless, companions of thieves, they all love bribes, and run after rewards. (Isaiah: 1:22-23).

Yes, America, now still near its apex, may be veering off its republican pathway into a system run by a chosen few who are highly protective of their rank, but this is the landscape of socialism. Rome and the old Soviet Union may have more in common, or even the new Russia, the Middle East, or Europe. The people of Europe, like those who received the dole in Rome, are compliant and sycophantic to their senators and emperors, worshipping them as celebrities. Longing to be united as one world, Europeans gathered 200,000 strong in Berlin in July 2008 to drink free beer and chant for the grace of Obama. They were joined in the new world by a crowd estimated at over 70,000 Seattle in May 2008.[22] We will be happy; we will be fed; but we will not prosper on the trajectory set by our republican founders, for socialism seeks the same goal in America, Europe or ancient Rome: the leveling of the masses and the exultation of those who govern over them. Capitalism may not be fair; by design it creates winners and losers. But when supported by a constitution that guarantees equality under the law, it permits the American Dream: to better oneself. Using the law to make us all equal regardless of our labors is a mandate for serfdom, whose name is socialism, be it in Rome or Washington, D.C.

# Part Six

# THE OBSOLESCENCE
# OF CHARACTER

The tremendous economic advances of the last century have elevated most Americans beyond a simple subsistence living to one when everyday goods are ridiculously inexpensive and available in countless variety at Wal-Mart. Once the baby boomers came of age and became the first generation to enjoy the wealth that capitalism and technological innovation has provided, they turned more to self-expression and self-actualization, rebelling against traditional lifestyles now known to us through iconic 1950s sitcoms such as *Ozzie and Harriet*. Cultural decadence embodied in events such as Woodstock invoked conservative horror. But by the 1990s the modern view was that this famed generation and those to follow had developed a new sensibility, a secular morality if you will, that reined in counterproductive rebelliousness and instead smartly produced doting parents willing to indulge their children's every wish. Inconvenient to the new levelheaded secularism, a revival of conservatism ran in parallel, particularly the emergence of the religious right which was personified in the election of George W. Bush.

This modern narrative is opposed in Part 6, "The Obsolescence of Character," where instead cultural decay is linked to the multigenerational financial excess coming to a head in the meltdown that began in 2008. The common theme is deferral of consequences. Fiat currency and even the gold-exchange standard departed from classical gold systems that provided our nation's most remarkable growth and prosperity by allowing financial actors to defer settlement of trade imbalances, avoid large bank insolvencies, and even sidestep entire economic recessions. Keynesian policies legitimized the putting off to children and grandchildren the cost of doling out generous entitlements to today's citizens. Now, the boomerang effect of systemic collapse, a product of continual stockpiling of future obligations, may force a reevaluation of the role of individual character as well as the secular societal revolution. It is hard to imagine a comeback of old-time religion, but clearly the stress of a severe downturn could produce soul-searching, if only because this setback removes an essential underpinning to the self-indulgent era, namely the assumption of abundance.

In Chapter 14 the observation that individual character has given way to the state's taking over responsibility for indiscretions, financial or otherwise, is developed. Chapter 15 further explores self-indulgence, tracing our modern economic behavior, such as the aversion to saving, to among other things a sexual revolution made possible through the advent of the birth control pill. With the family still under attack despite the claim by some in the libertarian camp that a modern sensibility has been regained, it has been natural for religion to fall by the wayside. In its place has been the installation of new commandments issued by the state, a culture of intense regulation and compliance, which is surveyed in Chapter 16 by recounting the explosive growth of regulation in the financial sector throughout the financial boom of the last 10 years, which oddly enough proved to be nearly completely ineffectual.

# Chapter 14

# Bending to the Modern World

*If you take your stand on the prevalent view, how long do you suppose it will prevail . . . All you can say about my taste is that it is old-fashioned; yours will soon be the same.*[1]

C.S. LEWIS, *EXPERIMENTS IN CRITICISM*, 1961

Why write about culture in a book that is primarily about money? Because money is neither gold any longer nor notes circulated with gold backing them. It is basically credit. It used to have a sliver of Treasury notes (less than $1 trillion) behind it, but even these have been largely swapped for, you guessed it, bad credit.[2] Credit has been socialized. That is: when it goes bad, the federal government steps in and cleans up, rescuing financial institutions, depositors, and through the "too big to fail" doctrine, large depositors at large institutions. Why was credit socialized? Because our culture demanded it. What shapes culture? Beliefs. Which brings us to character: whether individuals accept personal responsibility or instead place blame for economic outcomes on society as a whole. The resounding theme of this century has been that through government one might extract reimbursement for misfortune or bad decisions, or just walk away and not be concerned with the trail left behind.

Character might be built by man alone or through the traditions and morals preserved in religion. Good character attributes might be abundant in many religions, but the Judeo-Christian heritage seems to offer the complete package. The jury may be out on whether men living under that heritage behave better than secularists, but much evidence is in to support this thesis. Those who put man at the center of the universe depend heavily upon the systems of man rather than examine character, preferring scientific systems such as FICO scores or loan-to-value ratios to looking the borrower in the eye. They might beef up regulation and compliance, or they might staff comprehensive risk management departments, but somehow the frailty of man undoes the most elaborate of these controls.

The last century has witnessed the scientific awakening of man and the rise of the modern technocratic state. It has been accompanied by socialist governmental systems in most of the developed world, including the United States, and an era of fiat currency. C.S. Lewis, the great Christian thinker, devoted considerable time to reading old texts, quipping that this provided his mind with "the clean sea breeze of the centuries." His long-term perspective was encapsulated with the observation of the epigraph at the beginning of this chapter. What we have witnessed in a century stuffed with technological advancement rivaling that of all the Earth's before it, is a shift from concern with the character of the individual to obsession with constructing an all-encompassing state.

For the perspective on what this means in the world of money, who better than J. Pierpont Morgan to comment under oath when being browbeaten by Samuel Untermeyer, counsel to the House Banking and Currency Committee, a formative Wall Street lawyer who in 1911 first raised the specter of there being a "Money Trust" dominated by big New York banks:[3]

Untermeyer: Is not commercial credit based primarily upon money or property?

Morgan: No, Sir. The first thing is character.

Untermeyer: Before money or property?

Morgan: Before money or anything else. Money cannot buy it.

Untermeyer: If that is the rule of business, Mr. Morgan, why do the banks demand, the first thing they ask, a statement of what the man has got, before they extend him credit . . . He does not get it on his face or character?

Morgan: Yes, he gets it on character . . . Because a man I do not trust could not get money from me on all the bonds in Christendom.[4]

Men such as J.P. Morgan have been maligned for centuries. In the Iron Age, blacksmiths prospered above most farmers but were feared and relegated to outside the village, and they were thought to be mysterious for transforming materials. Similarly, centuries later traders and merchants, who trekked between villages and dealt with money, could take advantage of enormous arbitrage opportunities, possessing knowledge that others lacked. Like the blacksmith, they could make something out of nothing, and they were held in contempt by ordinary men and even intellects such as Plato and Aristotle.[5]

Morgan's perspective hails from Victorian ideals, which were popular and helped elect Theodore Roosevelt. Roosevelt was the model of masculinity: hunter, explorer, and soldier; he named himself the "Bull Moose" and the Teddy bear got its name from him. Consider this précis of how masculinity determined financial behavior in the Victorian era by Emily Rosenberg in her fascinating book about turn-of-the-century finance and culture, *Financial Missionaries to the World: The Politics and Culture of Dollar Diplomacy*:

In the formulation that was widespread among middle-class white men in the Victorian era, manliness emphasized strength of character, especially defined as self-control and self-mastery. According to the social evolutionary doctrine of the day, humans advanced by establishing mastery over themselves and the larger environment. The lack of self-discipline and ability to plan for the future marked a lower status. Thus, a worthy man had a duty to protect those who were weaker, self-indulgent and less rational: women, children, and nonwhite races. Manly restraint, both in monetary and sexual matters, would bring capital accumulation and family (thus social) stability. In this view, civilization advanced as men became more cognizant of manly duties . . . [6]

Rosenberg goes on to write throughout the book how the apostles of the gold standard were guided by this mindset and thought it their duty to spread a modern classical monetary order to the world. Charles Conant, an evangelist and moralist, was the pioneer in this regard and dominated this scene until he died in Cuba in 1915. Mexico, which switched to gold in 1905 at his urging, turned out to be an early setback, for its money supply had to shrink to meet its pegged value to gold, feeding grievances in all strata of society, leading to the Revolution of 1910. Conant was followed by Edwin Kemmerer, a trained economist, who built a fortune doing advisory work, which placed him in line to share fees based upon considerable seigniorage earned. Kemmerer continued Conant's work spreading the virtues of sound currency around the world, enabling America's open door policy to be quite potent without explicit colonization. By Kemmerer's time military interventions such as Smedley Butler's 1912 appearance in Managua with 2,000 U.S. Marines became passé, and "controlled loans" involving running the customs house were prevalent. By 1928, Kemmerer had spread the gold-exchange standard across the globe to 50 nations.[7]

Morgan rose to influence in an era when the accumulation of great wealth began to astound the ordinary man. As Nassim Nicholas Taleb observed in his book, *The Black Swan,* life is unfair, a theme the economist Sherwin Rosen, author of studies about the economics of superstars, develops as credited by Taleb. Rosen bemoans the high salaries of basketball stars and TV personalities, which he attributes to the "tournament effect," wherein someone who is marginally better can win the whole pot, leaving others with nothing. Taleb reminds us how this is so: We would rather buy a recording featuring the renowned Vladimir Horowitz for $10.99 than pay $9.99 for one of a struggling pianist.

However, ordinary men through democracy can band together to not only ostracize the J.P. Morgans from the village, but to strip them of tournament winnings. Just as important, they can redistribute them to those who struggle in the $9.99 bin. On the other hand, in the world of credit, democracy is a stranger. Should the rules be short circuited, wealth need not participate. Share prices for implicitly government-backed mortgage agencies can plunge from $60 to less than $1 in months. The Soviet Union learned this the hard way. Europe's unemployment rate during the boom times prior to 2008 stood at its 1932 depression level, its countries having not created more than a few million jobs in the last three decades. Yet somehow many think its system is still functioning relatively well.

By 1913, when J.P. Morgan appeared in the Pujo hearings, the era of lending money based upon character was beginning to have this determinant completely removed from the process, and the pendulum would shift 100 years later toward the ordinary man collectively mandating loans for everyone, eventually without even documentation or down payment. Or worse, smothering documentation would lend an air of legitimacy. Loans would be sliced and diced for general consumption, surrounded by the safety of telephone-book-sized prospectuses, overseen by thousands of regulations, and monitored by intricate risk models, none of which could put Humpty Dumpty back together. In the era leading up to Morgan, when character was put foremost, America had seen small percentages of banks fail in great panics, only to have most of their assets recover in value when liquidity returned. Now, thanks to modern practices, great numbers of giant-sized financial institutions have essentially failed. They must be kept on life support; because their assets are so tainted they may never recover in value.

## Secular Society

Is it possible to have character without religion? The question is unanswerable, and perhaps rightly so, because this is something for the individual and not the state to decide. The early Romans in the republican era were pagans and demonstrated character, at least until their values fell prey to their own imperial success. Imperial conquest led to a great transformation, literally turning Rome from red bricks to dazzling marble edifices at the center of 53,000 miles of highways whose length

approximated the U.S. interstate system. But the centralization of power
and economic decision making created a vastly distorted apparatus that
collapsed of its own weight within about 200 years, whereas the republic before it extended from the sixth century BC to 31 BC. When the
values of the republic failed, the result was not immediate, but its fate
may have been sealed. The man credited with Rome's defeat, Odoacer,
was in fact a Christian. But the empire he conquered had eliminated its
middle class, ceased to have meaningful world trade, had slipped into a
collection of large autarkic landholdings run by a shrinking aristocracy
that would not procreate, and had a large discontented mass of serfs that
centuries before had been independent farmers like Cincinnatus. The
great commerce of Rome had ceased nearly 300 years earlier.

It may just be coincidental that as our modern secular leaders complete the job of cleansing the nation of its Judeo-Christian traditions,
following Europe's lead, that our credit system becomes the turf of large
banks that are too big to fail and too big to succeed as well. Yet if there is
no connection, strangely the polarity of those who identify closely with
the Judeo-Christian traditions snaps to when placed against the mag-
netic axis of the conservative view that markets hold deep and complex
long-term interrelationships, which should not be bent by the machinations of man. Removing the premium garnered from Horowitz record-
ings and redistributing this to those with lesser talent would ensure that
no one would ever hear the music of great composers as it was supposed
to be played. And it would also mean that mankind would not advance,
but sink instead into another dark age of sorts. Perhaps its knowledge
would be safely encapsulated in monasteries on hills away from the rabble, waiting to return upon the discovery of a new world.

Like Europe, America too may evolve into a secular society. In that
configuration, we might preserve key elements of our morality, or any
other of the traditions that have been the bedrock of the success of this
country and of Western Civilization. Would we be capable of asking
if we are governing ourselves in ways that allow this secular majority
to trounce upon those of whom it disapproves, either through deceit,
through killing, through taking possessions by force, through not honoring fatherhood and motherhood, or through envy? Certainly it is
one's free choice whether or not to be religious, and to what degree
to embrace one's chosen religion. Importantly, this would also include
Islam, which has many American adherents who would not go the way

of the terrorist line and might be offended that one would think they would. But it is worth examining the record of secular societies to see if their modern sensibility is truly kind, tolerant, and capable of advancing economic growth.

One legacy of the last few decades has been a wholesale attack upon the Judeo-Christian heritage that has been leveraged upon the legal and government-controlled educational systems, which goes well beyond the intent of the Founding Fathers to merely ensure that the state would not endorse one particular theology. Another legacy, extant for nearly a century, has been the adoption of positions that embrace socialism and relativism, two isms that work to break down the morals developed over several millennia. If we are to live in such a secular society, who then *would* fight to preserve morality? Pol Pot? The Soviets, who would invade Georgia? Or, those such as the British, even the Archbishop of Canterbury, who would accommodate Sharia law? Would we not then soon see the dhimmi, the cutting off of hands, the stoning of homosexuals and adulterers? Would not the Canadian courts imprison Mark Steyn for being critical of Islamic fundamentalism? Should the United States adopt the fairness doctrine, would not conservative thinkers such as he have their right to freely speak political thoughts be regulated?

Is America's sense of fairness not distorted by the relativism of its second most wealthy individual, who taunts us by saying he bears a lower tax rate than the cleaning lady who works the night shift at his office, leading him to conclude taxes should be raised for the highest bracket of the middle class, 85 percent of whose wealth is confiscated by the time of death? How about by another billionaire, who would rank #32 on the Fortune 100 except that he donated two-thirds of his fortune, thus diverting a lifetime of taxes that might reduce the burden on others, toward political causes that he says are designed to "take down the American government"? Does not the United Nations embody what the secular and multicultural left wish we would meld our legal system and military into over time, following the lead of Pan-European awakening? Where is the evidence of that body's sense of justice, when it fills one-quarter of the seats of the Geneva-based Human Rights Commission with six of the 18 countries considered the world's biggest human rights abusers? How about when its leader's son would profit while his father endorses an oil-for-food program designed to benefit a tyrant condemned by 16 resolutions from that same body? Relativism allows us to comfortably make believe we have not moved too far from the goodness of the simple tenets preserved through religion over generations, and that we in fact understand the whys and wherefores better nowadays, for we grasp the nuance and complexity of the modern world.

Today's system of exchanging goods and services, which creates wealth through the productivity of specialization, has developed over the millennia. It improved upon the tribal systems, such as those in existence among native Indians and in Africa, to name two societies preserved in a savage and communistic state as near to today as two to three centuries ago. In these circumstances, principles such as government by chieftain and sharing of all resources served small units of population, particularly when animal attack or tribal war were everyday threats. But these collective systems were at odds with the bedrock of the exchange economy, such as the sanctity of contracts and private property. Secularism and relativism are premised upon man's assumed ability to control ethical behavior and redistribute through edict the gains from specialization of labor, and increasingly intellectual property, with the erroneous presumption that this would not undermine the incentive to produce in the least. Besides seeking freedom from the more onerous constructs of religion, socialists promise to liberate us from all the burdens of civilization: disciplined work, responsibility, risk taking, saving, honesty, or the honoring of promises (contracts). As Rousseau advocated, a return to the freedom of the noble savage, who knew nothing of private property or exchange, would discard such limiting traditions, returning man to his state of "being born free" rather than being "everywhere in chains."

A key element to continued prosperity is investment, which by definition equals savings. Edicts that punish and discourage savings for the good intention of aiding the tribe at large feel just in this ancient sense, but they cause society to digress. The recent experiments with classless national orders and eugenic pureness were abject failures, yet still the liberal mind gives no quarter to the possibility that distributed knowledge (that is, of prices, supplies demanded, return on capital) is superior to centralized control. And everywhere centralized control has been established, it being the essence of humanism, it must reject moralism.

Written in the Constitution is God's provision that we are equal before the law, but it does not say that the government ought to disproportionately share the fruits of our labor so that we would be more equal after our work is done. The Bill of Rights is predicated upon Judeo-Christian traditions of rules being set in place that ensure our freedom to pursue our dreams without the interference of other men. One should not covet the possessions of one's neighbor, steal, or bear false witness. But relativity chips away at such absolutes bit by bit. Taxes are levied, which in effect steal from those whose wealth is envied. The clear words of the Constitution are twisted to strip away freedom of political speech and gun ownership, to name a few false inventions of the jurists. It takes little effort to live for today and let others assume responsibility for one's welfare tomorrow.

Atheists ask why would God bring suffering into the world, knowing this is one of the most vexing challenges to belief. If man were given no moral judgments to make between good and evil, he would be like the animals, and if there were no pain, there would be no hot sun, no ice storms, no wild kingdom of predators, no livestock, no love, no hate—no spirit. The liberal wants Utopia, a tribal wholesomeness, a Garden of Eden with no God to judge; all can be plucked and eaten including the apple, and it is magically placed on the table each day. Like it or not, there is a direct connection between the religious concept of living in a world that contains pain and happiness, good and evil, and the parallel universe in capitalism where there are winners and losers. Wanting Rousseau's free world of the noble savage or John Lennon's imagining a modern equivalent of the Garden of Eden is no different than longing for economic equality and state provision for all our basic needs. To transform the tradition of the millennia, wherein individuals exchange specialized labor of their own free will because they wish to endure today's effort to stockpile for tomorrow or to benefit their offspring, today's so-called liberal must bit by bit reduce the rules that protect the pursuit of life, liberty, and happiness.

## Rational Man

Many breakthroughs marked the era just before and after the start of the 20th century. Two scientific observations which shaped ideas considerably by challenging classical order were Darwinism and relativity.

In Darwinism, the notion of the world being created in seven days through the design of a supreme being was shattered. Darwin was a rationalist, following an orderly scientific methodology to prove his case purportedly beyond doubt.

Einstein upended Newtonian physics by questioning the linearity of time. For the speed of light to remain constant (which it always does), two objects, one still and the other moving, cannot observe time or distance at the same rate. One's perspective determines speed (measured as distance over time), so that a ball thrown backward inside a train would appear to be standing still in the eyes of someone on a station platform. Eddington's 1919 test proving starlight was bent by the mass of the Sun confirmed Einstein's famous equation of relativity, $E = MC^2$, which held that mass was stored energy. To the surprise of Einstein, the unveiling of relativity and its undermining of Newtonian order, combined with a new hunger for scientific proof rather than belief in absolutes, was supportive of philosophic acceptance of relativism.

"Indirectly, driven by popular misunderstandings rather than a fealty to Einstein's thinking, relativity became associated with a new relativism in morality and art and politics. There was less faith in absolutes, not only of time and space, but also of truth and morality. In an editorial about Einstein's relativity theory, titled 'Assaulting the Absolute,' on December 7, 1919 the *New York Times* fretted that 'the foundations of all human thought have been undermined'" as noted in Walter Isaacson's excellent biography, *Einstein: His Life and Universe*.[8]

Although he was not religious, Einstein went on to resist the conclusions drawn by others from his work in particle physics as colorfully attested to by his quip, "God does not play dice with the universe." (Quantum physicists concluded certain particle movement is random and thus not governed by rules or equations.) He was horrified by the political and societal change in interwar Germany, which was the product of relativist deduction that replaced the morality of centuries with a grotesque and powerful statist doctrine, and which arose from the ashes of hyperinflation.

Unfortunately for the well-being of rich and poor alike, secularism, socialism, and relativism are linked conceptually, and they impact economics. These isms have been on the rise, and they offer some explanation why whenever there is a bump in the road there is strong popular approval for the socialization of debt, more transfer of income, preservation of failing industries or companies, more regulation of economic activity, and intolerance of recession. In 2008 the American people made another such easy choice for continuing "change." While one usually only thinks of secularism in the context of lacking religion, it is usually a cornerstone of statist control over the affairs of man and evident in monetary, fiscal, and redistributive schemes that sanction those in power to allocate economic resources rather than permit individuals to do so themselves.

Moreover, the development of rational thought as a replacement for traditions, morals, or restraints imposed by religious doctrine has formed the foundation for the growing acceptance of socialism, as described by Friedrich Hayek:

> The basic point . . . that morals, including, especially, our institutions of property, freedom, and justice, are not a creation of man's reason but a distinct second endowment conferred on him by cultural evolution—runs counter to the main intellectual outlook of the twentieth century. The influence of rationalism has indeed been so profound and pervasive that, in general, the more intelligent an educated person is, the more likely he or she now is not only to be a rationalist, but also to hold socialist views (regardless of whether he or she is sufficiently doctrinal to attach his or her views any label, including "socialist"). The higher we climb up the ladder of intelligence, the more we talk with intellectuals, the more likely we are to encounter socialist convictions. Rationalists tend to be intelligent and intellectual; and intelligent intellectuals tend to be socialists ... One's initial surprise at finding that intelligent people tend to be socialists diminishes when one realizes that, of course, intelligent people will tend to overvalue intelligence, and to suppose that we must owe all the advantages and opportunities that our civilization offers to deliberate design rather than to following traditional rules, and likewise to suppose that we can, by exercising our reason, eliminate any remaining undesired features by still more intelligent reflection, and still more appropriate design and 'rational coordination' of our

undertakings. This leads one to be favorably disposed to the central economic planning and control that lie at the heart of socialism.[9]

Once moral or constitutional absolutes are pushed aside, personal or political choices are no longer anchored but relative and shifting. The Founding Fathers chose to enshrine the Constitution with godly authority and to enumerate rights of citizens, which limited the role of government (free political speech, bearing arms, representative government, state's rights, etc.). By citing these powers as morally sanctioned and not established by man, the temptation for men to impose their will upon other men might be forestalled. Wisely, they knew an elite few backed by martial or police power or a tyrannous majority might have the potential to usurp the machinery of government and enslave the people. Today, anyone who might resist confiscation of his labor through the actions of the IRS must submit to judicial power.

The success of democracy requires citizens to jealously refrain from ceding authority to their governors—and unimagined by the Founding Fathers, to non-elected rulers, who have come to overshadow the people's representatives in influence and number. This latter downfall began when Congress created a technocracy unaccountable to voters under the inspiration of the political scientist Woodrow Wilson, who admired the Prussian bureaucracy and sought to insert a similar structure into U.S. government. This he did, and it was later entrenched when Roosevelt massively funded and expanded its operation. Wilson's famous *Study of Administration*, which advocated empowering administrations for regulation of business and the affairs of individuals flouts the Constitution:" . . . we need not care a peppercorn for the constitutional or political reasons which Frenchmen or Germans give for their practices when explaining them to us. If I see a murderous fellow sharpening a knife cleverly, I can borrow his way of sharpening the knife without borrowing his probable intention to commit murder with it . . . "[10]

Under Wilson the Fed was created, which did away with the need for sound banks as measured by today's capital requirements, and this along with the power to tax income through the Sixteenth Amendment converted a resilient banking system capable of bailing out a purposefully weak government into one where an omnipotent government would eventually be needed to bring us back from the abyss of systemic financial collapse. Should sharply increased taxes in the forthcoming administrations result in *decreased* revenue to the government as posited by supply-siders, complete debasement of the currency may follow, making the 95 percent dilution seen since the Fed began in 1913 seem mild in comparison.

Save for religious or the most strident conservative thinkers, most commentators fail to make the connection to the major contribution that the drift toward amorality inherent in relativism and secularism has been a root cause of today's political and economic struggles. For example, stock market guru Jim Cramer was profiled earlier in this work because he boasts about his immoral decision to personally profit at the hands of the taxpayer despite possibly knowing it would cause systemic damage. He would probably find conservative disdain for his actions risible.

Fed governors and in fact probably over 95 percent of the informed and uninformed of monetary policy alike have chosen not to address the structural problem of moral hazard, even though they may acknowledge its ill effect. In fact, they have pleaded for *more* government intervention instead of facing up to what is, deceptively, a moral predicament. Not necessarily would one need to be religious to see it as such. But the Judeo-Christian tradition would insist that we face painful choices head-on, rather than always opt to bite the proverbial apple. Consistent with J.P. Morgan's approach to lending, if participants in financial transactions strive to maintain character, then there would be a self-governing aspect to systemic risk, whereas today borrowers and lenders alike can abrogate responsibility to the state, meaning ultimately, other taxpayers.

Samuel Adams famously said, "It is not possible that any state should long remain free, where virtue is not supremely honored … when people are universally ignorant, and debauched in their manners, they will sink under their own weight without the aid of foreign invaders."[11] Nearly 200 years later, President Truman would witness firsthand the depravity of Nazi rule (whose German common name, *Nationalsozialismus*, belies its socialistic core). Likewise, Truman would declare that ". . . if we don't have the proper fundamental moral background, we will finally wind up with a totalitarian government which does not believe in rights for anybody but the state."

Why would Adams and Truman invoke the almighty, for are not men capable of having character without spiritual succor? Surely are we not in a more enlightened state than Adams, who inhabited an age so absent of modern science? Truman might be excused for having one foot in the past. The advances of the last hundred years have been staggering, and it is no wonder that humanism has begun to supplant divinity as a force in our lives. But has it led to outcomes beneficial to man, or has it frequently led to systemic collapses of government? How can one explain Mao (50 million dead), Stalin (20 million), Hitler (10 million), and others down the list such as Pol Pot (*only* two million)? Or merely misery, such as is seen in Africa or Cuba? Or the downtrodden state of women in the Islamic world? Or the failure to recognize the budding life of infants in the womb, snuffed out nearly 50 million times cumulatively in the United States alone? Might secularism foster economic collapse? Despite a horrendous civil war, two wars with Britain, and two world wars, never did we face a more protracted economic disaster than we did in the Great Depression. While liberals romanticize and elevate the changes Roosevelt forced upon the nation, never before had socialistic practices been brought to bear—both monetary and fiscal—and they achieved little, prolonging misery for a decade. Today we live in an era when the institutions born of that era have exploded horrendously, and perhaps in such a way that would pull the entire financial system under.

The injection of a religious foundation for the Constitution was an acknowledgement that man may want to establish orders that foster the advance of humanity, for men are prone to weakness. Relativism is a chain of actions that follows one another like a cats' feet in the night, so silent that they lead to collective evils beyond the pale, without leaving a trace of causation. After the fact, fingers can be pointed in any direction depending upon the consensus of the day.

## Occupying the High Ground

Are liberals immoral? No, not exactly, for they have belief systems. Can atheists be conservative? It is a little harder to say "no" to the second question, for conservatives have atheist friends, relatives, even spouses with whom they agree politically. Does it come down to nuance? After all, there are no atheists in foxholes as the saying goes. Alternatively, as James Burnham writes, "No one is willing to sacrifice and die for progressive education, Medicare, humanity in the abstract, the United Nations, and a ten percent rise in Social Security payments."[12]

Accusing a liberal of being immoral can be confused with calling him amoral. Merriam-Webster defines amoral as "neither moral nor immoral; lying outside the sphere to which moral judgments apply." But being amoral does not mean one is devoid of morals. Liberal secularists staunchly believe they are moral, for they strongly assert the rights of individuals, decry racism and sexism, believe in the right to dissent, and have compassion for the poor and disadvantaged. Why have those who strongly believe they have morals turned upon those who follow the tradition of Judeo-Christian values? Why would they not die for them as Burnham cleverly asserts, but the vast majority of those who put their lives on the line in Iraq profess religious belief? And what of soldiers for whom religion is not front and central, but simply whose patriotism runs deep? (After all, the Viet Cong fought well enough to defeat Americans 40 years ago.) Why wouldn't peace trump war on moral grounds, or alleviation of poverty be a more noble cause than the pursuit of wealth? This rift evokes one of the issues that split the Jew Jesus from his religion. He was a pacifist, but God in the Old Testament rewards his chosen with prosperity, sovereignty, and military victory when they heed his call and permits them to be utterly subjugated when they repeatedly drift into immorality.

A bedrock of liberalism is that the modern world has advanced because of science and rationalism, and these are noble disciplines that lie outside the sphere of moral judgments as Webster defines amorality. The notion is so strong that our culture now has begun to chide those with religious beliefs. Pope Benedict XVI in his trip to the United States in early 2008 was seen as peculiarly out of touch and "in need of being changed to reflect the way people live today." The quaintness of religion is even subliminally driven home to our children by Disney, whose young protagonist of its hugely popular movie *Air Bud*, Josh, befriends a stray dog, Buddy, and finds a place for them to develop amazing basketball skills together by chopping away old vines from a court belonging to an abandoned church. They might well have chosen a vacant lot aside an adding machine, icebox, or transistor radio factory, but Disney couldn't pass up a chance to subtly proselytize a captive audience in its formative stage.

There are two problems in the war of beliefs. One is that the liberal view is not passive; it is morphing into an insidiously totalitarian force. Herb London stresses that it creates a loss of nerve in foreign affairs. But like the downtrend in Rome traced in the last chapter, its empire succumbed to outsiders who had already been invited inside, notwithstanding attacks from neighboring opportunistic states that would be expected. The lifeblood of any nation is its economy. Problems in foreign affairs may just be a telltale sign that there is a loss of focus in business. Let's examine how changing cultural preferences and grasping for a utopian society may have become an obsession that has begun to weaken our character, slowly eroding givens such as contracts, debt repayment, and the ability to freely conduct business without governmental interference.

## Liberal Awakening

While the liberal awakening of the 1960s certainly had its militant moments, there was also a soft side that urged tolerance, being typified by the lyrics of Jesse Colin Young: "C'mon people now, smile on your brother, everybody get together try and love one another right now." Who could object to this? The problem is that these lyrics might be rewritten now that relativism has continually refined the notion of liberalism: Not only will you smile on your brother, you will give up 85 percent of your possessions to him by the time of your death. If he decides to live a life of crime and drug addiction, you will realize that isn't his choice because he has been disadvantaged, surrounded by others who did the same. He should not be punished, but given another chance. In the meantime if you were assaulted or your property stolen, please be tolerant and patient. If he was not disadvantaged but simply has not worked as hard or made sacrifices and saved as you did, it is probably because he was stuck in a low-paying job or was busy being cool in school rather than learning how to read and write well. If he borrowed too much money, it was probably the bank's fault. You are under strict orders not to make any suggestions that moral depravity or lack of character might be causing the problem.

Once we morph from mere tolerance of sexual deviance and drug use behind closed doors to hijacking the machinery of state and its laws to create social change, we have crossed a Rubicon to a form of soft totalitarianism. There is a huge difference between those who are productive but choose another sexual orientation or responsibly use alcohol or even drugs, even if these may turn out to be extremely poor decisions, and those who work to empower the state to tear down our moral fabric. The government is being called upon to assist or legitimize the destruction of character that can lead some of us to make poor choices in life. Propping up borrowers who overleveraged in the credit boom with funds from those who did not, teaches us that saving is bad and consumption is good. So does providing end-to-end bill payment for health care, education, and retirement. Strangling business with regulation and making it a honey pot for spurious litigation directs workers to be drones for large companies and broadcasts to them that it is dangerous to start up small enterprises without an expensive army of legal, tax, or compliance personnel. It also criminalizes trivial business behavior. In what is termed "the nanny state," government is proselytizing not through speech, but through fines and licenses, a new form of morality. Matters of smoking, trans-fatty acids, pesticide use, media fairness, cutting away brush near intermittent streams, drilling for oil in forlorn locales, the size of one's car, the use of child seats, or the generation of electricity through economic means such as coal or nuclear fuels come under heightened supervision by the state.

## Chilling of Inquiry

The tolerance that was once longed for in the late 20th century is slowly giving way to eradication of character development by the individual, and his intellectual freedom to challenge the assumptions behind the state's growing control over everything from everyday life to how business is conducted and consumers make decisions. In the words of Herb London, "Today the public square in the United States is clouded by confusion, misinformation, and misguided assumptions. A secularist agenda permeates so much of American culture—even the language we use—that serious discussion about secularism's implications is difficult. Any criticism of relativism, multiculturalism, or the postmodern outlook is muzzled by accusations of sexism, homophobia, or sheer intolerance, and defining an adversary's position as intolerant often ends the discussion."[13]

When the government controls the education system from kindergarten through 12th grade and through grants and direct support wields considerable authority over colleges and universities, the statist view becomes institutionalized. London continues:

> Without judgment, without discrimination, without a sense of right and wrong, taboos cannot exist. Removed from religion's timeless moral injunctions, secularists rely on the multiculturalist tendency to ask, "Who are we to condemn or censure? By what authority can we judge others?"

> Os Guiness explains that "naturally no one likes to be charged with racism, colonialism, or chauvinism. Nor does anyone want to be caught 'blaming the victim' or found 'misrepresenting the voice of the voiceless' with standards or categories 'imposed by outside cultures of domination.' But the upshot is a chilling of inquiry. Tough questions go unasked, serious investigations remain unpursued, spurious claims stay unchallenged." It is precisely that chilling of inquiry that colors the crusade for tolerance.[14]

The chilling of inquiry is so fundamental that it has invaded our court system, not just at the highest level where judges can abandon the laws crafted by elected representatives of the people in lieu of new directions they feel empowered to create, but in the lowest levels of meted justice.

From January to October 1995 the nation watched the murder trial of O.J. Simpson, culminating in a count of 150 million viewers when he was acquitted. Most of the nation (but not a majority of African Americans) when polled think he was guilty of killing his white wife, and that a stacked jury opted to engage in sheer "nullification" of the law, exhibiting racism in reverse. More than a decade later, he still draws the attention of millions; this was heightened by publicity surrounding a planned release of his so-called hypothetical tell-all book, *If I did it: Confessions of a Killer.* Although his aimless driving on L.A. freeways was a milestone for television viewing, perhaps giving birth to reality TV, the real significance of his trial was its inspiration to juries that might engage in nullification.

Some 13 years later, a study entitled *Disparities in Jury Outcomes— Baltimore City vs. Three Surrounding Jurisdictions—An Empirical Examination* conducted by Shawn Flowers of the usually left-leaning Abell Foundation showed there was a striking divergence between the outcomes of criminal trials in Baltimore City and its surrounding counties. Randomly examining 293 cases from mid-2005 to mid-2006, she found that conviction rates for the city were just 57 percent for drug defendants and 57 percent for those charged with personal offenses (murder, assault, or robbery), which was far lower than the counties' successful conviction of 95 percent and 69 percent, respectively. Flower developed a probability model that zeroed in upon the likelihood that a defendant would be convicted of the most serious charge against him, which was calculated at 2 percent in the city but 63 percent in the counties.

The study, originally slated for release in April 2008, was put on ice. Abell's President Robert Embry insists the delay was not caused by severe criticism by the Baltimore State's Attorney Patricia Jessamy. Jessamy said the study was "very flawed and needs a lot of work," and sent a letter to Embry asking that the study "be shelved" or its recommendations reworked. Flowers insists the conclusions are valid, and that she accounted for differences among the jurisdictions by using statistical controls and U.S. census data. Flowers lays the blame on theories such as the propensity for city prosecutors to "charge more aggressively" without allowing the plea bargaining process to equalize the punishment to fit the crime, for which she recommends creation of a regional jury pool. However, she does hint that jury nullification might be at work: The regional jury pool would "neutralize city residents' negative perceptions of the criminal justice system." Her solution would counteract that phenomenon, and it has nothing to do with the behavior of prosecutors. Yet the critique offered by Baltimore's Jessamy provides hints to Abell for rewriting the "potentially divisive" study. She thinks better training attorneys and police is "realistic," but this is already being done and the results are in. She writes, "I am simply appalled that in the name of science and research, you reach a conclusion that because a large number of city residents [live in poverty and among crime], they are incapable of performing their civic duty."

Maybe what is truly appalling is that it is true, and liberal policies and cultural norms do nothing but exact an atrocious human cost upon the people of Baltimore and other large urban centers that are dominated by Democratic political machines. The parallel with the media uproar after Hurricane Katrina, which similarly afflicted a Democratic fiefdom, is conspicuous. Over time, one would expect to see evidence mount of the effect of moral dissolution and systematic undermining of sound legal, tax, and educational systems such as documented by the Flower's study, and denial of the same to be shrill as it was in the case of Jessamy.[15]

## The Moral Vacuum

Secularism has banished the most inconvenient traditions of the centuries, and the moral vacuum left in its place is seen as liberation. People may behave as they wish, so long as they tithe support to the state. That we digress to savagery is pleasing as Rousseau would imagine, but it requires a bloated government machinery to pick up the pieces. Its political support rests upon two pillars: One is recruitment of more who work directly on its behalf at above private-market wages (public sector employees earn over $100,000 on average including benefits, a 50 percent premium to the private sector), and the second is a widening net of support directed at the bottom half of income earners.[16]

The tremendous advances yielded by capitalism continue to create wealth. Before the working wealthy were required to work five months per year for the government, and then turn over the fruits of another three upon death (plus one or more to pay property, excise, and other taxes), it was more common for successful individuals (more typically spouses) to become personally involved to aid the less fortunate, often under the mantle of their religious faith. Today, the rain of cash directed at society's needy falls from a distant cloud whose moisture is fed by Form 1040E, often subsidizing depravity and keeping misery from the view of rich neighborhoods.

We will probably never produce a Utopian classless society. However, progress toward the improvement of standards of living across this Earth should continue. Poverty may never disappear entirely, but economic advancement is lifting large swaths of humanity from it all over the world. The disparity between rich and poor should not be offensive, per se. What should be is the government's insertion between the relationship, which fractures any social bonds and moral common ground. Empathy for the poor, that the rich might have, has been replaced with faceless government programs. Those who build businesses and create jobs and wealth instead feel resentment that the government is draining their resources quite pointedly, and liberal politicians receive the approbation of the masses for playing Robin Hood. Never mind that Robin Hood's nemesis was the sheriff of Nottingham, the tax collector of the state who impoverished the populace with regressive taxation (much like the situation of Imperial Rome).

Secularists of all kinds maintain they occupy the highest intellectual ground. Like socialists who cannot grasp that the complex, unanalyzable, and unforecastable system developed through economic traditions is superior to those that are rational and devised by a few men, those who would reject the original Constitutional bounds are unwilling to recognize absolutes over centralized tinkering. This living, breathing interpretation of our political system is subject to man's attempts to subjugate other men through the power of the state, and substitutes the wisdom and desire of the few for the character of individuals.

Perhaps a secular nation can grow to respect absolutes such as the Founding Fathers' desire for limited, representative government. But it has failed thus far. The modern technocrat, filled with conceit that he can prove the benefit of each new regulation or social program exceeds its cost, will never favor the individual over the state, ever. What makes religion dangerous to him is that it, by contrast, does, in the sense that each person must establish character and weigh actions against certain moral absolutes. Yes, a social program may be kind to one group, but it usually has a negative secondary effect on another and the system as a whole. The impact usually is not in the near term, leading humanists to conclude there is proof that their policies are potent and for the good. However, usually a much larger problem, such as the moral and criminal collapse of the inner city or the failure of the Farm Credit System in the 1980s, occurs decades later, as we noticed with the boomerang of Depression-era housing policies in the credit crisis that emerged in 2008. John Maynard Keynes argued that it was better in the short run to save the system by setting in motion the powerful engine of government (the effectiveness of which in the 1930s may be debated), for "in the long run we are all dead." Yes, today he and his fellow progressives are dead. But we who live today are not, and it is we who now must deal with the consequences. As F. A. Hayek observed, Keynes' slogan is "a manifestation of an unwillingness to recognize that morals are concerned with effects in the long run—effects beyond our possible perception—and of a tendency to spurn the learnt discipline of the long view."[17]

How can the secularist not be blind to this unless he holds up a template of morality that questions the taking from one to give to another, or questions envy? Like the central planner, he is incapable of recognizing the power of traditions worked out in our Judeo-Christian culture that transcend seemingly correct decisions for certain individual circumstances. It may be that humans can establish an effective atheistic moral code, but in the end it would more closely resemble the Judeo-Christian ethic than what modern government is offering today, even in the United States.

Proof of concept can be deceiving. An important dividing line is what cannot be determined by science and evidence is not accepted as true. But this places an unfair burden upon spiritual matters, which belong to an invisible realm but are nonetheless felt by many and have been codified for the benefit of all humanity. Prior to the emergence of Jerusalem as a spiritual center, regard for human life was low, and many of the basest instincts prevailed. Is it no wonder that today's secular institutions are culpable for mass murder, numbering some 100 million massacred in the last century for political reasons? Yet secularists blame religion for today's conflagrations, particularly in the Middle East. Christians and Jews are painted as equally responsible as Islamists, yet there is no global network of Christian or Jewish terrorists. Moreover, we do not see Palestinians and Jews vociferously arguing about fine points of religious doctrine; rather their war is over real estate and regional sovereignty. Only Islam has an avowed religious goal of establishing statehood for a Caliphate spanning the globe.[18]

The economic, political, foreign policy, and religious debates of our time are hauntingly similar, which must give one pause as to whether the Founding Fathers were correct in their embrace of Judeo-Christian values as complimentary to the Constitution and to economic well-being: ". . . a society in which tolerance is the highest calling renders each man's judgment a law unto itself. And so the community standard becomes the lowest common denominator of human discernment and taste. This is what ails American culture, and only a sense of community and a sense of right and wrong can save it."[19]

# Chapter 15

# Self-Indulgence

*We labor to teach our children and adolescents and our dogs and, yes, ourselves the practical wisdom that keeps them and us from injuring or impoverishing or failing to develop themselves and others and ourselves . . . An imprudent person, someone who doesn't know the value of money and how to keep accounts, is a menace to his friends and family, and to his own developed self. And certainly he is a menace to his need in old age to provide, provide . . . without prudence he is a particular kind of fool, not virtuous as a whole. He is tragically or comically flawed, as most of us are, more or less . . .[1]*

McCloskey, Dierdre, *The Bourgeois Virtues:*
*Ethics for a Capitalist Age.*

P ain pills are a wondrous modern invention. They are perfect for headaches and fevers, which are temporary. They are also necessary for chronic pain, most often from the aging back. Within this nation obesity has emerged as commonplace. According to the Centers for Disease Control and Prevention, surveys show that prevalence has increased from 6.5 to 18.8 percent for those aged 12-19 over the past 25 years.[2] For adults, prevalence jumped from 15 percent to 32.9 percent.[3] Lack of exercise, poor diet, and overconsumption plague us. Certain of us will always develop bad backs. But without question fewer hours in front of the television and time spent maintaining muscle tone and properly feeding the body would put a major dent in the sales of pain pills taken for this chronic condition. It seems so logical, but when it comes down to it, there is a part of human nature that will always lead us to choose to put off or completely avoid things that we know are beneficial, and instead we fill the present with pleasure. In so many ways our culture has redefined its morality to reflect the deferral of consequences. While the scope of this book is mainly financial, one cannot ignore the effect of culture and its expression through politics upon attitudes about credit, which is after all what our money is now that it exists completely on a fiat basis.

What is confusing is that the delineation between liberal and conservative solutions in the world of finance in particular is misperceived. Those who are conservative wish government to leave us alone and single-mindedly be free to pursue money making without excessive regulatory interference and taxation. But in reality what most who are right of center do is neglect their civic duty. And what might that be? For one, it would be to engage the populace with ideas, which would be a short-term pain. But all too often they simply seek to maximize their earnings operating within the existing framework, no matter how odious. To make matters worse, they will run counter to conservative ideals and lobby the government for assistance or construct business models that would profit from its subsidization, figuring they might as well swing at whatever pitch is being thrown to them. Their second civic duty is to show some character and lobby against rather than for public subsidy. How different today is compared to when our country was founded! With an ocean between the king and his colonist subjects, rebellion was possible and ignited by the smallest kindling, which today would seem laughable compared to the yoke fitted upon the populace in most of the postwar era. Now we are more concerned whether the yoke fits well or looks good on us.

## The Inconvenience of Responsibility

The level of ignorance within the general population of the role of prices, taxation, and regulation in economic behavior can be stunning. Well-educated liberals who support socialized medicine wish to hold down the cost of health care. But when asked if price controls should be extended to the businesses that employ *them* (presuming they are not in academia or government as is often the case), they usually reject such a condition. This not-in-my-backyard (NIMBY) mentality is a rejection of the consistent application of principles (usually trampling constitutional rights). It is a defining mechanism of what liberals believe is democracy in action, which encases decisions in an influence-ridden process where economic determinations are stripped from individuals and granted to an all-knowing, supposedly apolitical panel of experts within the government. Such power being delegated outside the traditional structure of our three branches of government is the bedrock of constitutional abrogation in favor of socialism.

With the financial concept of moral hazard, pain is not merely put off—it gets shifted to an innocent party, and one in particular who might have been quite deliberate about foreseeing a problem and going out of his way to avoid it. Participants within financial markets from banks to institutional traders to individual homeowners, unwilling to experience hardship, are beginning to demand government solutions. Well before the credit markets began to boil over in 2008, the largest originator of subprime mortgages boasted of packaging below-grade mortgages into *prime* agency-backed securities (an inherently contradictory notion) at the behest of the government mortgage agencies seeking to help homebuyers with poor credit.[4] Testimony of CEOs in March 2008 in congressional hearings reinforced the notion, quite true, that their lending decisions had incorporated altruistic, socialistic considerations. Such public relations may be an insurance policy against the days that may come when their necks will be demanded as recompense for their misdeeds.

No longer burdened by the downside, which was transferred to taxpayers, lenders took advantage of the government guarantee to the hilt. They pleased the palate of the beast by grinding fat into its meat, manufacturing trillions of commoditized mortgages for its consumption, marbleized with sub-620 FICO score credit, with as much efficiency and copious output as was seen when our industry converted from producing goods to building tanks and planes in World War II.

For its part, in the credit bubble the public chose to be liberal rather than conserve its resources, for it, too, favored the pleasure of the present over the discomfort of saving for the future. Many took possession of better houses through interest-only variable rate loans with attractive teaser rates or at the very least supplemented their lifestyles with home equity withdrawals. Now, industry and government, listening to the clamor to continually defer pain, are busily concocting solutions that would offload their bad decisions to the most productive of society. Daresay this should ever be called abrogation of contracts, an essential underpinning of the Constitution and conventional morality. (Recall Shay's Rebellion: George Washington and the founders hastily convened the convention over one decade after victory over the British when they became alarmed by the demagoguery sprouting up in several states and the farmers of western Massachusetts abrogated contracts with Boston financiers under the crush of hard money deflation.)

No, the easier course is to rejoice at the awesome power of man's construction, which rewrites the rules and destabilizes the link between borrowers and lenders for good, substituting the risk of having the game rigged against capital and favoring those whose approval maintains the seat of power. When the most highly rated TV investing guru Jim Cramer publicly calls for a government bailout for mortgages, sees the Congress respond, and then crows that his investment in bank stocks will score a tremendous profit at the expense of taxpayers, he recognizes the moral dilemma but deliberately ignores it. He would make money, lots of it, now. But like Joe Boyd in the 1955 Broadway musical *Damn Yankees* who sells his soul to the devil to lead the hapless Washington Senators to victory in the World Series, he does not worry about his fate while it is perceived to be distant.

While Cramer favors squeezing more blood out of the taxpayer stone, the true foible is the government's operation of flawed monetary and tax machineries that encouraged moral hazard. The monetary system has spun out of control unchecked since ignorance is widespread, from the people to academia. The tax system likewise has preyed upon the complacency of the upper-middle class. Democracy has become the tool of a majority cognizant that it may exploit a minority, with the wrinkle that a plutocracy has masterfully composed the revenue code such that two very opposite schemes coexist parasitically, a Faustian bargain between the elite and the masses working against the middle. This combination has given birth to mandatory participation in the game of Russian roulette,

American style, in which anyone betting against the house odds that recessions would be mild and asset prices never fall for long would lose ground
economically. They would grow accustomed to the chink of the trigger hammer on the five empty chambers without thinking these would
unpredictably measure the intervals before the revolver would discharge.
The greatest moral flaw is our drift from freedom to central control in the
name of public benevolence, and the blindness that enables collusive takings of the individual.

The financial and political systems have reached several hinge
points in the last century or longer. The Wilson era laid essential
groundwork in several ways: It changed the pact that protected the
people from their government by permitting Congress to cede decision
making to bureaucracies staffed by dispassionate experts, thereby weakening the direct link to representative government. It gave the government the overwhelming power to tax with impunity the labor of its
citizens, and to direct this power against the chosen few who might be
targeted by a majority, eliminating the cherished equality of men under
the law. But this would not work in a world of hard money, for gold
would surely leave our shores, driving up interest rates and crippling
commerce.

So in compliment, the other feeding tube of governments, known
for centuries, would need to be attached: seigniorage. The establishment of the Federal Reserve System along with the movement to the
gold-exchange standard would be enough to give birth to a completely
elastic fiat currency. The nation received its first jolt of the heroin high
of elastic currency with substantial inflation in the late 1910s (whose
effects could never be reversed materially), robbing those who could
never imagine the 50 percent drubbing to the purchasing power of
billions of dollars of principal of 3.5 percent Liberty bonds they were
egged on to buy to support our entry into World War I (a large figure in that time, when a nickel was worth more than a dollar today).
Inflation overextended the commodity markets, resulting in plente-
ous capital investment and abundant, cheap goods in the 1920s, with
attendant preference for financial assets and the generous extension of
credit. However, the 1930s became another hinge point, building upon
the socialist fabric woven by Wilson. Unappreciated, like the strange
eggs discovered by space explorers in the classic sci-fi movie "Alien"

are the institutions of the Great Depression: the mortgage agencies; the FHA; and the Keynesian gift that keeps on giving, deficit spending. They had little salutary effect in that prolonged, lost decade. One of the last stages of incubation was Nixon's repudiation of international gold convertibility, which united the sperm and egg of monetary and fiscal lust into something as uncontrollably destructive as Rosemary's baby maturing to adulthood.

Ironically, like the prophesy of Lord Macaulay, the coalition of takers in a democracy will bellow for more bread. This time perversely the Cramers riding in carriages sipping champagne will throw crusts out the window as they pass by. The Founding Fathers desperately wished to build something more noble than the rabble of the French Revolution demanded and got, and like the greatest era of the Roman Empire, this lasted roughly 100 years. The second hundred years of the American republic have coasted upon the momentum of the first. Should scientific progress not be stifled by the emerging Islamo-fascist tide, the U.S. economy might blow along as under sail, alongside its aging parent, Europe, rather than have the locomotive of unrestrained capitalism speed us closer to a destiny of betterment. Or, should the substitution of belief systems of less successful cultures slowly immolate us, we may be like the second century Romans. They literally enjoyed the marvelous marble edifices built by their forebears, and so may we, blind to the not-so-civil wars within us that will lead to the coronation of our last leader, a barbarian such as Odoacer, continuing the state but losing its name and influence on history's stage until rediscovered by neoclassicists such as Washington in the millennia to come. It is ironic that even after it was over, the Roman Senate met to decide policy through roughly 524 AD, 50 years after the last emperor was deposed, and it ordered coinage to be struck with the motto, "Roma Invicta" or "Rome Unconquered," yet most of that once grand city's inhabitants had closed their shops and ventured to the country estates for a life of obligation to a lord.[5]

The mortgage mess is but one large manifestation of the moral rot that stems from literally everyone seeking at once to shift discomfort away from the present and substitute for it additional pleasure. The same may be said for almost every other governmental decision of our time. The voting majority has spoken, and it does not want in its own backyard the toxic waste product of banks, bombs, Social Security, or Medicare. The backyard is today and the dump is tomorrow, unless we shall soon see, with a Congress elected by a majority of whose voters pay no taxes (those who do vote for the other guys), that the mess could be dumped in the lap of luxury, for the greedy deserve it. The money culture, fraught with greed and high CEO pay, is fair game for vilification, but the concept of moral hazard is so distant from the lips of the citizenry that it would probably be mistaken for the wayward teachings of Reverend Wright, the spiritual advisor President Obama foreswore, in a Jay Leno man-on-the-street spoof. Being moral is so yesterday.

We are a society hooked on pain pills, ignoring our growing obesity that is the cause of what may be chronic financial back pain, complete with severe bubbles and meltdowns as symptoms. Perhaps the most telling sign of how we as a society would favor the quick win over saving for later is the ascendency of gambling. The American Gaming Association reports that the total revenue of the gaming industry, made up of U.S. companies that have only lately put a toehold into foreign refuges such as Macao, approached $100 billion in 2007.[6] This is now double the roughly $50 billion that Americans sock away annually for their retirement in 401K accounts.[7] Other signs of our willingness to do anything to defer pain and enjoy the moment abound; here are but a few inadequately resolved questions from the political debate of our time:

Ghetto kids not learning anything in school? Pass them for years and then let them drop out or graduate with worthless credentials. People not saving enough to retire? Promise them Social Security that you won't be able to fund 20 years from now. Does your little boy who watches television and plays video games endlessly annoy teachers when he wants to release nervous energy? Drug him on Ritalin. Don't want to muss up a measly 2,000-acre footprint of development within an area about the size of Delaware that is nearly void of life for nine months of the year? No sweat, just forego the equivalent of 30 years of Saudi oil. So what if there might be an oil crisis later! Want to tell voters you are doing something? Subsidize ethanol heavily, even if it is uneconomic and might cause food inflation. Too inconvenient to raise a child now? Abort it. Having a problem with Islamic terrorists who want to change your culture to a medieval, repressed society? Treat them well and maybe they will get to like you, and in the meantime you can spend the savings from cutting the military. Got elderly voters worried about medical needs? Maintain a government monopoly famous for miserly reimbursement of service providers, and shift the cost to the private sector, where employers face 15 to 20 percent increases annually. After years of cost-shifting, they will beg to abandon the "free market" and make camp under the government tent. Need more votes? Promise benefits that escalate such that Medicare nearly doubles as a percentage of national output in the next 20 years, even if that would break the system. Still not enough votes? Allow rapists, murderers, and thieves to cast ballots. Are conservatives complaining that what is being done is not moral, economically productive, or endangering our national security? Accuse them of being intolerant of other cultures, or worse—sexist, homophobic, or racist. While you are at it, pass a law to remove their right to political expression should they host shows on AM radio or place advertisements 30 days before an election, and in Orwellian doublespeak, call this media fairness. In relativism we reject absolutes such as hard money and prefer systems that allow beneficent technocrats to dial in adjustments that repeal economic cycles or remove the sting of bad decisions. Who would not vote for such heroes?

## Personal Liberation and the Business of Marriage

Author Lauren Belfer poignantly describes what it might have been like in America a century ago through her novel set in this era in Buffalo, NY—then a very happening place. The unwed protagonist, through an intermediary, hands her newborn over to a powerful businessman's family. The child avoids the horror of probable death from inadequate breast feeding at "the infant asylum."[8] Prior to the 1960s, our population would start families in their 20s. Women who became pregnant out of wedlock would keep their babies or put them up for adoption. Today there are no longer orphanages in the United States; anxious couples seeking to adopt must travel to Russia, Asia, or Africa and pay tens of thousands of dollars in what has become a worldwide market in child trafficking. Pop star Madonna purportedly paid

a Malawian village $3 million to rescue a 13-month-old boy whose
mother died of AIDS.[9] In that country 1.4 million, or one-quarter of
its population under the age of 14, are orphaned; the cause is mostly
the HIV epidemic.[10]

Two things happened beginning in the Viet Nam War era. The pill
became broadly available by the 1970s, and abortion became nationally ubiquitous and more commonplace, rather than confined to certain states. Abortions jumped from 16.3 per 1,000 women in 1973
to a peak of 29.3 in 1981.[11] Both became methods of birth control,
permitting the feminist movement to bloom in earnest. The issue of
abortion divides the nation almost evenly. As relativism would dictate,
young women typically are pro choice, while the older demographic
tilts toward appreciation of life above the convenience of terminating
unwanted children. Another encroachment of relativism is the left's
failure to acknowledge that infanticide is in reality a form of birth control, for it is used to terminate almost one-fourth of American preg-
nancies.[12] The flip side of abortion is illegitimacy, whose resulting cycle
of poverty is caused by social pathology.

Secularists would cure this ill through increased materialism, that is,
by dunning the rich so that the village might raise such children with
childcare, public education, and benefits. Indeed, most often cited as
reasons for not having a child are "not being ready for a child," "can't
afford a baby," and "would interfere with education or career plans."
The more completely the village steps into remove such parental
responsibilities, the more illegitimacy might be a positive life experience, but it is hard to imagine fewer abortions would result.[13]

The availability of birth control, a seemingly benign development
that is barely discussed as a societal factor even among conservatives,
has fostered an environment that reduced the value of marriage and its
linkage with child rearing. The institution of marriage remains popular
(90 percent participate), but it occurs in serial fashion (divorce probability is 50 percent) and is seen as a temporary romantic linkage for
the enjoyment of adults. Child bearing is increasingly a separate activity, with children born out of wedlock rising to nearly 40 percent of
all births nationwide, and 35 percent of these single-parent families
live below the poverty line. Thus, a rapidly expanding caste system has
developed that is particularly demanding of the fruits of socialism.[14]

The nation's youth was entranced with the self-empowerment to be completely free of any moral code or behavioral norm. LIFE magazine, now defunct but then a very popular periodical of extra-large photos, showed those who could not make the trek to upstate New York to attend Woodstock that it was possible to stand naked alongside millions, smoke pot, take LSD, and have sex freely—behavior that would be shocking now or anytime previously (save the times of Roman orgies). The zeal for such personal liberation was expressed by rock bands such as the Jefferson Airplane. This band renamed itself the Jefferson Starship, an act in support of the fantasy that the new generation might hijack the first NASA craft capable of transporting colonies of humans to other planets so that the new lifestyle might be codified in a new society. In an ode to this act of defiance written in 1970, they cry: "Free minds, free bodies, free dope, free music / The day is on its way the day is ours."[15]

What has emerged is the "hook-up" phenomenon that makes young women (and men) feel that it is natural to be promiscuous. The result has been a scourge of sexually transmitted diseases. Planned Parenthood's party line is that great epidemics such as those that followed World War I have been averted. But is that really so? Data collection of sexually transmitted infections (STIs) is incomplete, not including herpes and HIV at all in a national reporting system, and because many cases of others such as Chlamydia and HPV can be asymptomatic and go undetected. The CDC estimates that one out of five adolescents and adults have had a genital herpes infection, 7.4 million new cases of trichomoniasis occur annually, and 6.2 million Americans will get HPV each year. Those between the ages of 15 and 24 account for half of all STI diagnoses each year, even though this demographic only accounts for one-fourth of the sexually active population. The toll on the African American community, where cultural regard for the family has deteriorated the most, is disproportionately higher: The rate of Chlamydia among black women is nearly eight times that of whites. Blacks are 19 times more likely to get gonorrhea, and they account for half of all new HIV cases, despite being only 13 percent of the population. We most definitely have a cultural problem, which is linked to not just a laissez faire attitude about morality, but to a glorification of immorality.[16]

Much good has come from opening up society since that era; civil rights would top that list, and the possibility of career advancement for women has addressed a similar inequity. But spiritually there has been a subtle change, whether or not one practices the religion of her choice. Birth control liberated both men and women, but attitudinally its effect on women may have been far greater, because not having to bear children in one's 20s meant in practical terms that females would now be able to wait and see whether the male they would choose was well along the way to achieving material success. They would not have to rely solely upon an assessment of character to choose their mate. Relationships therefore could become more of a business deal than a spiritual expression of love and long-term commitment, a proposition that dovetailed nicely with the shift to no-fault divorce. Values in flyover country have nonetheless persisted, where the population is largely conservative and Republican, marries early, and reproduces at least one-for-one. But in the large urban centers on the coasts evidence of the transformation to no family or the new business of marriage is commonplace.

Nowhere is this more evident than in Manhattan. HBO's enormous success "Sex and the City" glorifies the lifestyle of 40-something single babes in Manhattan (though technically three of four main characters are purportedly in their 30s). As the characters mature, two marry rich men: Carrie lands "Big," a Wall Street tycoon; Charlotte finds Harry Goldenblatt, a Jewish divorce lawyer, after divorcing Trey, a heart surgeon with inherited wealth. Samantha, the sex addict dedicated to single life, has an extended relationship with a hotel magnate (Richard Wright), but rejects him for the considerably younger Jerry Jerrod, whom she remakes into Smith Jerrod, jumpstarting his acting career through her P.R. connections. Only Miranda Hobbes, Harvard graduate and corporate power lawyer, marries below her station, to Steve Brady, a bartender. Until Trey was dismissed from husbandly duties to Charlotte and replaced with Harry, this plebian bartender was the lone male character with emotional stability, a desire for family life, and a budding interest in entrepreneurism. Miranda rejects him when he is a bartender; she grows to accept him begrudgingly, and two seasons after he opens his own bar, she marries him more out of concern for her child and lack of alternatives than from admiration of his character, spiritual commonality, or love.

In the year 2000 census, Manhattan topped the list of single-person households, having 48 percent of households in this category; nearly double that of the United States, which has 21 percent. For the United States as a whole, single households have more than doubled since 1950.[17] Among the women who live in Manhattan, only 37 percent have ever married.[18] Few who are in their 20s can afford to live there. Yet they choose to do so, frittering away their incomes on closets filled with designer shoes to match whimsical, self-indulgent look-at-me outfits. With the lure of landing Big, Trey, or Harry Goldenblatt, who live in spacious Park Avenue digs or pop champagne corks in limos, many Steve Bradys get passed over. And who cares? According to Thomas Coleman, executive director of Unmarried America, "People living alone, especially unmarried women, used to be viewed with sadness ... Self esteem isn't based on having children and being married anymore."[19]

Alongside those who helped advance the noble aims of the "me" generation was a political movement that worked quietly on the legislative front to establish the welfare state. The less-told story is that the most concentrated block of single households resides in the African American community, as opposed to living the romanticized lifestyle of Sarah Jessica Parker's trendy Carrie Bradshaw or Candice Bergen's glamorous Murphy Brown. Single parents head 62 percent of families below the poverty line, and additionally 29 percent of people under the poverty line are not in families.[20] Marriage has become the exception rather than the rule among inner-city African Americans. This group continues to inhabit urban zones that have rapidly deteriorated from the 1960s onward coincident with a rise of single-parent families and toleration of the drug and "gangsta" culture. If one is content not to work and can obtain a large percentage of even a subsistence existence from government programs, then the government may be perpetuating a moral hazard, strangulating the urban poor. There is also a spill-over effect as middle-class youth emulate such self-destructive behavior, making this in more ways than one a moral hazard for society at large.

Conservative economist Walter Williams advises how not to be poor: "First, graduate from high school. Second, get married before you have children and stay married. Third, work at any kind of job, even one that starts out paying the minimum wage. And, finally, avoid engaging in criminal behavior. If you graduate from high school with a B or C average, in most places in our country there's a low-cost or financially assisted post-high school education program available to increase your skills." For this guidance, he is pilloried for being overly moralistic by the liberal bloggers who prefer to be "realistic" and advocate expanded government solutions.[21] He and other prominent conservative blacks are tarred as Uncle Toms by the liberal intellectual elite.

## Hippies Aging (Not So) Gracefully

Free of aspirations to settle down and raise families and encouraged to taste the fruits of personal liberation, the use of illegal drugs became widespread among all strata of society. Sympathy was engendered for lenient criminal prosecution of victimless crimes. In a cruel turnabout for the liberation movement of the 1960s and 1970s, with the boomers procreating late and crossing over age 50, they have become as a group conservative and backed Republican candidates, foregoing the vices of their youth. In contrast, the college-age crowd is liberal, thanks to a government controlled education system and liberally biased media. In mid-2008, supporters for Obama in this group outnumbered those intending to vote for McCain by about two-to-one. Once again the direction of where the culture may head—veering towards dependence upon the state or reliance upon individual character—lies with the youth. But youth, lacking wisdom, will almost always prefer instant gratification over moral and spiritual investment unless parents choose to imbue superior values by example and through teaching. The left's obsession to suppress Christianity and Judaism, even to the point that Sharia is welcomed, is validation that breaking this powerful link between generations is essential to the maintenance of its political majority. Conservatives know that the dissolution of the family as a social structure has powerful connections to poverty, crime, drug use, promiscuity, sexually transmitted diseases, and immorality in general.

The awakening of liberalism in the 1960s and 1970s has powerfully shaped the current era. That generation's pursuit of chemical and sexual pleasure along with yuppie-charged reaching for the brass ring was a confluence of factors that significantly delayed the establishment of families for the first time in human history; this has perpetuated youth and delayed the age-old constraints of adulthood. We are now feeling the reverberations in Social Security, the demographic implosion of Europe, Russia, and even China (with its one child limitation). It may even partly explain why the mortgage crisis occurred in the present time, for late family formation of the baby boomers along with the worship of material gain led to the McMansion craze as this generation hit its peak income level of 50-something. How many 30-year mortgages were purveyed to 45-year-olds who have inadequately saved (consuming through their extended youth) but plan to retire at age 65, much less fund college tuitions in their golden years?

Like the wonderful mental elevation experienced from the first hit off a sensimellia-filled bong or the snort of a line of cocaine, the "me" generation hopes for immediate gratification. Likewise, it would be removed from the necessity of working over time to achieve a financial— or familial—goal, perpetuating this rush. This is why spending in gambling parlors and for lottery tickets is double that of IRA contributions and it is also why the degradation of the culture may be linked to the present day credit crisis. If this behavior has finally been carried beyond the pale, it holds very significant implications for the well-being of everyone rich and poor, black and white, men and women, or any way we may be polarized politically.

# Chapter 16

# The New Commandments

*Private equity firms, investment banks, and financial services firms operate in an environment of terror.*[1]

ARTHUR LEVITT, FORMER SECURITIES
AND EXCHANGE COMMISSION CHAIRMAN

Almost unanimously the response to the financial panic of 2008 was that more, not less, regulation will be needed to prevent the abuse of the public by Wall Street. The myth invoked is that business has been lightly regulated or deregulated since the Reagan era began. This free market produced prosperity, but there is a natural tendency for capitalism to fail, and for certain operators to take advantage of a gullible public. Reagan indeed removed regulations. Pages in the Federal Register, which lists all regulations, fell from about 73,000 under Carter to fewer than 55,000 in the 1980s. But they rose again under Clinton to nearly 72,000, and then to over 75,000 when Bush was in power. Since 1980, employees at regulatory agencies expanded by 64 percent, to nearly 240,000 and regulatory spending tripled in inflation-adjusted terms over this interval, while the general population only rose by 33 percent. The largest areas are homeland security ($22 billion) and finance and banking ($2.6 billion), together forming over half of all regulatory spending.[2] The

314

formation of the Transportation Security Administration (TSA) contributed about 50,000 employees at a cost of $5 billion, so the large percentage increases reflect organic growth of other social and economic regulatory functions. An excellent breakdown is available through the Mercatus Center.

Alexis de Tocqueville warned in his classic oeuvre that the United States might one day degrade into "soft despotism," wherein its citizens would be subjected to a "network of small complicated rules."

> I think, then, that the species of oppression by which democratic nations are menaced is unlike anything that ever before existed in the world; our contemporaries will find no prototype of it in their memories. I seek in vain for an expression that will accurately convey the whole of the idea I have formed of it; the old words despotism and tyranny are inappropriate: the thing itself is new, and since I cannot name, I must attempt to define it.

> Above this race of men stands an immense and tutelary power, which takes upon itself alone to secure their gratifications and to watch over their fate. That power is absolute, minute, regular, provident, and mild. It would be like the authority of a parent if, like that authority, its object was to prepare men for manhood; but it seeks, on the contrary, to keep them in perpetual childhood: it is well content that the people should rejoice, provided they think of nothing but rejoicing. For their happiness such a government willingly labors, but it chooses to be the sole agent and the only arbiter of that happiness; it provides for their security, foresees and supplies their necessities, facilitates their pleasures, manages their principal concerns, directs their industry, regulates the descent of property, and subdivides their inheritances: what remains, but to spare them all the care of thinking and all the trouble of living?

> Thus it every day renders the exercise of the free agency of man less useful and less frequent; it circumscribes the will within a narrower range and gradually robs a man of all the uses of himself. The principle of equality has prepared men for these things;

it has predisposed men to endure them and often to look on them as benefits.

After having thus successively taken each member of the community in its powerful grasp and fashioned him at will, the supreme power then extends its arm over the whole community. It covers the surface of society with a network of small complicated rules, minute and uniform, through which the most original minds and the most energetic characters cannot penetrate, to rise above the crowd. The will of man is not shattered, but softened, bent, and guided; men are seldom forced by it to act, but they are constantly restrained from acting. Such a power does not destroy, but it prevents existence; it does not tyrannize, but it compresses, enervates, extinguishes, and stupefies a people, till each nation is reduced to nothing better than a flock of timid and industrious animals, of which the government is the shepherd.[3]

Even the most common man today is touched by an ever-expanding yoke of governmental control, all for his own benefit. At the airport old ladies are patted down; soft drinks are taken away from little children. Having more than a few ounces of moisturizer or nail scissors would be grounds for confiscation and chemical-based bodily review. In the car, seat belts must be fastened, child seats must be in place, and phones might not be used, but radio dials may be turned. At a restaurant or at work, smoking is not permitted. Carrying a gun? Not a good idea, unless you are a criminal. Want to transfer more than $10,000 by check or other means? Your bank is required to scrutinize this and report anything suspicious. Thanks to technological advances, big brother may soon be watching. In conjunction with its Local Update of Census Addresses (LUCA) program, field enumerators in the 2010 cycle will conduct an Address Canvassing Operation (ACO) using GPS-equipped hand-held computers. Roughly one-half million Census Bureau employees will be equipped with a smartphone pocket PC that includes a fingerprint reader. According to some sources the device will be used to photograph the entranceway of houses and record its exact location by satellite.[4] U.S. Transportation Secretary Ray LaHood proposed a vehicle mileage tax (VMT) in February 2009, which would require installation of a GPS chip in every vehicle. Oregon Governor Ted Kulongoski championed the cause, and his state conducted a pilot program with 300 cars. Five other states are considering the tax, which would make up for reduced collections from gasoline tax caused by widespread driving of hybrid cars. Might politically motivated government officials misuse GPS data? In the 2008 election, Ohio Secretary of State Helen Jones-Kelley resigned after denying she authorized a personal records search of Joseph Wurzelbacher, better known as "Joe the Plumber," after she had been put on leave for suspicions of using state email services to assist in Democratic Party fund raising. Wurzelbacher stopped working as a plumber after his employer was warned by the state that he was unlicensed.

The worst is reserved for businesses. Got a disgruntled employee at work who leaves a voicemail with the CFO about possible improprieties he might reveal if you fire him? Under the Sarbanes Oxley Act, you must initiate a multimillion dollar audit, even if it is an idle and baseless threat. Did your OSHA poster fall down? Pay a $300 fine. Forget to file a form qualifying you to do business in a state, or fail to apply for S-Corporation status for your small business? Too bad, you now owe substantial additional taxes or penalties. Manufacturing anything—meat, chemicals, toys? Get ready for inspection!

America's biggest businesses quickly grasped that if their industry gets smothered with a gaggle of rules, small businesses can be squeezed out. Jonah Goldberg, in *Liberal Fascism*, reveals the process of how large enterprises work to influence regulation for competitive advantage. He recounts how General Electric CEO Gerard Swope published "The Swope Plan" a year before Franklin Roosevelt took office, in which he proposed that the government should suspend antitrust laws so that collusion would be allowed to bring production in line with the reduced demand of the depression, and that the effort might be coordinated by a trade association and supervised by a government agency like the Federal Trade Commission.[5] Seventy-five years later, General Electric is once again on the bandwagon, this time in support of global warming initiatives through its program dubbed "Ecomagination."[6] In the company's 2007 Proxy statement, its board of directors recommended voting against a proposal by shareholders that would require it to disclose what scientific basis it had for its new position, what efforts it was making, and what the estimated cost and benefit to the company would be. The shareholders' proposal said, "... we believe that GE has gone beyond the bounds of simply helping customers to meet existing regulatory requirement. GE is working to impose new, more stringent government regulations that will raise energy costs and reduce energy availability without providing significant, or even measurable, environmental benefits. In particular, GE is lobbying lawmakers, and even supporting politicized activists in hopes of enacting greenhouse gas laws similar to the Kyoto Protocol . . . GE's business prospects ought not depend on government-mandated interest in certain of its products."[7]

A survey done by Clifford Chance LLP finds that "four out of every five company respondents expressed the view that more regulation is needed to drive business' response to climate change ... (and) are urging policy makers to take a more coordinated approach to climate change and introduce regulations to help them adapt."[8] General Motors gave the U.S. Climate Action Partnership (USCAP) a boost by joining its ranks of corporate members, "a landmark alliance of leading corporations and environmental leaders working together to urge the federal government to: cut greenhouse gas emissions 60 to 80 percent; create business incentives; and act swiftly and thoughtfully." The group has a list of members that varies from the most environmentally destructive, such as large mining companies, medical device manufacturers, and beverage companies.[9]

Yet not all large businesses start out with this goal. What brings them into the fold is when other competitors of material size decide to use the regulatory or legal framework to attack them. For years Wal-Mart and Microsoft eschewed lobbying (Gates had essentially one lobbyist), but both began to be voraciously attacked. Maryland, under the impetus of labor unions, placed an unconstitutional tax on Wal-Mart requiring the diversion of 8 percent of its payroll to health care, where non-compliance would require it to pay the difference into the state's Medicare program. Bankers used the government to block its entry into retail banking in-store. Beverage companies objected to its introduction of store-brand soda containing the artificial sweetener, *Splenda*.[10] As for Microsoft, it became the target of a gigantic anti-trust case, causing Gates to hire a battalion of lawyers, lobbyists, and consultants.[11] Who can recall what the outcome was, other than a magnificent show trial and some inconvenient workarounds for software engineers?

Goldberg makes an apt analogy that most businesses are like beehives. He explains:

> If government doesn't bother them, they don't bother government. If the government meddles with business, the bees swarm Washington. Yet time and again, the liberal "remedy" for the bee problem is to smack the hive with a bigger stick. There are hundreds of medical industry lobbies, for specific diseases, specialties, and forms of treatment, each of which spends a fortune in direct and indirect lobbying and advertising. Do you know which medical profession spends almost nothing? Veterinary care. Why? Because Congress spends almost no time regulating it. Why do pharmaceutical industries spend so much money lobbying politicians and regulators? Because they are so heavily regulated that they cannot make major decisions without a by-your-leave from Washington.[12]

## Compliance!

The 1967 Academy Award winning movie, "The Graduate," opens in a famous scene where a newly minted college graduate attends a party consisting of his parents' friends. A well-meaning businessman offers him career advice:

Mr. McGuire: I want to say one word to you. Just one word.

Benjamin: Yes, Sir.

Mr. McGuire: Are you listening?

Benjamin: Yes, I am.

Mr. McGuire: Plastics.

### *The Graduate* (1967)

Today Mr. McGuire might whisper into Benjamin's ear, "Compliance." There has been a persistent shortage of compliance professionals in the financial industry since the Internet bubble burst. Referring to the broker dealer side of the business: " 'Pay for compliance staff members has risen an average of 30% annually for the past three to five years', said Mitch Vigeveno, president of Turning Point, Inc., a Clearwater, Fla., industry recruiting firm."[13] As for banks, "Compliance spending grew 159 percent on average from 2002 to 2006," according to the report, *Navigating the Compliance Labyrinth: The Challenge for Banks*.[14] Investment advisors felt a similar crunch: "Compliance costs rose 65 percent from January 2007 through March 2008 for more than 400 investment advisory firms surveyed by four organizations involved in the advisory business."[15] Finally, Sarbanes-Oxley has been devastating to small corporations wishing to access capital markets: "For S&P 500 companies, (SOX) audit fees (are) up 189 percent since 2001."[16]

Most Americans don't know it, but the financial industry may be the most highly regulated sector in the economy. Because each new rule passed by FINRA, the SEC, or the five national banking regulators unquestionably works to the good of the hapless investor or depositor, none may be removed and only more may be added. With each new crisis, the Internet collapse or the credit crunch being the latest, another wave of reform ensues, so the cobweb of rules grows more complex and surer to snare those who would merely wish to be honest and benefit their customers. Yet even with this protection, the result seems to be an individual investor ever more willing to turn over his due diligence to the government apparatus. Moreover, larger and more complex messes keep erupting, such as the implosion of banks, hedge funds, government agencies, credit insurers, brokerage firms, and even whole towns such as Norvik, Norway, an arctic seaport that lost at least $64 million on securities that included California mortgages.[17]

Big brother is watching, even more carefully than the KGB was listening in Soviet Russia. Employees at many if not most financial industry firms no longer use email save to distribute preapproved material. Even the most innocuous, inadvertent slip of the finger on the keyboard could bar one from the industry for life. A senior manager at each firm must read through the email of all employees, plucking out potential violations, assigning retraining modules, and levying penalties. If the firm does not self-report problems (and not just those in email), it is doubly at risk with the regulators.

More is described by Pierre Lemieux:

The SEC plays a major role in the witch-hunt against corporate executives and financial wizards (the modern Salem witches), and in the governance fad. Through civil suits and administrative proceedings and orders, the SEC mandates securities registration, regulates brokerage, trading and disclosure, and helps enforce the prohibition of insider trading. It scares large companies into settling suits without trial. Royal Dutch/Shell paid a U.S. $120-million settlement. The agency also imposes fines and work bans. It regulates stock exchanges, which were historically private organizations. It files civil suits against violators of the Sarbanes-Oxley Act. The president of the SEC scolded American CEOs: "You must have an internal code of ethics that goes beyond the letter of the law to also encompass the spirit of the law." The problem is, where is the spirit of the law explained in writing, so that one knows what is required? Where is the rule of law? By mandating certain sorts of disclosure and preventing others, the SEC is, in fact, engaged in the control of information and speech. Where is the First Amendment?

The 2002 Sarbanes-Oxley Act imposes such wide-ranging requirements to corporations that they now compel their employees to change their computer passwords frequently. The risk of forgetting passwords (of course) increases, with the consequence that corporate employees resort to insecure tricks, like writing passwords on sticky notes affixed to their computers.[18]

Insider trading was once clear cut, such as buying before an announced takeover based upon information that was not disseminated to the public. Now it can be an analyst forgetting to put into a disclaimer his ownership of 100 shares of a company mentioned in passing in a report. Or if he trades in such a stock within 30 days of a routine quarterly earnings report that has no influence upon the price of said security, even if his holding *is* disclosed. Worse yet, he cannot even own 1 percent of a fund that holds a position in something he writes about. Even a financial advisor with the most limited scope of business and an intense amount of legal and compliance support staff quakes at the thought of a routine regulatory audit, for there is always something that could be written up. Not all auditors agree upon what rules apply and how to interpret them, opening up the possibility of debate wherein the wisest course of action is often to just agree with the government, since it could always threaten other, more stringent action. David simply cannot defeat Goliath when his slingshot is illegal.

## The (Growth) Business of Regulation

A story that never made it into the mainstream is the struggle for control of the National Association of Securities Dealers (NASD), the largest self-regulatory organization (SRO) in the United States. Now known as the Financial Industry Regulatory Authority (FINRA), its operations rival that of its regulatory overseer, the Securities & Exchange Commission (SEC). It conducts about 2,500 audits each year, nearly twice the amount of examinations that the SEC performs.[19] Chartered to provide a self-regulatory layer between the industry and the SEC, by law each of the more than 660,000 investment professionals engaged in the U.S. securities business must register with it and pass its examinations covering a broad range of topics. Until recent times it acted more as an industry group whose purpose was to maintain the good reputation of its member broker-dealers through weeding out the bad apples. However, perhaps awakened by the headline-grabbing persecutions of New York Attorney General Elliott Spitzer that started after the market peak in 2000, its organizational adrenaline began to flow freely. Regulatory fees and fines expanded at the astonishing rate of over 17 percent annually from 2000 to 2007 (even after adjusting for the addition of the NYSE's SRO into its fold in mid-2007).[20] Small firms began to suspect that it had become a self-perpetuating bureaucracy, and became frustrated by "vast compliance checklists that can trip up even the most honest firm ... (believing that) the NASD seems to want to play a game of gotcha, with the goal being to pry loose as big a fine as possible."[21]

Soon a mutiny began. The once sleepy election process for open seats on the NASD's 11 district committees began to get down and dirty, with broker-dealers putting forth alternatives to NASD-picked nominees that became known as "petition candidates" due to the arduous qualification process. In 2006, these renegade contenders won 19 of 37 open seats in the district committees, and two spots were seized on the National Adjudicatory Committee, a sort of Supreme Court for disciplinary cases. The most visible dissident was Richard Goble, the founder and principal shareholder of North American Clearing, Inc., a small clearing broker-dealer handling roughly 15,000 accounts for 40 corresponding firms. Goble established the Financial Industry Association, which began an aggressive campaign to contact NASD members and collect their alternative proxy ballots, thus being instrumental to petition candidate victories. Bolstering the discontent in the member community were quotations in trade newsletters such as *Investment News*:

> The NASD is too focused on technical violations that bring in money, such as unintentional late reporting of stock and bond trades, or failure to meet unreasonable demands for information in what are now routine sweep exams ... If a person forgets to report a bond trade within 15 minutes that should not be a $15,000 fine for a $5,000 (net capital) broker-dealer.
> "NASD Board Election Heats Up,"
> *Investment News*, January 23, 2006.

> Firms can face "major problems (when they fail to) dot an "i" or file a funny little form that's not a big deal," said compliance consultant Howard Spindel, owner of Trump Securities LLC in New York. "Members are very tired of being beat up over that kind of BS.
> "FINRA Board candidates Jockey for Position on Eve of Election," *Investment News*, October 8, 2007.

> The FIA argues that owners of small firms are often personally named in enforcement actions, unlike executives at larger firms.
> "FINRA Board candidates Jockey for Position on Eve of Election," *Investment News*, October 8, 2007.

Mr. Muh, a former partner at The Bear Stearns Cos. in New York, said he hadn't realized how small firms can be affected by rules written for larger firms until he formed his own firm 15 years ago.

"FINRA Board candidates Jockey for Position on Eve of Election," *Investment News*, October 8, 2007.

Adding to the feeling that the NASD was out of control was its enforcement track record, which reveals that in 2007 (a year of substantial improvement over 2006), some 29 percent of its cases were lost outright when brought to litigation, and among the 71 percent of cases won, half saw reduced fines.[22] This is well below the 92 percent success rate reported by the SEC.[23]

With a palace revolt going full tilt, it was not hard for the NASD's new CEO, Mary Schapiro, a former SEC commissioner appointed by Reagan and Bush and then named acting chairman by Clinton, to read the handwriting on the wall. The NASD proposed merging with the SRO of the NYSE, purportedly responding to the pleas from members about confusion from operating under two sets of rule books (the case for nearly 70 years). Efficiency would result; making two regulators one, but the reality for the industry is that since this time the total number of regulatory bodies has grown from 16 to 18 despite the merger. As an inducement to members, a $35,000 payout of equity would be made to each member broker-dealer when the merger went through.

Opponents of the deal objected to the change in governance proposed by the NASD, such that its members would no longer be entitled to nominate or elect a majority of the board of governors. With the broker-dealer community disenfranchised, the elites in control of the new organization, FINRA, would be able to control its own makeup. It would be immune from influence from its members or a wider audience, save its government overseer. To those who voted against the merger, the $35,000 per member payout seemed paltry compared with the equity of the NASD, which held some $1.6 billion of reserves, or about $300,000 per member firm. There were also complaints about heavy-handed and ill-timed investigations directed against firms that were vocal and whose principals had been nominated for board slots.

In January 2007, 64 percent of NASD members approved the deal, which became effective the next July, creating FINRA. Ironically, as the credit crunch began to take hold, North American Clearing, the firm owned by the dissident's ringleader, Richard Goble, became a victim. The SEC obtained an asset freeze and alleged fraud and other violations at this firm, among other things contending that it began to access customer funds to pay for daily business obligations. The SEC's case states that North American Clearing began to experience a severe financial decline precipitated by the departure of a large client, which had held collateralized mortgage obligation securities, and that the firm had incurred a multimillion dollar loss in connection with customer transactions in a penny stock company.[24] One successful member of the group of petition candidates thought Goble was the victim of SEC persecution, but added that he sometimes was a little loose with the facts and had a paranoid view of the world in which there was a conspiracy against small firms. Instead, this observer characterized the new FINRA as an "equal opportunity fuck everybody" organization that "enforces laws which have long outlived their purpose," hinting that should another SRO be formed as an alternative to FINRA, broker-dealers would flock to it en masse, a scenario that seems impossible.

These are strong words and there remain strong feelings among the few who care about such things in the broker-dealer community. Most simply helped in the fight when the few such as Goble carried the torch. FINRA does indeed help investors, and its new CEO, Mary Schapiro, has displayed level-headedness and stressed the need for regulatory balance. Fines in 2007 fell 37 percent to $48 million, but regulatory fees increased over 11 percent (excluding the addition of the NYSE to 2007 and the rebate to members). This still leaves one wondering if there was a virulent outbreak of white collar crime in this decade, or rather if there wasn't after all a zealous grab for revenue from bureaucrats, like a town police force gone wild with speed traps. Compounded growth of 17 percent annually is astounding. (Compounding at this rate doubles a sum in four years). To praise a lesser rate of increase is to accept the notion that the new, higher level of intervention into the affairs of business is essential to the smooth functioning of capital markets. Schapiro rescued the NASD from comprehensive internal reform instigated by small firms, but in so doing she isolated its governance forever from this influence. The current leadership of the organization may (or may not) be benevolent now, but future management could set up even more speed traps. Of course, fundamentally FINRA is a self-regulatory body, not a government agency as is the SEC. What fundamentally has happened is that it has simply evolved into being a regulatory agency in everything but its legal structure.

In early 2009, President Obama nominated Mary Shapiro to head the SEC. After the disgrace of not having discovered the largest Ponzi scheme in history at Bernard L. Madoff Investment Securities, the appointment is seen as a way of tapping into the auditing machine of FINRA, which is viewed as extensive and thorough. It may be, but within the industry SEC audits are feared more and broker-dealers and investment advisors usually prefer to have former SEC prosecutors on their team when challenged by regulators. A stumbling block to the nomination is a lawsuit filed in December 2008 by A.H. Seidle, a former lawyer at the SEC who investigates pension fraud and other financial abuses. Seidle sued the NASD in 2002 when that agency had blocked the publishing of his book about disciplinary proceedings. On behalf of NASD member firms Seidle's newest action alleges that during a vigorous campaign to sell the benefits of the merger into the new FINRA, Shapiro misrepresented an IRS position against the NASD's having a $35,000 limit per member firm payout offered as the sweetener. In fact, the IRS had made no such ruling until after the deal was completed. The IRS ruling is alleged by Seidle to contain evidence contradicting Shapiro's view, but it remains under seal along with an independent fairness opinion on the deal by Houlihan Lokey Howard and Zukin Financial Advisors. Seidle's case continues along with another class action that was filed a year earlier that was lost but taken to the U.S. Court of Appeals. The cases will be won or lost on their merits eventually, but in the meantime Shapiro's having increased her compensation from under $2 million to more than $3.1 million on account of the merger's consummation now appears to taint her objectivity. Other key FINRA executives received salary raises of about 20 percent. The lead lawyer for the two cases, Jonathan W. Cuneo, summed it all up: "Our cases raise questions about the transparency, truthfulness and candor of the NASD and its leadership in a major financial transaction with its own members ... It's certainly ironic that the case involves the NASD, which is charged with policing these values in others."[25]

Meanwhile, the trend toward investing in hedge funds may also be seen as an anti-regulatory backlash. The hedge fund industry is estimated at $1.8 trillion worldwide (not double counting fund-of-funds), which by comparison is still less than 10 percent of assets under management within all investment advisors registered with the SEC.[26] The high fee structure possible in limited partnerships has attracted analytical talent from the traditional money management community. Most of the money is concentrated in the largest firms (75 percent is in the top 100), so the bulk of those working in the industry reside at its roughly 10,000 small mangers, whose shops are derisively referred to within the industry as "two guys and a Bloomberg." In these cases specifically, the enhanced top line helps some, but the reality is that the absence of regulation may be their key enabler. Analysis of the figures of the industry's growth indicates that while the largest firms are expanding, outside of the top 100 firms there had been no growth for the two years that preceded the 2008 meltdown.

In December 2004 the SEC proposed to regulate the hedge fund industry, adopting a new rule requiring registration by February 2006 at the latest.[27] However, this was challenged by Phillip Goldstein, a hedge fund manager who sued the SEC in federal court and won in a decision handed down in late June 2006. The SEC is alarmed that any assets have begun to leak outside its control. Our culture is such that the populace demands investigations of the regulators when failures unfold such as Madoff or Stanford, which were not hedge funds but instead were broker-dealers or investment advisors. Predictably SEC commissioners would testify before sympathetic congressmen that if they had only been granted oversight over hedge funds, they might have been able to stop the terrible damage that was wrought upon innocent investors. Not that they were able to do anything about other previous scandals before they occurred, or of failed firms that did fall under their jurisdiction, such as Madoff or Stanford. However, regulators have become fantastically successful at extracting enormous sums from the financial industry after the fact for infractions such as mutual funds permitting "timers" to arbitrage percentage moves based upon global time zone differences or analysts being shills for corporate finance departments. While both are examples of clearly undesirable behavior, the justice meted had more to do with the deep pockets of the perpetrators than anything else. To this day analysts carefully follow new rules that delineate their coordination with corporate finance, but nonetheless they coincidently suck up to managements of companies under stock research coverage in an attempt to woo underwriting for their firms.

The actions of Elliott Spitzer galvanized the SEC to action and led to two large efforts: First was the Global Settlement, an enforcement agreement reached in April 2003 that led to a record $1.4 billion of disgorgement and penalties.[28] Then, in fiscal year 2005 it assessed $700 million against three mutual fund companies,[29] following up on $700 million it had collected from six complexes the year before, in matters relating to market timing and late trading at mutual funds.[30] In February 2003 the SEC received approval to hire over 800 new staff members, and its FTEs numbered over 3,500 in FY 2008.[31] Disgorgements and penalties have fallen off to less than $500 million in FY2007, but this is well above the $216 million seen in the quiet year of 2004.

The SEC's budget, or appropriated funding as it is known, was $906 million for FY2008, having risen 11.5 percent annually since 2001. Investor complaints however, have barely increased. From 2001 to 2007 their annual growth was just 1.6 percent.[32] According to a Rand Corporation study of investment advisors and broker-dealers registered with the SEC, the combined total of these grew at an annualized rate of just 3.4 percent over the five years 2001-2006, but this growth rate was skewed by some 700 hedge funds that subsequently deregistered after the study's end point; excluding these the annualized growth would shrink to just 2.5 percent. All of the growth has come on the investment advisor side, and these are typically very small operations compared to broker-dealers.

So similar to the story of the NASD, the data support the case that absent a sudden behavioral shift towards an epidemic of white collar crime, the SEC is a self-perpetuating bureaucracy bent on growing rapidly, which increasingly burdens the much slower growing sector that it regulates. The sensational case regarding conflicts between research and investment banking has only slightly rolled back the linkage of these two activities through barring direct ties between these departments at the large investment banks. The $400 million directed as a subsidy to independent research is set to expire in 2009, with no one clamoring for its extension. The mutual fund trading scandal has continued the new tradition for mega-settlements, enabling SEC commissioners such as Roel Campos to crow that "American mutual fund investors have been under attack," and "billions of dollars were literally stolen from investors by executives . . . (who) participated in sweetheart schemes in which privileged third parties such as hedge funds were allowed to market time mutual funds and engage in late trading ..."[33] Were it not for the shaky condition of the financial markets, we would see major settlements from the largest financial institutions once again, including possibly the GSEs, which instead now appear on the road to becoming full-fledged government agencies.

Merriam-Webster defines despotism as "a system of government in which the ruler has unlimited power." The government may never nationalize its financial institutions, but despotism amounts to something worse. Like citizens of the former Soviet Union, its officers and employees are asked to be both jailer and inmate, informer and informant, with no crime having yet been committed. Yes, there are those who would commit fraud. But the burden upon those who sincerely aim *not* to do so is extraordinary, and it is getting heavier with the passage of each new rule.

Somehow it seems that ill-intentions might be mostly a function of human nature, and thus would not be reduced by the tightening net of the law. If as Dostoevsky's Ivan Karamazov contended that if there is no God, everything is permitted, then in reality into this vacuum rushes the state. It is a merciless, cold master rather than a forgiving father. When a people lose their respect for morality and spiritual absolutes, then investors no longer can weigh the measure of a man, but must look to the state to impose a gaggle of restrictions in a costly and barely effective trap to catch the truly criminal. They feel relieved of having to perform due diligence, but in so doing make themselves more vulnerable, because as we have found in the meltdown of so many financial entities lately, schemes to part the public with its money are always with us.

No one declared before its toppling that the pleasingly high-yielding Bear Stearns hedge funds were filled with toxic investments. Or more fittingly, such declarations were actually yelled from the treetops in the dense jungle of private placement memoranda heavy as small town phonebooks. Because of the intense regulation and threat of liability, the makers of such investment vehicles all manufactured hundreds of pages of documentation requiring signatures and initials. In so doing, they release themselves of guilt should anything go wrong (which happens to some percentage of any risky investment by nature), but investors learn to ignore this rubbish and even associate the better-run firms with the most official looking and weightiest paperwork.

In the end, the despot takes his cut, the investors lose out and honorable money managers are burdened. Fraudsters such as Bernie Madoff or Allen Stanford, both major Democratic Party supporters, might escape the long arm of the law indefinitely unless a super-bear market exposes missing funds when redemptions are requested, especially if they make well-placed donations to political campaigns as did Marc Rich (through his wife), earning him a pardon by the ultimate wizard of relativism, President Bill Clinton. For his part, in the last election cycle Stanford placed contributions to numerous Democratic politicians for over $30,000, but covered all bases by also making a $28,000 one to the National Republican Committee. Stanford reports donations using various addresses and permutations of his name, and in one case happens to erroneously report the recipient as Stanford Financial Group, as if he filled in the wrong box on the form. Who did that one go to? His 35-year-old CIO, who had no previous investment experience before working at Stanford but was responsible for running $15 billion, saw fit to donate $2,300 to Chris Dodd in March 2007, who happens to chair the Senate Banking Committee. Madoff was less bipartisan, making several Democratic gifts topped off by writing one $50,000 check to the Democratic Senatorial Campaign Committee. His lone Republican beneficiary, who returned the gift well before the Ponzi scheme was exposed, was Andrew Saul, the chairman of the Federal Retirement Thrift Investment Board.

It seems that being in charge of regulation making can be profitable outright, much less through the revolving door that connects the job market in New York with Washington D.C. It is no wonder that financial behemoths that took on too much risk must be preserved at all costs and that regulation of them should become ever more complicated and extensive, for it grafts their flesh to the government's. And nationalization will surely be temporary, for if it were not, jobs in the financial sector might not be as lucrative for old hands from the political sphere. Freddie and Fannie were goldmines for ex-Clinton aides such as Franklin Raines, because that problem of pay grades goes away in the private sector. There is more to regulation than simply protecting the innocent.

# Part Seven

# THE FUTURE

Murray Rothbard, in the tradition of Mises, explains that in a period of extreme financial crisis businessmen as a group make a "cluster of errors," an unusual occurrence that contrasts with their usual prescience and money making ability. To blame for this phenomenon is the fiat currency system and a central bank policy of setting interest rates so low that prices of securities and assets such as real estate get priced at artificially high levels. Even if one wholeheartedly embraces the Austrian School view, it is impossible to know whether the bust will happen now, or whether it could be forestalled by hyperinflation.

Chapter 17 reveals two elephants in the room that are responsible for the crisis: socialism and fiat currency. By now the reader is intimately familiar with the interaction of the two and their economic impact. Rather than rehash that, their influence is recounted from the perspective of two notable super-rich elites and their coterie in the recent movie "I.O.U.S.A." The film was developed to educate the pathetically ignorant citizenry of the United States, which is now tasting the consequences of decades of economic illiteracy. It is so widespread, thanks to misinformation spread by academia, that even politicians and businessmen still have no familiarity with the ignominious record of debt imbalances capable under centrally managed fiat currency systems, but they should certainly know better.

Chapter 18 shows what the world would look like if gold were to replace the mountain of debt-backed currency that has been printed globally. It presents the hope that the present crisis may have a cleansing effect that would lead to America retaining her cultural, moral, and economic beacon, thus remaining truly unconquered. The Roman Empire ironically succumbed to government ineptitude, the greed of its aristocracy, and infiltration of barbarians, the latter arguably a good thing for its people. Chapter 19 reviews America's future in this context. America has a better chance to succeed, with its colonial heritage remembered by more than a few and a vibrant conservative ideological core that is honing its communications skills and bringing the sunshine of logic to the American people.

# Chapter 17

# Elephants in the Room

*"The future ain't what it used to be"*

YOGI BERRA[1]

I n July 2008 on the eve of substantial financial destruction, a documentary film, "I.O.U.S.A.," was released that discusses the perils of our federal indebtedness. It is a wake-up call that winds up being an impassioned plea for a bipartisan solution, which of course means that there should be some spending restraint by the government combined with some sort of tax increase. To pass on such debt to the next generation of Americans would be, it claims, immoral, in essence having one group spend and enjoy, while another generation pays for it. A reviewer for the *Washington Post,* Philip Kennicott, thought the film was O.K., but it ". . . just isn't, well, very *interesting."* As for American's penchant for spending over saving, the *New York Times'* Jeannette Catsoulis says, "Good luck, boys: Suze Orman has been working on that for years." The *Miami Herald's* Robert Butler adds, "it's important," but ". . . we go to the movies to escape bad news, not wallow in it."

On opening night movie theatres broadcast a town hall meeting featuring David Walker, former comptroller general of the United

States; Blackstone group's billionaire founder Pete Peterson; Warren
Buffett; William Niskanen, chairman of the Cato Institute; and Bill
Novelli, CEO of AARP. Walker, an appointee of various administrations for 25 years who was fired by Bush in 2007, appears the most
bipartisan and has credibility, having the longest involvement in warning the public about the crisis. But his alarmism earns him the title
"Chicken Little" from a second reviewer from the *Washington Post*,
Frank Ahrens, as well as the more respectable "Cassandra." Cato is libertarian, so Niskanen seems to do everything to muster restraint in
a forum that clearly would not welcome ideas out of right field. His
presence is a lone and reserved one that confers an air of collegial-
ity. With Ron Paul having been drubbed badly and marginalized by a
press that portrayed him as a bit flaky in the 2008 primary, Niskanen's
spending capital to earn a seat at this table may have been worthwhile
just to stimulate interest in his organization from a receptive audience that at least is willing to examine facts and figures for two hours
and 45 minutes. Likewise, Novelli swallows his left-wing partisanship,
apparently posturing to salvage the best outcome for his very narrow
interest group of seniors in the fiscal war of attrition sure to heat up
once the entitlement squeeze will be on some five to 10 years from
now. Nebraska billionaires and friends Buffett and Peterson are peas in
a pod that have profited enormously from both the tax code and more
importantly from the fiat money system, which has made credit abundant and let inflation escalate the value of assets levered with either
debt or tax-protected insurance company capital—take your pick. Not
introduced by moderator Becky Quick nor addressed by any of the
panelists were two elephants also present in the room: socialism and
the fiat currency system.

The greatest issue of our time is the resolution of a now over
century-long debate to determine the superiority of capitalism over
socialism. Socialists are hopeful that their doctrine is a natural evolution of the developed world, and evidence abounds that it has indeed
been adopted in Europe and America. Central to this battle is decid-
ing whether the hand of government can move the chess pieces of the
economy efficiently or if individuals left alone are better positioned to
respond to price and investment signals. As Keynes did, socialists would
advocate the use of tax policy to shift income to the lowest levels

where the propensity to consume is greatest; supply-siders stress the disruptive effect this has in allocating scarce capital away from productive investment and by reducing savings.

By grinding the axe that capitalism is meant only for the rich, socialists chop away at its strength, which is the use of incentives to coax entrepreneurial behavior, thus fostering a healthy and growing middle class. Socialism's progressive tax policies retard capital formation among this group, but somehow get skirted by the über-rich, who as often as not politically support the left so long as they can exploit the system. This recalls the century or more when the aristocracy of Rome destroyed that empire's yeoman landholder class and turned the screw on what became a peasant-citizen class, all the while increasing the dole made to them and entertaining them with games and baths to quell desires for revolution. It also recalls the astonishingly flat societal structures headed by an oligarchy in the Soviet Union, China, Latin America, and Africa—all regions of the world where economies reverted to barely functional states of economic penury.

Europe's currency and economy is praised in the media, and its socialistic model is emulated by Democrats, particularly those who ran against each other in the 2008 Presidential primary. With light dependence on oil and fleets of mini-cars, it is painted as prudent and foresighted, sometimes even the victim of the United States with European banks suffocating under a blanket of AAA-rated CDO mortgages gone wrong. They would have us believe that the greed of Wall Street touched off the credit crisis, which could be seen as a failure of unbridled American capitalism. But soon the social disaster of Europe may unfold. The untold story is that its welfare state is at risk, too. In cultural synchronicity with American socialism, it too has had huge deficit spending since the 1980s, with public sector spending trending just above or below 50 percent of GDP for at least 20 years. Its surfeit of public debt is comparably as unhealthy as that of the United States as a percent of GDP, but its unfunded pension liabilities average 285 percent of GDP, with the United Kingdom the most disciplined but Spain and Greece being off the charts. It, too, has printed money excessively, living in a culture of credit gone wild, as measured by M3 growth exceeding real economic growth by 5 percent ever since the Euro was launched. It has a rapidly aging population and some 19 million unemployed, but some such as Martin De Vlieghere and Paul Vreymans write that these figures are faked and might realistically be double this, thinking real unemployment stands at the level of the 1932 Depression.[2]

Is it not heartening to politicians to seize and distribute today's wealth and promise more in future obligations knowing that erosion of the value of fiat currency will reduce the burden of government debt incurred? Is not their public debt simply a scorecard representing the cumulative transfer of wealth mostly driven by past entitlements, for which politicians lacked the chutzpah to lay at the feet of the taxpayers? To erase it with excessive printing of money would silently extract value from savers and investors, and most importantly cause capital to flee or be hoarded and essential investment to be foregone.

Does anyone expect the bill to be paid with 2009 constant-value dollars when it comes due in another generation's time? Does the burden vanish, or is it socialized, and if so, to whom? Will it be borne by the population today, most of which pays almost no income tax through relegating the burden to the upper-middle class, which ever since World War I has been taxed by the Treasury and the states at between a 40 percent and 90 percent rate? Or will it be transferred to a population of tomorrow, whose less affluent may suffer real wage erosion and not enjoy the benefit of the heavy investment in capital stock that has made today's prosperity possible? What incentive exists for wealth to remain still in the crosshairs of an untaxed rabble, which thinks it moral, even righteous to stake a large claim on another man's paycheck and remove half the unspent remainder when he dies, not to mention the cacophony of other taxes government imposes?

The second elephant in the room at the I.O.U.S.A. town-hall meeting was fiat currency. The pleasant and fatherly Warren Buffett assures us that the economic pie always grows, and that if we were from Bangladesh we would gladly "bid" as if in an auction to pay a high tax rate on income should we be allowed to emigrate, because things are so great here. Buffett's highly public backing of higher income and death tax rates is analogous to Mark Twain's Tom Sawyer, who convinces the boys of his neighborhood that whitewashing a fence is not work. Sawyer "was a poor poverty stricken boy in the morning," but is "literally rolling in wealth" by the afternoon and "(plans) the slaughter of more innocents."[3] Buffett exhorts us to *like* the inevitable tax increase in the offing as well as a slight reduction in entitlements. Yet this is the best outcome of all for this billionaire, because it will maintain the stability of the dollar and it might keep inflation from completely coming uncorked but still preserve its gentle upward trajectory. It would avoid the diminution of his wealth through excessive printing of money. Importantly, it also ensures that the bar tab for the binge we have enjoyed as a country gets picked up by the middle class; as for his own tax liability, that is probably shielded by insurance company tax breaks, offshore legal structures, or donations he directs to his or Bill Gates's foundation. He is no casual Pollyanna, having been buying downtrodden banks and other financial stocks with both hands, although these mega positions are probably not material to his financial condition.

The author of the book upon which the movie is based has been advising his newsletter clients that to survive the coming financial Armageddon, we must buy gold. Having sold the movie rights to the private equity billionaire Pete Peterson, the ending has been rewritten, and this outcome is completely missing! No one, certainly neither Buffett nor Peterson, would warn us that the collapse of the purchasing power of the dollar could result from the need to reflate. The slick graphics of the movie show how we as a nation have always paid down the piles of debt amassed when during wartime. But the elephant cannot be talked about; historically in each case the CPI-U vaulted to a new plateau, and as if sprayed with *Roundup*, inflation takes the green of savings and whithers it to a brown crisp.

No, instead we pretend the winds of history would never blow this way again. Fiat currency has had a drug-like effect, taking the edge off of the pain of business cycles for decades. It has been so effective a medicine that Republicans, traditionally conservative, gave up the fight for fiscal responsibility by the time of the younger Bush. Neither Ronaldus Maximus in the 1980s nor Newt Gingrich holding a contract with America in hand in the 1990s could negotiate any spending discipline from their Democratic counterparts, but they certainly tried. Naively at first they thought tax reductions might force the issue, but the positive feedback from supply-side economics seemed to only open up the nation's pocketbook to keep expansion of entitlements on a roll. George W. Bush might even be seen as cynical, upping the ante at the poker table by wagering a larger stack of entitlement chips, or history might see him as a Herbert Hoover, a Republican wholeheartedly embracing liberal government fixes to emerging economic demands. Clinton is hailed as the lone sensible voice, balancing the unified budget for three years, but this still only addresses the traditional debt and says little of the Democrats' desire to add entitlements. Remember, with future entitlements added, the GAAP liability on the U.S. balance sheet jumps nearly seven-fold.

Leaving blame aside, neither Republican nor Democrat nor these supposed nonpartisans of the town hall can look history or the future in the eye and not see that politically there has never been a resolve to *completely* address the overall credit problem. They don't have the guts to tell us they never will ask the truly difficult questions that would reveal why our system has a built-in tendency to misappropriate funds and encourage accumulation of excessive government obligations and also private sector debt. If the bipartisans succeed, there might be a deferral of consequences. But like an alcoholic that tries to limit himself to two drinks per night, another irresistible moment may likely present itself. Interestingly, all the panelists of the I.O.U.S.A. town hall agree that cultural change and a better informed populace are desperately needed. During the Volcker experience of 1979–1980, fiscal consciousness was raised, but hardly enough to think about throwing off more than one side of the yoke of socialism (think of taxes and spending as the two oxen). And it took nearly 20 percent interest rates to get there. What sort of shock would be needed now to entice voters to swallow the movie's bitter pill?

# Chapter 18

# The Elephant Killer—Gold

The mellow stock market decline through mid-2008 (measured by historical yardsticks) and the bull market in U.S. Treasuries of all maturities belied not a crisis but some dreadful disease that had been effectively quarantined. Perhaps as in history's great epidemics, the doctors in this case had not seen this sort of sickness before and had yet to understand completely what strain of bug was at work. Although having DNA similar to pathogens seen in wartime debt buildups, this season's strain encoded itself with the pattern of socialism: entitlements, bloated and intrusive government, and punitive taxation exclusively directed at the top brackets. Its vector of transmission is fiat currency. Our culture leaves the body politic and the investment community with no antibodies to recognize this threat. In earlier eras such as the 1980s, the bond vigilantes watched the money supply and government outlays closely. At the turn of the century, leading bankers looked over their shoulder for signs of the next wave of panic from others who might have lent speculatively, and they kept their balance sheets in good shape for that rainy day. Today, those who took defensive action through short selling or exchanging their money for commodities were instead pilloried in public hearings and damned for being speculators.

Even before the stock market panic that began in 2008, lenders were willing to accept historically low returns on short- and long-dated treasuries even if these nominal returns were being eroded by a CPI-U that pierced through 5 percent from June through August, or worse, by that and taxation, too. The low interest rates then may have anticipated the risks revealed once the stock market collapsed. More joined this wary camp to push nominal returns below zero once deflation became evident. It may be this contagion is a virus capable of fooling the body's defenses, sort of an HIV look-alike, since with long-term Treasury rates in the low single digits and a public that is not alarmed (or even aware) of the dangers of $60 trillion of national obligations, a message is being sent to the government that it might have unlimited supplies of free money that it might spend.

Private debt of $40 trillion plus $60 trillion of public debt and entitlements might have been enough moisture to feed a hurricane. But it might just as well require more, due to the behavioral aspects of the system and its complexity, so no economist might know what the breaking point may be. Unfortunately, sometimes markets, like ocean skies, can be clear before bed but stormy in the morning. The storm that could break hardest would be the downgrading of the credit rating of the United States. For if we expect to pay off the obligations of the government through concentrating tax increases on the top brackets, foisting debts of somewhere between $500,000 and $2 million upon each rich household (depending on where the cut-point is drawn), no longer would the Treasury have the resources to honor its obligations. Yes, complete dismantling of the socialist entitlement state would fix the problem. But the political will to do something this drastic could never come out of thin air; it would only come once we as a society as a whole hit rock bottom.

## Keeping the Genie in the Bottle

The fiat currency system is elegant and innovative. It has served us well, and might continue to do so if we could as a society change our culture so drastically that we might reign in credit growth—both public and private—responsibly. This would be the fairy-tale solution, one where the paper and electronic money supply behaves as if it were backed by gold, but actually isn't. But that restrictive system would institutionalize mild deflation as the deterrent against runaway credit. Instead, central bankers everywhere aspire to target inflation at a minimal nominal percentage, say 1 to 2 percent. Even so, saying and doing are two very different things. For starters, central bankers cannot address fiscal issues, and their pegging the cost of money at friendly levels encourages the government to pursue policies of cutting taxes and increasing spending simultaneously, which has been the practice since the Reagan era. Central bankers are also trusting the fox to guard the henhouse, for they accept that inflation is low despite considerable tinkering of methodology maintained by the U.S. Commerce Department that may understate it by 3 to 4 percent. However, as established in the monetary section of this book, the built-in bias towards inflation of asset values, such as real estate and stock prices, is not reflected in tame inflation yardsticks. A fiat money supply will forever encourage the amassing of debt by the private sector and the government alike. That, in turn, makes it only a matter of years before another financial calamity destroys the hopes of another generation. We may no longer operate fiat currencies as clumsily as did Massachusetts of 1690 or the French Assembly. Instead, we may be more like the Roman Empire, charted upon a course of slow decline, run by arrogant but physically fit potentates with exceptional or miserable oratorical skills, as you like.

In an act of intellectual finesse, in November 2005 the Fed stopped publishing its estimate of M3, the broadest measure of money, at a time when its running three-month growth rate had probed solidly into double-digit territory.[1] It gave up targeting money supply in the mid-1980s, this turning out to be a brief attempt to synthetically replicate a hard currency. Abandoning it succeeded then because (as in the 1920s) overinvestment in commodity production had paved the way for disinflation for years in the 1980s and 1990s. Fed actions also easily kept inflation at bay initially because the systemic growth of credit of today had not yet reached the extreme level where it is now (though some seers at that time thought that it had). In the last decade or so, the additions of tens of millions of low-wage workers from around the globe have lowered manufacturing costs.

The bogey of merely restraining inflation was achieved easily. It enabled the banking system to print enormous sums of money, trillions of dollars, seemingly without consequence. But there is never a consequence felt while the bubble is inflating, because interest and principal can be financed by new debt. When debt reaches an untenable height relative to income or equity, the system becomes susceptible to the most minor cyclical downturn, with years of accumulated excess to be purged.

What new developments might cause the supposedly $1 trillion to $2 trillion of popularly expected losses from the credit crisis to break the quarantine the Federal Reserve and the Treasury wishes to maintain to such an extent that they would overwhelm the economy? For starters, the savings-rich trading partners of the United States or other investors generally might demand our adoption of a hard currency of some sort. This they could accomplish by rapidly converting their holdings to gold (and not other currencies). It could be that another country, such as Switzerland, might seize the opportunity to operate a new high-level reserve currency. Or, countries such as Japan or the United States might suffer extreme economic contraction from the sharp appreciation of their currencies in the floating foreign exchange markets that, like the gold standard in the 1930s, they would reject the fiat-floating model of trade. Similar to the heresy of going off gold then, today these governments might likewise conclude that floating exchange rates are inexplicably hurting their terms of trade, forcing dramatically lower industrial production and employment relative to currencies that have depreciated greatly. If this were judged to be the root of the problem, governments would jump ship, something they could only do by reverting to gold. Even with a tarnished financial reputation, it is difficult to imagine that the United States would not still be able to capitalize upon its position as the strongest country in the world, even if it lost control of the world's reserve currency.

If a consensus between the Fed and the Treasury could be reached, federally chartered banks might back the dollar with gold again, or the issuance of private currency could be authorized. It would be smartest for the Treasury to quietly buy in massive quantities of gold before such a strategy became known. Then like Roosevelt did, it could anchor the dollar at a higher level, perhaps $2,000 or $5,000 per ounce. But as the lessons of the interwar era taught us, this carries a substantial risk and as shown in calculations to follow these prices would excessively trigger gold reserve redemption. Now as then, the correct peg level is unknowable, and the success of such a measure is dependent upon the price central banks of foreign nations would establish (even if they opted for a gold exchange standard). The temptation would be for each country to lock in a trade advantage, which would force deflation and higher interest rates upon the United States, an unwanted outcome. A critical problem to be addressed before such a change could happen would be how to treat the national debt, and for that matter the even greater debt held by the U.S. citizenry.

## Flexible Gold

Probably the most workable solution would be a new gold standard that would be flexible. Countries could establish the value of their currency in ounces of gold, but vary this price depending upon international confidence in it and the terms of trade. If, for example, the United States believed its major trading partner, China, was maintaining its currency at low levels to maximize export earnings, it would have the option to devalue the dollar relative to gold instead of accusing China of manipulation. In today's system, China can exercise considerable power to softly peg the yuan to the dollar. But if under a gold standard it fixes its paper to a commodity equivalent, gold, it would be forced to export that commodity upon demand if it made an ounce equivalent to too many yuan. That would happen if it chose to competitively devalue in synchronization with the United States—but only if the U.S. dollar was not itself undervalued also. In that case, both countries would suffer a drain of gold.

The U.S. dollar and all other fiat currencies, having been printed relentlessly since the abandonment of the gold standard, would all need to be reset at a price which equilibrates a high number of currency units per ounce of gold, otherwise there would not be enough gold to be used for currency value linkage, and because debt would be overvalued and a run on gold reserves would ensue. In 2008 and 2009 there has been a substantial amount of currency volatility, which confirms that the massive trade imbalances of many countries (particularly the United States and China) are in need of settlement but may not have a mechanism through which to clear. Gold may be that tool. In the past, a chief objection to its use was the volatility it might introduce into price-rigid world economies, heightening unemployment. But with permission to revalue and devalue, currency volatility would be no more than it is now, and in the world's shaken and unstable environment, high unemployment is likely anyway.

There still would be political obstacles to restoring gold. For one, China has had a policy that encourages exports and retention of savings. Facing its own recession, it can hardly induce its citizens to step up consumption of imports now. But its government could import a proxy for commodities—gold. If the United States and other countries were part of a flexible gold standard, then the drain of gold from countries that have large trade deficits, such as the United States, would cause pressure for them to increase their local price of gold. This would stimulate gold production or dishoarding, but longer term the beneficial effect would be to engender the development of industries that would suddenly be that much more competitive globally at the new exchange rate. Alternatively, if the United States chose to maintain a high level of consumption and not join the new flexible gold standard, then China could continue to convert dollars into gold. In the past this would have seemed irrelevant or barbaric, but in the aftermath of the great financial bubble, it may be exactly what is required to unlock the credit markets *and* balance trade (classifying gold as a commodity proxy). Yes, the dumping of dollars would transmit a measure of inflation to the United States, but with deflation and conventions that make prices and wages sticky to the downside, that may be a welcome surprise. In essence it would be the mirror image or reverse of the low consumer price inflation and rapid revaluation of asset prices seen during the great financial epoch, for there would be a rebalancing that shifts the upward price movement back into the real (and productive side) of the economy, while prices of nonproductive assets, such as real estate and overpriced stocks, might remain depressed or rise comparatively less.

Even after a 20 percent equity market selloff in the first three months of 2009, most institutional money managers and analysts assigned a very low probability that the countries of the world would ever return to a gold standard. Instead, they would hold out for a conventional recovery driven by the white knights at the Federal Reserve System, the natural cyclical forces of capitalism, or if they have faith in Democratic solutions, the American Recovery and Reinvestment Act of 2009. So, besides the geopolitical obstacles, it is hard to imagine much popular passion for gold restoration. One must turn to scenario analysis, where a possibility that unusual world financial events could suddenly lead to this outcome. The most interesting case is a scenario that eerily echoes the events of May 1931, when the collapse of Creditanstalt triggered a wave of currencies defaulting on gold exchangeability by the fall of that year.

European banks as a whole took on more leverage than their U.S. counterparts, because capital risk weighting guidelines allowed them to borrow almost with impunity against AAA-rated investments, which included many of the mortgage pools assembled into CDO securities by U.S. investment banks. Also largely represented in AAA holdings are securitizations of credit cards and corporate loans. Note that in this sense government regulation in Europe may have been the proximate cause of the mortgage bubble, along with the complicity of Fannie Mae and Freddie Mac. This vulnerability is compounded by these banks having acquired Eastern European banks and having made loans in these nations, often low-interest-rate mortgages denominated in what are today very strong currencies: the yen, Swiss franc, or compared to local scrip, the euro. Since the borrowers' income is denominated in heavily compromised local currencies, defaults have risen rapidly. It is not hard to imagine the unexpected failure of a significant Central European bank under the circumstances. In 1931, Creditanstalt received a rescue package, just as today the IMF has been injecting funds into the region to keep it propped up. In the 1930s, even the Fed was involved in the rescue, and today it is no different with the largest item on its newly ballooned balance sheet being currency swaps with foreign central banks. Some believe the IMF itself could be insolvent, which might trigger it to dump its 3,200 metric tonnes of gold onto the market. The holdings of the IMF are second only to the United States (8.1 thousand tonnes) and Germany (3.4 thousand tonnes), and are 11 percent of all central bank reserves.

China could step in and offer to quietly do a block trade at a firm price, thus saving the IMF from pressuring the gold market (disrupting the market is actually codified as against IMF policy). Such a transaction would not be large compared to the international currency markets, for at nearly $1,000 per ounce the IMF holdings are worth just over $100 billion, which would be a fraction of Chinese holdings of U.S. government securities. However, such a trade would be viewed dimly by the United States, because it would underscore the fundamental weakness of the dollar and it would release a small but significant quantity of U.S. government bonds for sale by the IMF to help clean up the mess in Eastern Europe. Like China National Offshore Oil Corporation's $18 billion tender offer for Unocal that was nixed in August 2005 as a security threat, such a transaction could be vetoed as well. But China is in a stronger position today, and the necessity of bailing out the IMF might bring the world's countries together in conference to distribute the gold and establish a rejuvenated Bretton Woods system that would signal a tilt back toward the usage of gold to restore confidence in the dollar and the health of central banks generally. Perhaps with this in mind in April 2009 China revealed that it had been buying gold, increasing its reserves from 600 tonnes (in 2003) to 1,054 tonnes five years later. In late 2008 rumors that China was buying gold surfaced. Note that China has grown its M2 money supply at double digit rates historically, and by April 2009 monetary stimulus advanced at a 26 percent clip. China would likewise need to buy massive amounts of gold to back the yuan, and it would face devaluation compared to gold and perhaps even the dollar. Despite the aforementioned leaks about its increasing gold reserves, China has accumulated even greater levels of foreign exchange reserves, diluting the hard backing of its currency.

When Roosevelt devalued the dollar in 1934, this turned the tide and fostered monetary expansion that transformed deflation into slight inflation. Before that point, savings had begun to increase as well, another prerequisite for a sound banking system. However, relative to the Roosevelt era, as discussed earlier in the book's inflation-adjusted bracket analysis, nowadays taxes are already high. Moreover, state and federal governments occupy a greater percentage of the economy than they did in the 1930s. Consequently, Roosevelt-inspired fiscal tinkering may be of diminished benefit, if indeed one could concede that it had any positive effect in the first place back then. The proclivity of government to borrow and spend puts pressure on the Fed to be accommodative and makes further increases in taxes politically thorny and perhaps even revenue reducing outright. Should a return to gold or silver be forced upon us through world events, there might be an irresistible run on Treasury gold or silver unless very harsh fiscal restraint was exercised. About the only imaginable way that this could come to be would be if politicians knew they were cut off from the unlimited funding they enjoy through the Sixteenth Amendment, which enables government to expropriate property. A political backlash strong enough to bring this about might be the predation of IRA accounts or pension funds, which of course would be foisted onto the public as a temporary necessity.

If a new Bretton Woods meeting does not produce a flexible gold standard, the free market may move toward the adoption of an ETF-like currency, anyway, whose value is expressed in the weight of the gold or silver backing it. This was the original meaning of the "pound" adopted by Britain, and in fact the "dollar" is a name derived from a 16th century Bohemian coin known as the "Joachimsthaler," shortened to "thaler," which was defined by weight.[2] This concept of having currency based upon the physical metal is known as free metallism. Gresham's law dictates that the current poorly backed currencies would keep new well-backed ones from emerging, so long as countries are willing to accept payment for their exports and return of their capital in the form of depreciating paper currencies. But in reality gold and silver never disappeared. Rather it was held by the populace in savings and withdrawn from usage to transact business and pay taxes, for which inferior currency was used. Conversely, paper currency was no longer useful for savings. The specie that disappeared from circulation in the 18th century was not destroyed; it was exported to nations that honored sound money, or it was hoarded.

As an alternative to the inflationist view, demand for gold may continue to rise even though a deflationary threat emerged in late 2008. U.S. citizens fearing encroaching statism and reckless finance may see physical gold and ETFs as an alternative store of value. Investment demand has soared. Physical gold purchases doubled in 2008, reaching almost 800 tonnes, and ETFs added over 300 tonnes that year, a 24 percent rise. Since 2000, investment demand has grown by 900 tonnes, nearly offsetting an almost 1,100 tonne falloff in jewelry demand. Once investment demand more than backs out jewelry usage, the price of gold is likely to reset closer to its equilibrium point for utility as money rather than where supply and demand for ornamentation sets its value. Some think ETFs could fail because the custodians of their gold may be leasing out their deposits to traders at bullion banks who are selling the metal short to earn an interest spread. This may explain the churning in the gold markets in 2008-2009 and the heavy technical resistance seen at about $1,000 per ounce. In response to this fear, many have begun to buy specie instead, which would reveal this subterfuge and also suspected naked short selling by bullion banks generally. An interesting alternative to specie is digital gold, essentially deposit accounts that enable electronic transactions for commerce that are 100 percent reserved. James Turk pioneered this product, goldmoney.com, which had about $700 million of holdings in mid-2009. To alleviate the credit crunch of 2008, politicians are considering unprecedented increases in government spending and borrowing. This in turn has begun to trigger monetization of government debt through the direct purchase of such obligations by the Fed, which could expand. A key element of a successful currency is its scarcity. Borrowing can be discouraged by concerns over creditworthiness, to which even the United States might be subject. Unbacked currencies have been shunned before, and they tend to reach a tipping point as was seen after World War I in Europe. When money moves to a natural, unleveraged form, it starves oxygen from bubble-fed assets and securities, which are much riskier.

The question was asked of the "I.O.U.S.A." town hall panelists whether our trading partners might sell off their holdings of Treasury notes. Warren Buffett offered that they not only would not, they could not, because they would need to convert into some other currency, which would be little better than ours. The other panelists concurred by silence. Enter the elephant of fiat currency: Buffett's answer assumes that there is no alternative, because for generations all the world's currencies have been backed only by the promise that governments would accept them in payment of taxes. But that ignores a currency that has been used effectively by man for thousands of years: gold. China and other countries might exchange their U.S. dollars for it now.

Clearly Buffett and other billionaires benefit from a fiat currency system, because it provides gently rising asset prices against which they can borrow to obtain cash flow in a tax-free manner. The derivatives market can even take out the repayment risk by maintaining a floor for collateral valuation. So the last thing Buffett would want to do is to alert the movie's viewers to the possibilities of using gold to back the dollar, for it would cut off the über-rich's tax-free ATM machine. Speaking at Harvard in 1998, Buffett said "gold gets dug out of the ground in Africa or someplace. Then we melt it down, dig another hole, bury it again and pay people to stand around guarding it. It has no utility. Anyone watching from Mars would be scratching their head."[3] Yet when governments are undisciplined spenders and wish to monetize their debt, gold is the only means investors may have to preserve their wealth; in this case it possesses unparalleled utility. Mr. Buffett is a humanist with absolute conviction that man can construct economic and governmental systems that are failsafe. Those who see the train wreck central planning will nearly always produce (as long as enough time has elapsed) realize they would rather place their faith in something absolute as opposed to paper money, which is readily manipulatable by men.

## If Gold Were Money Again

Why not gold? Even though it made an advance to some $1,000 per ounce by mid-year 2008, shortly thereafter it plunged to less than $700 per ounce. At $800, on an inflation-adjusted basis it would only be worth a little over $300 per ounce in 1980 dollars. After fully feeling the monetary discipline of Volcker and reflecting the collapse of oil in the glut of the mid-1980s, it could not sink much below $250, a level of support it maintained for years. One could overanalyze the investment rationale of our trading partners, but for those who are not blessed with generous supplies of oil, holding reserves in gold at these levels rather than in U.S. dollars would appear to be a no-brainer. However, there are some reasons why these countries would not. Foreign governments operate fiat currencies, and these are a backdoor means of taxing wealth and also forcing it to remain inside their borders. As for the oil exporters, gold being very closely correlated with oil would magnify commodity risk for them, so they might not opt for this solution, unless perhaps asked to do so for political reasons by influential fundamentalists.

The largest stumbling block toward the adoption of gold as a currency reserve is the severe discipline it injects into the fiscal and monetary policy-making process. In recent years, the U.S. government has maintained an approximately $3 trillion budget in a $13 trillion economy with annual deficits in the hundreds of billions. Its monetary authority, the Federal Reserve System, has permitted the money supply to double in the last seven years, continuing a post-war trend of quantitative looseness. In contrast, the world's supply of gold grows slowly over time, roughly in line with population. Annual mine production is 2.2 million tonnes. However, much of this output becomes one or more steps removed from satisfying future demand, because it is mixed with alloys for American grade jewelry or it goes into gold bonding wire or gold-plated contacts and connectors used in industry. Above-ground stocks are estimated at 161,000 tonnes (5.2 billion ounces) by GMFS Limited, an independent research organization in London, which says that these have increased by 2 percent per year over the 10 years through 2007.[4] All the gold in the world could fit into a two Olympic-sized swimming pools.[5] During the Internet boom, gold-bugs used to say that the value of all gold was lower than the market capitalization of Microsoft. With gold set at a high price, such as the $10,000-an-ounce level, mine production would rise from its current 2 percent tendency to increase the total world supply of gold to something greater, but nowhere near the double-digit M3 growth rates seen in the early part of the 21st century.[6]

Whether or not we adopt gold, we may be forced to choose between national default combined with massive private bankruptcies or accepting deliberately manufactured inflation. The Federal Reserve has attempted to liquefy the system with trillions of dollars of loans, but loans do not restore equity, per se. TARP funds placed into preferred stock of financially strapped banks and brokers may be converted to common equity or repaid with Fed loans. However, under a quasi-nationalized banking system managers of these institutions appear capable of destroying this equity through following orders to shovel in good money after bad for multibillion-dollar commercial real estate loans to failing gambling houses in Las Vegas or hopelessly high-cost automakers.

Although the bond market obligingly consumed large quantities of newly issued Federal debt at almost nonexistent interest rates throughout 2008, at some point investors might care less about liquidity and more about national creditworthiness. Such a switch in sentiment would then force the issue, causing the Federal Reserve to become a large direct buyer of Treasury bonds, as it was in the early 1950s. The country might then be in a position similar to where it was in 1817, when the Second Bank of the United States cut a deal with the states to inflate bank credit-based money by $6 million, a very large sum at the time, to entice them to agree that any notes they had issued that were not redeemable in specie would no longer be considered legal tender for the payment of federal obligations.[7] In essence, it might be necessary to avoid default with one last inflationary push before resumption.

If the United States were to back its currency with gold, it would have two options: It could replenish its gold reserves through purchases at market rates, or it could revalue the dollar today by announcing it would be convertible at a specific price, using the backing that it currently has. Table 18.1 shows how gold reserves rose in the Great Depression partly due to Roosevelt's confiscation of private wealth, and its runoff under the Gold Exchange Standard and Bretton Woods is evident as well. No one could know what percent of the currency

### Table 18.1: Theoretical Equilibrium Price of Gold

| Year | Reserves (Mil Oz.) | M3 ($ Bil) | Gold Price ($/Oz.) | Reserve Ratio (%) |
|------|--------------------|------------|--------------------|-------------------|
| 1930 | 204 | 46 | 21 | 9.2% |
| 1940 | 628 | 55 | 35 | 39.8% |
| 1950 | 652 | 135 | 35 | 16.9% |
| 1960 | 509 | 315 | 35 | 5.6% |
| 1970 | 316 | 677 | 35 | 1.6% |
| 1980 | 264 | 1,996 | 615 | 8.1% |
| 1990 | 262 | 4,155 | 383 | 2.4% |
| 2000 | 262 | 7,118 | 279 | 1.0% |
| 2008 | 262 | 14,000 | 850 | 1.6% |
| ???? | 262 | 14,300 | 11,000 | 20.1% |

Note: U.S. reserves and money supply used in calculations. 1930 M3 is assumed to equal M2 since non-M2 in M3 was minimal prior to 1950.

would need to be backed by gold, for public confidence is the most essential input to that equation. With less confidence, a higher ratio is necessary. The government could double its quantity of physical metal by buying gold in the open market, but that would certainly escalate the price to at least $2,000 per ounce. With that guess, the total outlay would be some $570 billion, a large number, but not all that different from those bandied about by the Fed and the Obamian stimulus wonks. However, this would still leave the heavy lifting of taking gold backing from roughly 4 percent to 20 percent to devaluation, which would be measured in orders of magnitude. Even this small initial purchase would require finding sellers willing to part with 2.3 times the annual supply of gold, so the effect on price would probably be larger. Moreover, other governments might want to soak up some of the roughly 100,000 tonnes not held by central banks.[8] Table 18.1 calculates an equilibrium price of gold of some $11,000 per ounce, which would arise from a base case of our not buying any metal openly. If the Treasury were able to double its stock of gold through open market purchases, it would ameliorate some of the devaluation.

In his short but trenchant analysis in 1994 of fractional reserve banking, *The Case Against the Fed*, Murray Rothbard laid out another methodology for establishing an benchmark price of gold based upon liquidation value of the Federal Reserve. For perspective, in 1994 gold closed the year at $384/ounce, while the broadest measure of money having been printed in the United States (M3) stood at $4.4 trillion, or only 31 percent of its 2008 quantity.[9] When he performed this exercise using the balance sheet of April 6, 1994, he calculated that shutting down the Federal Reserve and distributing gold bullion to its creditors would reset the dollar's value to $1,555 per ounce.

The balance sheet of the Fed ballooned during 2008 in response to the freezing up of the credit markets and the collapse of equities. Table 18.2 is a condensed Fed balance sheet with year-end 2008 and mid-October data. Basically what Rothbard does in his liquidation is cancel any government-to-government obligations, regardless on which side of the balance sheet they reside. What remains are reserve deposits of the commercial banking system and currency (the monetary base) less any assets of the Fed that might be sold off. At the time of Rothbard's writing, these other assets might be buildings

Table 18.2: Federal Reserve Liquidation Analysis ($ billions)

| Assets | 22 Oct '08 | 31 Dec '08 | Comment |
|---|---|---|---|
| Gold | 11 | 11 | 260 mil oz. |
| Treasuries & Agencies | 491 | 496 | Cancel |
| Repos | 343 | 80 | Liquidate at par |
| Term Auction Credit | | 450 | To Soc Security |
| Comm. Paper Funding Facility | | 334 | To Soc Security |
| Other Loans | 408 | 194 | To Soc Security |
| Other Assets | 551 | 701 | ~$400 B |
| **Total** | **1,804** | **2,266** | |
| **Liabilities** | **22 Oct '08** | **31 Dec '08** | **Comment** |
| Reserve Balance | 221 | 860 | Pay in gold |
| Currency | 820 | 853 | Gold Certif. |
| U.S. Treasury Deposit | 615 | 365 | Cancel |
| Reverse Repos | 96 | 88 | Net against repos |
| Other | 12 | 58 | Pay in gold |
| Capital | 40 | 42 | Write Off |
| **Total** | **1,804** | **2,266** | |
| Net Liquidation Liability | 660 | 2,630 | |
| Necessary Gold Value | $2,500 | $10,100 | |

Note: Totals may not add due to rounding.
Methodology developed by Murray Rothbard.

or miscellaneous accounts. Today there are a host of credits provided by the Fed to weak banks, which are collateralized by troubled assets. There has also been a large swap program with foreign central banks. For the purpose of this update, the loans to weak banks are assumed to have zero value, for calling these loans and reinjecting the collateral back into the system now might initiate rapid monetary contraction. (However, it might be possible to extract some value from these for the taxpayers by transferring them to the Social Security trust fund.) The Fed has been opaque in disclosing precisely what is occurring with its currency swap lines; it is unclear whether these are tied directly to the Treasury's supplemental financing account, which is projected to run off. Regardless how one sees these fine points, the basic notion is that the gold would need to be revalued to match the monetary base.

What is interesting is that, as the credit crisis unfolds, there is a convergence between the Rothbard approach and the conclusion drawn if gold were to simply back 20 percent of the broad money supply. The reason is that central bankers have been injecting borrowed reserves into the banking system, which expands the monetary base, the numerator above the divisor of Fed gold holdings. If Fed spokespersons who have hinted that the Fed balance sheet might stretch to $3 trillion of assets by the end of 2009 are correct, then reserves would swell to some $2.2 trillion (assuming banks do not lend against this liquidity). That would boost the gold revaluation to over $10,000 per ounce, nearly reaching the $11,000 projected by the money supply approach. What this is saying is that the banking system needs to deleverage, and the borrowed reserves need to be converted into equity or non-borrowed reserves. At that point, borrowers and lenders would probably feel comfortable with the amount of debt they carry, and normal lending might resume. However, this unabashed printing of money would likely create inflation (making debt repayment easier for the private and public sectors alike), so it is entirely possible that the public would regard borrowing as a hedge against the loss in purchasing power that would result. By announcing a definitive date for the resumption of a gold standard, even if it were to occur at an undetermined price or solely by weight (free metallism), the public and the federal government would be put on notice that inflation would not be a permanent condition, and in fact slow, controlled deflation would be the new long-term tendency. Such was the case in the six years leading up to the resumption of 1879.

Confiscation of gold was an option that Roosevelt employed in the last great crisis. In the 1930s, many citizens were still alive who had lived under the gold standard of the late-19th century. This especially socialistic and totalitarian presidential order was pernicious, because it essentially was a tax that could not even be offset against income. However, today it would be unlikely to happen, since gold is no longer broadly owned. Globally, investment holdings are estimated at 26,500 tonnes, or just 16 percent of all above-ground stocks at the end of 2007. At $800 per ounce (about 32,150 troy ounces per tonne), the value of private holdings of everyone in the world is just $700 billion, or just over 1 percent of U.S. household net worth as of June 2008. By comparison at that same date, in the U.S. alone net equity in real estate was $8.8 trillion, stocks and mutual funds were worth $9.8 trillion, and accrued pensions held $12.3 trillion.[10] Confiscation of gold today would arbitrarily target those few who fear the consequences of government policies that caused the banking system to become uniformly weak over the last century, and who rationally made a decision to avoid risky paper assets.

Probably most of those who read Rothbard's musings when they were published well before the credit meltdown began in 2008 doubted that the fiat currency system could ever unravel to the extent that it did. All of us suffer from a recent past bias that makes us disbelieve great financial changes might occur. Chapter 3 recounted the monetary history of the United States, which clearly shows a pendulum-like tendency of swinging between hard money and fiat currency, but transitions can take decades. During times of fiat currency use, anyone who prophesied that a complete collapse would usher in hard money would have been dismissed by the experts of his time. Likewise, once gold and silver had been written into the Constitution, no one might have thought that it would be replaced by paper within 60 years. Skeptics of greenbacks probably got a better hearing and were able to successfully push for an agenda of gold resumption. But before the London Economic Conference of 1933, the world would be shocked by Roosevelt's rejection of the gold standard. It is possible that somehow the simple injection of massive amounts of fresh credit might forestall the crisis unleashed in 2008 from leading to a call for hard money. But if leverage remains high, almost certainly a series of crises such as was the case in Rome might ultimately bring the pendulum back toward gold.

# Chapter 19

# America Invicta

Federal Reserve officials refer to the period of economic recovery that followed the collapse of the Internet bubble as "The Great Moderation," because inflation, interest rates, and the volatility of financial markets were low. The credit meltdown was unexpected, and it has spawned conflicting prognostications ranging from deflation to hyperinflation. Unprecedented fiscal and monetary policy stimulation has been undertaken, but the possibility of hindering growth through higher taxation looms. For the first time in nearly a century, the possibility of a gold standard is imaginable, although remote in the eyes of the mainstream financial commentators. Support for it is already building internationally, not openly by world leaders but as evidenced by China's accumulations. Moreover, individuals are quietly amassing holdings of specie and ETFs. These actions are likely harbingers of a complete change in world finance that would occur once the pressure of excessive monetary growth, which paralleled the credit expansion prior to the crisis, would become impossible to restrain. At the same time, America faces external threats, and a "great moderation" of world peace could similarly be challenged. The Unites States and particularly the United Nations are unwilling to police the world or to develop human intelligence, to check the rise in military strength and nuclear capabilities of rogue nations, and they seem increasingly powerless to influence global political change that might swerve towards belligerence, hastened by economic weakness.

Should financial turmoil lead to the adoption of a gold-based monetary system, American fiscal and monetary policy would enter a new era of unprecedented vigorous growth, much as was the case following the resumption of 1879. The same could be said for the world. The Chinese would no longer hoard treasury securities; instead they could buy American goods. Likewise, importation and integration of trade with the Middle East would occur, too, if international accounts were forced to be settled up on an immediate basis. This brief chapter outlines the recent events and concerns with finance and an assessment of external threats considered together. It concludes that America need not fear the development of disturbing new events that could follow the moderation to which we have grown accustomed, as long as we stiffen our character and raise our consciousness to recognize the tremendous exposure to risk that has been built by our economic, legal, intelligence, and military policies.

## The End of Moderation

The pressures of integrating vast populations involved on the periphery of the world economy played an important role in the formation of the financial bubble at the turn of the millenia and the subsequent meltdown. World integration, while hardly new, accelerated greatly after the fall of the Berlin Wall. Probably within a half century it may be largely over, save for pockets around the globe that may remain backwards due to Islamic fundamentalism, communism, or despotism. Population growth, once a scare akin to global warming today, peaked at 2.4 percent in the 1960s in developing regions. While the first response of poor people to exposure to newfound wealth may be the instinct of procreation to provide for them in their old age, such customs die off. China once feared a population explosion, but within decades it will experience an aging demographic due to its one-child policy.

At first in 2008 Wall Street excitedly embraced the concept that Brazil, Russia, India, and China (the "BRIC" countries) could grow independently of the rest of the world, and in so doing maintain upward pressure on commodity prices. Despite the pressure from integration into the world capitalist system of former communist and socialist states global demand probably did not expand much more than population growth. Frank Veneroso, in a June 2007 presentation to the World Bank, meticulously established that consumption of commodities grew only about 2 percent in this cycle, but "apparent" demand was manipulated through parking physical stocks in China, for instance. He alleges that cheap capital, especially the leverage effect of OTC derivatives, hyper-charged the speculation.

The unusual movement of commodities in this cycle merely was a secondary effect of far deeper economic phenomena. Operating cen-trally controlled fiat currencies in nations throughout the world per-mitted the accumulation of massive trade imbalances, as well as the buildup of private and public debt throughout the developed world. The purchase of cheap goods from China and other low-wage coun-tries that were integrating poverty-stricken peoples into a manufactur-ing economy did not have to be settled by the exchange of goods or services in return. Nor did the provisioning of government services or the transfer of entitlements in the United States. A portion of our trading partners' export earnings poured into their local economies (by exchange with local scrip), where inflation became prevalent. U.S. dol-lars got channeled into purchases of world commodities like steel, copper, and oil, where price increases of mid-2008 defied prediction. These basic materials, including oil, are a small portion of the U.S. economy. During the boom, America enjoyed deflation in costs from imported items which embedded cheap labor, and also from immigration. Thus, consumer price inflation was successfully cordoned off into the world's backyard and safely kept out of America's. Until the financial meltdown began in late 2008, a stability of sorts existed, because the pain of having transferred wealth abroad was not matched by a decrease in wealth here. Specifically, differ-ences in international accounts have not been required to settle up since the world abandoned the gold standard in 1913 (replacing it with the gold exchange standard). Rather than feel impoverished by exchanging debt for imports, Americans felt wealthy because monetary expansion enabled tax-free extraction of cash from the rising value of residential real estate.

Monetary actions by the Fed (and other printers of the world's fiat currencies) were not factored in much to economic forecasts by finan-cial gurus until they were asked to explain why credit dried up and stocks collapsed. By the latter half of 2008 gold prices were closer to inflation-adjusted lows than highs. U.S. Treasuries reflected little fear of either inflation or the inability of the government to collect taxes at a significantly heightened rate structure, much less any urgency for doing so. The substantial money creation instigated by the Fed in late 2008 and 2009 might cause stagflation, a condition whose Cassandras are led by one John Williams, who publishes an alternative calculation of M3 and other economic indicators in his economic newsletter, *Shadow Government Statistics*. As of December 2008, Williams estimated that if the CPI-U, which placed inflation at just 0.1 percent, were measured using pre-Clinton methodology, it would be closer to 8 percent. Williams has also been pounding home the point that officially measured GDP is gamed to be larger than it actually is, because it is a calculation derived from nominal dollar output that is deflated by an intentionally under-estimated price deflator. Williams carefully tracks the watering down of the CPI-U by government bureaucrats through hedonic, geometric, substitution, owners' equivalent rent, and bogus seasonal adjustments to the official yardstick. He recalculates government statistics the way he believes they would have been reported before the process was gradually degraded through political intervention.

However, the amount of leverage in the private sector is unprecedented, so from the vantage point of late 2008 it looked like deflation would occur, a scenario that was ruled out by most prognosticators in March 2009 when the stock market rebounded from a plunge that started the year before. In fact by May the consensus swung to recognition of "green shoots" that a full-scale cyclical recovery was just around the corner. However, it was hard to imagine at that time that stability at a lower level of income would be capable of servicing the excessive debt accumulated in the last cycle. Eventually, the disruption to the world economy is likely to attenuate, not because of government fixes but in spite of them. As the financial system emerges from the malaise, world integration should resume, returning prosperity as long as socialism does not permanently distort the modern economy. In the medium-term government meddling is likely to repress output even if growth resumes, much like the "recovery" that occurred in the late 1930s. Moreover, deleveraging and preference of individuals and central banks to convert paper into gold could reveal weakness in the financial system far deeper than the stress tests of early 2009 did. This would force resolution of the imbalances that have built up, ushering in a system of robust, balanced world trade and healthy domestic savings.

## Barbarians at the Gate

After having cashed in the check from the peace dividend received when the Berlin Wall fell in late 1989, begrudgingly America has been brought back into conflict. The United States looked the other way when al Qaeda launched repeated, minor strikes in the 1990s, but we were forced briefly into a new perception of who our enemies were on September 11, 2001, when the nation was attacked in New York and at the Pentagon. With a weakened intelligence capacity, no one is completely sure whether Iran is on the brink of becoming a nuclear power, and it has pledged to destroy Israel. The Russian attack upon Georgia in 2008, although initially shrugged off by financial and commodity markets as inconsequential, may embolden this former enemy and signal the restart of another Cold War. Foreign policy has thus shifted from being an "unknown unknown," as Rumsfeld would say, to being a "known unknown." With an intelligence service that is not hamstrung by conferring Constitutional rights to alien combatants, from rights to trials in the U.S. justice system to blocking the monitoring of phone calls between aliens on foreign soil, less would be unknown.

Human intelligence, which is essential in the fight against terrorism, was decimated first by the Church Committee in 1975, the application of the Torricelli Principle (1995), and President Clinton's Directive 35. The Torricelli Principle requires all spy recruits to have a lily-white background, essentially sealing the CIA off from recruiting sources of information abroad. For example, obtaining knowledge of the importation of nuclear devices through Mexican drug tunnels or corrupt port workers is virtually impossible. The United States has little if any presence inside Iran, and Clinton as president placed the MEK, a shadow government group friendly to our intelligence gathering, on a watch list that precludes their being a source.

In the mid-1990s President Clinton issued Directive 35, which reduced the CIA's extension to the point that his director, John McLaughlin, testified to the Senate that his agency was "in Chapter 11." By 1995, only 25 new case officers a year graduated from the agency's training center known as "The Farm," while 2,000 terrorists per year were instructed at al Qaeda camps in Afghanistan.[1]

Fewer than 10 percent of CIA employees speak any foreign language, and only a handful of Arabic-speaking translators have classified clearance. In the past, with human intelligence spread too thin to corroborate anything, the agency has relied heavily upon agents such as "Curveball," who earned this nickname from CIA operatives because he supplied erroneous information. In his notorious *60 Minutes* appearance (April 23, 2006), Tyler Drumhelter said he relied upon this spy, yet he was championed by the liberal press as a whistleblower who alleges President Bush cherry-picked intelligence to support the case to invade Iraq.[2] Author Rowan Scarborough lays out the history of Curveball's revelations, as well as the claims of Drumheller, whom many in the CIA label a "pathological liar," in his excellent book, *Sabotage: America's Enemies Within the CIA.*[3]

Some downplay a threat on U.S. soil from al Qaeda, thinking that the organization's priority is to establish its authority on Muslim land. The argument is that another 9-11 would invite the U.S. invasion of tribal areas in Pakistan, perhaps a message relayed by the now deposed Musharraf. Yet a more disturbing conclusion is that bin Laden, with his fighters in Iraq in disarray, would not launch an attack that has a low death toll, because it would convey weakness in its comparison to 9-11. Al Zawahiri abandoned a chemical attack on the New York subway 45 days before it was to take place in March 2003, perhaps for this reason.[4] Journalist Paul Williams has tried to alert the public to the possibility of a nuclear suitcase bomb attack within the United States, but he says that given servicing requirements, a need for forward deployment, codification for detonation, site preparation, and the precise coordination with scattered cells necessary to attack with multiple nuclear suitcase bombs, it may take time to pull off such an audacious plot. Osama bin Laden's favorite verse from the Quran is "I will be patient until patience is outworn by patience." One of the few journalists to interview bin Laden, Hamid Mir, has published interviews that confirm that this group may indeed be keeping its powder dry for a truly devastating attack.

In 2008 a far-reaching U.S. Supreme Court ruling, if literally read, would completely undermine the essential function of soldiers in war nearly as effectively as replacing metal bullets with Nerf darts. The case conferred a citizen-like right to trial in the United States to nonuniformed enemy soldiers captured in battle. Using the justice system to conduct warfare against terrorists reduces the effective scale of combat. In more than a decade, legal prosecutions of terrorism acts have been pitifully low—numbering in the double digits. Moreover, they were conducted at a staggering taxpayer cost, compared with the efficient actions of killing tens of thousands of terrorists in Iraq.[5]

Pakistan has the potential to at some point succumb to Taliban influence with the ouster of Pervez Musharraf, although most Pakistanis clearly do not support fundamentalist terrorism. However, there is considerable disquiet among that country's populace, which was irritated by an inflation rate that was logged at 24.3 percent in July 2008. The country's current account deficit was 9 percent of GDP in 2007–2008, and its budget deficit was 7 percent of GDP (this would be roughly twice that of the United States). Pakistan's foreign exchange reserves fell from $16.5 billion in October 2007 to $9.9 billion on August 9, 2008. The Karachi 100 stock market index collapsed 44 percent through August from its all-time high in April, even before Musharraf had left office or the meltdown of global bourses had occurred. The Taliban's aggression in May 2009 was a natural consequence of a weakened financial condition in Pakistan.

The list of known unknowns seems to be growing larger each day, and it may be traceable to the self-destructive policies of the left that undermine national security. But one must also ask if the interaction of socialism and fiat currency has not weakened America such that our enemies may have calculated that America would face financial difficulty to gear up the sort of military force that would be necessary to fight in multiple hotspots. Is this not precisely what Ronald Reagan calculated when he initiated an arms race against the Soviets, knowing this would cause *their* fiscal instability? His timing could not have been better, given the washout of oil and other basic commodities that the Soviet Union's creaky economy could not withstand. Thinking that the worm had turned in favor of oil and other hard commodities, whose supply-demand imbalance might not have been rectified for years, what is to say that Vladimir Putin did not wager a similar gamble by invading Georgia, thinking turnabout is fair play? Moreover, the deep opposition to the Iraq war seen coming from the radical left is encouragement enough that building forces through a draft would be nigh impossible. However, the enemies' possible miscalculation here is that in the event our sovereignty, oil supply, or other strategic interest were in jeopardy, America's response would be strong and the red tape would quickly be cut.

What other known unknowns exist, military or otherwise? Many have been mentioned already. Russia's intrusion into Georgia probably presages the fall of other former satellite states should Russia regain its footing, and the Ukraine bears watching. It could also set up other confrontations, such as over Poland regarding its new missile pact, or even another Cuban missile crisis. Venezuala's dictator, Hugo Chavez, has bought $6 billion of sophisticated weapons from Russia and China and has formed links to Hizbollah and Hamas, so he could be working behind the scenes to promote a crisis. In a bid for Eastern European influence, Germany might ally with Russia concerning certain territorial spheres. But otherwise, Russia appears weak economically and demographically. China might overtake Taiwan, or even other Asian targets. Iran might flex its muscles, either directly or through its foreign force, Hezbollah. Any of these or other known unknowns might alter supply relationships for crude oil.

Financially there are many unknowns. Besides having our own problems with which to contend, the world's countries operate fiat currencies and have been universally lax with spending, debt, and entitlement programs. Unlike the United States, they do not enjoy the status of being the reserve currency of choice for other nations. A shove from the globalization of the credit crisis might trigger devaluations, runaway inflation, or national defaults. The success of the euro has been predicated upon countries exercising fiscal restraint (which has not been followed despite lip service that it has), including off-budget items such as entitlements, which are gaining visibility now that the demographic is aging nearly everywhere. In 2008, spreads on default insurance began to diverge for individual countries in the European Union. Comparing January 2009 with the previous September, credit swaps jumped from 51 basis points to 1.2 percent for Spanish sovereign debt, Greece increased from 1.6 percent to 2.4 percent, and Ireland rose more than seven-fold to 2.2 percent. This may be the wedge that pries apart the unified currency structure, and it may explain why the dollar and the yen resumed their steep ascent at year-end 2008.[6]

America is still quite strong, and most of its fiscal problems stem from entitlements, which might be reduced or eliminated. So it is possible that war might be financed and armies manned. But war usually causes debt and tax rates to increase. America is for the first time fragile on both accounts *before* facing such a crisis. We should heed the words of George Washington from his farewell address of 1796:

> As a very important source of strength and security, cherish public credit. One method of preserving it is to use it as sparingly as possible, avoiding occasions of expense by cultivating peace, but remembering also that timely disbursements to prepare for danger frequently prevent much greater disbursements to repel it, avoiding likewise the accumulation of debt, not only by shunning occasions of expense, but by vigorous exertion in time of peace to discharge the debts which unavoidable wars may have occasioned, not ungenerously throwing upon posterity the burden which we ourselves ought to bear. The execution of these maxims belongs to your representatives, but it is necessary that public opinion should co-operate.[7]

In his era, the Revolutionary War had caused debt to rise to $84 million in the year of his speech, and it had been climbing slightly in the previous five years (1791 is the earliest record kept by the U.S. Treasury) after having run up to finance the war. Washington's warning was indeed heeded, for the nation paid down its obligations to $45 million by 1812, enabling the young nation to resist a second British conflict by borrowing another $82 million by 1816. (It also built a strong Navy to resist the Muslim Barbary pirates, who impressed over one million on the high seas, condemning them to slavery in North Africa.) Twenty years later, the country would be essentially debt free. Washington goes on to say that as citizens we should be willing to accept taxation to pay down debt from unavoidable wars:

> To facilitate to them the performance of their duty, it is essential that you should practically bear in mind that towards the

payments of debts there must be revenue; that to have revenue there must be taxes; that no taxes can be devised which are
not more or less inconvenient and unpleasant; that the intrin-
sic embarrassment, inseparable from the selection of the proper
objects (which is always a choice of difficulties), ought to be a
decisive motive for a candid construction of the conduct of the
government in making it, and for a spirit of acquiescence in
the measures for obtaining revenue, which the public exigen-
cies may at any time dictate.[8]

Washington lived in a time when there was no income tax, much
less a progressive version. Hence he speaks of choosing "objects" to tax,
such as tea or stamps (which were affixed to items). His message to
accept taxation applies to the citizenry as a whole, not to a situation as
it exists today when the top 25 percent of earners pay 86 percent of all
income tax, which would have been unimaginable in his time.

Unlike the citizens of Rome who had no say about their level of
taxation, Americans could seize the moment and elect a slate of candidates that truly would abandon the formula of the last century, rather
than just tweak the dysfunctional structure of the present in a bipartisan compromise. The trajectory begun under Wilson and Roosevelt
has led to a bloated government structure with a fourth branch composed of unelected rule makers—yet another concept inconceivable in
Washington's time. Today's government spends heavily, and our elected
representatives within it compete for our vote by making promises to
spend at an ever-higher level, which has resulted in GAAP obligations
that are more than six times greater than the over $10 trillion of public
debt outstanding today. Such wanton extravagance is the polar opposite of what Washington advocated, and it is precisely the fallacy which
Lord Macaulay predicted.

As surely as the War of 1812 followed the Revolutionary War,
another threat from the known unknown of Islamic jihad could erupt, or
seemingly from out of the blue such as the Russian advance on Georgia.
And if it would not, as even the supposed bipartisans who thoughtfully
pontificated on the I.O.U.S.A. town hall panel admitted, the persistence
of entitlements and the debt they would perpetuate or grow at a reduced
rate would be immoral. What is missed in their argument is that we have

already crossed the Rubicon, for the magnitude of present levels of debt spread over the 25 percent who pay nearly all taxes would place them deeply into bankruptcy. The remaining majority of the citizenry that has shirked its civic obligation by egging on its representatives to dig surrounding our foundation will ultimately lose the most, for they may be condemning themselves or their children to lives of serfdom. It is a privilege to have democracy, for which the blood of Washington's soldiers was spilled. For the people to expend it by seizing it for socialistic aims is the veritable immorality of our times.

# Epilogue

There are two types of people who will read this book. One will feel empowered and may rediscover his civic duty. He is also likely to act by reallocating his investment choices, thinking he now has insight as to where we are headed. The second type of reader will feel somewhat impotent and overwhelmed by the changes at hand. But both camps of individuals have more in common with each other than they would like to admit.

You may wonder why, despite some strong observations, my musings on the future are couched in ambivalence. The reason is stated in the book's early chapters and reinforced throughout. As Nassim Nicholas Taleb and Friedrich Hayek point out, we are part of a much greater system. It is reactive and made up of people, many people, making decisions that influence each other's outcome. Think about some of the changes in history. Would Germany have instigated World War II without Hitler? Yes, there were other voices advocating racial purity and socialism in Germany after the First World War, and maybe another would have risen in his stead. Would the silver market have spiked as it did in 1980 without Bunker Hunt attempting to corner it? Who knows, but there aren't too many billionaires who get pulled in to one idea this deeply, unless they have delusions of either grandeur or financial suicide; there is a parallel with Hitler trying to corner the market for government in Europe maybe. Never before has one man—Soros—spent more money, $5 billion, to shape public opinion, much of it directed to "organize" local communities and influence the national media. What would have happened without this? Was his influence counteracted by another phenomenon, Rush Limbaugh? Didn't he singlehandedly rescue radio from oblivion and fashion it into a powerful megaphone to sway millions, loosening the liberal death grip on the dissemination of news and editorial opinion? In 2008, the arrival of an obscure politician, Governor Sarah Palin of Alaska, came close to changing the outcome of a national election at what may turn out to be a hinge point in our history more significant than 1913. What if she had never been born, perhaps aborted by a mother wanting to enjoy a social life or to hold out for Big, Harry Goldenblatt, or Trey, who might serve up a long driveway instead of the life of a spouse to an oil-field worker and commercial fisherman?

Since we are at best signal-men with only glimmers of the future, the most we might do is to rely upon a hunch or the insight of the material in this book and see a range of possibilities: America may degrade into an Argentinean experience, or the ship may right itself in the waters of a more spiritual cultural sea, or it could perhaps simply adopt the mores of the Roman republicans, honoring familia, virtus, and dignitas. Regardless, how the financial winds would swirl above that sea will never be precisely known in advance; the National Hurricane Center is far from perfect. I am in the business of investing money of institutions and the wealthiest individuals in the United States. Unlike the writers of doomsday financial books, I will not know how to bullet proof their portfolios from financial Armageddon. In the scenarios I weave in this book, stocks could drop precipitously as the investing public accepts the radically revised and weakened underpinnings of the monetary and fiscal systems. In that case, shorting equities would look smart. But if we reflate, as is likely, the Dow could very well go to 35,000. Just one small problem: Your next car might cost $175,000.

At the money management affiliate that I founded in 1995, just after year-end 2008 we had sizable short and long positions in equities, and similarly we were significantly invested in gold mining stocks. But by the time you read this book, our investment strategy may have changed from being fairly defensive to betting on a recovery, albeit one probably driven by monetization of debt. But given the generational rarity of witnessing a systemic financial meltdown, we would not be inclined to reinvest based upon models of recovery based upon the modern financial record. Rather, it is based upon the occurrence of substantial change. Company selection—our specialty—seeks to place us in strong, competitively advantaged firms likely to find opportunities amid turmoil, although as our disclaimer warns, past performance might not be indicative of future results. One thing seems certain. Since we may be entering a homolog of the Great Depression, we citizens will need to evolve differently to get out of it, and this will require searching within oneself for character instead of relying upon the tribe for protection, as if attacked by an outside invader. Godspeed to you on that journey.

## Policy Solutions

Some who read this in manuscript before its publication asked what solutions might I offer to get out of the current financial crisis? It's a natural and legitimate question, since by intent there was no specific chapter devoted to this topic. Some think of this book as just another rant against socialism, therefore a rejection of solutions that would involve extensive use of government. But sprinkled throughout the book are not-so-subtle hints of what actions to take and, equally important, which solutions could potentially prove harmful.

What is being missed by nearly everyone in Washington D.C. and by those on Wall Street who were fattened by the bubbles and lobbied hard for a bailout is that the cause of our problem is moral hazard. Moral hazard is an artificiality, a false signal that contravenes the working of the marketplace, for it severs the age-old relationship between risk and return. Borrowers and lenders will become ebullient or fearful, and they will always do so in tandem, never in opposition. About the only thing that can constrain excessive behavior is to promote the development of contrary thinkers at both extremes of the cycle.

We desperately need sound banks. There are none, despite what managements in this sector or stress testers will tell you. They all clustered at the edge of employing extraordinary leverage, both on and off their balance sheets, and they exposed themselves to nearly unquantifiable counterparty risk. They did so because government stepped in to insure deposits, and it preempted the role of safekeeping. The elastic nature of fiat currency intervention at the bottom of economic cycles transmitted a message that systemic risk did not exist any longer.

Yet at exactly this moment, government became least able to provide a backstop to deposits and counterparty failure, because it had leveraged its own balance sheet, whose debts are those of the people (the upper-middle class to be specific—since they are nearly exclusively called upon to fund government). Government also succumbed to moral hazard, for legislators felt they could propose and approve spending programs that would be enjoyed by a majority of citizens but be paid for by a smaller, separate group. Like the banker who shifted risk to government and retained the profit, an electoral majority clamored for more stuff: medical care, retirement income, education, lower mortgage payments and down payments, support for almost any social hardship imaginable, as long as somebody else was picking up the tab. It's like having a charge card whose bill goes to another person—not necessarily one such as a parent, who out of love would hold you accountable, but a faceless group in another tax bracket for whom you might even hold animosity for their success.

Separating the giving from the getting creates moral hazard. It takes almost inhuman moral fortitude to refuse the largesse. It is not a coincidence that both the private and public sectors would fall prey to moral hazard at exactly the same moment. It happened because our culture changed over the last century. Our ancient tribal instinct of collectivism returned. We turned away from acknowledgement that an economic and social system operates in another dimension far more complex than that which man can control, and we tinkered with it at our own peril.

The early Romans honored familia, virtus, and dignitas, but the later citizens of the Empire exalted the machinery of the state and fell from excessive hubris. History has shown that the regressive tax scheme of ancient Rome wiped out its middle class. If America crafts a bipartisan solution to the financial crisis, it is sure to have an even more progressive tax scheme that would eviscerate the middle class of today. The über-rich can and will take care of themselves, for their influence has been unmistakably great, in ancient Rome as well as in modern America.

Robert Schiller of Yale is one of our most credible observers of the financial situation, for his gift of insight that the Internet bubble and later the real estate bubble would end badly was remarkable. So what wisdom does he offer? He says our financial system failed to practice "enlightened risk management," encouraging people to borrow heavily against their life savings to buy houses. He therefore recommends giving different advice to people engaging in the mortgage process, and planning ahead with them through writing into their contracts how a loan would be modified in the event monthly payments could not be made. Such a mortgage would be called the "continuous workout mortgage," and it would not cost more than a regular one, because it would have reduced foreclosure costs, and it would benefit society through reducing the pain of "neighborhood effects." New and better government agencies would improve upon Great Depression solutions, offering insurance for default. In his words, his solution would, just like the innovation of moving from three- and five-year mortgages to 30-year loans, advance us out of the Stone Age of real estate finance.

One would think that super-bright professors like Schiller would understand moral hazard. Surely he is familiar with the concept, but this solution brushes it aside in the most condescending terms. If he thought moral hazard were an important ingredient in the crisis, he would know it would never be the case that a speculating public could be met by bankers consistently counseling less usage of the commodity they sell. In every major up-cycle, willing lenders supplied other people's money—deposits—to willing borrowers. Animal spirits of bull markets run in herds. How would a "continuous workout mortgage" not invite default, and why would it ultimately not develop into a system where large financial institutions become REITs that rent real estate to tenants month after month—ultimately dooming the middle class to lose title to its lands through subtle changes in legal definition just as happened in ancient Rome? Schiller once had enormous vision to see that the great Internet craze was a giant bubble. But today he sees the financial mess too narrowly. It is a subprime problem. Like modern liberals who believe socialism failed in the past only because it had not yet been perfected or expanded adequately, Schiller's viewpoint of evolutionary finance believes the penetration of finance into the fabric of the economy is an advancement that failed because it was not innovated upon adequately. Instead, the financial calamity begun in 2008 is broader, an infection of both the monetary and the fiscal regimes; it is moral hazard.

Still, you say I offer the reader no solution. But the sad truth is that asking what my solution is reveals a subconscious denial that the answer is everywhere in this book. If we continue to run with the herd and not demonstrate character or exercise self-discipline, we will prescribe more of the same medicine: higher taxes, bigger transfer payments, more crowding out of the private sector by government, more regulation, absorption of more lending risk, and big business favored over small business. How can we escape the conceit of thinking we can solve our own problems from the top down? What feeds character and self-discipline, our innate tools for doing the job right? Was not religion devised to remind us that we are weak and fall prey to our own desires? Does it not try to awaken us to a higher, more complex logic that by our nature we can never completely understand? If we reject humanism, relativism, and the urge to play God and arrange layer upon layer of intricate rules and laws that become our own undoing, then a simple gift results: The beauty of our condition is that once we submit ourselves to respect others and not envy them, there is a natural tendency for betterment and harmonious behavior.

So now, with great humility, I offer some thoughts for solutions. I place these before you with sadness, because with our culture having decayed and hubris and condescension never having been so palpable, surely they are far less likely to be followed than the great ideas of the Schillers of the world. We need strong banks. Not behemoths that cannot be allowed to fail. Small ones, medium-sized ones, inevitably some large ones. If deposits are known to be at risk in banks generally, then bank managements will resume the role of safekeeping. Not to compete for depositors based upon safety would risk a migration of deposits to safer competitors. Stop encouraging large semi-weak banks to take over large weak banks, with the Fed providing a backstop for these transactions. Instead let these more poorly run banks fail. For a time, print money to make good on deposits and accounts held at these banks and brokers. It's only fair, because there have been no safe financial institutions for people to use, thanks to bad governmental policy. Eventually, close down the SIPC and the FDIC. Remove the tax loss carry forwards of the large banks, for with those in place along with refreshed balance sheets no small, sound bank could possibly compete against them. As bad banks fail, money will be printed in accommodation, lots of it. While this riles the libertarian sensibility, morally it is reprehensible that a populace trained for nearly 100 years to entrust deposits to banks should be impoverished as if they had been duped by Bernie Madoff.

The taxpayer should never again be called upon to subsidize anything other than government's duty as originally enumerated in the Constitution: national defense, border security, yes; entitlements, no. Of course, those who are old and dependent should still be taken care of. But phase it out—all of it—according to a preannounced timetable. With a dramatically shrunken government, there will be less need for taxes. But there will still be an overhang from past debt and entitlements (even if they are reduced), which vastly exceeds the capability for their servicing by those in today's top brackets.

The printing of money used to replenish the financial system may cause inflation—whether or not this series of radical measures is adopted. It will monetize public and private debt, and the key to not letting the surge in inflation become embedded permanently will be the taking of a credible stance to redraw our system with reduced liability going forward. While we are printing money, our government should quietly (if possible) buy gold with which it would promise to redeem dollars beginning at some point when our economic recovery is certain. No doubt this would be at a price that might shock the world today: perhaps $5,000, $10,000, or higher. Let the market bracket the possibilities; perhaps gold ETFs or digital gold accounts such as those at goldmoney.com would be our new private currency, and we could get out of the money-printing business once and for all.

Taxes, like death, are inevitable. But they do not have to be destructive and pit one element of society against another. The current system of having Warren Buffett pay 17 percent and the upper-middle class owe 35 percent plus another 5 to 10 percent to state government is unacceptable.

Some have proposed a flat tax on income or consumption. These suggestions are intriguing and should be considered. But for millennia mankind has instead existed with wealth taxes. One's gross assets would be subject to tax, so the use of leverage, which today is used in a fiat currency environment to perpetually defer the payment of taxes by the über-wealthy, would become very unappealing. The result would be less leverage, ergo less systemic risk. With income taxed 0 percent at the margin, an incentive to produce would be unleashed unlike anything seen since the age of Augustus, when Roman prosperity reached its zenith. Fairness would also result, just as long as strong limits on progressivity or regressivity were codified, because no longer would the über-wealthy be able to minimize W-2 or ordinary income and extract cash through borrowing against constantly appreciating assets.

There would also need to be a plethora of other changes, mostly to dismantle the chokehold regulation has on much of the economy—such as the farcical cancerous growth rates of financial regulators who could neither anticipate nor control what may go down in history as the largest financial meltdown of our nation. Yes, there are some very appealing aspects of regulation: safe drugs, prevention or at least prosecution of outright financial fraud, and certain environmental protections. Keep them; jettison everything else. Moreover, craft a new apparatus that harnesses the creativity and millions of hours that independent research analysts might perform to reveal risk and gauge opportunity for investment in everything from stocks, bonds, commodities, credit ratings, off balance sheet conduits, investment advisors, broker-dealers, you name it. To do this, firms that engage in corporate finance and trading (banks and broker-dealers) would be strictly prohibited from being in the research business. Moreover, publicly traded companies and these banks and broker-dealers would not be allowed to pay independent firms for research. They would be paid either directly by investors, small and large, or through directed commission flow from mutual funds or other accounts managed for them. Those disbursements, in turn, should be disclosed and transparent. To aid their work, securities-issuing companies would be required to make much greater disclosure of the things these analysts need to look at, such as off balance sheet structured vehicles. The SEC could reexamine its mission thusly and get creative about what that might be. Such a system would cost almost nothing. It would provide gainful employment for many laid-off Wall Streeters (not that anyone cares!). And it would uncover more fraud than an army of technocrats looking for documentation of every move financial industry employees make.

I can say with 100 percent certainty that these solutions would not even come close to seeing the light of day in today's fractious political environment. At the moment, we are in the midst of a civil war of ideas. Great concepts such as the abolition of slavery or the establishment of our democracy were born out of conflict—literally armed conflict. The one silver lining above this struggle is that like other transformative events, World War II for example, it will touch all of us together, which opens up the possibility of some unanimity of opinion. All that is needed is a two-thirds majority. Another is that it should not come to mortal blows as true war would. The greatness of America has been its ability to come together in adversity and to recall great ideals that were immortalized by our founders. We were not descended from kings, emperors, or pharaohs. Our strength is in each other. If we can reclaim our moral clarity, we may resume our path to the great destiny that inspired us over two centuries ago.

But casting these solutions as moral is sure to infuriate the humanists, secularists, and socialists among us. It begs another issue raised in the book, that those who would use government as an agent to rearrange society feel they are in sole possession of morality and that the capitalists are heartless. As this is being written today, the fix is nearly in. The Fed has begun to print money that is monetizing federal debt and mortgages. It may not be adequate to produce enough nominal income to make servicing debt that reached nearly four times GDP easy. Additional waves of printing might be politically necessary, although it is highly unlikely we would go to the extreme seen during the Civil War or under the French National Assembly of the 1790s. In the French experience, money transformed from hard to soft, sewing the seeds of temporary affluence that gave way to economic ruin. Consider what happened at the end of the 18th century in that country:

> ... there appeared another outgrowth of this disease . . . This outgrowth was a vast debtor class in the nation, directly interested in the depreciation of the currency in which they were to

pay their debts. The nucleus of this class was formed by those who had purchased the church lands from the government. Only small payments down had been required and the remainder was to be paid in deferred installments: an indebtedness of a multitude of people had thus been created in the hundreds of millions.... these were speedily joined by a more influential class;—by that class whose speculative tendencies had been stimulated by the abundance of paper money, and who had gone largely into debt looking for a rise in nominal values. Soon demagogues of the viler sort in the political clubs began to pander to it; a little later important persons in this debtor class were to be found integrating in the Assembly—first in its seats and later in more conspicuous places of public trust. Before long, the debtor class became a powerful body extending through all ranks in society.... All were apparently able to demonstrate to the people that in new issues of paper lay the only chance for national prosperity. This great debtor class, relying on the multitude who could be approached by superficial arguments, soon gained control ... while every issue of paper money really made matters worse, a superstition gained ground among the people at large that, if only enough paper money were issued and were cunningly handled the poor would be made rich. Henceforth all opposition was futile.[1]

The Fed has encouraged banks to print in large quantities since its inception. After the Internet bubble burst, it stepped up the pace of the printing press, which bestowed an opulence across the country through the real estate boom in particular. Rather than admit M3 growth was out of control (over 8 percent since 1970, and surprisingly 10.6 percent year-over-year in December 2008), it chose to ignore it and eventually even stop reporting it.[2] The elites who are above the grip of the gluttonous taxes on ordinary income and estates in the United States have a huge vested interest in continuance of the fiat money system operated at the hands of a central bank, for it enables profit to uniquely accrue through appreciation rather than through income. Furthermore borrowing against the buildup of wealth allows cash to be extracted without taxation.

The French wound up breaking and burning their printing presses on the 18th of February, 1796, at nine o'clock in the morning. They made a brief comeback, but the era ended shortly thereafter. When Napoleon Bonaparte took over, government debt remained high and taxes could not be raised. When asked how he would pay for the expenses of government, including his army, he replied "I will pay cash (meaning specie) or pay nothing." It took 40 years for the French economy to recover.

So what would the best solution for the United States be? Moving back to a simpler government organization, a fairer and less onerous tax mechanism, and a harder currency that must be settled up makes sense to me, but somehow these ideas are off the table in our national discussion. Still, somehow we need to make good on the most essential of our promises: to depositors not offered safe banks, to the poorest of the elderly who need medical attention. I have offered a solution that may be immoral, for it contemplates something akin to the French National Assembly's first infusion of 400 million livres worth of assignats to accommodate those caught in the crosshairs of our collapsing socialist system. Have I thus done what Google's founders did when they were a party to Chinese oppression and censorship, justifying this by weighing evil on a scale? Perhaps. But this is why I simultaneously propose certain measures to remove us from this hell into which we placed ourselves.

We need to promise that never again will we let ourselves get this deeply into debt, confiscate the estates of the middle class, or let money supply growth outpace what is needed to maintain normal real economic growth. Once enough money is printed to not let deposits fail, a gold-backed currency would fulfill this pledge. George Washington was right. We must settle up our accounts promptly. Quoth Shakespeare's Polonius: "Neither a borrower nor a lender be." The cracks in the house that credit built, or houses that credit built if you prefer, are showing. This is a chance for a renewed national discussion of fundamental governmental banking principle; we should do everything we can to escape the folly of socialism and promote the reestablishment of a nation as Washington and his peers envisioned.

# Notes

**Chapter 1: Unknown Unknowns**

1. Grant's Interest Rate Observer (New York).
2. John Brooks, *The Go-Go Years* (New York: Weybright and Talley, 1973), 218–221.
3. Lou Barnes, "FED Gets It: Credit Crisis Trumps Inflation," *Inman News*, August 29, 2008, http://www.inman.com/buyers-sellers/columnists/loubarnes/fed-gets-it-credit-crisis-trumps-inflation.
4. Eugenia Levinson, "Bill Miller: Toughest Market I've Seen," *Fortune*, August 1, 2008, http://money.cnn.com/2008/07/31/news/companies/miller_levenson.fortune/index.htm?postversion=2008080107.
5. Bill Miller's Letter to Investors, taken from Eugenia Levinson, "Bill Miller: Toughest Market I've Seen," *Fortune*, August 1, 2008, http://money.cnn.com/2008/07/31/news/companies/miller_levenson.fortune/index.htm?postversion=2008080107.
6. Daniel F. Cuff, "For Chemcapital Head, New Role, New Risks," *New York Times*, June 17, 1987.
7. 2008 Ibbotson Stocks, *Bonds, Bills, and Inflation Classic Yearbook* (Chicago: Morningstar, Inc., 2008), 27, 29.
8. Ibid., 299.
9. John Brooks, *The Go-Go Years* New York: Weybright and Talley, 1973, 153

10. U.S. Department of Defense, Public Affairs, *DoD News Briefing—Secretary Rumsfeld and Gen. Myers* (February 12, 2002).

11. Nassim Nicholas Taleb,. *The Black Swan: The Impact of the Highly Improbable* (New York: Random House, 2007), xix, 152–53, 156.

12. Ibid., 154.

13. Art Lindsley, *C.S. Lewis's Case for Christ: Insights from Reason, Imagination, and Faith* (Downer's Grove, IL: InterVarsity Press, 2005), 19, 41.

**Chapter 2: Wings of Wax**

1. Anthony S. Kline, *Ovid's Metamorphoses, Book VIII* (2000), http://etext.virginia.edu/latin/ovid/trans/Ovhome.htm.

2. Franklin Raines, Testimony before a House subcommittee in late 2004, http://www.youtube.com/watch?v=_MGT_cSi7Rs.

3. Dean P. Foster and H. Peyton Young, *The Hedge Fund Game: Incentives, Excess Returns, and Piggy-Backing*, November 2007, http://knowledge.wharton.upenn.edu/papers/1352.pdf.

4. James B. Kelleher, "Buffett's 'Time Bomb' Goes Off on Wall Street," *Reuters*, September 18, 2008, http://www.reuters.com/article/newsOne/idUSN1837154020080918.

5. International Swaps and Derivatives Association (ISDA) Market Survey June 30, 2008.

6. Ibid.

7. William C. Powers Jr. et al. Report of Investigation, Special Investigative Committee of the Board of Directors of Enron Corp., February 1, 2002, 23.

8. Malcom Gladwell, "The Formula: Enron, Intelligence, and the Perils of Too Much Information," *The New Yorker*, January 8, 2007.

9. Bill Gross, Beware Our Shadow Banking System, *Fortune*, November 28, 2007.

10. David Reilly, A Way Charges Stay Off Bottom Line, *Wall Street Journal*, April 21, 2008.

11. Yalman Onaran, Banks Keep $35 Billion Markdown Off Income Statements (Update1), *Bloomberg*, May 19, 2008.

12. Harry Marcopolos, *The World's Largest Hedge Fund is a Fraud*, November 7, 2005. Copies circulate on various Internet sites, including http://www.berniemadoffsec.com/the-worlds-largest-hedge-fund-is-a-fraud.html.

13. Nassim Nicholas Taleb, *The Black Swan: The Impact of the Highly Improbable* (New York: Random House, 2007), 229–252. A sprightly discussion of this is in *The Black Swan's* Chapter 15: "The Bell Curve, That Great Intellectual Fraud."

14. Zillow, *The Majority of U.S. Homeowners Thinks Their Home is Insulated From the Housing Crisis* (August 6, 2008), http://zillow.mediaroom.com/index.php?s=159&item=64.

## Chapter 3: The Rise and Fall of Hard Money

1. Laurence H. Meyer, *Remarks by Governor Laurence H. Meyer*, December 5, 2001, www.federalreserve.gov/boarddocs/speeches/2001/20011205/default.htm.

2. Murray N. Rothbard, *The Case Against the Fed* (Auburn, AL: Ludwig von Mises Institute, 1994), 42.

3. Ibid., 30.

4. Michael David Bordo, "The Classical Gold Standard: Some Lessons for Today," *Federal Reserve Bank of St. Louis*, May 1991, 5.

5. Sidney Homer, *A History of Interest Rates* (New Brunswick, NJ: Rutgers, the State University of New Jersey, 1963, 1977), 29.

6. Murray N. Rothbard, *A History of Money and Banking in the United States: The Colonial Era to World War II* (Auburn, AL: Ludwig von Mises Institute, 2002), 52–54.

7. Ibid., 54.

8. Farley Grubb, "Benjamin Franklin and the Birth of a Paper Money Economy," *Federal Reserve Bank of Philadelphia*. Essay based upon speech of March 30, 2006, http://www.philadelphiafed.org/education/ben-franklin-and-paper-money-economy.pdf.

9. Murray N. Rothbard, Conceived in Liberty, Volume III, *Advance to Revolution 1760–1775*, Mises Institute, Auburn AL, 1999, 44–45, 67.

10. Mark, Skoosen, *The Completed Autobiography of Benjamin Franklin*, Washington D.C., Publishing, Regnery 2006, pp. 39–43.

11. Murray N. Rothbard, *A History of Money and Banking in the United States: The Colonial Era to World War II* (Auburn: Ludwig von Mises Institute, 2002), 59–61.

12. Ibid., 62–63, 70.

13. Howard Bodenhorn, *State Banking in Early America: A New Economic History*, New York, Oxford University Press, 2003, 15.

14. Ibid.

15. Murray N. Rothbard, *A History of Money and Banking in the United States: The Colonial Era to World War II* (Auburn: Ludwig von Mises Institute, 2002), 73–76.

16. Thomas Perkins Abernethy, *The Formative Period in Alabama 1815–1828*, The University of Alabama Press, Revised Edition 1965 (Original 1922), 6.

17. Ibid., 86–89.

18. Ibid., 101. Rothbard cites a 1935 book by Reginald McGrane, *Foreign Bondholders and American State Debts*.

19. Howard Bodenhorn, *State Banking in Early America: A New Economic History* (New York: Oxford University Press, 2003), 148–153.

20. Murray N. Rothbard, *A History of Money and Banking in the United States: The Colonial Era to World War II* (Auburn: Ludwig von Mises Institute, 2002), 112–113.

21. Murray N. Rothbard, *The Case Against the Fed* (Auburn, AL: Ludwig von Mises Institute, 1994), 75.

22. Murray N. Rothbard, *A History of Money and Banking in the United States: The Colonial Era to World War II* (Auburn: Ludwig von Mises Institute, 2002), 141–148.

23. Ibid., 150–156.

24. J. Laurence Laughlin, *The History of Bimetallism in the United States* (New York: D. Appleton & Company, 1885), 75.

25. Geoffrey Wheatcroft, *The Randlords: The Exploits & Exploitations of South Africa's Mining Magnates* (New York: Atheneum, 1986), 120.

26. Murray N. Rothbard, *A History of Money and Banking in the United States: The Colonial Era to World War II* (Auburn, AL: Ludwig von Mises Institute, 2002), 157–158.

27. Ibid., 66, 157.

28. Ibid., 159–166.

29. Ibid., 189.

30. Ibid., 158–59.

31. Ibid., 160.

32. R.F Bruner and S. D. Carr, *The Panic of 1907: Lessons Learned From the Market's Perfect Storm* (Hoboken, NJ: John Wiley & Sons, 2007), 58.

33. James Grant, *Money of the Mind* (New York: Farrar Straus Giroux, 1992), 46, 63, 117–118.

34. Murray N. Rothbard, *A History of Money and Banking in the United States: The Colonial Era to World War II* (Auburn, AL: Ludwig von Mises Institute, 2002), 209.

35. Ibid., 46, 63, 117–118.

36. Ibid., 211.

37. Timothy Green, "Central Bank Gold Reserves: An Historical Perspective Since 1845," *World Gold Council*, November 1999, 17.

38. Lawrence H. Officer,, *Gold Standard*, EH.Net Encyclopedia, http://eh.net/encyclopedia/article/officer.gold.standard.

39. Timothy Green, "Central Bank Gold Reserves: An Historical Perspective Since 1845," *World Gold Council*, November 1999, 17.

40. W. Arthur Lewis, *Economic Survey 1919–1939* (London: George Allen and Unwin Ltd., 1949), 21, 25.

41. John Maynard Keynes, *The Economic Consequences of the Peace* (New York: Harcourt, Brace & Howe, 1920), 229.

42. Lewis, W. Arthur, *Economic Survey 1919–1939* (London) George Allen and Unwin Ltd., 1949, 49.

43. W. Arthur Lewis, *Economic Survey 1919–1939* (London: George Allen and Unwin Ltd., 1949), 32, 47.

44. Benjamin M. Anderson, "Cheap Money, Gold, and Federal Reserve Bank Policy," *Chase Economic Bulletin*, 4, no. 3, (August 4, 1924), 1–2, 5.

45. Emily S. Rosenberg, *Financial Missionaries to the World: The Political and Culture of Dollar Diplomacy, 1900–1930* (Durham and London: Duke University Press, 2003), 171–174.

46. W. Arthur Lewis, *Economic Survey 1919–1939* (London: George Allen and Unwin Ltd., 1949), 35, 39.

47. Murray N. Rothbard, *A History of Money and Banking in the United States: The Colonial Era to World War II* (Auburn, AL: Ludwig von Mises Institute, 2002), 401–406.

48. Ibid., 356–359.

49. W. Arthur Lewis, *Economic Survey 1919–1939* (London: George Allen and Unwin Ltd., 1949), 32–33, 98.

50. Timothy Green, "Central Bank Gold Reserves: An Historical Perspective Since 1845," *World Gold Council*, November 1999, 13–14.

**Chapter 4: Flat Earth Economics**

1. Undoubtedly some would claim that the existence of one data point that is apparently anomalous (1929–1940) is suspect, but in reality this is a cluster of 11 years. It would likely be joined by another cluster post-2008 if money supply is allowed to shrink. However, far more likely will be considerable debt monetization that would more than offset falling velocity of money. In that case, if the theory that money supply growth is best for real growth when maintained at a moderate pace is to hold, then under that scenario the ex-ante claim would expect a new data point to present itself lower and farther to the right along the downward slope of the curve. Of course, should the Fed succeed in dialing in just the right amount of money supply in the wake of the 2008 panic, real growth would resume. This would probably still require a prodigious quantity

of federal debt to be monetized, resulting in high nominal (inflationary) economic growth. Many, such as those in the Austrian School, posit that the printing of money through direct monetization cannot stimulate this outcome of strong real growth. They are probably correct; therefore the most likely scenario is a cluster of years at one or the other tail of the distribution.

2. J. Laurence Laughlin, *The History of Bimetallism in the United States* (New York: D. Appleton and Company, 1885), 115–6.

3. Ibid., 122.

4. Sidney Homer, *A History of Interest Rates* (New Brunswick, NJ: Rutgers, the State University of New Jersey, 1963), 318.

5. Table H.6 Money Stock Measures, *Federal Reserve Statistical Release*, http://www.federalreserve.gov/releases/h6/. Estimates by Shadow Government Statistics.

6. Bob McTeer, "The Fed's Balance Sheet," *Forbes*, October 29, 2008.

7. Paul Comly French, "$3,000,000 Bid for Fascist Army Bared," *Philadelphia Record*, November 20, 1934.

8. Jules Archer, *The Plot to Seize the White House* (New York: Hawthorn Books, 1973), 139.

9. Ibid., 9.

10. Franklin Roosevelt, *Executive Order Number 6102*, April 5, 1933.

11. Robert R. Prechter, *Conquer the Crash* (Gainesville, GA: Elliott Wave International, 2002), 213.

12. *Historical Statistics of the United States: Colonial Times to 1957*, Series X 285–298 Currency in Circulation, by Kind: 1860–1957 (U.S. Department of Commerce, 1960), 648. Specie in 1925 was $718 million compared to M2 of $42 billion.

13. *Historical Statistics of the United States: Colonial Times to 1970*, Series X 410–419 Money Stock-Currency Deposits, Bank vault Cash, and Gold: 1867–1970 (U.S. Department of Commerce), 992.

14. W. Arthur Lewis, *Economic Survey 1919–1939* (London: George Allen and Unwin Ltd., 1949), 92, 94, 95.

15. Robert Higgs, "Higgs on the Great Depression," *Library of Economics and Liberty*, December 15, 2008, www.econtalk.org/archives/2008/12/higgs_on_the_gr.html.com.

16. Robert Higgs, "Wartime Prosperity? A Reassessment of the U.S. Economy in the 1940s," *The Journal of Economic History* (March 1, 1992), Table 4: Alternative Estimate of Real Personal Consumption per Capita.

17. Robert Higgs, "Higgs on the Great Depression," *Library of Economics and Liberty*, December 15, 2008, www.econtalk.org/archives/2008/12/higgs_on_the_gr.html.com.

18. W. Arthur Lewis, *Economic Survey 1919–1939* (London: George Allen and Unwin Ltd., 1949), 113

19. Ben S. Bernanke, *Money, Gold, and the Great Depression*, Speech to the Federal Reserve Board, March 2, 2004, http://www.federalreserve.gov/boarddocs/speeches/2004/200403022/default.htm.

20. Ehsan U. Choudhri and Levis A. Kochin, "The Exchange Rate and the International Transmission of Business Cycle Disturbances: Some Evidence from the Great Depression," *Journal of Money, Credit, and Banking*, 12, no. 4 (November 1980): Part I, 565–574.

21. Michael D. Bordo and Barry Eichengreen, "The Rise & Fall of a Barbarous Relic: The Role of Gold in the Monetary System," *Essays in Honor of Robert Mundell* (Cambridge, MA: MIT Press, 2000), 6.

22. Lawrence H. Officer,, *Gold Standard*, EH.Net Encyclopedia, http://eh.net/encyclopedia/article/officer.gold.standard.

23. Sidney Homer, *A History of Interest Rates* (New Brunswick, NJ: Rutgers, the State University of New Jersey, 1963, 1977), 560

24. W. Arthur Lewis, *Economic Survey 1919–1939* (London: George Allen and Unwin Ltd., 1949), 48, 65.

25. Stanley G. Payne, *A History of Spain and Portugal, Vol. 2*, http://libro.uca.edu/payne2/spainport2.htm.

26. Sven-Olof Olsson, "*Nordic Trade Policy in the 1930s*," (paper presented at the XIV International Economic Congress, Helsinki, Finland, August 21–25, 2006, Session 91) http://www.helsinki.fi/iehc2006/papers3/Olsson.pdf.

27. W. Arthur Lewis, *Economic Survey 1919–1939* (London: George Allen and Unwin Ltd., 1949), 86.

28. Sven-Olof Olsson, "*Nordic Trade Policy in the 1930s*," (paper presented at the XIV International Economic Congress, Helsinki, Finland, August 21–25, 2006, Session 91) http://www.helsinki.fi/iehc2006/papers3/Olsson.pdf.

29. Barry Eichengreen and Jeffrey Sachs, *Exchange Rates and Economic Recovery in the 1930s*, National Bureau of Economic Research, Working Paper #1498, November 1984, 2–3.

30. Belgium devalued March 30, 1934, otherwise it would rest precisely on the regression line. Just before devaluation it lost 2,360 million francs worth of gold, but this loss was minor compared to its accumulations in the preceding years. It would keep accumulating gold after the devaluation.

31. James Fallows, "Be Nice to the Countries that Lend You Money," *The Atlantic*, December 2008.

32. Steve Stroth and Jessica Brice, "China May Add 4,000 Tons to Gold Reserves, Guangzhou Daily Says," *Bloomberg*, November 19, 2008.

33. James Fallows, "Be Nice to the Countries that Lend You Money," *The Atlantic*, December 2008.

34. Barry Eichengreen and Peter Temin, "The Gold Standard and the Great Depression," *National Bureau of Economic Research*, June 1997, 2. Eichengreen's best know work is *Golden Fetters: The Gold Standard and the Great Depression, 1919–1939* (1992) and Temin's is *Did Monetary Forces Cause the Great Depression?* (1976).

35. Barry Eichengreen and Kris Mitchener, *The Great Depression as a Credit Boom Gone Wrong*, May 2003, 26.

36. Ibid., 23–24.

37. William, Greider, *Secrets of the Temple: How the Federal Reserve Runs the Country*, (New York: Simon and Schuster, 1987), Chapter 2: In the Temple.

38. Barry Eichengreen and Kris Mitchener, *The Great Depression as a Credit Boom Gone Wrong*, May 2003, 49–50.

39. Michael D. Bordo and Barry Eichengreen, "The Rise & Fall of a Barbarous Relic: The Role of Gold in the Monetary System," *Essays in Honor of Robert Mundell* (Boston: MIT Press, 2000), 13.

40. Ibid., 3.

41. Michael D. Bordo and Anna J. Schwartz, "Transmission of Real and Monetary Disturbances Under Fixed and Floating Exchange Rates," *Cato Journal*, 8, no. 2 (Fall 1988), 452.

42. Ibid., 468.

43. Irving Fisher, "Fisher Doubts Market Crash," *New York Times*, September 6, 1929.

44. Murray N. Rothbard, *A History of Money and Banking in the United States: The Colonial Era to World War II* (Auburn, AL: Ludwig von Mises Institute, 2002), 303.

45. Giovanni Pavanelli, "The Great Depression in Irving Fisher's Thought," *Universita di Torino* (December 2001): 6–10.

46. Ibid., 13.

47. David L. Porter, "Ramseyer's Battle for Monetary Reform," *University of Iowa*, (April 1981), http://www.lib.uiowa.edu/spec-coll/Bai/porter.htm.

48. Alain Pilote, "Social Credit in the United States in 1932," *The Michael Journal*, September–October 1996.

49. Giovanni Pavanelli, "The Great Depression in Irving Fisher's Thought," *Universita di Torino* (December 2001): 15–16.

## Chapter 5: Spitting Into the Wind

1. Irving Fisher, "The Debt Deflation Theory of Great Depressions," *Econometrica* (March 1933): 339.

2. Ben S. Bernanke, *Deflation: Making Sure "It" Doesn't Happen Here*, November 21, 2002, http://www.federalreserve.gov/BOARDDOCS/SPEECHES/2002/20021121/default.htm.

3. Ibid.

4. John Cassidy, "Anatomy of a Meltdown," *The New Yorker*, December 1, 2008, http://www.newyorker.com/reporting/2008/12/01/081201fa_fact_cassidy. Quoted from Ben Bernanke's speech to the Federal Reserve Board, "Asset Price Bubbles and Monetary Policy," October 15, 2002, http://www.federalreserve.gov/boarddocs/speeches/2002/20021015/default.htm.

5. Ibid.

6. "Assets, Liabilities, and Net Worth of U.S. Commercial Banks, Thrift Institutions and Credit Unions as of June 30, 2002" (latest available data as of August 19, 2008), *Federal Financial Institutions Examination Council, Annual Report 2002*, http://www.ffiec.gov/PDF/annrpt02.pdf.

7. Charles I. Plosser, "The Financial Tsunami and the Federal Reserve," Federal Reserve Bank of Philadelphia, December 2, 2008, http://www.philadelphiafed.org/publications/speeches/plosser/2008/12-02-08_university-of-rochester.cfm.

8. "Assets and Liabilities of Commercial Banks in the United States (H.8)," Federal Reserve Statistical Release, January 2, 2009, http://www.federalreserve.gov/releases/h8/.

9. *Forbes*, April 8, 2008.

10. Yalman Onaran, "Banks' Subprime Losses Top $500 billion on Writedowns" (Update 1), *Bloomberg*, August 12, 2008, http://www.bloomberg.com/apps/news?pid=20601087&sid=a8sW0n1Cs1tY&.

11. Eric Martin and Rhonda Schaffler, "Roubini Sees Worst Recession in 40 Years, Stock Drop" (Update 3), *Bloomberg*, October 14, 2008, http://www.bloomberg.com/apps/news?pid=20601087&sid=asxXHEAn1glc&refer=home#.

12. "BB&T Chief Executive Slams Bailout Plan," *Business First of Louisville*, September 26, 2008, http://louisville.bizjournals.com/louisville/stories/2008/09/22/daily53.html.

13. Minutes of the Federal Open Market Committee, December 15–16, 2008, pp. 5, 8, 9, http://www.federalreserve.gov/monetarypolicy/files/fomcminutes20081216.pdf.

14. Before it went under, Lehman claimed it had reduced leverage from the high 20s to the low 20s (evident in actual balance sheet 10Q disclosure). Several other banks made this same claim immediately after the September forced government investment in their preferred shares. Although preferred shares are a form of equity, they behave much like unsecured debt.

15. Irving Fisher, "The Debt Deflation Theory of Great Depressions," *Econometrica* (March 1933): 341.

16. Kris Hollington, "Lost in Space," *Fortean Times*, July 2008, http://www. forteantimes.com/features/articles/1302/lost_in_space.html#.

**Chapter 6: Moral Hazard**

1. Shocking Video Unearthed Democrats in Their Own Words Covering Up the Fannie Mae, Freddie Mac Scam That Caused Our Economic Crisis, YouTube.com, accessed April 30, 2009, http://www.youtube.com/watch?v=_MGT_cSi7Rs.

2. Emergency Order Pursuant to Section 12 (k)(2) of the Securities Exchange Act of 1934 Taking Temporary Action to Respond to Market Developments, SEC Release No. 34–58592 (September 18, 2008) http://www.sec.gov/rules/other/2008/34–58592.pdf. Shortly later the list was expanded to 898 firms.

3. Although Cramer has not managed money in recent years, purportedly his hedge fund performed well during previous years before he devoted himself to public appearances.

4. Bill Gross, "There's a Bull Market Somewhere?," *Investment Outlook, PIMCO,* September 2008, http://www.pimco.com/LeftNav/Featured1Market1Com mentary/IO/2008/Investment1Outlook1Bill1Gross1Sept120081Bull1Marke t.htm. Accessed September 10, 2008.

5. Paul McCulley, "In the Fullness of Time," *Global Central Bank Focus, PIMCO,* September 2008, http://www.pimco.com/LeftNav/Featured1Market1Com mentary/FF/2008/Global1Central1Bank1Focus1McCulley1Sept120081In1t he1Fullness1of1Time.htm. Accessed September 10, 2008.

6. TheStreet.com, *Inc.*, Free Encyclopedia of Ecommerce, http://ecommerce. hostip.info/pages/985/Thestreet-Com-Inc.html.

7. Blogger IrvineRenter, "Rudolph the Red-Nosed Reindeer," Irvine Housing Forums, comment posted November 27, 2007, http://www.irvinehousing-blog.com/blog/comments/rudolph-the-red-nosed-reindeer/.

8. *Summary of Deposits,* FDIC, http://www2.fdic.gov/sod/pdf/ddep_2008.pdf.

9. Rebecca Wilder, "TARP: Totally Aggravating for Reasonable People," October 3, 2008, http://www.newsneconomics.com/2008/10/tarp-totally-aggravating-reasonable.html.

10. *2008 Ibbotson Stocks, Bonds, Bills, and Inflation Classic Yearbook* (Chicago: Morningstar, Inc., 2008), 31.

11. "The Out of Control Tax Code," Don't Mess With Taxes weblog, April 17, 2008. Information sourced from the CCH Standard Federal Tax Reporter, a

Walters Kluwer business. http://dontmesswithtaxes.typepad.com/dont_mess_with_taxes/2008/04/the-out-of-cont.html.

12. Limbaugh, Rush, *Who Do You Trust?*, Opening Monologue: September 25, 2008, http://www.rushlimbaugh.com/home/daily/site_092508/content/01125108.guest.html.

13. Ibid.

14. Andy Kessler, "The Paulson Plan Will Make Money for Taxpayers," *Wall Street Journal*, September 25, 2008, http://online.wsj.com/article/SB122230704116773989.html?mod=googlenews_wsj.

15. Rush, Limbaugh, *Who Do You Trust?*, Opening Monologue: September 25, 2008, http://www.rushlimbaugh.com/home/daily/site_092508/content/01125108.guest.html.

16. *Rush Limbaugh Show*, Hour Two, December 17, 2008.

17. Donald Lambro, "GOP Aims For New Economic Agenda," *The Washington Times*, November 23, 2008.

## Chapter 7: The Rich Are Different From You and Me

1. More often the above is misquoted with the glib follow-on that the rich are different because they have more money, an actual conversation attributed to Hemmingway but more properly to a literary reviewer of the time, Mary Colum.

2. Sidley Austin LLP website, http://www.sidley.com/tax_derivatives/. Accessed September 17, 2008. Italics and bold added by author.

3. Wikipedia, "Bernardine Dorn," http://en.wikipedia.org/wiki/Bernardine_Dohrn, accessed October 15, 2008.

4. International Swaps and Derivatives Association (ISDA) Market Survey June 30, 2008. "US Credit – Lehman Threatens CDS Market With First Real Test," *Reuters*, September 14, 2008, http://www.reuters.com/article/rbssInvestmentServices/idUSN1472586720080915.

5. James Wesley, "Derivatives – The Mystery Man Who'll Break the Global Bank at Monte Carlo," Survival Blog website, http://www.survivalblog.com/derivatives.html.

6. A very important driver of the economics of the insurance industry are tax preferences. Life insurance premiums accrue income tax free, subsidizing their use as an investment vehicle in competition with traditional investment products. Annuities can be structured to remove assets from students or seniors seeking to obtain government subsidies for health care costs and tuition. In these transactions, income is realizable in amounts over time that would be low enough to enable applicants to qualify for subsidies but high enough over future periods that students or seniors would be willing to exchange their

assets for them. Public demand for annuities also is strong among individuals seeking to avoid the death tax, but a close examination of such a strategy can show that it still may be preferable to structure one's estate to invest in high-return equities that can be placed into trusts to lock in the exclusion before appreciation occurs.

7. Mollenkamp, Carrick, "UBS Move Will Affect U.S. Clients," *Wall Street Journal,* July 18, 2008.

8. Rachel Breitman and Del Jones, "Should Kids be Left Fortunes, or Be Left Out?" *USA Today,* July 26, 2006.

9. Dwight Garner, "The Season of the Heirheads," *New York Times,* November 16, 2003, http://query.nytimes.com/gst/fullpage.html?res=940DE4D71F39 F935A25752C1A9659C8B63.

10. See the opening paragraph of the "American Dream" section for calculation of the tax burden on lifetime income.

11. Phil Kent, *Foundations of Betrayal: How the Liberal Super Rich Undermine America* (Johnson City, TN: Zoe Publications, 2007), 37–38.

12. Ibid., 27.

13. Ibid., 47–65.

14. Ibid., 17–18.

15. Ibid., 47–65.

16. Ibid., 20–22.

17. Ibid., 35.

18. The Open Society Institute is tax exempt under Section 501(c)(3). The Open Society Policy Center (OSPC) is "a non partisan public policy organization organized under Section 501(c)(4)."

19. "George Soros: The Man, The Mind, And The Money Behind MoveOn," *Investor's Business Daily,* September 20, 2007, http://www.ibdeditorials.com/ ibdarticles.aspx?id=275181103776079.

20. S.S.M., "*Wash. Times Op-ed Expanded on O'Reilly's False Attacks on Soros and Media Matters,*" May 9, 2007, http://mediamatters.org/items/200705090002?f=s_search

21. Ibid.

22. Michelle Malkin, "The Democrat Party Platform's Hidden Soros Slush Fund," August 20, 2008, http://michellemalkin.com/2008/08/20/ the-democrat-party-platforms-hidden-soros-slush-fund/.

23. O'Reilly Factor, Interview with Howard Wolfson, Fox News Channel, July 30, 2008.

24. MoveOn.org, from http://www.moveon.org/ and https://pol.moveon.org/ obamabuttons/?rc=homepage, accessed July 30, 2008.

25. Jeff Birnbaum, "Rove Urges Donations to Non-GOP Attack Groups," *The Washington Times*, September 8, 2008.

26. "George Soros: The Man, The Mind, And The Money Behind MoveOn," *Investor's Business Daily*, September 20, 2007, http://www.ibdeditorials.com/ibdarticles.aspx?id=275181103776079.

27. John Fund, "Obama's Liberal Shock Troops," *Wall Street Journal*, July 12, 2008, Page A11.

28. Sol Stern, "ACORN's Nutty Regime for Cities," *City Journal*, Spring 2003.

29. *Top 50 Federally Focused Organizations*, Center for Responsive Politics, http://www.opensecrets.org/527s/527cmtes.php?level=C&cycle=2004.

30. William Baker, *Study of Fortune 100 Donors to 527 Groups*, Commissioned through the Center for Responsive Politics, September 2008.

31. Michelle Malkin, "Kill the Bailout: More ACORN Funding?!," September 26, 2008, http://michellemalkin.com/2008/09/25/kill-the-bailout-more-acorn-funding/.

32. Congressman John Culberson, "*Glen Beck: Fed Up*," October 13, 2008, http://www.glennbeck.com/content/articles/article/196/16704/.

**Chapter 8: Sharecroppers**

1. Estimates above are based upon the author's analysis of actual tax rates. A thorough analysis of the total tax burden can be found at the Tax Foundation web site, http://www.taxfoundation.org/taxdata/.

2. When one makes between $360,000 and $5 million, the average rate falls below the marginal rate by about 10 percent. The range presented above tries to capture this effect, so its low end overstates the government take by a few percentage points but the high end accords the maximum benefit.

3. U.S. Census Bureau, http://www.census.gov/hhes/www/income/income06/statemhi2.html

4. IRS Selected Income and Tax Items, 2006, http://www.irs.gov/pub/irs-soi/06in11si.xls

5. TreasuryDirect, U.S. Treasury, http://www.treasurydirect.gov/govt/reports/pd/pd.htm.

6. "Budget Deficit in 2008 Hits New All-Time High," CBS/Associated Press, October 14, 2008, http://www.cbsnews.com/stories/2008/10/14/business/main4522293.shtml.

7. IRS, Individual Income Tax Returns with Itemized Deductions: Sources of Income, Adjustments, Itemized Deductions by Type, Exemptions, and Tax Items, by Size of Adjusted Gross Income, Table 2.1 Tax Year 2006, http://www.irs.gov/pub/irs-soi/06in21id.xls.

8. U.S. Treasury per table from the Tax Policy Center, http://www.taxpolicyc-enter.org/taxfacts/Content/PDF/distribution_taxes_2000.PDF.

9. U.S. Treasury, Fact Sheet: *Who Pays the Most Individual Income Taxes?*, March 2, 2005.

10. "Returns with Positive Adjusted Gross Income (AGI): Number of Returns, Shares of AGI and Total Income Tax, etc. Tax Years 1986–2005," Internal Revenue Service, http://www.irs.gov/pub/irs-soi/05in05tr.xls, accessed August 19, 2008.

11. U.S. Census Bureau, http://www.census.gov/hhes/www/income/income06/statemhi2.html.

12. IRS Selected Income and Tax Items, 2006, http://www.irs.gov/pub/irs-soi/06in11si.xls.

13. *Boston Globe,* Editorial Board interview, October 11, 2007.

## Chapter 9: The Heart of the Financial System

1. Marcus Junianus Justinus, *Epitome of the Phillippic History of Pompeius Trogus*, translated by the Rev. John Selby Watson (London: Henry G. Bohn, York Street, Covent Garden, 1853).

2. *Federal Financial Institutions Examination Council, Annual Report 2002*, Assets, Liabilities, and Net Worth of U.S. Commercial Banks, Thrift Institutions and Credit Unions as of June 30, 2002 (latest available data as of August 19, 2008), http://www.ffiec.gov/PDF/annrpt02.pdf.

3. Damian Palea, Jon Hilsenrath and Deborah Solomon, "At Moment of Truth, U.S. Forced Big Bankers to Blink," *Wall Street Journal*, October 15, 2008, http://online.wsj.com/article/SB122402486344034247.html.

4. Stan Liebowitz, "The Real Scandal: How Feds Invited the Mortgage Mess," *New York Post*, February 5, 2008.

5. Countrywide Credit Investor Conference Call, July 24, 2007, p. 13. John McMurray SMD, chief risk officer: "There is s belief by many that prime FICOs stop at 620. That is not the case. There are affordability programs and Fannie Mae, expanded approval, as an example, that go far below 620, yet those are still considered prime. Documentation and leverage are also impor-tant factors. So if you have the existence of one of these high risk factors or the combination of several of these factors in a prime loan, it is going to exhibit higher delinquencies."

6. Office of Federal Housing Enterprise Oversight (OFHEO), *Report of the Special Examination of Fannie Mae*, May 2006, Updated January 2008. p. i.

7. Ronald Utt, "Time to Reform Fannie Mae and Freddie Mac," *Heritage Foundation Backgrounder No. 1861* (June 20, 2005): 3.

8. Susan Davis, "McCain Attacks Obama on Ties to Former Fannie Mae CEOs," *Wall Street Journal,* September 19, 2008, http://blogs.wsj.com/wash-wire/2008/09/19/mccain-attacks-obama-on-ties-to-former-fannie-mae-ceos/.

9. Office of Federal Housing Enterprise Oversight (OFHEO), *Report of the Special Examination of Fannie Mae,* May 2006, updated January 2008, 2.

10. "Shocking Video Unearthed Democrats In Their Own Words Covering Up the Fannie Mae, Freddie Mac Scam That Caused our Economic Crisis," YouTube, September 26, 2008, http://www.youtube.com/watch?v=_MGT_cSi7Rs.

11. Ronald Reagan, Inaugural Address, January 20, 1981, http://www.reaganfoundation.org/reagan/speeches/first.asp.

12. Ronald Utt, "Time to Reform Fannie Mae and Freddie Mac," *Heritage Foundation Backgrounder No. 1861* (June 20, 2005): 8.

13. Particularly those not represented on the inflation-adjusted chart reviewed earlier, which were above the $16 million of annual income measured in 2007 equivalent dollars.

14. Justin Fox, "Fannie, Freddie, Ginnie Now Account for 130% of Mortgage Lending in U.S.," Time Magazine Blog. http://time-blog.com/curious_capitalist/2008/07/fannie_freddie_ginnie_now_acco.html.

15. *The State of the Nation's Housing,* Joint Center for Housing Studies of Harvard University, July 2008.

**Chapter 10: A Return to Malaise**

1. *Public Debt Reports,* TreasuryDirect, U.S. Treasury, http://www.treasurydirect.gov/govt/reports/pd/pd.htm.

2. M. De Vlieghere and P. Vreymans, "Europe's Ailing Social Model: Facts & Fairy Tales," *Brussels Journal,* March 23, 2006.

3. *Promises, Promises: A Fiscal Voter Guide to the 2008 Election,* Committee for a Responsible Federal Budget, August 2008, updated August 29, 2008, 5, http://www.usbudgetwatch.org/files/crfb/usbw082908promises.pdf.

4. Daniel John Zizzo and Andrew Oswald, *Are People Willing to Pay to Reduce Other's Incomes?* Oxford University, July 2, 2001.

5. IRS, Selected Income and Tax Items, 2006, http://www.irs.gov/pub/irs-soi/06in11si.xls. The effective average tax rate hits a peak and rests at about 24 percent for brackets between $500,000 and $5,000,000 of adjusted gross income less deficit. For those who report over $10,000,000, their effective average tax rate is only 20 percent, reflecting the diminished contribution of ordinary income. Thus, the second $5,000,000 of a $10,000,000 earner's reported income would need to be taxed at 16 percent to bring down the average rate to 20 percent, which is just about equal to the 15 percent long-term capital

gains rate. Once one gets above the strata of small businessmen, few therefore choose to monetize their earnings through directly flowing through income. They would, however, need to convert their S-corporations into C-corporations, which are subject to a 35 percent tax; another approach would be to use offshore entities.

6. In the years 2005-2007, Berkshire Hathaway averaged paying just 25 percent of its pretax earnings to governments for taxes (Source: Berkshire Hathaway 2007 SEC Form 10K).

7. Jimmy Carter, Crisis of Confidence Speech, July 15, 1979, http://www.pbs. org/wgbh/amex/carter/filmmore/ps_crisis.html.

8. Paul Volcker, Speech to the Economic Club of New York, New York City, April 8, 2008.

## Chapter 11: Democracy: The Achilles' Heel of Capitalism?

1. Russell Kirk, Speech at the Heritage Foundation, July 14, 1987.

2. Laura Ingraham, *Power to the People* (New York: Regnery Publishing, 2007), 135–6.

3. Adolfo Sturzenegger and Ramiro Moya, "Economic Cycles," in *A New Economic History of Argentina*, Paolera and Taylor (Eds.). (New York: Cambridge University Press, 2003).

4. W. Mark Crain, "The Impact of Regulatory Costs on Small Firms," *Small Business Research Summary*, Number 264, September 2005, p. 1. http://www. sba.gov/advo/research/rs264tot.pdf.

5. Bill Bonner, "Eternal City, Chronic Rubble," *The Daily Reckoning*, May 7, 2008, http://dailyreckoning.com/eternal-city-chronic-trouble/.

## Chapter 12: From the Golden Era to Totalitarianism

1. Gaius Sallustius Crispus, *Conspiracy of Cataline*, translated by Rev. John Selby Watson, 1867.

2. Cullen Murphy, *Are We Rome? The Fall of an Empire and the Fate of America* (New York: Houghton Mifflin Company, 2007), 38–39.

3. F. A. Hayek, *The Fatal Conceit: The Errors of Socialism* (Chicago: The University of Chicago Press, 1988), 43.

4. Keith Hopkins, "Taxes and Trade in the Roman Empire (200 BC–AD 400)," *The Journal of Roman Studies*, 70 (1980): 106.

5. Ibid.

6. H.J. Haskell, *The New Deal in Old Rome*, (New York: Alfred A. Knopf, Inc., 1939), 29.

7.  Hopkins, Keith, Taxes and Trade in the Roman Empire (200 B.C. – A.D. 400), *The Journal of Roman Studies*, Vol. 70 (1980), 102–109.

8.  Jean Andreau, *Banking and Business in the Roman World* (New York: Cambridge University Press, 1999), 39–40, 131–132, 146.

9.  Ibid., 136

10. Bruce Bartlett, "How Excessive Government Killed Ancient Rome," *The Cato Journal*, 14, no. 2 (Fall 1994), http://www.cato.org/pubs/journal/cjv14n2–7.html.

11. H.J. Haskell, *The New Deal in Old Rome*, (New York: Alfred A. Knopf, Inc., 1939), p. 85.

12. Ibid., p. 83.

13. Keith Hopkins, Taxes and Trade in the Roman Empire (200 BC–AD 400), *The Journal of Roman Studies*, Vol. 70 (1980), 106–110.

14. H.J. Haskell, *The New Deal in Old Rome*, (New York: Alfred A. Knopf, Inc., 1939), p. 187.

15. Ibid., p. 20.

16. Ibid., p. 124.

17. Gaius Sallustius Crispus, *Conspiracy of Catialine, and The Jugurthine War*. Literally translated with explanatory notes by Rev. John Selby Watson, 1867. Intro by Edward Brooks ([1896]).

18. Bruce, Bartlett, *How Excessive Government Killed Ancient Rome, The Cato Journal*, Volume 14 Number 2, Fall 1994. http://www.cato.org/pubs/journal/cjv14n2-7.html.

19. Julian Fenner, *To What Extent Were Economic Factors to Blame for the Deterioration of the Roman Empire in the Third Century?*, 7, http://www.roman-empire.net/articles/article-018.html.

20. Ibid.

21. Ibid.

22. Bruce Bartlett, "How Excessive Government Killed Ancient Rome," *The Cato Journal*, 14, no. 2 (Fall 1994), http://www.cato.org/pubs/journal/ cjv14n2-7.html.

23. Cullen Murphy, *Are We Rome? The Fall of an Empire and the Fate of America* (New York: Houghton Mifflin Company, 2007), 100.

24. Douglas C. Smyth, "Why the Ruling Ideology Makes Me Do It," www.roman-empire-america-now.com.

25. Julian Fenner, *To What Extent Were Economic Factors to Blame for the Deterioration of the Roman Empire in the Third Century?*, 10, http://www.roman-empire.net/articles/article-018.html.

## Chapter 13: Other Perspectives

1. But note that a vomitorium is in actuality a passage situated below or behind seats of an amphitheatre into which an audience exits at the end of a performance. Myth has it the Romans had such "rooms" for relief of drunken excesses.

2. Julian, Fenner, *To What Extent Were Economic Factors to Blame for the Deterioration of the Roman Empire in the Third Century?*, 9, http://www.roman-empire.net/articles/article-018.html.

3. Cullen Murphy, *Are We Rome? The Fall of an Empire and the Fate of America* (New York: Houghton Mifflin Company, 2007), 31.

4. Peter Heather, "Why Did Rome Fall? Its Time for New Answers," History News Network, George Mason University, July 16, 2007, http://hnn.us/articles/40538.html.

5. Keith, Hopkins, "Taxes and Trade in the Roman Empire (200 B.C.–A.D. 400)," *The Journal of Roman Studies*, 70 (1980), 101–125.

6. *Zimbabwe Inflation Hits 11,200,000 Percent*, CNN.com/World Business, http://edition.cnn.com/2008/BUSINESS/08/19/zimbabwe.inflation/?iref=mpstoryview.

7. *Population Historic/Projections Africa 1950–2050*, GeoHive, http://www.geo-hive.com/earth/his_proj_africa.aspx.

8. The web site www.roman-empire-america-now.com is an extensive collection of writings from Douglas C. Smyth, who integrates his commanding knowledge of the Roman Empire with his deeply socialistic beliefs. An interesting read for those attempting to understand the socialist perspective on the topic.

9. Cullen Murphy, *Are We Rome? The Fall of an Empire and the Fate of America* (New York: Houghton Mifflin Company, 2007), 106–107.

10. Ibid., 108–116.

11. Thomas Sowell, *Economic Facts and Fallacies* (New York: Basic Books, 2008), 9.

12. Cullen Murphy, *Are We Rome? The Fall of an Empire and the Fate of America* (New York: Houghton Mifflin Company, 2007), Chapter Two: The Legions.

13. HS is used to account for large sums; technically it is the Sesterius, a coin containing 25 grains of orichalcum, which equaled 4 denarii, which held 3.8 grains of silver content under Augustus. A excellent reference of Roman currency containing conversion tables, history, and explanations is available at a web site "Roman Currency of the Principate" hosted by Tulane University, http://www.tulane.edu/~august/handouts/601cprin.htm.

14. Keith Hopkins, "Taxes and Trade in the Roman Empire (200 B.C.–A.D. 400)," *The Journal of Roman Studies*, 70 (1980): 116–120.

15. Base Structure Report Fiscal Year 2007 Baseline, Department of Defense, http://www.defenselink.mil/pubs/BSR_2007_Baseline.pdf.

16. *Active Duty Military Personnel Strengths by Regional Area and by Country (309A) June 30, 2007*, Department of Defense, http://siadapp.dmdc.osd.mil/person-nel/MILITARY/history/hst0706.pdf.

17. Cullen Murphy, *Are We Rome? The Fall of an Empire and the Fate of America* (New York: Houghton Mifflin Company, 2007), 73–4. Murphy credits Edward Luttwak, senior advisor at the Center for Strategic and International Studies, for analysis of Roman military strategy in his book, *The Grand Strategy of the Roman Empire: From the First Century A.D. to the Third* (Baltimore: Johns Hopkins Press, 1978).

18. Ibid., 67.

19. Branko Milanovic, *Roman Empire 14 CE – A Social Table*, November 10, 2007, http://gpih.ucdavis.edu/files/Roman_Empire_14CE.pdf.

20. *NATO Handbook*, 2006, p. 247, http://www.nato.int/docu/handbook/2006/hb-en-2006.pdf.

21. Rabbi Daniel Lapin, *Genesis Journeys: Tower of Power*, Audio CD 2008, rabbi-daniellapin.com.

22. "Free Concert by Popular Band Preceded Obama's Big Rally," *Free Republic*, May 20, 2008, http://www.freerepublic.com/focus/f-news/2018898/posts. Also: "Germans LOVE a Free Rock Concert!," *No Quarter*, July 27, 2008, http://noquarterusa.net/blog/2008/07/27/200000-germans-love-a-free-rock-concert/. Left out of the press reports of the large Obama crowds was mention of popular bands The Decemberists (Seattle) and Reamonn (Berlin).

**Chapter 14: Bending to the Modern World**

1. C.S. Lewis, *An Experiment in Criticism*, (New York: Cambridge University Press), 105–106, 1961.

2. The Federal Reserve balance sheet is published weekly at http://www.federalreserve.gov/releases/h41/.

3. James Grant, *Money of the Mind* (New York: Farrar Straus Giroux, 1992), 124–125.

4. R.F. Bruner and S.D. Carr, *The Panic of 1907: Lessons Learned From the Market's Perfect Storm* (Hoboken, NJ: John Wiley & Sons, Inc., 2007), 182–183. References *Money Trust Investigation: Hearings, I*, p. 1084, U.S. Government.

5. F.A. Hayek, *The Fatal Conceit: The Errors of Socialism* (Chicago: The University of Chicago Press, 1988), 90.

6. Emily S. Rosenberg, *Financial Missionaries to the World: The Politics and Culture of Dollar Diplomacy*, 33.

7. Emily S. Rosenberg, *Financial Missionaries to the World: The Politics and Culture of Dollar Diplomacy* (Durham & London: Duke University Press, 2003), 21, 24, 77, 154.

8. Walter Isaacson, *Einstein: His Life and Universe* (New York: Simon & Schuster, 2007), 278.

9. F. A. Hayek, *The Fatal Conceit: The Errors of Socialism* (Chicago: The University of Chicago Press, 1988), 53–4.

10. Ronald J. Pestritto, *Woodrow Wilson and the Roots of Modern Liberalism* (Lanham, MD: Rowman & Littlefield Publishers, 2005), 232.

11. The Founders' Constitution, Volume 1 Chapter 18, Document 6, http://press-pubs.uchicago.edu/founders/documents/v1ch18s6.html.

12. Herbert, London, *America's Secular Challenge: The Rise of a New National Religion* (New York: Encounter Books, 2008), 10. James Burnham as quoted by Herb London.

13. Ibid., 94.

14. Ibid., 76–77.

15. Julie Bykowicz, "Jury Study Raises Hackles in City," *Baltimore Sun*, August 18, 2008.

16. Grover Norquist, *Leave Us Alone: Getting the Government's Hands Off Our Money, Our Guns, Our Lives*, (New York: Harper Collins Publishers, 2008), 36.

17. F. A. Hayek, *The Fatal Conceit: The Errors of Socialism* (Chicago: The University of Chicago Press, 1988), 57.

18. D'Sousa, Dinesh, Speech at CPAC, February 7, 2008.

19. Herbert, London, *America's Secular Challenge: The Rise of a New National Religion* (New York: Encounter Books, 2008), 80.

## Chapter 15: Self-Indulgence

1. Dierdre McCloskey, *The Bourgeois Virtues: Ethics for a Capitalist Age* (Chicago: University of Chicago Press, 2006), 195–196.

2. Centers for Disease Control and Prevention, Data from two NHANES surveys (1976–1980 and 2003–2004), http://www.cdc.gov/nccdphp/dnpa/obesity/childhood/prevalence.htm, accessed August 12, 2008.

3. Prevalence of Overweight and Obesity Among Adults: United States, 2003–2004, National Center for Health Statistics, http://www.cdc.gov/nchs/products/pubs/pubd/hestats/overweight/overwght_adult_03.htm, accessed August 12, 2008.

4. Countrywide Credit Investor Conference Call, July 24, 2007, p. 13.

5. Cullen Murphy, *Are We Rome? The Fall of an Empire and the Fate of America* (New York: Houghton Mifflin Company, 2007).. Excerpt from http://www.npr.org/templates/story/story.php?storyId=11074833.

6. American Gaming Association, Gaming Revenue: 10-Year Trends, www.americangaming.org/Industry/factsheets/statistics_detail.cfv?id=8.

7. IRS, *Taxpayers with Individual Retirement Arrangement (IRA) Plans, by Size of Adjusted Gross Income*, Tax Year 2004, http://www.irs.gov/pub/irs-soi/04in02ira.xls.

8. Laura Belfer, *City of Light* (New York: Random House, 1999).

9. Mary Mitchell, "Madonna's Adoption," *Chicago Sun-Times*, October 26, 2006, http://blogs.suntimes.com/mitchell/2006/10/madonnas_adoption_1.html.

10. Brigitte Zimmerman, "Orphan Living Situations in Malawi: A Comparison of Orphanages and Foster Homes," *The Review of Policy Research*, November 1, 2005.

11. *Facts on Induced Abortion in the United States*, Guttmacher Institute, July 2008, http://www.guttmacher.org/pubs/fb_induced_abortion.html.

12. National Right to Life, http://www.nrlc.org/abortion/facts/abortionstats2.html.

13. Laura Ingraham, *Power to the People* (Washington, DC: Regnery Publishing, 2007), 342–343.

14. Kay Hymowitz, *Marriage and Caste in America: Separate and Unequal Families in a Post Marital Age*, Speech at The Heritage Foundation, January 30, 2007, http://www.heritage.org/press/events/ev013007a.cfm.

15. Paul Kantner, Grace Slick, Marty Balin & Gary Blackman, Jefferson Starship, "Hijack," from *Blows Against the Empire*, 1970.

16. *Facts on Sexually Transmitted Infections in the United States*, Guttmacher Institute, August 2006, http://www.guttmacher.org/pubs/fb_sti.html.

17. David Caruso, "Manhattan Leads Single-Living Trend," *Associated Press / Washington Post*, September 3, 2005, http://www.washingtonpost.com/wp-dyn/content/article/2005/09/02/AR2005090202189.html.

18. Andrew Beveridge, "Women of New York City," *Gotham Gazette*, March 20, 2007, http://www.gothamgazette.com/article/demographics/20070320/5/2126.

19. David Caruso, "Manhattan Leads Single-Living Trend," *Associated Press / Washington Post*, September 3, 2005, http://www.washingtonpost.com/wp-dyn/content/article/2005/09/02/AR2005090202189.html.

20. U.S. Census Bureau, Income, Poverty, and Health Insurance Coverage in the United States: 2006.

21. Walter E. Williams, http://www.gmu.edu/departments/economics/wew/.

**Chapter 16: The New Commandments**

1. David Dickson, "The SEC 'Has Been Grievously Hurt,'" *Washington Times*, March 30, 2009, 17.

2. Veronique deRugy and Melinda Warren, Regulatory Agency Spending Reaches New Height: An Analysis of the U.S. Budget for Fiscal Years 2008 and 2009, Annual Report, August 2008, Mercatus Center George Mason University and Weidenbaum Center, Washington University, 6.

3. Alexis De Tocqueville, *Democracy in America*, Volume II, Book 4, Chapter 6(1835).

4. Will Park, "2010 Census Goes High Tech With Data-Only HTC 'Census' GPS Smartphone," *IntoMobile*, April 4, 2007.

5. Jonah Goldberg, *Liberal Fascism: The Secret History of the American Left From Mussolini to the Politics of Meaning* (New York: Doubleday, 2007), 294–5.

6. Marianne Lavelle, "Can Industry Spread its Green Fever?: General Electric Puts New Focus on Global Warming," *U.S. News & World Report*, May 29, 2005, http://www.usnews.com/usnews/biztech/articles/050606/6warm.htm.

7. GE 2007 Proxy Statement, Shareowner Proposal Number 7: Global Warming Report, http://www.ge.com/ar2006/proxy/sprop7.htm.

8. "Businesses Favor Global Warming Regulation: Three Quarters See Business Opportunity," *The Daily Green*, December 3, 2007, http://www.thedailygreen.com/environmental-news/community-news/business-global-warming-66120301.

9. *Top Firms call for Climate Action*, Environmental Defense Fund, May 8, 2007, http://www.edf.org/article.cfm?contentID=5828.

10. Amy Menefee, "*Wal-Mart: Always Under Attack. Always*," *Business & Media Institute*, February 22, 2006, http://www.businessandmedia.org/news/2006/news20060222.asp.

11. Jonah Goldberg, *Liberal Fascism: The Secret History of the American Left From Mussolini to the Politics of Meaning* (New York: Doubleday, 2007), 294–295, 303–304.

12. Ibid., 305.

13. Dan Jamieson, "Broker-dealers Hurting for Pros in Compliance," *Investment News*, September 18, 2006, http://www.investmentnews.com/apps/pbcs.dll/article?AID=/20060918/SUB/609180730/1009/TOC&ht=&template=printart.

14. Sara Hansard, "Bank-Compliance Costs Soar, Says Study," *Investment News*, January 14, 2008, http://www.investmentnews.com/apps/pbcs.dll/ article?AID=/20080114/REG/805128168/1094/INDaily03&ht=.

15. Sara Hansard, "Compliance Costs Soar," *Investment News*, July 21, 2008, http://www.investmentnews.com/apps/pbcs.dll/article?AID=/20080721/REG/ 486077376/1024&ht=.

16. *Study Tracks Cost of Sarbanes Oxley*, Pensions & Investments, August 2, 2007, http://www.pionline.com/apps/pbcs.dll/article?AID=/20070802/DAILY/ 70802012/1034/PIDAILYMM.

17. Mark Landler, "U.S. Credit Crisis Adds Gloom to Norway," *New York Times*, December 2, 2007, http://www.nytimes.com/2007/12/02/world/europe/02norway.html?pagewanted=1.

18. Pierre Lemieux, *The Idea of America* (Alberta, Canada: The Western Standard, Calgary, 2008), Part I, 6.

19. *Putting Investors First*, http://www.finra.org/InvestorInformation/Investor Protection/PuttingInvestorsFirst/index.htm, and *2007 Performance and Accountability Report*, Securities & Exchange Commission, p. 28, http://www.sec.gov/about/secpar/secpar2007.pdf#sec1.

20. 2007 FINRA Year in Review and Annual Financial Report, p. 9, and 2000 NASD Annual Financial Report, p. 14.

21. "Small Firms Need Voice At Trade Group," *Investment News*, November 20, 2006.

22. Andrew Coen, "Brokerage Firms Win Fewer Suits Against FINRA," *Investment News*, June 2, 2008.

23. *2007 Performance and Accountability Report*, Securities & Exchange Commission, p. 27, http://www.sec.gov/about/secpar/secpar2007.pdf#sec1.

24. FINRA BrokerCheck Report #96756-83014 generated August 14, 2008.

25. Stephen Labaton, "Named to Head S.E.C., and Named in Lawsuits," *New York Times*, January 12, 2009, B1–B2.

26. FY 2009 Congressional Justification, U.S. Securities & Exchange Commission, February 2008, 7.

27. *Registration Under the Advisers Act of Certain Hedge Fund Advisers*, Securities & Exchange Commission 17 CFR Parts 275 and 279 [Release No. IA-2333; File No. S7-30-04] RIN 3235-AJ25, December 7, 2004.

28. "Ten of Nation's Top Investment Firms Settle Enforcement Actions Involving Conflicts of Interest Between Research and Investment Banking," Joint Press Release of the SEC, NY State Attorney General, NYSE, NASAA, and NASD, April 28, 2003, and "It's Only Fair: Returning Money to Defrauded Investors," Testimony before the U.S. House of Representatives Subcommittee on Capital Markets, Insurance, and Government Sponsored Enterprises, February 26, 2003.

29. *2006 Performance and Accountability Report*, Securities & Exchange Commission, p. 10, http://www.sec.gov/about/secpar/secpar2006.pdf.

30. Roel Campos, "Mutual Fund Governance – Response to the Remand," speech by the commissioner, June 29, 2005.

31. FY 2009 Congressional Justification, U.S. Securities & Exchange Commission, February 2008, 1.

32. *2002 Performance and Accountability Report*, Securities & Exchange Commission, p. 25, and *2007 Performance and Accountability Report*, Securities & Exchange Commission, p. 37

33. Roel Campos, "Mutual Fund Governance – Response to the Remand," speech by the commissioner, June 29, 2005.


## Chapter 17: Elephants in the Room

1. Yogi Berra, *The Yogi Book* (New York: Workman Publishing, 1998), 118–119. "I just meant that times are different. Not necessarily better or worse. Just different."

2. Martin De Vlieghere and Paul Vreymans, "Europe's Ailing Social Model: Facts & Fairy Tales," *The Brussels Journal*, March 23, 2006, www.brusselsjournal. com/node/933.

3. Mark Twain, *The Adventures of Tom Sawyer* (1876), Chapter Two.


## Chapter 18: The Elephant Killer – Gold

1. Federal Reserve Statistical Release: H.6 Money Stock Measures, November 10, 2005, http://www.federalreserve.gov/releases/h6/20051110/.

2. Murray N. Rothbard, *A History of Money and Banking in the United States: The Colonial Era to World War II* (Auburn, AL: Ludwig von Mises Institute, 2002), 217. Spanish pieces of eight began to be called dollars after 1690, according to this same source.

3. Warren Buffett, Harvard University Speech cited on en.wikipedia.org.

4. *SPDR Gold Trust Prospectus*, August 22, 2008, 15.

5. *CitiFX Technicals – Chart of the Week*, Citi Foreign Exchange, November 26, 2008.

6. *SPDR Gold Trust Prospectus*, August 22, 2008, 15.

7. Murray N. Rothbard, *A History of Money and Banking in the United States: The Colonial Era to World War II* (Auburn: Ludwig von Mises Institute, 2002), 83–84.

8. One tonne is equal to 2,204.6 pounds.

9. Murray N., Rothbard, *The Case Against the Fed* (Auburn, AL: Ludwig von Mises Institute, 1994), 145–149.

10. *Flow of Funds Accounts of the United States (2Q08)*, Table B.100 Balance Sheet of Households and Nonprofit Organizations, Federal Reserve Statistical Release, p. 102. http://www.federalreserve.gov/releases/z1/Current/z1.pdf.


## Chapter 19: America Invicta

1. Diamond, John, "CIA's Spy Network Thin," *USA Today*, September 21, 2004, http://www.usatoday.com/news/washington/2004-09-21-cia-spies_x.htm.

2. *A Spy Speaks Out: Former Top CIA Official on "Faulty" Intelligence Claims*, CBS News – 60 Minutes, April 23, 2006, http://www.cbsnews.com/stories/2006/04/21/60minutes/main1527749.shtml.

3. Rowan Scarborough, *Sabotage: America's Enemies Within the CIA* (Washington D.C.: Regnery Publishing, 2007), 94–100.

4. Chris Quillen, "Three Explanations for Al-Qaeda's Lack of a CBRN Attack," *Terrorism Monitor*, 5(3), The Jamestown Foundation / Global Terrorism Analysis (February 15, 2007).

5. Andrew McCarthy, *Willful Blindness: A Memoir of the Jihad* (New York: Encounter Books, 2008), 310.

6. John Glover and Abigail Moses, "Credit Swaps on Ireland, Spain Rise on Ratings Threat" (Update 1), *Bloomberg*, January 14, 2009, http://www.bloomberg.com/apps/news?pid=newsarchive&sid=a7GQeqld1g3o.

7. http://www.yale.edu/lawweb/avalon/washing.htm

8. Ibid.

## Epilogue

1. Andrew Dickson White, *Fiat Money Inflation in France: How It Came, What It Brought, and How It Ended* (Boston: IndyPublish.com), 8. Reprint of original believed published in 1914.

2. John Williams, *Shadow Government Statistics*, www.shadowgovernmentstatistics.com. Accessed January 12, 2009.

# About the Author

For over 25 years William W. Baker, CFA has been an equity money manager or investment research analyst in an institutional setting. More than half of these years he has spent concurrently developing two companies: GARP Research & Securities Co. (member FINRA, SIPC) and Gaineswood Investment Management, Inc. (an SEC registered investment advisor). Before this he was at Reich & Tang, Oppenheimer Funds, and Van Kampen American Capital, being directly responsible for mutual funds or institutional accounts during most of that interval. One of the funds he managed at Oppenheimer was awarded a five-star rating in November 1990 shortly before he left the firm. Mr. Baker received his master of business administration from the Amos Tuck School at Dartmouth College in 1980, and he was granted a bachelor degree in economics in 1978 from the University of Pennsylvania. He is vice president and a trustee of the Harbour League, and he recently founded ConservativeEconomist.com.

# Index